A MEDIEVALIST
IN THE EIGHTEENTH CENTURY

ARCHIVES INTERNATIONALES D'HISTOIRE DES IDEES

INTERNATIONAL ARCHIVES OF THE HISTORY OF IDEAS

83

GEOFFREY WILSON

A MEDIEVALIST
IN THE EIGHTEENTH CENTURY

A MEDIEVALIST
IN THE EIGHTEENTH CENTURY

LE GRAND D'AUSSY AND THE FABLIAUX OU CONTES

by

GEOFFREY WILSON

MARTINUS NIJHOFF – THE HAGUE – 1975

TO MY WIFE

PRINTED IN THE NETHERLANDS

TABLE OF CONTENTS

ACKNOWLEDGMENTS

I am grateful for this opportunity to offer my thanks publicly to Professor L. Gossman of the Johns Hopkins University. Through his pioneering study of La Curne de Sainte-Palaye, but more especially through the advice and guidance he so freely gave in correspondence, Professor Gossman has put me greatly in his debt.

An even greater debt is owed to Professor C. E. Pickford of the University of Hull whose inaugural lecture, *Changing attitudes towards medieval French literature*, first suggested this study in eighteenth-century medievalism and whose example has been an constant source of inspiration throughout its execution. Whatever merits this work may finally have are due entirely to my "premier maître." Its faults are solely mine.

INTRODUCTION

It is a common belief that in France the study of medieval literature as literature only began to gain recognition as a valid occupation for the scholar during the nineteenth century. It is well known that historians of the sixteenth, seventeenth and eighteenth centuries looked to the literary productions of the Middle Ages for materials useful to their researches, but it is only recently that the remarkable frequency of this reference has been appreciated and that scholars have become aware of an unbroken tradition of what might best be described as historically ori ented medievalism stretching from the sixteenth century to our own. The eighteenth century has drawn the greatest number of curious to this field, for it is evident that the surprisingly extensive researches undertaken then do much to explain the progress made a century later by the most celebrated generation of medievalistst. Very slowly we are coming to see the value of the contribution made by little known scholars like La Curne de Sainte-Palaye, Etienne Barbazan and the Comte de Caylus.

This appreciation marks an advance, of course, but it must be said that the credit given falls far short of that which is due. The eighteenth century has been singled out for special praise because the volume and exactitude of researches then undertaken overshadow all that had gone before. Since the sixteenth century interest in the Middle Ages had been steadily increasing and more and more experience had been gained in the techniques of historical research. The eighteenth-century medievalist has learned by the mistakes of his predecessors, his projects became much more ambitious and his results were vastly superior. He is the strongest link in the chain of that tradition handed on by Fauchet, Pasquier and Duchesne, and he merits respect as such. But he remains only a link and scholars of a much later generation were to exploit the researches he pursued.

La Curne de Sainte-Palaye and his contemporaries are thus remembered for their industry and thoroughness but denied any real originality. And yet this is where their merit chiefly resides. That this should be
much ignored is perhaps no disgrace when one considers how little
work has so far been carried out in this relatively new field of eight-
teenth-century medievalism, where we are only now beginning to see
beyond a veritable ocean of source materials. The truth is that while
eighteenth-century scholars followed their predecessors in studying the
literary productions of the Middle Ages principally for the light these
shed upon the manners, customs, laws and institutions of the period,
while they whole-heartedly embraced that tradition of historically
oriented medievalism passed on by Fauchet and his fellows, they did in
addition significantly enrich it and can be said to have begun a gradual
process of redirection from within, preparing the ground for a new enlightened appreciation of medieval literature as literature. This process of redirection is best evidenced in Pierre-Jean-Baptiste Le Grand
d'Aussy's *Fabliaux ou Contes*, the first successful attempt to render medieval French literature popular with a mass reading public made little
short of two centuries ago.[1]

The medievalists of eighteenth-century France fall roughly into three
categories. Foremost amongst the scholars was La Curne de Sainte-
Palaye. To his nineteenth-century successors he bequeathed a vast
fund of copies and notices of medieval literary manuscripts which bears
testimony to a lifetime of the most meticulous research. No one in the
France of his day knew more about the literary productions of the
twelfth and thirteenth centuries. But equally no one thought less of
them as literature. Sainte-Palaye was first and foremost historian. He
rarely gave more than a moment's thought to the artistic abilities of the
"anciens rimeurs," never once thinking to set them against their
eighteenth-century brethren. For him they simply did not bear comparison. They were worthy of recall and close study because in their
works they mirrored the manners and customs of the society in which
they had flourished. But Sainte-Palaye did go a little beyond Fauchet,
insisting that contemporary historians treat these fictional sources with
the deference hitherto reserved for chronicles and legal documents.
Thus, in one way at least, he did contribute to the elevation of medieval

---

[1] *Fabliaux ou Contes du XIIe et du XIIIe siècle, traduits ou extraits d'après divers manuscrits du
tems; avec des notes historiques et critiques, et les imitations qui ont été faites de ces Contes depuis leur
origine jusqu'à nos jours*, Paris (Eugène Onfroy) 1779, 3 vols. in-8. A fourth volume, *Contes
dévots, Fables et Romans anciens*, was added in 1781.

literature, although at the same time clearly consolidating the historical tradition.

At the opposite end of the scale are those who can be said to stand
outside his tradition, the "remanieurs," men like the Comte de Tressan
and A. G. Contant d'Orville, who adapted the efforts of France's earliest poets to the tastes of their more enlightened age. Some, it is true,
did strive for a certain degree of fidelity in their modern renderings, the
Marquis de Paulmy, for example, originator of the *Bibliothèque des
Romans*, whose purpose was to convey a concise and yet complete impression of the original. But Paulmy stands in almost complete isolation as one who had studied his sources well. Moreover, he was using
the "anciens rimeurs" to acquaint a wide readership with medieval
French society, not to gain a literary reputation for himself at their expense. His less scrupulous and more successful fellows cared little what
remained of their sources, even, in extreme cases, inventing their own
twelfth and thirteenth-century classics. It might at first appear that
such works could serve only to lessen the status of medieval literature.
And yet their value becomes clear when one considers that initially the
mass of the eighteenth-century reading public had no other recourse.
The learned few might turn to the scholarly papers read before the
Académie des Inscriptions et Belles-Lettres, but the uninitiated would
have continued for some time in total ignorance of a medieval literature had it not been for those most diverting publications of Tressan
and his colleagues. Their contribution was to promote a wide interest
in the efforts of France's earliest poets. By popularizing these pseudo-
medieval texts they were in fact helping to create the atmosphere essential to a "serious" popularizer like Le Grand d'Aussy.

Le Grand stands somewhere between La Curne de Sainte-Palaye
and Tressan. One might say that he is scholar turned "vulgarisateur."
But this alone cannot explain his originality. There is nothing really
new in Le Grand's belief that certain of the efforts of the "anciens
rimeurs" remain valid as literature even when measured by the standards of his own day. The great scholars of the sixteenth and seventeenth centuries all had their especial favourites amongst the romances
and the fabliaux, although it would never have occurred to them to
publish these for their literary value. Even so, Le Grand was not the
first to combine such an appreciation with the desire to popularize.
This honour must go to Etienne Barbazan who in 1756 published a
three-volume collection of *Fabliaux et Contes* intended for a mass public.[2]

---

[2] *Fabliaux et Contes des Poëtes françois des XII, XIII, XIV et XVes siècles, tirés des meilleurs
auteurs*, Paris (Vincent) and Amsterdam (Arkstée and Merkus) 1756, 3 vols.

The collection can be said to have failed, Barbazan, who presented his texts in the original old French, expecting far too much of the average, non-specialist reader. Le Grand's originality resides then in a combination of three essential elements, a belief in the enduring validity of some medieval literature as literature, a desire to render the delights this affords accessible to a wide reading public and an understanding of the very real limitations of that public. This distinguishes Le Grand from all other medievalists of his day.

It must not be thought that the *Fabliaux ou Contes* represents a departure from that traditional historical bias of the scholars. Le Grand was himself a scholar, a pupil of Sainte-Palaye, and he would end his career as Keeper of Manuscripts at the Bibliothèque Nationale. He was not so far ahead of his time as to think a collection of "fabliaux ou contes" worthy of publication on literary merit alone. Indeed, he makes it bundantly clear in his compilation that to produce evidence of the artistic abilities of the "anciens rimeurs" was the least of three major aims envisaged here. In examining this work we have devoted a separate chapter to each of these aims, preserving Le Grand's own order of priority and, after an introductory biography, beginning therefore, in Chapter I, with his concern to establish the particular historical utility of this genre, "fabliaux ou contes," and through it to convey to his readers an accurate impression of life in medieval France. Chapter II considers a second defence of the "anciens rimeurs" on historical grounds, examining Le Grand's efforts to demonstrate the importance of their contribution to the "perfection" of French literature, to ensure that they finally receive the credit due to them as the authors of a European literary renaissance. It is only in Chapter III that we begin to consider Le Grand's desire to establish the enduring validity of certain medieval tales as literature. We could not have expected Le Grand to adopt any different order of priority and it would be improper for us to tamper with this ourselves. The *Fabliaux ou Contes* did not alter the course of medieval studies overnight, but it did contribute more than any comparable eighteenth-century work to what we have previously termed a gradual process of redirection from within.

Chapter IV of this study is devoted to the sources of the *Fabliaux ou Contes*. Only once does Le Grand rely upon the printed word, the remainder of his extracts being drawn from medieval manuscripts or, more frequently, from copies of these executed for, and annotated by, his friend and benefactor Sainte-Palaye. It is important for us to appreciate the nature of the gulf existing between what Le Grand was working from and what was acceptable to the public he wished to reach. The problems he confronted in his efforts to bridge this gap and the solutions he found are the subject of Chapter V, where one of the more useful extracts, with which the author thought to serve all three of his primary ends, is examined in some detail. It is hoped that this will prove the justice of the distinctions awarded to Le Grand in the final chapter of this study.

If the plan of this work can be said to have evolved naturally from the subject-matter, then it was no less obvious from this that the enquiry should centre upon the first three volumes of the *Fabliaux ou Contes* and Le Grand's own defence of these, the *Observations sur les Troubadours*, which appeared as a supplement.[3] The extracts of "contes dévots," fables and romances which Le Grand was to add to his collection were meant to complete the picture and we in turn have exploited them for the added light they shed upon their author. But it was with the first three volumes of his collection, the "fabliaux ou contes" proper, that Le Grand thought to realize his three primary objectives and these are our main concern. Equally, it must be said, we have limited ourselves to Le Grand's own very loose definition of the genre with which he was concerned. While the eighteenth century did make some effort to distinguish between the fabliaux and similar "contes à rire," Le Grand himself was not greatly interested in this distinction and a detailed examination of his understanding of the term "fabliau" could thus serve little useful purpose. Nevertheless, it has been thought worthwhile to include in this study a table showing the precise number of manuscripts preserving accepted fabliaux known to Le Grand and his predecessors.

Passing mention only has hitherto been made of Part I of this work. Since the purpose of this study is in part to "rehabilitate" Le Grand d'Aussy, it was thought that rather more should be known about his life, which is his work, than can be gleaned from the few comments which biographers and bibliographers have afforded him thus far. As founder of the Bibliothèque de l'Arsenal the Marquis de Paulmy draws the attention of Henry Martin in his history of that famous library,[4] Henri Jacoubet made the Comte de Tressan the subject of a

---

[3] Paris (Eugène Onfroy) 1781, 1 vol. in-8.
[4] *Histoire de la Bibliothèque de l'Arsenal*, Paris (Plon) 1899.
[5] *Le Comte de Tressan et les Origines du Genre Troubadour*, Paris (Imprimerie des Presses Universitaires de France) 1923.

study in 1923,[5] and four years ago Dr. Lionel Gossman of the Johns Hopkins University published the first major work on La Curne de Sainte-Palaye.[6] While it must be said that Dr. Gossman's book represents an enormous advance upon all previous studies in eighteenth-century medievalism, providing the present researcher with the ideal introduction to this area of study, yet it could not hope and indeed was not meant to cover this whole vast field. Le Grand d'Aussy remains in semi-oblivion.

We can perhaps never know what Le Grand d'Aussy looked like,[7] but we can and should know much more of the life he led, of his ambitions and of his achievements. Given the number and value of these latter, it is nothing less than astonishing to discover that Alexandre Cioranescu should have deemed him unworthy of a separate entry in his *Bibliographie de la Littérature française du dix-huitième Siècle*.[8] The greatest modern student of the fabliaux, Joseph Bédier, appears to have been unaware that a Le Grand d'Aussy ever existed.[9] And yet the man must have had some merit when one considers that a scholar of Sir Walter Scott's calibre thought his *Fabliaux ou Contes* important enough to own two separate editions together with English translations.[10] Perhaps the most significant move towards "rehabilitating" Le Grand has already been made with the reprinting of his collection.[11] It is hoped that the present study will complete the process.

---

[6] *Medievalism and the Ideologies of the Enlightenment. The World and Work of La Curne de Sainte-Palaye*, Baltimore (The Johns Hopkins Press) 1968.

[7] All efforts to trace some portrait have been fruitless.

[8] Paris (Editions du Centre National de la Recherche Scientifique) 1969, 3 vols.

[9] There is no mention of him in Bédier's *Les Fabliaux*, 6th edition, Paris (Champion) 1964.

[10] Cf. Sir Walter Scott, *Catalogue of the Library at Abbotsford*, Edinburgh (T. Constable) 1838, pp. 40, 118, 185 and 187. Scott also makes reference to Le Grand's collection and to an English translation in his *Sir Tristrem: a Metrical Romance of the Thirteenth Century*, 4th edition, Edinburgh (A. Constable) 1819, pp. 306 and 361 respectively.

[11] Slatkine Reprints, Geneva, 1971. All credit for this is due to Professor C. E. Pickford who first brought the work to Slatkine's attention and suggested a reprint.

PART ONE

THE LIFE AND WORK OF LE GRAND D'AUSSY

A. THE EARLY YEARS: LE GRAND AND THE SOCIETY OF JESUS

Pierre-Charles Lévesque sets the tone for his "Notice historique sur Legrand d'Aussy" with the following remark:

C'est dans la médiocrité, souvent même dans l'indigence, qu'ont pris naissance la plupart des hommes qui se sont distingués dans les sciences, dans les lettres et dans les arts.[1]

If this is true in the case of Pierre-Jean-Baptiste Le Grand, born in Amiens on June 3rd 1737 to parents of only moderate means, it certainly does not apply to a number of those with whom he was to rub shoulders in his researches on the Middle Ages and medieval literature. The Marquis de Paulmy[2] and the Comte de Tressan,[3] for example, later to be editors of the *Bibliothèque universelle des Romans* upon which Le Grand would collaborate, were clearly of quite different origins:

De brillantes perspectives s'ouvrirent pour lui [Tressan] quand sa grand'-tante, la duchesse de Ventador, gouvernante du Roi, le fit admettre parmi les jeunes nobles qui partageaient l'éducation de Louis XV.[4]

Nevertheless, if Le Grand did not come from the most wealthy of families, he was fortunate to have in his father, Pierre, an employee of the "fermes générales," a man who recognized the importance of education and who was willing to make sacrifices in order that his three sons should not be deprived of this.

His efforts do not appear to have been in vain. Le Grand's two younger brothers both entered the Church, Pierre-Théodore-Louis

[1] The "Notice" was published in the *Mémoires de l'Institut National des Sciences et Arts. Sciences morales et politiques*, vol. IV (Paris, Baudouin, 1802) pp. 84–95, and also prefaces Le Grand's own *Vie d'Apollonius de Tyane*, published posthumously, Paris (L. Collin) 1807, 2 vols.

[2] Marc-Antoine-René du Voyer, marquis de Paulmy d'Argenson, 1712–1787.

[3] Louis-Elisabeth de La Vergne, comte de Tressan, 1705–1785.

[4] Henri Jacoubet, *Le Comte de Tressan et les origines du genre troubadour*, Paris (Presses Universitaires de France) 1923, p. 196.

Augustin dying curé of Beauchesne near Vendôme, Alexandre while
serving the parish of Saint-Roch in the capital. Le Grand himself began
his academic career at the Jesuit college of Saint-Nicolas in Amiens,
entering the Society of Jesus novitiate on October 5th 1753. The Jesuits
were a powerful force in the France of the day and particularly in the
field of education. Nowhere might Le Grand have found better and
more diversified instruction. There can be little doubt that the passion
and talent for literature, for linguistic studies, for history, geography
and even the natural sciences which Le Grand was later to show were
first fired by his teachers at the Collège Saint-Nicolas which amongst
its scholars could boast such names as Voiture, Du Cange, Gresset,
Nicolas Sanson and Philippe Briet.[5] Le Grand himself can have had no
little success here. The Jesuits were in the habit of earmarking their
most gifted students for the service of the Society and when Le Grand
left Amiens it was to take the chair of rhetoric at their college in Caen.[6]
But he lacked the time to distinguish himself in his new post. The ene-
mies of the Society were now beginning to make their influence felt and
although they were not finally suppressed until 1773, a decree from the
provincial capital of Rouen banished the Jesuits from Normandy more
than a decade earlier in 1762. The college at Caen was vacated on
July 1st in that year. This was a turning-point in Le Grand's life. He
was now twenty-five years old.[7]

B. THE APPRENTICESHIP

While Le Grand may well have been introduced to medieval studies at
the Collège Saint-Nicolas in Amiens, it is probably correct to say that
his real initiation into this field came only with his move to Paris. For
it was here that he became involved with researches being undertaken
for the *Glossaire de l'ancienne langue françoise* projected by La Curne de
Sainte-Palaye[8] and collaborated on the *Bibliothèque universelle des Romans*, first directed by the Marquis de Paulmy and later by the Comte
de Tressan, and on the *Mélanges tirés d'une grande Bibliothèque,*co-edited

---

[5] On the Collège Saint-Nicolas, cf. P. Delattre, *Les Etablissements des Jésuites en France
depuis quatre siècles*, vol. I (Enghien, Institut supérieur de théologie and Wetteren, Imprimerie
de Meester frères, 1949) cols. 180–202.

[6] The noted scientist Pierre Simon Laplace was amongst his students. François Mézeray,
Pierre Daniel Huet and Voltaire attended the college. Cf. Delattre, *op. cit.*, vol. I, cols. 991–
1007.

[7] Since he was so young when his career with the Jesuits ended, it would seem unlikely
that Le Grand was ever ordained.

[8] Jean-Baptiste de La Curne de Sainte-Palaye, 1697–1781.

by Paulmy and A. G. Constant d'Orville. With his scholarly background Le Grand seemed well suited to this new-found employment.[9] More important, he was serving under some of the most distinguished masters of his day, engaged upon significant projects of differing substance which reveal to some extent not only the scale but also the range of the work undertaken at this time on the Middle Ages and medieval literature. It is certainly to this apprenticeship that we must look to find both the inspiration behind Le Grand's own work on the fabliaux and the experience which ensured its success.

In the first place there was the detailed study of Old French demanded by the *Glossaire*, intended as an aid to the proper understanding of medieval texts and documents.[10] The idea of a comprehensive dictionary of Old French had originally been that of Camille Falconet,[11] but it was Sainte-Palaye, a member of Falconet's circle, who undertook the work and, in the *Projet d'un glossaire françois*, emphasized its purpose.[12] It was not to be an end in itself then, but the means to an end. Others had tried to reduce the distance separating the eighteenth century from the Middle Ages with dictionaries and glossaries of Old French, but none could match the meticulous zeal of Sainte-Palaye whose researches into vocabulary, using innumerable manuscripts in several different countries, stretched to thirty-one volumes in-folio. Le Grand's participation in these researches was obviously to stand him in excellent stead for the handling of the enormous volume of manuscript material basic to his own work.

The experience gained elsewhere was hardly less valuable. The purpose of the *Bibliothèque universelle des Romans*[13] and of the *Mélanges tirés d'une grande Bibliothèque*,[14] an attempt, amongst other things, to popularize the literature of the Middle Ages by making not inconsiderable sections of it readily accessible to a wide reading public, is clearly akin

---

[9] Rentré dans le monde, il s'y tint étranger, et ne connut, au milieu de la capitale, que des savants et de vieux livres. (P.-C. Lévesque, "Notice historique.")

[10] *Dictionnaire historique de l'ancien langage françois, ou Glossaire de la langue françoise depuis son origine jusqu'au siècle de Louis XIV*, Niort (L. Favre) 1875–1882, 10 vols.

[11] Falconet put forward the idea in a paper entitled "Sur nos premiers traducteurs françois, avec un Essay de bibliothèque françoise" which he read before the Académie des Inscriptions et Belles-Lettres on January 28th 1727. Cf. L. Gossman, *Medievalism and the Ideologies of the Enlightenment. The World and Work of La Curne de Sainte-Palaye*, Baltimore (Johns Hopkins) 1968, pp. 163–168. Cf. also Gossman's article "Old French scholarship in the eighteenth century: the 'Glossary' of La Curne de Sainte-Palaye," in *French Studies*, vol. XII (1958) pp. 346–358.

[12] *Projet d'un glossaire françois*, Paris (H.-L. Guérin and L.-F. Delatour) 1756.

[13] Paris, 1775–1789, 112 vols. A Reprint of this work, in 28 volumes in-4, has recently been issued by *Slatkine Reprints*, Geneva, 1970.

[14] Paris, 1779–1788, 39 vols.

to that of the *Glossaire*. Indeed, La Curne de Sainte-Palaye had himself expressed the desire to see the compilation of "une bibliothèque générale & complète de tous nos anciens Romans de Chevalerie."[15] Nevertheless, the task in hand was of a different order, affording Le Grand an invaluable insight not only into the question of general approach, but also into the practical difficulties of presenting medieval literature, in particular here the romances, to the eighteenth-century reading public, into the merits of the summary or extract in modern translation as a solution to the problems posed. For, concerned as they were with varying priorities, Le Grand's employers were by no means all at one over this question of method. This meant, of course, that before embarking upon similar work himself, Le Grand was well aware not only of the difficulties he would have to face, but also of the possibilities that lay open to him.

Le Grand was indebted to his employers in one other important respect, perhaps the most important of all. His participation in the researches of Paulmy and Sainte-Palaye gave him access to two of the richest privately owned collections of the day. Paulmy's in particular was of startling proportions. Many of the thousands of volumes it comprised bear notes in the collector's own hand or dictated by him.[16] But Sainte-Palaye's own library was no mean one, particularly his collection of manuscripts and copies of manuscripts, a considerable number of the latter either made or annotated by Sainte-Palaye himself. Le Grand makes it clear that without these he would have had neither the inspiration nor the necessary source material to embark upon the collection of *Fabliaux ou Contes*:

Je dois à M. de Sainte-Palaye les premiers matériaux avec lesquels j'ai commencé cet Ouvrage, & qui m'en ont même inspiré le projet.[17]

---

[15] "Mémoire concernant la lecture des anciens Romans de Chevalerie" read before the Académie des Inscriptions on December 13th 1743 and published in the Académie's *Mémoires*, vol. XVII, pp. 787–799.

[16] Le Grand more than once testifies to the size and value of Paulmy's collection: "...une bibliothèque immense, dont la formation seule suffirait pour faire une réputation à tout autre que lui, et dont pourrait se glorifier en Europe plus d'un Souverain." (*Ms. Paris, Arsenal 6588*, fol. 77ro.)

The collection forms the nucleus of what is now the Bibliothèque de l'Arsenal where the Marquis took up residence in 1767. Cf. Henry Martin, *Catalogue des Manuscrits de la Bibliothèque de l'Arsenal*, vol. VIII, *Histoire de la Bibliothèque de l'Arsenal*, Paris (Plon) 1899. A marginal note to an extract prepared for the *Bibliothèque universelle des Romans* shows just how well Le Grand knew Paulmy's library: "M. le Mis. de Paulmi, a, si je ne me trompe, cette seconde partie du Roman, sous le nom du Comte de Ponthieu, dans les ms. de Barbazan qui sont entre la fenêtre et la cheminée." (*Ms. Paris, Arsenal 6608*, fol. 7ro.)

[17] *Fabliaux ou Contes* (1779) vol. I, preface, p. lxxxix.

Before becoming engaged upon the *Bibliothèque universelle des Romans* Le Grand had, in 1770, been nominated Secrétaire de la Direction des Etudes at the Ecole Militaire and a little later had been charged to complete the education of the son of a "fermier général." Yet teaching is no longer his first love. It seems his association with Sainte-Palaye has confirmed him as a medievalist and he is soon collaborating with Paulmy. Before long he is preoccupied with collecting and translating the fabliaux, although not, as he will later claim, with a view to publishing:

Heureux et content dans mon obscurité, je me flattois de pouvoir cultiver en paix les lettres, qui, toute ma vie, avoient fait mes délices; mais, dans le système de bonheur que je m'étois formé à moi-même, ma première loi avoit été de ne jamais écrire. Je craignois de risquer mon repos et ma tranquillité sur ces mers remplies d'écueils, couvertes d'ennemis, et sans cesse infestées de pirates.[18]

Written as they are in retrospect, when Le Grand had become only too well acquainted with the inherent "risks" of a literary career, we may well have good reason to doubt the sincerity of these lines. Nevertheless, he sees fit to relate the turn of events which, as he would have us believe, was to force his reluctant hand.[19]

C. THE *FABLIAUX OU CONTES*

It appears that Le Grand found himself one day in the company of a group of people whose conversation had turned to the subject of the Middle Ages:

... et l'on en parloit avec ce mépris insultant qu'ont inspiré mal à-propos quelques-uns de nos historiens.

Provoked by such injustice, he immediately leapt to the defence of the "siècles d'ignorance" in an effort to enlighten his misguided companions:

Je pris la liberté de dire que, pour le style, le goût, la critique, pour tout ce qui tient à l'art, il ne falloit point le chercher dans les ouvrages de ce temps; mais que si l'on vouloit se contenter d'esprit et d'imagination, on pourroit, à

---

[18] *Fabliaux ou Contes*, third edition (1829) vol. II, *Observations sur les Troubadours*, p. 4. Le Grand appears to have held the post of private tutor for some considerable time. A letter from the Marquis de Paulmy dated June 5th 1779 is addressed to him ',Chez M. De la Borde, Fermier Général, Place du Carrousel." (*Ms. Paris, Arsenal 6588*, fol. 77 vo.)

[19] *Observations sur les Troubadours*, pp. 4–6. All references to the *Observations*, which did appear separately, are to that version appearing in the third edition of the *Fabliaux ou Contes* (1829) Vol. II, pp. 1–166.

une certaine époque, en trouver chez nos vieux poètes; et j'ajoutai qu'il nous restoit d'eux, en ce genre, des choses fort agréables qui méritoient d'être connues.

Evidence to support this claim was requested and three or four days later Le Grand returned with a translation of some of the fabliaux he had come to know through Sainte-Palaye, together with a copy of the originals. The reaction, as he had foreseen, was a favourable one, but in removing a prejudice Le Grand had apparently kindled the curiosity of his hostess:

La maîtresse de la maison m'en demanda quelques autres. j'y consentis, sans prévoir où alloit m'engager ma complaisance; mais quand elle en eut en main un certain nombre, elle exigea de moi que j'en publiasse le recueil, et, en cas de refus, me menaça de publier elle-même, sous mon nom, ceux qu'elle possédoit, malgré l'état d'imperfection où nécessairement ils étoient encore.[20]

Thus obliged, he says, to take the publication of the collection upon himself, he nevertheless hoped to retain something of the peace and tranquillity he had formerly enjoyed by remaining anonymous. He was soon to realize the futility of this desire. Not only was it his duty to express his gratitude to those who were of service to him in his researches, but critics exposed him when denouncing certain of the opinions put forward in the collection. He regretfully decided to name himself in the fourth volume:

...quoique tout ceci détruisît pour jamais le système de vie qui m'avoit rendu heureux....

However great Le Grand's alleged initial reluctance to put pen to paper, his first literary effort, the three volumes of *Fabliaux ou Contes* which appeared in 1779,[21] the year following that which had seen the death of both Rousseau and Voltaire, was enthusiastically received by a number of contemporary critics:

Le goût & l'érudition, Monsieur, paroissent avoir également présidé à la rédaction de cet ouvrage, le plus complet de tous ceux qu'on nous a donnés

[20] A remark made in the introduction to the section "Fabliaux" in the *Bibliothèque universelle des Romans* for February 1777 makes it clear that Le Grand had begun to work seriously towards publication by this date: "Nous ne pouvons, dans un article consacré aux Romans de Chevalerie, parler des autres Fabliaux, qui, d'ailleurs, doivent faire l'objet d'un Recueil que l'illustre Académicien (La Curne de Sainte-Palaye) fait composer sous ses yeux." (p. 87.)

[21] *Fabiaux ou Contes du XIIe et du XIIIe siècle, traduits ou extraits d'après divers manuscrits du tems; avec des notes historiques & critiques, & les imitations qui ont été faites de ces Contes depuis leur origine jusqu' à nos jours*, Paris (Eugène Onfroy) 3 vols. in-8. Except where otherwise stated, all references to the *Fabliaux ou Contes* shall be to this first edition.

dans ce genre, & qu'on peut regarder comme un recueil d'excellens mémoires, propres à servir à l'histoire de notre ancienne poésie.[22]

The eighteenth-century reading public was not, of course, entirely unprepared for such a collection, as the *Journal Encyclopédique* makes clear in its review:

Il semble que le succès de la 'Bibliothèque des romans' ait inspiré à plusieurs gens de lettres le désir & le courage de revenir à l'étude de notre ancienne littérature françoise, presque entièrement négligée de nos jours. C'est depuis la publication de cet ouvrage qu'on a tenté de ressusciter nos vieux poëtes; & les auteurs des 'Annales poétiques'[23] ont présenté au public un choix ou un extrait de leurs ouvrages les meilleurs ou les plus supportables....[24]

Numerous collections, poetry, "vieilles chansons," anecdotes and "contes," in fact preceded those mentioned above.[25] Some, like Bonafous' *Le Parterre du Parnasse*[26] and Le Fort de la Morinière's *Bibliothèque poétique*,[27] consider nothing before the sixteenth century. Sinner, on the other hand, restricts himself entirely to the Middle Ages[28] and Monnet goes as far back as the thirteenth century with his *Anthologie françoise*.[29] Nevertheless, to judge from the *Journal de Littérature, des Sciences et des Arts*, Le Grand's collection appears to have compared favourably with those of his predecessors:

Vous ne confondrez pas, Monsieur, l'intéressante production que je vous annonce avec tous ces misérables Recueils, dont la médiocrité féconde nous afflige, qui n'ajoutent rien à la masse de nos richesses littéraires, & ne font

[22] *Journal de Littérature, des Sciences et des Arts*, 1779, vol. VI, pp. 102–103. The *Mercure de France* will take up Le Grand's nautical metaphor and congratulate the lady who obliged him to break his vow of silence: "Nous aurions trop perdu s'il avoit pu garder sa résolution. Le repos ne convient qu'aux gens incapables de braver les dangers & de franchir les obstacles. Les eaux stagnantes sont plus nuisibles à l'humanité que les mers orageuses & les torrens dévastateurs. Les Pirates ne doivent point empêcher Cook & Bougainville de faire le tour du monde & de découvrir de nouveaux rivages. Les Pirates Littéraires sont trop vils & trop méprisés pour être redoutables." (May 1782, p. 129.)

[23] *Annales poétiques, ou Almanach des Muses depuis l'origine de la poésie françoise*, Paris (C. S. Sautreau de Marsy and B. Imbert, editors) 1778–1788, 40 vols.

[24] *Journal Encyclopédique ou Universel*, 1780, vol. II, pt. I, p. 72.

[25] It is interesting to note that already in 1747 the *Mercure* had begun to publish the works of France's medieval poets. The periodical did much to secure the popularity of Old French literature, although the editor adopts a rather patronizing attitude in this instance, refusing to publish more than one piece at a time: "...nos anciens poètes ne sont que des enfants et vous sçavez que les enfants peuvent amuser un quart d'heure, mais qu'à la longue ils se rendroient insupportables." (September 1747.) Cited by H. Jacoubet, *Le Comte de Tressan*, pp. 169–170.

[26] *Le Parterre du Parnasse françois, ou Nouveau recueil des pièces les plus rares et les plus curieuses des plus célèbres poëtes françois, depuis Marot jusqu'à présent*, Amsterdam (E. Roger) 1710.

[27] *Bibliothèque poétique, ou Nouveau choix des plus belles pièces de vers en tout genre, depuis Marot jusqu'aux poëtes de nos jours*, Paris, 1745, 4 vols.

[28] *Extraits de quelques poésies du XIIe, XIIIe et XIVe siècle*, Lausanne, 1759.

[29] *Anthologie françoise, ou Chansons choisies, depuis le XIIIe siècle jusqu'à présent*, Paris, 1705, 3 vols.

que transporter dans un livre ce qui existoit déjà dans un autre. Celui-ci est un Ouvrage véritablement neuf, & le premier qui nous offre des Mémoires d'une certaine étendue sur les Monuments de notre ancienne Poésie.[30]

However successful, the collection as it stood was not complete. In a note concluding the third volume Le Grand points out that it had been his intention to complement the fabliaux with a number of "contes dévots" or "miracles."[31] In view of their length, however, he announces that, together with a number of the fables of Marie de France and extracts from some of the old romances, these tales are now to form a separate fourth and, as he hopes, final volume. Not that he intends to abandon his literary career once the collection is complete, for another important project is already well under way:

...avant de tracer le tableau de nos moeurs & de nos usages, je veux avoir fini celui de notre ancienne littérature.[32]

It would seem that Le Grand was to make no attempt to return to the peace and tranquillity of obscurity.

Although essential to his purposes, this additional volume, *Contes dévots, Fables et Romans anciens; pour servir de suite aux Fabliaux*, which did not appear until 1781,[33] clearly in the author's eyes contained nothing to match the fabliaux. The fables and the romances do, he says, have a certain appeal and there are even those "pious" tales which he considers to be not entirely without merit:

...il se trouve plusieurs de ces Contes qui offrent de l'imagination, de l'esprit, de l'intérêt même, & jusqu'à une sorte d'art dans la narration.[34]

Three such examples were included amongst the fabliaux and two or three more are to appear in the present volume.[35] As for the remainder, however, Le Grand can only hope that they will please his readers by their originality, since little else can be said in their favour:

---

[30] *Journal de Littérature*, 1779, vol. VI, p. 73.
[31] Cf. *Fabliaux ou Contes*, vol. III, pp. 439–441.
[32] P. 441.
[33] Paris (chez l'Auteur, quai de l'Ecole, maison de M. Juliot; et aux Adresses ordinaires) 1 vol. in-8. Except where otherwise stated, all references shall be to this edition of the *Contes dévots*.
[34] *Contes dévots*, Discours préliminaire, p. xxxix.
[35] Those "contes dévots" inserted amongst the fabliaux in the first three volumes of the collection are: "Merlin" (vol. I, pp. 1–8); "De l'Hermite que l'Ange conduisit dans le siècle" (vol. II, pp. 1–13); "Du Prud'homme qui avait été Marchand" (vol. III, pp. 183-190). Cf. the note concluding the third volume of the *Fabliaux ou Contes*, pp. 440–441.

... Je sens trop la différence qu'il y a entre de pareils sujets & ceux des Fabliaux; & je ne dois pas me flatter, pour ce Volume, du même succès qu'ont eu le bonheur d'obtenir les trois autres.[36]

Le Grand was apparently to feel that he had been correct in this assumption. In any event a supplement containing the remaining three out of the four romances he had hoped to include in this volume and which he promised would appear if the reception of "Parténopex" proved their publication worthwhile,[37] did not follow. The plural "s" is significantly dropped from the word "Romans" on the title-page of the second edition of the collection, *Fabliaux ou Contes du XIIe et du XIIIe siècle, Fables et Roman du XIIIe*, which in fact appeared in the same year as the *Contes dévots*, 1781.[38] But whatever doubts Le Grand may have had regarding the success of this additional volume and the reception of "Parténopex,"[39] he appears to have had few qualms about the popularity of the collection as a whole. As we can see, the first edition is hardly complete before the second is available for purchase.

Apart from being of a far more convenient and much cheaper format, a point which the *Journal de Littérature* rightly sees as worthy of note,[40] this second edition differs principally from the first by the addition of the *Observations sur les Troubadours*,[41] of which a number of copies were printed separately in octavo format for the benefit of those possessing the earlier edition.[42] In a note contained in the *Contes dévots* Le Grand had promised to reply to criticism of the opinions he had expressed, in the preface to the first volume of the collection, upon the relative merits of the "trouvères" and the troubadours.[43] In the *Observations sur les*

---

[36] *Contes dévots*, Discours préliminaire, p. xl.

[37] Cf. the note concluding this volume of *Contes dévots*, pp. 399–400.

[38] *Fabliaux ou Contes du XIIe et du XIIIe siècle, Fables et Roman du XIIIe, traduits ou extraits d'après plusieurs Manuscrits du tems; avec des Notes historiques & critiques, & les imitations qui ont été faites de ces Contes depuis leur origine jusqu'à nos jours. Nouvelle édition, augmentée d'une Dissertation sur les Troubadours*, Paris (E. Onfroy) 5 vols. in-12.

[39] This does not in fact appear to have been too discouraging. The *Année littéraire*, for example, is particularly enthusiastic and anxious to read the romances to follow: "M. le Grand se propose de donner dans un supplément les trois autres Romans qu'il a annoncés. S'ils sont aussi intéressans que celui-ci, il ne peut trop tôt acquitter sa parole." (1781, vol. V, p. 252.)

[40] 1782, vol. IV, p. 50.

[41] Vol. II, pp. 1–114.

[42] Paris (E. Onfroy) 1781. The *Journal des Sçavans* is well pleased by Le Grand's consideration for his readers: "L'Auteur, en faisant imprimer à part ses Observations en faveur de ceux qui ont la première Edition, a fait une chose d'un très-bon exemple & a donné une forte leçon à de grands Ecrivains qui n'en ont pas usé si bien envers le Public." (November 1782, pp. 742–743.)

[43] The note follows the Discours préliminaire.

Troubadours he fulfils this promise and thereby strikes a further blow in what the *Année littéraire* was to term "une espèce de guerre littéraire."[44]

D. THE *OBSERVATIONS SUR LES TROUBADOURS*

The dispute between the northern and southern provinces of France as to which might claim responsibility for the renaissance of letters in that country, the "querelle des trouvères et des troubadours" as it came to be known, was nothing new. The view that it is to the Midi that one must look to discover the origins of French poetry had begun to insinuate itself well before the turn of the century and, given frequent expression in such works as the Abbé Guillaume Massieu's *Histoire de la Poésie françoise*[45] and Charles Noblot's *L'Origine et le Progrès des Arts et des Sciences*,[46] soon came to be quite widely accepted as an incontestable fact of history. There was some considerable opposition, notably from Lévesque de la Ravalière and the Abbé Goujet who did much to reinstate the North as the true birthplace of the fathers of modern French poetry.[47] Nevertheless, it was not until the publication of the *Fabliaux ou Contes* that matters were really brought to a head. The question is clearly one of importance to Le Grand and central to his purposes.

The intention underlying the remarks made in 1779, in the preface to the first volume of the collection, is stated categorically in the *Observations sur les Troubadours*:

Ma dissertation, puisque c'est ainsi qu'on l'a nommée, avoit pour but de prouver que les troubadours ne méritent pas à beaucoup près la renommée dont ils jouissent, et qu'au contraire, les troubadours qui ont écrit en romane francoise n'ont pas obtenu toute celle qu'ils méritent.[48]

We know already the outcome of this attempt to remove "a prejudice to which time had lent the appearance of historical fact."[49] Le Grand exposed himself to those "marauders" who, as he would have us believe, had made him so reluctant ever to embark upon a literary career:

J'ai débuté dans la littérature par une querelle, moi qui n'estime rien sur la terre au prix de la paix et du repos, moi qui, comme Sosie, voudrois être l'ami de tout le monde.[50]

---

[44] 1782, vol. IV, p. 329.
[45] Paris (Prault) 1739.
[46] Paris (H. L. Guérin) 1740.
[47] On the early history of the dispute, cf. H. Jacoubet, *Le Comte de Tressau*, pp. 70–77.
[48] Pp. 9–10.
[49] *Fabliaux ou Contes*, vol. I, preface, p. v.
[50] *Observations sur les Troubadours*, p. 7.

Le Grand's argument, although favourably received by certain of those periodicals reviewing the first three volumes of the *Fabliaux ou Contes*,[51] brought forth a storm of protest from the "provençalistes."[52] In his "Observations critiques sur les 'Fabliaux ou Contes des douzième & treizième siècles,' " Charles-Joseph de Mayer comes to the defence of his "homeland" with a "Tableau Historique de l'ancienne Littérature Provençale" which would prove this latter "la mère de la Françoise incontestablement."[53] Summoned to take up the cause by the Abbé de Fontenay,[54] Papon, noted historian of Provence,[55] publishes his *Voyage littéraire de Provence* in which are contained five letters combating at length the views of Le Grand and reaffirming the preeminence of the troubadours.[56] The letters will demonstrate the insignificance of their northern counterparts:

... quand cette discussion sera faite, vous serez étonné de les voir dans un dénuement total de tout ce qui peut attirer l'attention; dépourvus d'imagination & de sentiment, réduits à nous présenter pour toute preuve 'de cette vertu créative & de cette fécondité de production'[57] dont on les gratifie si libéralement, quelques fabliaux insipides, remplis de choses triviales & froidement contées.[58]

The Abbé de Fontenay would appear to regard Papon's remarks as conclusive:

... ces maussades plagiaires des troubadours sont remis à leur vraie place.[59]

Le Grand himself remains unshaken:

... je crains bien qu'il n'ait rendu ma cause meilleure encore qu'auparavant.[60]

---

[51] For example, cf. *Journal de Littérature*, 1779, vol. VI, pp. 75–84; *Journal Encyclopédique*, 1780, vol. II, pt. I, pp. 73–78.

[52] Les journaux de 1780 et 1781 sont remplis de la querelle des trouvères et des troubadours. (René Lanson, *Le Goût du Moyen Age en France au XVIIIe siècle*, Paris and Brussels, G. van Oest, editor, 1926, p. 21.)

[53] Cf. The "Observations" appear in the *Mercure*, April 1780, pp. 147–160.

[54] Cf. *Affiches de Province*, 1780, no 8.

[55] Jean-Pierre Papon compiled a certain *Histoire générale de Provence*, Paris (Moutard) 1776–1786, 4 vols.

[56] *Voyage littéraire de Provence, contenant tout ce qui peut donner une idée de l'état ancien & moderne des Villes, les Curiosités qu'elles renferment, la position des anciens Peuples, quelques Anecdotes littéraires, l'Histoire Naturelle, &c. & cinq Lettres sur les Trouvères & les Troubadours*, Paris (Barrois l'aîné) 1780. A second edition appears later in two volumes, Paris (Moutard) 1787.

[57] Cf. *Fabliaux ou Contes*, vol. I, preface, p. liii.

[58] *Voyage littéraire de Provence* (1787) vol. II, pp. 173–174.

[59] Cf. *Observations sur les Troubadours*, p. 9.

[60] Cf. the note following the Discours préliminaire to the *Contes dévots*.

Deeming the letters unworthy of a reply, his first intention had in fact been to ignore them completely. But Papon was not Le Grand's only critic and, realizing that silence on his part might well be misconstrued as an acknowledgment of defeat, he promises to respond to his various detractors:

> En attendant, je supplie mes Lecteurs de ne point prononcer contre moi encore, & de suspendre leur jugement jusqu'à ce qu'ils m'aient entendu.[61]

If the *Observations sur les Troubadours*, published "pour achever d'éclaircir la question,"[62] were meant to put an end to the dispute, then Le Grand did not achieve his aim. Certainly his efforts did not remain unapplauded and the *Année littéraire* for one found his arguments convincing:

> ... M. le Grand remet enfin les Provençaux à leur place.[63]

In gaining support, however, Le Grand had attracted fresh and determined opposition in the form of Bérenger, "le tenant par excellence de la bonne cause,"[64] who begins his campaign with the *Porte-feuille d'un Troubadour*.[65] In this latter is contained a "Lettre à M. Groslei de l'Académie des Inscriptions & Belles-Lettres, sur les Troubadours," where this new adversary, drawing upon the findings of fellow "provençalistes" and numerous historians of literature, respectfully denounces Le Grand in no uncertain terms:

> Il est certain que l'effet de la nouvelle brochure, je n'ose dire son but, pourroit être comme vous le remarquez très-bien, Monsieur, non-seulement d'armer la France contre elle-même, mais encore de nous jetter dans une erreur de vocation dont les suites seroient aussi funestes qu'irréparables...[66]

This was but the start of a campaign which Bérenger was to pursue fervently and at length, until the justice of his cause appeared proven beyond all doubt, the victory of the "troubadours" conceded and universally applauded.[67]

In fact this was by no means final victory. If Le Grand remained

---

[61] *Ibidem.*
[62] *Ibidem.*
[63] 1782, vol. IV, p. 329. Cf. also, *Journal de Littérature*, 1782, vol. IV, pp. 49–61; *Mercure*, May 1782, pp. 127–133.
[64] Cf. H. Jacoubet, *Le Comte de Tressan*, pp. 349–351.
[65] Marseille and Paris (Nyon l'aîné) 1782.
[66] P. 108. Bérenger had earlier referred to a suggestion made by Le Grand: "...savoir que notre jeunesse méridionale peut espérer plus de succès en se livrant au genre grave de la morale, qu'en suivant son penchant pour les ouvrages d'imagination." (P. 106.)
[67] Cf. H. Jacoubet, *Le Comte de Tressan, loc. cit.*

silent it was not because he considered himself defeated or even seriously threatened:

Lorsque j'entrepris d'examiner la question des Troubadours, je cherchais la
vérité. A force de recherches je crus l'avoir trouvée, et alors je publiai mes
remarques, qui par la faiblesse des réponses qui m'ont été faites jusqu'ici me
paraissent aujourd'hui démontrées.[68]

When preparing a third edition of the *Fabliaux ou Contes* in later years he
did indeed make many important additions to the *Observations sur les
Troubadours*. Although he himself never published these, the fact that
Antoine-Augustin Renouard finds it important to include them in his
own edition of the collection, which appeared nearly thirty years after
the original author's death, half a century removed from those remarks
which had instigated the dispute, this is evidence enough both of the
value attached to Le Grand's arguments and of the sustained impetus
of the "querelle":

... réimprimer les dissertations sans leurs nouveaux développements eût
été priver l'auteur des avantages d'une légitime défense, et passer condamnation sur des reproches dont il démontre l'injustice.[69]

Although Le Grand had been well aware that he would not go unchallenged, he could hardly have foreseen the real consequences of his
first literary efforts:

Au reste, il m'étoit aisé de prévoir que mon insurrection trouveroit des contradicteurs, et je devois m'y attendre ... Mais ce à quoi je ne m'attendois
pas, c'est la chaleur que certaines personnes ont mise à me combattre.[70]

The question of the "trouvères" and the "troubadours" would be debated for some time to come.

E. THE *HISTOIRE DE LA VIE PRIVÉE DES FRANÇAIS*

Whether or not Le Grand had genuinely been reluctant to embark
upon a literary career, a dispute of this kind clearly represents the kind
of publicity for which authors crave and which, in itself, is frequently
enough to ensure success. It might be unfair to suggest that the "guerre
littéraire" instigated by the *Fabliaux ou Contes* had been planned. Nevertheless, for a man who valued peace and tranquility so highly Le Grand

---

[68] *Ms. Paris, B.N.n.a.f. 6227*, fol. 24ro. These lines appear to have been written some time
after 1790.
[69] *Fabliaux ou Contes* (1829) vol. I, Avis de l'éditeur, p. vii.
[70] *Observations sur les Troubadours*, p. 7.

began his career as a writer with a period of great productivity and some turbulence. Firstly, he seems to have been unable to put down his pen having once set it to paper. Already when the first three volumes of the *Fabliaux ou Contes* appear in 1779 mention is made of the projected *Histoire de la Vie Privée des Français*.[71] The first part of this is published only three years later in 1782,[72] and yet by this time the first collection is complete in its five volumes and a second edition has already appeared. In the second place, Le Grand seemed fated to be involved in controversy of one kind or another. While engaging in public debate to prove the "trouvères" of the North the true fathers of modern French poetry, he is at the same time fiercely contesting ownership of the aforementioned *Histoire de la Vie Privée des Français*, still only a "projet de publication." This work was clearly considered to be of some importance and the dispute to which it gave rise is itself not insignificant, of special interest to us for the insight it affords into Le Grand's character in particular, but also into that of his opponent, the Marquis de Paulmy.[73]

All credit must be given to Paulmy for this idea of a history of French manners and customs. Although himself not in a position to undertake the vast researches necessary, he did draw up a plan of the work in 1776 and set the project in motion by entrusting its execution to Contant d'Orville. Unfortunately this latter appears to have been unprepared for such a task and the results produced during the eighteen months he spent engaged upon the work fell far short of what Paulmy had expected of his deputy. By this time Le Grand had become a frequent visitor to Paulmy's library, already collaborating with the Marquis on other work, as we know, and preparing his own collection of *Fabliaux ou Contes*. It was not long before he had been informed of the position and had himself agreed to replace Contant d'Orville. Clearly Paulmy had no little confidence in the ability of Le Grand who began working from the original plan, having taken the first part of Contant d'Orville's script into his possession.

Paulmy appeared at first to have chosen wisely, for the researches Le Grand had been compelled to undertake for the *Fabliaux ou Contes* had furnished him with a great deal of material relevant to the new task in

---

[71] Cf. vol. I, p. 242, note (g); vol. III, note, p. 441.

[72] Paris (PH-D. Pierres) 3 vols.

[73] For a summary of the dispute, cf. H. Martin, *Histoire de la Bibliothèque de l'Arsenal*, pp. 43-46. The account which follows is taken from correspondence with Paulmy preserved in the Bibliothèque de l'Arsenal, *Ms. Paris, Arsenal 6588*, ff. 75ro-91ro: "Correspondance et pièces relatives au différend survenu entre Legrand d'Aussy et le marquis de Paulmy, au sujet de l' 'Histoire de la vie privée des Français' 1779-1781."

hand. However, much remained to be done and Le Grand began work in earnest, sparing himself no pains, as he later points out in a letter to the Marquis outlining the principal causes of the dispute:[74]

J'entrepris donc un travail immense. Je parcourus et dépouillai nos vieux Historiens, nos Légendaires &c, en un mot une quantité incroyable des livres de votre bibliothèque. J'employai à cela plus d'une année, me refusant tout plaisir, travaillant dix à douze heures par jour, et n'interrompant guère que pour aller dîner chez vous: car vous m'aviez fait l'honneur de m'admettre à votre table, et je me le rappelle avec reconnaissance.[75]

Certain of Paulmy's suggestions, it seems, did not meet with Le Grand's approval, but the two men continued on good terms until the Marquis was called away to Versailles and, realizing that his stay might well be lengthy, decided to take Le Grand's notes with him in order to correct and edit them.[76]

At Versailles, however, Paulmy not only completed the task of revision but, no doubt unable to resist so illustrious an audience, read the manuscript before distinguished company, including the King's physician, and announced that it was shortly to be published under his name. Hearing of this from someone who had attended one of Paulmy's readings, Le Grand found himself in a most difficult position. He had no wish to offend the Marquis, but nor was he prepared to renounce all claim to an enterprise which had cost him more than a year's hard work. After some hesitation he finally decided to explain to the Marquis that, having himself shown the manuscript to a number of men of letters amongst his friends, it was now impossible for him to relinquish the project without loss of face. Paulmy, needless to say, was far from pleased and so replied to Le Grand that the latter withdrew in anger, resolved never again to accept the Marquis' services or use his library, more important, to leave his material unpublished but prevent anyone else from bringing the project to fruition.

Both men subsequently realized that they had been precipitate and within the space of two months, by the end of April 1779,[77] they are once again communicating, the Marquis requesting Le Grand to explain to his secretary the terms on which he is prepared to continue

---

[74] *Ms. Paris, Arsenal 6588*, ff. 86ro–89ro, rough draft.

[75] Fol. 87vo.

[76] Marie-Antoinette was about to give birth to her first child. Paulmy, who had held various high offices, would have been listed amongst members of the court and dignitaries requested to attend at the birth.

[77] Le Grand appears to have begun work on the *Histoire de la Vie Privée des Français* in the last months of 1777. He had come to know of Paulmy's plan to publish the work under his own name towards the end of February 1779.

with the project. This Le Grand does, leaving with Paulmy's secretary, Soyer, a note to the effect that, while he is only too pleased to acknowledge his indebtedness to the Marquis for the plan of the project, he himself claims full credit for its execution and will allow no name other than his own on the title-page of the finished work:

> Je demande maintenant à faire l'ouvrage en entier, à le faire seul, et à y mettre mon nom.[78]

Thereupon Le Grand leaves for the country, for Corbeil, to give his full attention to the printing of the *Fabliaux ou Contes*.

On Monday June 1st 1779 Le Grand is invited to dine with the Marquis and it is agreed that the latter shall be permitted to publish his plan for the proposed work and read it before the Académie, that thereafter he will take no active part in it and leave all credit to his colleague.[79] Paulmy is a little annoyed that Le Grand should have omitted to name him when referring to the project in a note contained in the first volume of the *Fabliaux ou Contes*[80] but he is quickly appeased when the author proposes that he dictate a short notice, clarifying his part in the enterprise, which might be inserted in all copies of Le Grand's collection remaining to be sold. The two men now seem to understand each other perfectly, and yet only four days later Le Grand receives the following letter from Soyer:

> M. le Marquis de Paulmy veut absolument, mon cher Ami, lire à l'Académie le plan de son ouvrage, et le faire imprimer. Vous travaillerez après cela avec luy, si cela vous convient, sur le pied que les choses étoient cy-devant, sur un autre, si vous aimez mieux que ce soit ainsy. Tout l'honneur des recherches vous sera donné en entier. C'est luy qui fera généralement les avances de tout; bien entendu que dans ces avances n'entreront, ni ce qu'il a pu donner déjà à M. D'Orville, quand il a commencé à l'occuper à cet ouvrage, ni ce que vous sçavez. Il désire seulement (et cela luy paroît comme à moi juste) que dans le bénéfice, un tiers soit pour M. D'Orville.[81]

Le Grand takes this to mean that the Marquis has had a change of heart and intends after all that the work be published under his name. He is bewildered and outraged at Paulmy's attitude. Once again their association is in jeopardy.

On June 8th Le Grand sends Soyer a lengthy and unequivocal reply.[82] The Marquis may please himself as to what use he makes of his

---

[78] *Ms. Paris, Arsenal 6588*, fol. 77ro, rough draft.
[79] Le Grand, of course, is to be welcome once again in Paulmy's library.
[80] P. 242, note (g).
[81] *Ms. Paris, Arsenal 6588*, fol. 76ro-vo.
[82] *Idem*, ff. 78ro–79vo, rough draft.

plan, which after all is no more than a series of divisions and subdivisions of chapters. But that he should put his name to the completed work when he knows nothing of the enormous volume of meticulous and painstaking research involved, this is unthinkable:

Vous n'avez certainement pas voulu me proposer de n'avoir dans un travail tel que le mien que la peine et l'ennui seuls pour mon partage; et de m'employer comme un manoeuvre à tirer pendant plusieurs années des pierres d'une carrière, à les tailler, à les mettre en place, tandis que d'autres mains en auroient l'honneur sans aucune peine. Vous savez sur cela ma façon de penser; je vous l'ai déclarée, et jamais elle ne changera.[83]

Similarly there can be no question of Contant d'Orville sharing in whatever profit is made from the enterprise. He was, it appears, quite handsomely paid for the eighteen fruitless months he spent engaged upon the project. He cannot seriously hope to benefit from his failure a second time. His abortive efforts have been of no use whatsoever,

... fatras que je compte tellement pour rien que pour ce qui me reste à achever je ne veux pas même voir la suite de sa compilation....[84]

Le Grand's position is greatly strengthened by the fact that he now feels himself able to decline Paulmy's offer of financial backing. He leads, he says, a very simple life and in any event, given that his collection of *Fabliaux* is successful, could probably raise any capital required for the new project through public subscription:

Pour la dernière fois qu'il ne soit point entre nous question d'argent pour prix de mon travail. Je ne veux point absolument en entendre parler. Faire ma besogne seul la faire pour l'honneur qui peut m'en revenir, voilà deux points dont jamais je ne me départirai.[85]

It may have been that Le Grand simply misinterpreted Soyer's letter or that the Marquis was indeed disturbed by this obvious threat that the enterprise could and would continue without him, but relations were quickly restored, Le Grand returning to his researches in Paulmy's library. His stay would not be a long one. It had been agreed that the Marquis should be allowed to publish his plan of the *Histoire de la Vie Privée des Français*. When the third volume of the *Mélanges tirés d'une grande Bibliothèque* appeared Le Grand was shocked to discover that it

---

[83] Fol. 79ro.

[84] Fol. 78vo. Even Paulmy's hallowed plan for subsequent parts of the work, the first being completed, will, it seems, very probably need modification since the Marquis has not seen the materials amassed for these. Le Grand, however, is prepared to follow the Marquis' outline as closely as possible since his colleague values it so highly.

[85] Fol. 79ro.

contained not only the plan but a detailed summary of the whole work:[86]

Quelle fut ma surprise, lorsque parut votre troisième volume des 'Mélanges,' et que je vis ce plan prétendu, que j'avois toujours cru une distribution méthodique de l'ouvrage, être devenu un précis contenant un volume entier, c'est-à-dire l'ouvrage en petit.[87]

This time Le Grand decided to remain silent until he had finished work upon his first collection when he might give his full attention to the task of reasserting his rights over the *Histoire de la Vie Privée des Français*. The fourth volume of his *Fabliaux ou Contes* opened with a "Prospectus d'un Ouvrage intitulé: 'Histoire de la Vie Privée des Français,' depuis l'origine de la Nation jusqu'à nos jours. Par M. Le Grand."[88] Paulmy's name is not mentioned here.

Outraged the Marquis decides to use his position and influence to discredit Le Grand, having a six-page printed account of the affair read before the Académie Française and distributed to its members and to those of the Académies des Inscriptions et Belles-Lettres.[89] Le Grand for his part pleaded that one or other of the two Académies settle the dispute, but neither would hear of his proposal or even listen to his reply.[90] On February 2nd 1781 an article by Paulmy decrying his adversary appears in the *Journal de Paris* and is answered by Le Grand in the number for the 5th of the same month.[91] On February 15th the journal publishes what the Marquis intends will be the last word on the matter.[92] He has obtained an order from the Garde des Sceaux prohibiting the publication of any reply from Le Grand. On February 21st 1781 the author of the *Fabliaux ou Contes* writes to the Garde des Sceaux, pleading to be allowed to defend himself publicly:

J'ose donc supplier votre grandeur de lever la défense qui a été faite à mon sujet et de donner ordre aux deux journaux en question d'admettre chacun ma réplique.[93]

---

[86] *Précis d'une histoire générale de la vie privée des Français dans tous les temps et dans toutes les provinces de la monarchie*, formant le volume C des *Mélanges tirés d'une grande Bibliothèque*, Paris (Moutard) 1779.

[87] *Ms. Paris, Arsenal 6588*, fol. 88vo. Le Grand was particularly annoyed to note that much of this summary had been taken almost verbatim, yet without acknowledgment, from La Curne de Sainte-Palaye's unpublished *Dictionnaire des antiquités françoises*. He himself had arranged with Sainte-Palaye, "mon premier maître, mon ami, mon bienfaiteur" (*ibidem*), that this should be loaned to the Marquis.

[88] *Contes dévots*, pp. (1)–(8).

[89] *Lettre à l'Auteur des Fabliaux*, n.p.n.d. Paulmy had been a member of the Académie Française since 1748 and of the Académie des Inscriptions since 1756.

[90] Cf. a brief summary of the dispute by Le Grand, *Ms. Paris, Arsenal 6588*, fol. 84ro–vo.

[91] *Journal de Paris*, volume for January–June 1781, pp. 132 and 143 respectively.

[92] *Idem*, p. 183.

[93] *Ms. Paris, Arsenal 6588*, fol. 81ro, rough draft. The *Journal de Littérature* had also carried Paulmy's articles against Le Grand.

The request is refused. As a last resort Le Grand now begins a private campaign to clear his name, and on March 26th he informs the noted historian Louis-Georges de Bréquigny, former protégé and very good friend of the now deceased Sainte-Palaye, member of the Académie des Inscriptions and one of the few to side with Le Grand,[94] that irrefutable proof of the justice of his cause can be viewed by any of his detractors at his residence:[95]

Je supplie les Gens de Lettres, les Membres des différentes Académies, les parens mêmes et les amis de M. le Marquis de P. . . de me faire l'honneur de venir chez moi se convaincre, par leurs propres yeux, si je suis inexcusable ainsi qu'il l'a fait dire à deux journalistes, même avant que ces MM. m'eussent entendu. Toutes les personnes qui se présenteront pour me demander mes preuves, seront reçues de moi avec reconnaissance. Si elles ne sont pas convaincues, je leur aurai fourni de quoi me déshonorer publiquement.[96]

In his last letter to the editors of the *Journal de Paris* Paulmy had formally stated that he no longer cared what became of his project:

Au reste, j'abandonne cette discussion, comme je laisse la liberté à M. le Grand, ou à tout autre de composer dorénavant sur la vie privée des François, tels gros ouvrages qu'ils jugeront à propos, en suivant ou ne suivant pas ce que j'ai déjà publié sur cette matière.[97]

In 1782 Le Grand proceeds to publish the first part of the *Histoire de la Vie Privée des Français* and in the "Avertissement" is careful not only to give the Marquis full credit for the plan of the collection,[98] but also to thank him for his advice and for the use of his library. But there has been no reconciliation. Le Grand remains bitter:

Je me fais un devoir de lui en témoigner ici ma reconnaissance; & je ressens d'autant plus de plaisir à être juste envers lui, que depuis un certain tems il ne l'a pas été, il s'en faut de beaucoup, envers moi.[99]

And in case there should be the least doubt as to his feelings, he concludes the preface by vehemently reiterating his claim:

Quelque soit au reste l'ouvrage qu'on va lire, il est le mien, le mien tout entier; & je défie qui que ce soit au monde d'en revendiquer la moindre

[94] Cf. a letter from Paulmy to Bréquigny, dated February 7th 1781, complaining of the latter's sympathy with Le Grand's cause, *Ms. Paris, B.N. fonds Bréquigny 165*, fol. 206ro–vo.
[95] Quai de l'école, maison de M. Juliot.
[96] Rough draft of this letter, *Ms. Paris, Arsenal 6588*, ff. 90ro–91ro. For the fair copy sent to Bréquigny, cf. *Ms. Paris, B.N. fonds Bréquigny 165*, ff. 208ro–209ro.
[97] Volume for January–June 1781, p. 813.
[98] He adds, however, that Paulmy's four main headings, "logement, nourriture, habillemens, divertissemens ou jeux," are obvious and nothing new.
[99] Vol. I, p. viii.

chose. Ce qui a paru sous le même titre & sur la même matière précédemment à moi, m'appartenait; on l'a extrait de mes cahiers. Malheureusement,
il ne m'est pas permis d'en dire davantage sur cet objet; une loi sévère, que
je suis obligé de respecter, m'impose, une seconde fois, le silence sur mes
droits.[100]

For a man who claims to have had a "système de bonheur" founded
upon the private cultivation of letters in the peace and calm of obscurity, it is surprising to see the lengths to which Le Grand is prepared
to go in order to establish and advertise himself as sole author of what
was to prove a difficult and most demanding piece of work.

The projected history of French manners and customs in fact represented no easy path to literary fame and in all fairness to Le Grand
it must be said that few men would be prepared to undertake a task of
this immensity without the promise of proper recognition. For, whatever assistance he might have had, the bulk of the work was his to do:

... renonçant à tous les plaisirs, travaillant dix à douze heures par jour,
extrayant, copiant sans cesse: enfin, pareil en quelque sorte au Saturne de
de la Fable, je ne vêcus presque plus que pour dévorer des livres. Et quels
livres, juste ciel![101]

If we remember that the work was divided into four sections and look
to the lengthy and highly detailed plan for the first of these,[102] alone to
occupy three volumes, then it is not difficult to understand the need for
such industry. Nor is it indeed surprising that even Le Grand should
find himself discouraged when faced with the task of bringing order and
sequence to the material amassed:

Je me trouvai possesseur de plusieurs milliers de bulletins, dont le plus long
offrait quelques lignes. A la vue de ce chaos effroyable, avec lequel il me
fallait cependant composer une histoire suivie, tout mon corps frissonna, je
l'avoue: je restai quelque tems dans une sorte de stupeur & d'abattement;
& actuellement encore que l'ouvrage est fini, je ne puis me rappeller ce
moment d'efffroi sans éprouver de nouveau un sentiment de terreur in-
volontaire. Quel métier, bon Dieu! que celui de compilateur![103]

This was clearly to be a collection involving no little effort on the part
of the author. But it was not only the author himself who saw the
undertaking as worthwhile and regarded the effort as well-placed:

---

[100] P. xiii.
[101] *Histoire de la Vie Privée des Français*, Avertissement, p. viii.
[102] Cf. the "Prospectus" in the *Contes Dévots* of 1781.
[103] *Histoire de la Vie Privée des Français*, Avertissement, pp. viii–ix.

Cette histoire peut devenir très-curieuse entre les mains d'un homme habile à faire des recherches, & déjà muni de nombreux matériaux.[104]

In fact the project was to prove something of a disappointment both to the author and his critics. For Le Grand's part it was not the scale of the researches to be undertaken that proved discouraging:

... toute fatiguante qu'était cette partie de ma tâche, ce n'est pas celle qui m'a coûté davantage.[105]

As we know, the compilation of the *Fabliaux ou Contes* had furnished him not only with the necessary experience but also with a good deal of material useful to the new collection. The disappointment lay in the subject itself:

Au premier coup-d'oeil, peu de sujets m'avaient paru aussi séduisans que la vie privée des Français; à l'exécution, peu me parurent aussi décourageans. Presque tous les détails qui s'offraient à moi étaient froids, secs & minutieux.[106]

The history of French manners and customs, which had seemed so full of promise, proved in fact to be barren ground and the disappointed Le Grand thus found himself obliged to render his subject attractive by artificial means, by inserting here and there in his text some curious anecdote, some interesting digression which might veil the aridity of his material:

Semblable à un Décorateur auquel on aurait donné des jardins à tracer dans un terrein vaste & pittoresque, mais sec & montueux, presque à chaque pas je me disais à moi-même: que placerai-je ici? Comment m'y prendre pour cacher cette difformité?[107]

Whether or not this would be sufficient to redeem the work remained to be seen.

It was certainly a brave attempt and when the three volumes of the first section, under the general heading "Nourriture," appeared in 1782, it did not go entirely unapplauded:

Il ne s'est pas dissimulé la sécheresse de son sujet; mais il a sçu l'égayer par une multitude de traits historiques qui réveillent l'attention, & sur-tout par plusieurs digressions intéressantes sur le jardinage, sur la chasse, sur la pêche, &c.[108]

---

[104] *Année littéraire*, 1781, vol. V, pp. 252–253.
[105] *Histoire de la Vie Privée des Français*, Avertissement, p. x.
[106] *Ibidem.*
[107] P. xi.
[108] *Année littéraire*, 1783, vol. II, p. 251. The article on the *Histoire de la Vie Privée des Français* occupies pp. 217–251.

But was this enough? While yet appreciative of Le Grand's efforts, this same critic, Geoffroy, concluded his article with the following remark:

Le public en rendant justice à ses travaux, paroît désirer qu'il choisisse avec un goût plus sévère les détails qui doivent entrer dans les parties suivantes, qu'il évite les circonstances minutieuses & frivoles, pour ne s'attacher qu'aux usages qui peignent les moeurs & le caractère national.[109]

The *Journal de Monsieur* was particularly anxious to show Le Grand that he was not alone in his disappointment:

Jamais je n'éprouvai de surprise égale à celle que m'a donnée la lecture de cet ouvrage, par le peu de rapport que j'ai trouvé entre sa valeur réelle & l'idée que je m'en étois faite.[110]

And if le Grand had feared how easily a work such as his might be ridiculed,[111] then this same periodical did its utmost to prove those fears justified:

Si dans les siècles reculés, quelque savant vient à parcourir ces trois volumes, ne croira-t-il pas qu'on y a voulu faire l'histoire privée du peuple le plus gourmand qui ait existé, & que l'Auteur de l'histoire étoit pour le moins un Maître-d'hôtel ....[112]

The feeling was that Le Grand had failed to treat the subject which his title announced and which he had promised earlier, that he had occupied himself only with the "détails froids, secs & minutieux" of which he speaks in his preface:

Dans ces trois volumes d'histoire de vivres & de nourritures, l'érudition est épuisée sur des vétilles qui n'intéressent personne; & la partie des moeurs, de la vie privée des François, qui étoit le sujet de l'Auteur, n'est pas même effleurée.[113]

And yet, strangely enough, there was no suggestion that Le Grand would have done well to return the project to Paulmy, no suggestion that the Marquis might have found another deputy more capable of giving the work the "proper" emphasis and of producing the results expected, although we know that Paulmy and Le Grand had been at variance over the direction to be taken in the collection. On the contrary, both the *Année littéraire* and the *Journal de Monsieur* found the basic plan to be at fault, a plan which Paulmy himself appears to have

---

[109] P. 251.
[110] 1783, vol. I, p. 250. The article occupies pp. 250–281.
[111] Cf. *Histoire de la Vie Privée des Français*, Avertissement, p. x.
[112] *Journal de Monsieur*, 1783, vol. I, p. 254.
[113] *Idem*, p. 281.

approved.[114] In the view of these periodicals, Le Grand could not hope to justify his title if he kept to the present plan and approached the remaining three sections as he had this first:

Si M. Legrand continue son ouvrage avec la même abondance pour les chosés inutiles, & la même stérilité pour les choses essentielles, il compilera une douzaine de volumes qui laisseront encore à désirer un ouvrage intéressant & fait avec goût sur le même sujet.[115]

One begins to wonder what results Paulmy himself could have produced in this case.

It would be wrong to accept these findings without reservation. If the intention so far has been to demonstrate that the *Histoire de la Vie Privée des Français* fell far short of what had been expected, especially in view of the prolonged dispute which had centred upon it, then the justice of this emphasis has not been deduced solely from the bitter disappointment shown by certain critics when reviewing the first section of the work. This latter had found favour in certain quarters:

Dans cette première partie le style pourroit être beaucoup mieux soigné, plus aisé, &c; mais le fond nous semble devoir mériter à l'auteur des éloges très-distingués, de même que tous les encouragemens & les secours dont il a besoin pour compléter une histoire si intéressante.[116]

The primary consideration is the disappointment shown by the author himself, the result of his failure to foresee the difficulty of the task in hand given the materials to be used. No attempt is made to conceal this discouragement in the preface to the first volume, where Le Grand seems almost to acknowledge defeat in anticipation:

... je veux prévenir seulement que j'ai connu les principales difficultés de mon entreprise; que j'ai cherché à les vaincre; & que si je n'ai pas mieux fait, il n'était pas dans mes facultés de faire mieux.[117]

It appears that Le Grand had been obliged to interrupt the work because of his health, which had suffered from the excessive efforts demanded by the collection. But he promises that the task will be re-

---

[114] Cf. the draft of one of Le Grand's irate letters to the Marquis, *Ms. Paris, Arsenal 6588*, fol. 87ro: "Or l'ordre que j'ai mis dans cette partie, les divisions et sous-divisions que j'ai imaginées pour sa distribution, tout cela est de moi; et en vérité je n'y attache pas un grand mérite. Cependant ce qui me feroit croire que mon ordre de matières étoit bon, c'est que vous m'avez fait l'honneur de l'adopter dans votre précis."

[115] *Journal de Monsieur*, 1783, vol. I, p. 281. Cf. also, *Année littéraire*, 1783, vol. II, pp. 218–219.

[116] *L'Esprit des Journaux Français et Etrangers*, May 1783, p. 45. Cf. also, *Mercure*, May 1783, pp. 59–70.

[117] *Histoire de la Vie Privée des Français*, Avertissement, p. xi.

sumed with renewed vigour if, despite their many faults, these first three volumes find favour with his readers.[118] In what might almost be interpreted as a last desperate attempt to save the project he assures these latter that those sections still to appear will have neither the defects nor, more important perhaps, the volume of the first:

Peut-être aussi, à l'aspect de ce qu'a fourni le seul article de la nourriture, craindra-t-on de voir ces volumes se multiplier en proportion pour les parties suivantes, & devenir assez nombreux pour effrayer d'avance. Mais on sera rassuré, quand j'aurai prévenu que cette première partie est seule aussi abondante que les trois autres ensemble.[119]

The *Histoire de la Vie Privée des Français*, in public at least, never progressed beyond these first three volumes. Several factors might account for Le Grand's silence, personal disappointment, perhaps simply continued poor health. In any event, he could not have been too discouraged by the reception of this first part which, as we saw earlier, had not gone entirely without applause. Indeed, it was to draw attention for a number of years to come. In 1800, the year in which Le Grand died, a history of fruit-growing in France extracted from his work was published in Germany,[120] and as much as twenty-six years later a group of writers were inspired by it to produce a *Vie publique et privée des Français*.[121] But by far the most significant evidence of the value attached by some to this unfinished collection came in the interim period, in 1815, with its re-edition.[122]

J. B. B. de Roquefort had no difficulty in justifying a second edition of this lengthy historical account of the sustenance of the French nation:

Le succès de la 'Vie privée des François' étoit assuré depuis long-temps; La Nation et particulièrement les Etrangers accueillirent cet ouvrage avec bien-

---

[118] Cf. a note, vol. III, p. 346.

[119] Avertissement, p. xii.

[120] *Versuch einer Geschichte des Obstbaues in Frankreich*, Frankfurt (P. H. Guilhauman) 1800. The translator considers that Le Grand's article "Des Fruits" will be of considerable interest and value to German fruit-growers: "Bey der sich immer weiter verbreitenden Liebhaberey an dem Gartenwesen, kann es wohl nicht fehlen, dass der Inhalt derselben manchem Liebhaber der Obstkunst unterhaltend und unterrichtend ist, indem man hier aus alten und neueren Schriftstellern und sonsten mit Mühe und Fleiss dasjenige ausgehoben und zusammengestellt findet, was zur Geschichte der Obstbaumzucht in Frankreich dient; und da die Franzosen im Gartenwesen unsere Vorgänger und Lehrer waren, so wird das Büchlein gleiches Interesse Deutschland haben." (Translator's preface.)

[121] *Vie publique et privée des Français, à la ville, à la cour et dans les provinces, depuis la mort de Louis XV jusqu'au commencement du règne de Charles X, pour faire suite à la 'Vie privée des Français' de Legrand d'Aussy*, Paris (Mlle Sigault) 1826, 3 vols.

[122] Paris (Simonet and Laurent Beaupré) 3 vols.

veillance à l'époque où il parut (en 1782). Devenu rare et d'un prix fort élevé, il importoit d'en publier une nouvelle édition ....[123]

There were numerous additions and corrections to be made and the new editor, like the original author, found his task a tedious one. But the work needed to be done and there were compensations:

Au surplus si un travail aussi fastidieux que celui que j'ai entrepris admet quelque consolation qui puisse me dédommager de l'ennui qu'il entraîne, c'est le plaisir de pouvoir de temps en temps louer avec sécurité ma patrie qui, malgré les malheurs qu'elle vient d'éprouver, possède assez encore pour ne pouvoir être abattue et briller d'un nouvel éclat.[124]

Le Grand would presumably have been well pleased by these patriotic intentions for he had himself found similar consolation in his own work. On more than one occasion in the *Fabliaux ou Contes* he declares his primary concern to be the Nation's honour, the glory of France.[125] The emphasis remains unchanged in the *Histoire de la Vie Privée des Français*. If the intimate domestic life of the great Roman people could prove a fascinating study, then so too would that of the French, themselves able to boast no mean achievement:

Eh! pourquoi quelqu'un qui voyant les Français devenus, par l'aménité de leurs moeurs & par la supériorité de leurs écrivains, l'une des premières nations de l'Europe, ne se flatterait-il donc pas d'inspirer un intérêt semblable, en leur présentant les moeurs, les usages, en un mot la vie domestique de leurs Ancêtres.[126]

The publication of this second edition of the *Histoire de la Vie Privée des Français* more than thirty eventful years after the first was in itself something of a tribute to the work which, after all, represented only the first part of a collection left largely unfinished, at least unpublished, by its author. We know that the three volumes had been well received by certain critics and J. B. B. de Roquefort testifies to their popularity both in France and abroad. And yet, when compared with the *Fabliaux ou Contes*, this second literary venture can be regarded only as a limited success. It may have been as a result of the plan or the material used or even the manner in which these were approached, but in a

---

[123] Vol. I, Avis de l'éditeur, p. i.
[124] *Idem*, p. v.
[125] Cf. for example vol. I, preface, p. c.: "L'amour-propre trouvait peu d'aliment dans un Ouvrage qui ne demandait que beaucoup de lecture & quelque goût; mais cet Ouvrage tenait en quelque sorte à la gloire de ma Patrie; il renfermait nos titres d'aînesse littéraire; & dès-lors il m'est devenu précieux."
[126] *Histoire de la Vie Privée des Français*, Avertissement, p. vi.

project which appeared to have immense possibilities, possibilities worth fighting for, Le Grand found frustration and disappointment. It was J. B. B. de Roquefort's intention to complete the collection.[127] It is perhaps significant that he failed to do so.

Before turning our attention from the *Histoire de la Vie Privée des Français* we might note that the title-page to the first volume of the edition of 1782 bears the name Le Grand d'Aussy. The origin of this rather ennobling appendage to the family name is not difficult to trace for Le Grand's father was a native of Auxi-le-Château in the Pas de Calais. But if this was not a family title, then why had Le Grand suddenly seen fit to adopt it? Was it simply that he found it more fitting to his newly acquired status as a man of letters? This is certainly a possibility. But perhaps the proper explanation is indicated in the note which concludes the preface to the *Histoire de la Vie Privée des Français*:

Depuis quelque tems, les papiers publics ont annoncé & publié, sous un même nom que le mien, différens Ouvrages, &, entr'autres, plusieurs Pièces de vers, que certaines personnes m'ont fait gratuitement l'honneur de m'attribuer. Comme aucune de ces productions ne m'appartient, je déclare que jusqu'ici il n'a paru de moi dans le public que les 'Fabliaux,' & la partie de la 'Vie privée des Français,' qu'on va lire.[128]

The name of Le Grand was by no means uncommon and it is understandable that this could lead to some confusion. Were it not for the above declaration, we might still easily be misled, for example, by Grimm's *Correspondance littéraire*:

On a donné à la Comédie Française, le 4 de ce mois,[129] la première représentation du 'Bon Ami,' comédie en un acte et en prose, par M. le Grand.[130]

Although, as suggested earlier, there may well have been other considerations, it was surely with the primary intention of removing the possibility of such confusion that the author of the *Fabliaux ou Contes* became Le Grand d'Aussy.

---

[127] Cf. de Roquefort's edition of the work (1815), vol. I, note to p. vi; also vol. III, note to p. 402.

[128] P. xiii.

[129] November 1780.

[130] *Correspondance littéraire, philosophique et critique, adressée à un souverain d'Allemagne, depuis 1770 jusqu'en 1782, par le baron de Grimm et par Diderot*, Paris (F. Buisson) 1812, vol. V, p. 209. The third volume of the *Correspondance* contains an article on a one-act verse comedy "d'un certain M. Legrand" entitled *La Rupture ou le Malentendu* (pp. 315-316).

F. THE EXCURSIONS TO AUVERGNE

It was not until 1787 that Le Grand indulged himself with what was his first real excursion into the provinces since his arrival in the capital well over twenty years earlier. In that year he set out for Auvergne to visit the brother he so cherished, Pierre-Théodore-Louis-Augustin, then prior of the abbey of Saint-André in Clermont.[131] Unaware on leaving that other delights would be added to the joys of the reunion, he had intended to stay only a month. Almost five months elapsed before he returned to Paris, so enthused as to want to publish his observations, ample testimony to the pleasure and fulfilment brought by this temporary departure from a life of secluded scholarship.

As had apparently been the case with the *Fabliaux ou Contes*, the *Voyage d'Auvergne* came to be written almost by chance.[132] Quite apart from the idea of publishing his observations Le Grand had not originally intended even to record these, and it was only at the request of a friend, the Abbé de F...,[133] that he promised to do so:

... comme, dans un pareil voyage, je devais à-coup-sûr rencontrer plus d'un objet curieux, l'Homme-de-Lettres dont je viens de parler, m'avait prié de lui donner quelques détails sur ceux qui me paraîtraient les plus piquans. Je le promis, sans savoir à quel point je m'engageais, mais j'étais bien éloigné de croire que de cette promesse résulterait un livre.[134]

Yet as le Grand himself willingly admits, it was precisely this promise which, urging him to close and careful observation and forbidding exaggerated confidence in the powers of the memory, rendered the excursion itself, quite independent of the object, the reunion with Pierre-Théodore, a most rewarding experience, so rewarding that he believed others might wish to share in it:

Il m'a semblé que ce que j'avais eu tant de plaisir à voir, d'autres peut-être auraient encore du plaisir à le lire; & c'est dans cet espoir que, de retour à Paris, après cinq mois de courses, j'ai rédigé mon travail & l'ai mis en état d'être publié.[135]

---

[131] Pierre-Théodore had earlier been prior of Licques in the diocese of Boulogne.

[132] *Voyage d'Auvergne, par M. Le Grand d'Aussy*, Paris (E. Onfroy) 1788.

[133] Le Grand describes him simply as "Rédacteur d'un Journal." This was very probably the Abbé de Fontenay, editor of the *Affiches de Province*, who had earlier spoken for the South in the "querelle des trouvères et des troubadours."

[134] *Voyage d'Auvergne*, Avertissement, p. vi.

[135] *Idem*, pp. vii–viii. It appears that before the appearance of the *Voyage d'Auvergne* the Abbé de F... had published two articles from it in his journal, one concerning the Puy de Dôme and the other la Limagne (*ibidem*).

Le Grand's observations were first published more or less in their original form of a report made out to a friend, which does much to explain
the spontaneity and enthusiasm found in this first edition of the *Voyage
d'Auvergne*, so sadly lacking in the *Histoire de la Vie Privée des Français*:

> Primitivement ce n'était qu'un compte rendu à mon ami. Je lui écrivais
> dans l'effusion de mon âme, & lui parlais autant de ce que j'avais senti que
> de ce que j'avais vu. Il m'en eût coûté trop de tems pour changer cette
> forme; je l'ai conservé. Au reste, l'Ouvrage appartenait en partie à M. L'Ab-
> bé de F...; puisque d'abord c'était pour lui qu'il avait été entrepris.[136]

And yet this same enthusiasm, even a certain degree of spontaneity, of
immediacy, marks the second edition, published several years after a
second visit to Auvergne in 1788, where Le Grand found order and
sequence an unavoidable discipline.[137]

The second excursion had been planned even before the first had
come to an end, for although extended this had allowed Le Grand
enough time to acquaint himself with only a small part of the region
and much remained to be seen. [138] Clearly anxious to return to the
delights of this new experience, he was not to be disappointed by a
return visit of a further five months, which he had originally intended
should provide a second volume on similar lines to the first. However,
the various districts visited frequently resembled those treated earlier
in so many respects that, rather than risk frustrating his readers with
constant references to the first volume or boring them with the reproduction of almost identical observations, Le Grand decided to revise
the whole of the material collected on both occasions and publish a
completely remodelled second edition, enlarged to three volumes:

> ... j'ai pris le parti de refondre en entier mes matériaux, de leur donner une
> autre forme, de réunir sous de mêmes cadres tous les objets de la Haute et de
> la Basse-Auvergne dont les rapports étaient communs; en un mot de varier
> mes tableaux, en même tems que je les agrandirais.[139]

To judge from the author's sustained enthusiasm in this second edition,
the return visit to Auvergne proved, as indicated already, no less a

---

[136] *Ibidem.*

[137] *Voyage fait en 1787 et 1788, dans la ci-devant Haute et Basse Auvergne, aujourd'hui départemens
du Puy-de-Dôme, du Cantal et partie de celui de la Haute-Loire, Ouvrage où l'on traite ce qui regarde la
nature du sol, les révolutions qu'il a éprouvées, ses productions, climat, météores, produits de volcanisation,
mines, carrières, lacs, eaux minérales, moeurs des habitans, constitution physique, population, arts, commerce, manufactures, industrie, etc. etc'.* Paris (chez le directeur de l'Imprimerie des Sciences et
Arts) an III de la République française (1795) 3 vols.

[138] Cf. first edition, p. 27.

[139] Second edition, vol. I, Avertissement, pp. ix–x. This second edition is written as a
series of letters addressed "Au cit. Le B...."

pleasure than had the first. In view of the promise made to the Abbé de
F..., Le Grand had initially felt obliged to take proper and careful
note of all he saw that was of interest. But he was soon to realise that
this was no imposition. It was as if he was learning for the first time to
make use of his latent talents and to enjoy the rewards they offered:

... j'ignorais, quand je quittais Paris, tous les plaisirs qui m'étaient préparés ... Que vous dirai-je; je me proposais de rester en Auvergne un moi; j'y
en ai passé près de cinq; & à mon départ, je regrettais encore de n'avoir pu
en passer davantage.[140]

This was very probably the first time that Le Grand had allowed himself to be seriously distracted from his scholarly researches in the capital
and clearly he was delighted by the quite unexpected results.

The strength of the *Voyage d'Auvergne*, particularly in its first but also
in its more carefully ordered second edition, lies in the great diversity
of the observations made and the ensuing diversity of the style used to
convey these, the variety born of unfailing interest:

J'ai visité l'Auvergne, mon ami. Tu avais soupçonné, comme moi, que ce
canton ignoré devait être intéressant; et aujourd'hui, que j'en suis revenu,
tu me demandes ce que j'en pense. Le voici. De toutes les anciennes provinces de France, il n'en est point assurément qui soit moins connue; et parmi
toutes peut-être, il n'en est point, qui, pour le physicien et le naturaliste,
pour le peintre et le voyageur, mérite de l'être davantage.[141]

The author in fact becomes all of these in turn and more besides and
this is surely the key to his enthusiasm. Compelled as it were to bring
into play facets of his imagination and intelligence which he had hitherto ignored or been unable to exploit in the capital, Le Grand now
draws upon these resources and finds a new fulfilment.

In one respect at least the *Voyage d'Auvergne* resembles the *Histoire de
la Vie Privée des Français*, for at the simplest level it might be described
as a catalogue of facts. The work, especially in the enlarged second
edition, contains a fund of information on Auvergne with its numerous
villages and small townships. History, geographical situation and geo-
logical structure, climate, agriculture and commerce, art and architecture, laws and customs, little of relevance goes without mention, including the physical and moral characteristics of the region's inhabitants, and there is even an itinerary suggested for those who might like
to follow in the author's footsteps and take the best possible advantage

[140] First edition, p. 304.
[141] Second edition, vol. I, p. 1.

of a visit to Auvergne.[142] But already this new field of inquiry is to be distinguished by its immense scope and flexibility. More important, the method of inquiry is somewhat different. Although in the edition of 1795 Le Grand freely admits that he has consulted and incorporated in his work whatever relevant information he could find, information gleaned as much from the archives of the local government offices as from the numerous scholarly works published on this region,[143] yet no longer does he depend exclusively upon the written word for his material. The *Voyage d'Auvergne*, and this is particularly obvious in the earlier version, is written from first-hand experience. The author is personally involved with the object of his researches, observing and discovering for himself, although never failing to seek advice when necessary or to welcome those who came forward with the offer of assistance.[144]

For a man of letters Le Grand appears to have had something of a passion for the sciences, a latent talent finally brought to fruition by this excursion into the provinces. The natural history of Auvergne he found to be a particularly fascinating object of study, although he admits to only "shallow knowledge" of this field in which he would not presume to rely upon his own judgement:

> ... ce n'était pas à moi, Homme-de-lettres, de parler d'une science, dans laquelle je n'ai que les connaissances superficielles qu'on peut aquérir, quand, comme moi, on a seulement suivi quelques cours, lu quelques livres, & parcouru quelques cabinets.[145]

Instead he sollicited the help of a certain M. Mossier, magistrate of the town of Clermont, an apothecary by profession but also an accomplished naturalist, who gave his services most willingly and even accompanied Le Grand and his brother on some of their expeditions:

> Nous devons à sa complaisance de nous avoir accompagnés dans quelques voyages; moi je dois à l'amitié qu'il m'a témoignée pendant tout le tems de mon séjour, des conservations particulières dont j'ai souvent profité pour l'Ouvrage qu'on va lire.[146]

---

[142] In the second edition Le Grand takes up more than twenty separate points on the town of Clermont alone, including such details as "la tortuosité des rues."

[143] Cf. vol. I, Avertissement, pp. xii–xvi.

[144] Second edition, Avertissement, pp. xii–xiii: "Connu dans la contrée à mon second voyage, parce que le premier m'y avait annoncé, j'ai trouvé par-tout des secours plus étendus et plus nombreux. Médecins, négocians, ingénieurs, tout ce qui alors portait le nom de curé, de gentilhomme, d'homme de loi, de chanoine et de religieux, s'empressa de satisfaire à mes questions, de me donner les renseignemens dont j'avais besoin, et de me conduire même aux lieux qu'il croyait pouvoir être intéressans pour moi."

[145] First edition, Avertissement, p. ix.

[146] *Idem*, pp. ix–x.

Le Grand was clearly to owe a great deal to the numerous individuals who were of service to him in his varied researches, men who shared Mossier's ability to communicate not only knowledge but, more important, enthusiasm. Perhaps their task was made easy. Certainly the pupil was most willing to learn and himself not altogether uninspired.

As a student of natural history Le Grand is interested in everything from the great variety of minerals found in Auvergne to the vicissitudes of climate experienced in that region. But rarely are his observations purely factual or coldly objective. Although much of this immediacy is lost in the second edition, the "reportage" is generally lively and marked by a certain spontaneity, interrupted here and there by some interesting digression upon the utility of lightning-conductors or by the relation of some curious anecdote attached to a particular mineral, some fable concerning an extinct volcano. As a scientist he has noted and will describe for us "les différens corps que peut produire un volcan,"[147] but then in his enthusiasm he will go on to suggest how man's knowledge of those substances and of the volcanoes themselves might be greatly increased. He proposes that one of Auvergne's volcanic mountains should literally be laid open for scientific inspection. The high cost of such excavations would quickly be met by a fresh influx of sightseers and the rewards to science would be immense:

Après avoir vu l'abîme, examiné son foyer & parcouru son aire, on allumerait des flambeaux pour visiter les cavernes. C'est-là que, transporté de plaisir, le Naturaliste trouverait des coctions, des fontes & des vitrifactions à tous les degrés possibles, des substances nouvelles & que nous ne connaissons probablement pas, enfin des effects du feu en grand, & mille accidens divers, dont nous ne pouvons avoir d'idée, & qu'aujourd'hui il n'est pas même possible pour lui de deviner.[148]

That an accomplished man of letters like Le Grand can apply himself to any kind of real scientific observation is surely to his credit. That he should do so with such fervour is quite remarkable. It is as if Le Grand would allow of no half measures. Having himself tasted of the delights offered by the study of natural history he would have others share in these delights and suggests that a "cabinet d'Histoire-naturelle" be established in each and every province of France, first and foremost in Auvergne "... qui de toutes peut-être est la plus riche en accidens & en singularités ...".[149] But having made the suggestion he is not con-

---

147 First edition, p. 454.
148 *Idem*, p. 493.
149 *Idem*, p. 26.

tent to sit back and await results. Already during his first stay in the region he and his brother are out conducting experiments and gathering samples to begin a collection.[150] Scrambling over rocks, falling into streams, cutting and bruising himself at every step but slowly acquiring a certain technique and clearly savouring every moment, what a change from the life he had led in the capital,[151] and what enthusiasm from a man already well into middle age:

L'air des montagnes, quand elles n'ont qu'une hauteur médiocre, a une élasticité qui se communique à notre machine & lui donne du ressort. Peut-être le plaisir que j'y éprouvais animait-il mon courage; mais quoi-qu'ac-coutumé à la vie sédentaire d'un Homme-de-lettres, & par conséquent peu fait à marcher, jamais je n'y ai senti une vraie fatigue. Cent fois il m'est arrivé d'y passer six ou sept heures de suite, sans m'asseoir un seul instant; & je ne m'apercevais de quelque lassitude que quand j'étais dans la plaine.[152]

Le Grand had grown particularly fond of this idea of establishing in Auvergne what might be described as a museum of natural history:

Ce projet m'est devenu cher, je l'avoue; j'y mets un intérêt infini, & je serais désolé de le voir échouer.[153]

But in other fields too he displays this same inability to remain detached, this same need for complete personal involvement. What he has to say about the Auvergnats themselves, for example, amounts to little less than a sociological survey, interested as he is in everything from the clothes they wear to the diseases from which they suffer. More important, living amongst these people he became genuinely concerned about their condition, feeling it his duty to help in any way open to him. To judge from certain remarks made in the second edition of the *Voyage*, his efforts for Auvergne do not appear to have been entirely wasted:

Ce que j'avais dit sur les impôts excessifs dont elle était accablée, sur l'émi-gration forcée à laquelle sont réduits la plupart de ses habitans, etc. m'y a mérité quelque reconnaissance; par-tout, sur ma route, on me l'a témoignée.

---

[150] *Idem*, p. 27: "A quelques morceaux près, que je rapporterai à Paris avec moi, tout le reste a été placé chez lui [Pierre-Théodore]; & si, l'an prochain, 1788, je retourne en Auvergne, comme je m'en flatte, nous augmenterons encore la collection."

[151] *Idem*, pp. 306–307: "Combien de fois ai-je passé cinq ou six heures de suite avec un habit mouillé de sueur! Combien de fois suis-je revenu avec des contusions & des déchirures! Dans les commencemens, l'ardeur emporte; on ne peut se contenir, on s'expose; & d'ailleurs on est un peu gauche au métier. En voulant casser une lave, je me suis emporté l'ongle du pouce. En voulant, au Mont-Dor, sauter sur une pierre pour traverser La Dordogne, je suis tombé dans l'eau."

[152] *Idem*, p. 308.

[153] *Idem*, p. 27.

La commission intermédiaire elle-même, dans un mémoire, qu'elle a présenté en 1788 au ministère, pour demander un allégement à tant de maux, m'a fait l'honneur de me citer en témoignage, et de copier une partie de ce que j'en avais dit. J'ai dû parler pour l'Auvergne, et je l'ai fait. Hélas! pourquoi ne m'est-il pas donné de pouvoir davantage?[154]

As we are already aware, this enthusiasm, this need for complete and intimate involvement had brought Le Grand far more personal rewards.[155] Others yet awaited him. On setting out for Auvergne Le Grand had promised the Abbé de F... that he would observe closely and report upon anything he considered striking or worthy of note. Although himself not a scientist he found the region to be particularly interesting for its "détails d'Histoire-naturelle" and therefore plunged himself with fervour into this new field. The results, as we saw, were quite unexpected. What might have been an imposition became a pleasure, a pleasure developing into a passion which offered a new kind of fulfilment. But it must also be remembered that Auvergne is an area of great natural beauty, natural beauty of a kind almost unknown to Le Grand after more than twenty years in the capital. Once again he applies himself with the same fervour, and once again the results are quite unanticipated:

Pour moi qui, depuis vingt six ans ne suis guères accoutumé qu'aux beautés froides & à l'art compassé des environs de la Capitale, je fus ravi, je l'avoue. Jamais mes yeux n'avaient vu un théâtre aussi riche, aussi vaste, & aussi grandement dessiné. Je ne pouvais me lasser de l'admirer; & comme Argus, j'eusse voulu en ce moment être tout oeil. Ma vue se portait de la plaine aux montagnes, & des montagnes à la plaine. En vain j'essayais de la fixer sur un objet, un autre objet plus beau encore l'appellait vers lui; & près de celui-ci j'en découvrais vingt autres qui me paraissaient plus piquans encore.[156]

This confrontation seems to have brought Le Grand to a true awareness of the delights which the senses could afford. The experience had come late in life but in no way did this diminish its effects. On the contrary, the years of what might almost be described as deprivation could have served only to heighten his susceptibility. He himself speaks freely of the violence of the impression made, his soul as it were exhausted by the constant flow of new sensations and ideas which he feels must be communicated:

---

[154] Second edition, vol. III, pp. 158–159.
[155] Paradoxically it was most probably this enthusiasm which caused the "failure" of the *Histoire de la Vie Privée des Français*, due if anything to an excess of zeal on the author's part.
[156] First edition, pp. 10–11.

L'homme qui, en ce moment, m'eût empêché d'écrire, m'aurait imposé un supplice affreux.[157]

In this state of mind Le Grand sees only through the poet's subjective eye, his observations acquiring a lyrical quality, perhaps indicating a certain talent in this direction hitherto unexploited:

On dirait que ce mont célèbre[158] est placé-là, comme par magie. Il ferme la valée, de sa large base; s'arrondit autour d'elle, en demi-cercle; et s'élevant par une pente peu rapide, forme un vaste amphithéâtre qu'occupe une forêt de sapins. Tu vois s'épanouir devant toi, les uns au-dessus des autres, ces arbres à tige élancée, à feuilles de dard; et leurs cîmes caduques, ainsi que leur physionomie sauvage, produisent-là un effet inconcevable.[159]

It is as though he is almost at a loss to set down his impressions despite his need to do so. Indeed, there are occasions when his feelings are such that he can find no words to describe them, occasions when he is totally given over to the sensations of the moment, an altogether new experience for Le Grand:

Dans certains momens, les idées venaient m'accabler; mais elles étaient incohérentes, & se succédaient avec la rapidité d'un éclair. Dans d'autres j'étais absorbé; je ne pouvais plus penser, & je n'avais que des sensations; c'était vraiment un état d'ivresse. Enfin que vous dirai-je; j'éprouvai là une impression très-profonde, une émotion délicieuse; mais ce qui se passait en moi était si subordonné, si confus, qu'il me serait impossible de vous en rendre compte.[160]

Equally at ease when reporting an experiment to discover how noxious is the air in certain caves situated in the vicinity of Clermont[161] as when evoking the play of light filtering through one of the many water-falls found in this region,[162] one begins to wonder at Le Grand's ability to apply himself in such diverse ways. Is he poet or scientist? Is there no dichotomy? The question had obviously occurred to Le Grand himself for he speaks of his natural bias as a man of letters, convinced of his own shortcomings in other directions:

Nous autres gens-de-lettres, trop futiles dans nos études, trop superficiels dans nos écrits, nous prisons trop le coloris du style et point assez les connaissances de l'esprit. Les savans ont le tort contraire. Il nous manque, à nous, la culture; et à eux, l'ornement. Pour l'avantage des uns et des autres,

---

[157] *Idem*, p. 305.
[158] Mont-Dore.
[159] Second edition, vol. II, p. 65.
[160] First edition, p. 167.
[161] These are known locally as "étouffis." Cf. first edition, p. 116.
[162] Cf. second edition, vol. II, pp. 85–86.

il faudrait un temple commun, dans lequel ils sacrifieraient aux grâces, et nous aux sciences.[163]

But the reader is never aware of any such imbalance and in reality Le Grand had just as little experience as a writer of descriptive prose, for which he had earlier lacked both opportunity and inspiration, as he had as a student of natural history. The truth of the matter would seem to be that, applying himself with his accustomed fervour in hitherto unexplored spheres of activity, he was surprised by his own capabilities. It is the enthusiasm resulting from this sense of new achievement that is communicated to the reader.

Le Grand had waited more than twenty years before thus indulging himself and his patience had been well rewarded. But if the days spent in Auvergne were clearly to count amongst the most enjoyable that he would know, then this was due almost entirely to the promise he had made the Abbé de F... shortly before departing upon the first excursion in 1787. It was this which had led to his exploiting neglected or little used talents and which to the satisfaction of this new fulfilment had eventually added the pleasure of enabling others to share a most rewarding experience.

In fact Le Grand sincerely hoped that the *Voyage d'Auvergne* would encourage others to follow in his footsteps and in this hope, as we know, he suggests a possible itinerary for those interested, ensuring that their time be not wasted, almost guaranteeing enjoyment. But to this is added the promise of quite unexpected delights, his first recommendation being that from time to time they allow themselves the freedom to wander through the region at will, seeking their own adventures like the knights-errant of old:

L'Auvergne est un pays si extraordinaire & si peu connu, qu'infailliblement, si j'en juge d'après ce que j'ai presque toujours éprouvé, ils n'auront qu'à se féliciter de leur curiosité; & que probablement même leurs aberrations amèneront des découvertes nouvelles.[164]

As a further inducement Le Grand had originally intended that the work should be furnished with a number of illustrations, an idea which he had eventually been obliged to abandon having found no one in a

---

[163] Second edition, vol. III, p. 150.
[164] First edition, p. 512. In the second edition the itinerary occupies pp. 353–432 of the third volume.

position to undertake the work.[165] Certainly this would have been an improvement, but as it stood the *Voyage d'Auvergne* seems to have drawn considerable praise from contemporary French critics and to have been deemed worthy of translation into at least one foreign tongue.[166] Although an opinion which Le Grand in his modesty will dispute, several periodicals apparently considered the work a worthy example for others to follow,[167] a view shared by the Censeur Royal:

Cet Ouvrage m'a paru fait pour servir de modèle, & tel qu'il seroit à désirer que l'on en publiât sur chacune des Provinces de France. Je crois donc qu'il ne peut qu'être fort utile, soit par ce que l'on y apprendra, soit aussi par ce qu'il pourra faire naître, à des hommes suffisamment instruits, le désir d'en publier de pareils sur les lieux de leur résidence.[168]

G. A NEW CAREER? THE YEARS OF SILENCE

Following the obvious frustration and disappointment which the compilation of the *Histoire de la Vie Privée des Français* had brought Le Grand, the success of his excursions to Auvergne and of the ensuing publications might be seen to indicate that he had earlier failed to realize his true vocation in life, at least that the time was now right for a change of occupation. This was the first time that he had allowed himself any real freedom, the freedom to pursue other interests, to allow other talents to develop naturally and of their own accord, and the results of what proved a most satisfying experience had not been altogether without merit. Then perhaps he should embark upon similar journeys into other provinces of France, even into other lands, seeking adventure and fulfilment as an explorer and chronicler of such voyages of discovery, like François Levaillant whose account of a second expedition into the African interior Le Grand helped to complete.[169]

[165] A fold-out illustration of Clermont and its immediate surroundings opens the first edition, but there are no others. In the third volume of the second edition Le Grand lists those objects he himself considers worthy of illustration in the hope that amongst his successors there may be one with the necessary talent and inclination to take up the project: "Il pourra choisir dans ce nombre ceux qu'il croira dignes de son crayon." (Pp. 432–436.)

[166] Cf. a German translation of the work, revised with notes and additions: *Reisen durch Auvergne von Legrand. Umgearbeitet mit Anmerkungen und Zusätzen von Heinr. Fr. Link, Professor zu Rostock*, Göttingen (Vandenhöck und Ruprecht) 1797. The translator mentions a German rendering of the first edition, published in Bayreuth in 1791.

[167] *Voyage d'Auvergne*, second edition, vol. III, p. 157: "Je ne m'abuse point sur les éloges qu'ont daigné me prodiguer les journalistes; et n'ai garde, sur-tout, de croire, comme l'ont dit la plupart d'entre eux, que je doive servir de modèle en ce genre."

[168] First edition, Approbation.

[169] *Second Voyage dans l'Intérieur de l'Afrique, par le Cap de Bonne-Espérance; dans les années 1783, 84 et 85; par F. Levaillant*, Paris (H. J. Jansen) an III de la République une et indivisible (1795) 3 vols. It is difficult to know the extent of Le Grand's participation in this work. The British Museum catalogue simply notes that he completed it, the catalogue of the Bibliothèque Nationale that it was both completed and published by him.

Clearly Levaillant must have been a man Le Grand both envied and admired. Indeed, the two were much alike. An accomplished student of natural history, it was Levaillant's passionate interest in this field which had led him to spend almost five years in Africa, not only observing the wild-life but collecting innumerable specimens for close examination.[170] His first expedition into the interior had lasted sixteen months,[171] but as had been Le Grand's experience in Auvergne, this had only left him anxious to return at the first opportunity:

Seize mois de courses et de chasses continuelles dans l'intérieur de l'Afrique méridionale n'avoient pu ralentir mon zèle, ni combler tous mes souhaits: cette passion toujours plus impérieuse d'accroître mes connoissances en histoire naturelle naissoit de la multitude même de celles que je venois d'amasser.[172]

As can be seen from the account of this second journey, it was not only within the sphere of his researches as a student of natural history that Levaillant displayed such enthusiasm. Like Le Grand he allowed himself complete freedom, putting time and opportunity to their fullest use by giving this attention to all he found worthy of it. This might be anything from the manners and customs of the various peoples he encountered to the scenes of great natural beauty upon which he stumbled, a sunset viewed from Table Mountain:

On pourroit dire que c'étoit l'arrivée du maître de la nature aux bornes du monde. Je vis ce globe de feu se plonger et disparaître avec majesté dans les eaux. Quel ravissant spectacle il offrit à mes yeux étonnés, lorsque, rasant la surface des mers, il parut tout-à-coup en embrasser l'abîme, pour rejoindre, comme le dit Ossian, l'immense palais des ténèbres.[173]

And this is the style used more or less throughout the three volumes, that same lively "reportage" found in the first edition of the *Voyage d'Auvergne* which gives the impression almost of a diary kept for the benefit of a friend that he might share a most enjoyable and a most rewarding experience. Little wonder then that the accounts of Levaillant's exploits, as enthralling as any adventure story, for adventures there were in plenty, should prove extremely popular with the contemporary reading public both in France and abroad.[174]

---

[170] A keen ornithologist, he speaks at one point of having collected well over a thousand birds. His ornithological writings appear to have enjoyed great success.

[171] 1781–1783.

[172] *Second Voyage dans l'Intérieur de l'Afrique*, vol. I, p. 3.

[173] *Idem*, p. 125.

[174] An account of Levaillant's travels between 1780 and 1785 appeared in 1790 (Paris, Leroy, 1 vol. in-4, 2 vols. in-8) and there was at least one later edition (Paris, Crapelet, an VI, 2 vols). But the two expeditions were also treated separately, these individual accounts

Comparing the *Voyage d'Auvergne* with the *Second Voyage dans l'Intérieur de l'Afrique* it becomes evident that Le Grand had a great deal in common with Levaillant, so much in common that one feels he would have gained equal fulfilment from such voyages of discovery. He must surely have envied the man his opportunities for the talents brought to fruition by the excursions to Auvergne would seem almost to have destined Le Grand for this kind of life. Already in 1782, when reviewing the second edition of the *Fabliaux ou Contes*, the *Journal de Monsieur* had suggested that the author would do well to make better use of his natural ability:

> ... il feroit plus d'honneur à notre siècle si, en se livrant à son propre génie, il quittoit le pénible métier de Traducteur & d'Editeur, pour un emploi plus brillant & plus flatteur que son mérite naturel doit lui procurer.[175]

Was it now possible that he would heed this advice? It must be remembered that the year in which the *Second Voyage dans l'Intérieur de l'Afrique* appeared, 1795, was also the year which saw Le Grand's fifty-eighth birthday, hardly the time of life to begin a career of exploration and adventure in foreign parts. But the greater part of France remained as yet unknown to him and even within the capital itself there was surely ample opportunity for him to exploit his many varied abilities. What use would he make of the few years left to him?

In attempting to show that Le Grand was a man of many talents we have purposely avoided all mention of the manuscript work undertaken after 1782. But Le Grand was first and foremost a scholar and his researches had not ceased with the publication of the *Histoire de la Vie Privée des Français*. The latter may have brought him frustration and disappointment but in no way could this dampen his enthusiasm. In 1795 these scholarly researches became once more his sole preoccupation, a most regrettable error of judgement in the view of Pierre-Charles Lévesque who in respect of the *Voyage d'Auvergne* will later remark:

> C'est là qu'on peut reconnoître quels succès il auroit obtenu dans l'art d'écrire, s'il n'avoit pas consacré sa vie presque entière à l'étude de productions barbares.[176]

apparently proving equally popular. The *Second Voyage* which Le Grand helped to complete reappeared at least twice after 1795, in the an IV of the République (Paris, H.-J. Jansen, 2 vols.) and in 1803 (Paris, Crapelet, 3 vols.). There were numerous English and German translations of these works, the *Second Voyage* appearing in London in 1796 under the title *New Travels into the interior parts of Africa* (3 vols.).

[175] *Journal de Monsieur*, 1782, vol. III, p. 327.
[176] "Notice historique sur Le Grand d'Aussy."

But was this such a mistake? In the first place we could not agree that the time Le Grant spent compiling the *Fabliaux ou Contes*, for example, had been in any way wasted. More important, if Le Grand was to end his days in devoted study amidst the manuscripts of the Bibliothèque Nationale, then not only would the scope of his researches allow him the freedom to pursue his diverse interests, the very nature of the work undertaken would oblige him to do so, even demanding inquiry into hitherto unexplored fields and so further enriching his experience. Le Grand was finally to combine all his talents. The last five years of his life were not to be without their rewards.[177]

It must of course be remembered that since Le Grand's return to the capital after his second excursion into the provinces France had gone through a most difficult period in her history, knowing the joys but also the sorrows of a revolution whose effects were to be felt in every sphere of human activity. If the second edition of the *Voyage d'Auvergne* did not appear until 1795 then it was not because the author had required seven years to complete the work. The fall of the Ancien Régime disrupted the lives of all Frenchmen, but nowhere could this disruption have been more immediate or more violent than in Paris itself where Le Grand had made his home. We cannot know what were his feelings as he witnessed the events taking place about him but in one way at least he might be said to have made his own contribution to the Revolution. It will be remembered that in the first edition of the *Voyage d'Auvergne* he had done what he could to draw attention to the plight of the Auvergnats, often forced to leave their own province in order to seek a livelihood and overburdened with taxes if they remained. His remarks would appear to have been well in keeping with the new movement:

... comme il gémit sur le sort des opprimés! comme il tonne contre l'atrocité des oppresseurs! comme il s'indigne de l'indolence des puissans, quand il s'agit de soulager des misérables![178]

---

[177] Nevertheless, the eleven-page *Lettre sur la communauté des Guittard-Pinon* (Clermont, Thibaud-Landriot frères, n.d.) which Le Grand had been inspired to write after his second visit to Auvergne in 1788, shows that the return to a solitary, sedentary life in the capital can have demanded no little sacrifice of him: "J'allai, avec la troupe, m'asseoir et causer sur tout ce qui la concernait. Les mères vinrent se placer et se serrer autour de moi; leurs enfans s'approchèrent pour me caresser; les hommes firent cercle et nous entourèrent: c'était à qui me témoignerait plus d'amitié. Emu, jusqu'aux larmes, par ce spectacle attendrissant, bientôt je le fus davantage encore par ce que j'entendis. Tout ce que me disaient ces braves gens, tout ce qu'ils répondaient à mes questions, me les montrait doux, simples, bons, et, quoiqu'-infiniment respectables, plus aimables encore. Je me voyais dans le séjour du bonheur et de la vertu; il me semblait être sous un autre ciel et avec une autre espèce d'hommes." (P. 8.)

[178] P.-C. Lévesque, "Notice Historique sur Le Grand d'Aussy."

This is not to suggest that Le Grand had any major rôle to play in the events which took place during these turbulent years or even that his sympathies were with the revolutionaries once the violence began. It may even have been that the second visit to Auvergne, if not the first, had been prompted to some extent at least by the desire to be out of the capital at this critical period, although in this case he had seriously mistimed his absence. Certainly his apparent silence between the years 1788 and 1795 would seem to indicate if anything that he was preoccupied with his own well-being.[179]

If we cannot say precisely how Le Grand himself fared during these years then we do know something of the fluctuations in contemporary literary tastes caused by the Revolution and its aftermath and from this it is possible to draw certain tentative conclusions regarding Le Grand's own career. He may never have abandoned his scholarly researches into the life and literature of the Middle Ages and yet after 1782 he failed to make the fruits of these available to the general reading public. We know of course that he had been disappointed by the *Histoire de la Vie Privée des Français* and we shall in fact see that he fully intended to continue his work popularizing the literature of medieval France. But to the majority of those who had read and enjoyed the *Fabliaux ou Contes* it must surely have seemed that Le Grand had altogether lost interest, finally choosing to turn his attention elsewhere.

This question of public demand is all-important. There can be little doubt that a second collection of medieval tales on similar lines to the *Fabliaux ou Contes* would have brought Le Grand renewed success in the early 1780's. But his third major work did not appear until 1788 by which time there was considerable evidence of a decline in the popularity of such tales, a decline in the popularity of medieval literature generally in whatever guise it might be presented. With the approach of the Revolution the period of the Middle Ages began to be viewed with increasing disfavour, gradually yielding to the "new" movement, a return to antiquity. Already in 1771 Rigoley de Juvigny had heralded the coming of a new classical era, denouncing current trends in a century which had sullied everything that was of value, and now it seemed the romances of chivalry were to be replaced by classical verse.[180] The

[179] This is perhaps understandable since his father was listed amongst the "condamnés." Cf. a letter, dated the 16th frimaire an VI, from the Minister of the Interior, Letourneux, to the keeper of the Dépôt des Cordeliers: "Je vous autorise, Citoyen, à rendre au Cit. Le Grand, moyennant récipissé, la Bibliothèque de son père, Pierre Jacques Le Grand condamné, existante dans le Dépôt des Cordeliers." (*Ms. Paris, Arsenal 6498*, fol. 219 ro.)

[180] Cf. the "Discours sur le Progrès des Lettres en France" in Rigoley de Juvigny's edition of the *Bibliothèques françoises* of La Croix du Maine and Du Verdier (Paris, Saillant et Nyon 1772–1773, 6 vols.) vol. I, pp. 19–92.

publication of the *Bibliothèque des Romans,* which had been selling at a reduced price, was interrupted in 1788 and then again in 1789 after which time the collection was not to re-appear until the an IX of the République.

Yet this was not simply a question of literary tastes evolving naturally to take an opposite direction, as is so often the case. Soon the political spirit of the age would begin to make itself felt and in the new order of things the literature of medieval France appeared to lose all relevance:

Tout changement arrivé dans le gouvernement ou dans les moeurs d'un peuple doit nécessairement amener des révolutions dans son goût; d'un siècle à l'autre un peuple est différemment frappé des mêmes objets, selon la passion différente qui l'anime. Or nous ne sommes plus dans le temps de l'héroïsme fabuleux de la chevalerie; le récit des actions héroïques est sans objet dans un siècle éclairé et dans les nobles mouvements qui agitent maintenant tous les esprits on réserve exclusivement son admiration pour les objets utiles.[181]

In fact this reaction would not endure and already by 1795 it was becoming clear that the heroes of the romances were soon to regain their popularity.[182] But while the unsympathetic mood prevailed the Middle Ages and its literature were so effectively discredited that it must surely have seemed as though the death-blow had finally been dealt.[183] The question is to what extent did this influence Le Grand's own career? It would be wrong to presume that he had anticipated the decline, but its effects must eventually have become obvious to him.[184] If even the Comte de Tressan's works were selling at greatly reduced prices, then how might others hope for success?[185] It is quite possible that the author of the *Fabliaux ou Contes* had felt himself obliged to turn his attention from the Middle Ages, publicly at least, in order to be at all sure of a future as a man of letters.

H. FINAL RECOGNITION. THE LAST AMBITIOUS YEARS

Whatever the reasons for the apparent break with the past Le Grand acquitted himself so well with the *Voyage d'Auvergne* that one might

---

[181] Vozelle in a review of Florian's *Gonzalve* in the *Journal des Sçavans* for March 1792, pp. 131–142. The quotation is used by H. Jacoubet in his survey of the effects of the Revolution and its aftermath upon the popularity of medieval literature. Cf. *Le Comte de Tressan,* pp. 371–381.

[182] Cf. H. Jacoubet, *Le Comte de Tressan,* pp. 382–390.

[183] Jacoubet notes that in 1794 Paris theatre-goers were entertained with an opera entiled *Alisbeth ou les Crimes de la Féodalité.*

[184] It should be remembered that Le Grand had at one time been employed on the *Bibliothèque des Romans.* He would surely have been aware of the failure of the collection.

[185] Cf. H. Jacoubet, *Le Comte de Tressan,* p. 380.

fully have expected him to take this as the basis for a whole new career. Yet we know already that within a short space of time he would once again be totally preoccupied with the kind of scholarly researches he had undertaken for his earliest works. For if it had in fact been this rejection of a feudal past inspired by the Revolution which had made it difficult for Le Grand to follow his true vocation, then precisely the counter-reaction, the renewed enthusiasm for the Middle Ages and all that period had to offer, would mean that he could once again resume his life's work. We had said that there was evidence of a revival already by 1795. For Le Grand at least this marked the turning-point. In that year he was honoured with an appointment to the position of Keeper of Manuscripts at the Bibliothèque Nationale, a position he would hold until his death.

Le Grand was an obvious candidate for the post, not altogether a stranger to the manuscript room of this great library which at one time he had practically made his home. The compilation of his first collection, the *Fabliaux ou Contes*, had entailed endless searches in the "département des manuscrits" and we know that much of the material used for the *Histoire de la Vie Privée des Français* had been gathered here, Le Grand having felt obliged to withdraw from Paulmy's collection in view of his quarrel with the Marquis. These two works alone were ample testimony to his ability, and it seems that no one could have been more appreciative of the honour or indeed more enthusiastic about the possibilities of the new appointment. For Le Grand's nomination as Keeper of Manuscripts at the Bibliothèque Nationale was doubly rewarding. Firstly the nomination itself obviously implied recognition of his work as a scholar which he must surely have found most gratifying. More important, the new post finally made it possible for him to set in motion a project which had been haunting his imagination for a considerable number of years, in fact ever since he had come to compose the *Fabliaux ou Contes*:

Ce qui me flatta le plus, quand j'appris que la Convention m'avait nommé Conservateur de la Bibliothèque nationale, fut de me voir à portée d'exécuter enfin le projet que je méditais depuis si long-tems.[186]

Clearly the year 1795 marks a climax in Le Grand's career.

The project in question, a history of French poetry from its origins to modern times, was in itself nothing new and Le Grand was fully aware of this. But if others had treated the subject then the period of

---

[186] *Ms. Paris, B.N.n.a.f. 6228*, fol. 70.

the Middle Ages had invariably been misrepresented. Massieu may have published a short treatise on old French verse as early as 1721 but he had done so without first consulting the manuscripts available and for Le Grand this rendered the work invalid:

Cet homme qui entreprenait de nous faire connaître nos vieux Poëtes, n'en avait pas lu un seul en manuscrit. Tous les Romanciers, Chansonniers, Fabliers, Dramatistes et autres Rimeurs des trois siècles antérieurs à la découverte de l'Imprimerie (et ce nombre est immense) lui étaient totalement inconnus. Le peu qu'il en dit est copié d'après les notices erronées ou très imparfaites qu'a publiées Fauchet sur quelques-uns d'entre eux; et l'histoire de notre Poësie reste encore à faire en entier.[187]

Then if the project itself was nothing new, at least Le Grand proposed to treat it in an original manner, firmly convinced that any such work must necessarily be based upon the author's personal and intimate acquaintance with all relevant source material. It was precisely this conviction which had prevented him from embarking upon the project earlier, for he knew that he would need to have the vast resources of the then Bibliothèque du Roi entirely at his disposal, an impossible condition as it then appeared. In 1795 this condition was fulfilled and all obstacles removed:

Aussi, du moment où j'entrai en fonctions, je m'y livrai tout entier; et il a été exclusivement, depuis près de trois ans et demi, la seule occupation de toutes mes journées.[188]

Although he had originally intended to restrict himself to the history of French poetry, Le Grand soon realized that the majority of his readers, unaccustomed to the language of the "anciens rimeurs," would find little value in such a work if left to their own devices or forced to rely solely upon brief notes for their enlightenment. If subtle variations in style and idion were not to be lost to his public, then Le Grand felt he must trace the history of the language in which this verse had been written, a prospect which he did not find too disconcerting, a new challenge:

En prenant la langue à son origine et en suivant jusqu'à nos jours sa marche et ses progrès, j'avais à traiter un sujet neuf et curieux, que personne n'avait entrepris encore; et je n'hésitai point.[189]

---

[187] *Ibidem.*

[188] *Ibidem.* These and preceding lines are taken from a full account of the project, written early in 1799 and headed "Notice sommaire sur les trois ouvrages auxquels je travaille," contained in *B.N.n.a.f. 6228.* Folios 49–69 represent a first draft of the "Notice," folios 70–80 a second version, corrected and with additions.

[189] Fol. 71.

Then again, experience had taught him that it was impossible to treat the literature of the past without reference to the manners and customs of the period in question, which, as we shall see in the *Fabliaux ou Contes*, might entail explanatory notes upon anything from contemporary architecture to the musical instruments played at the time. But once again Le Grand was not too dismayed:

... je savais en même tems, par expérience, que pour un auteur rien n'est plus difficile que de faire comprendre par écrit ces sortes de matières, et qu'avec plusieurs pages de description qui lui auront donné bien de la peine, il sera moins entendu qu'avec une simple gravure, quelque médiocre qu'elle soit.[190]

Certainly a few simple illustrations would greatly reduce the time required for this particular aspect of the work and perhaps time had now become an important factor. Already when the newly appointed Keeper of Manuscripts had decided he might finally embark upon the long-nursed project it had represented a quite formidable task. But how the task had grown since then.

If Le Grand appears to have had few qualms about the ever increasing dimensions of his project, then he was certainly perturbed by the highly unstable political situation of the day. For if anything it was this, he felt, which would eventually prevent him from completing the work, some fresh crisis depriving him of his new position and thereby also of the freedom to forage at will for his material in the manuscript collection of the Bibliothèque Nationale. So real was the threat that he decided to seek government sanction for the venture, submitting a detailed résumé of the proposed work to the Minister of the Interior who then forwarded it to the Commission d'Instruction Publique for examination. The report received by the Minister, Bénézech, would appear to have been a most favourable one. Le Grand was given every encouragement:

... il m'écrivit une lettre très flatteuse, par laquelle non seulement il m'autorisait à entreprendre l'ouvrage et m'incitait même à y donner tous mes soins et tout mon tems, mais il y attachait en outre, comme dédommagement et comme indemnités des frais de copie, traduction, dessins, gravure &c, auxquels je serai nécessairement obligé, un traitement annuel de six mille francs, pendant six années; et cette somme qui n'était point réductible dans la supposition d'un changement de monnaie, devait être prise sur les fonds affectés à la Cinquième Division, et commencer à être payée le premier nivôse de l'an 4.[191]

[190] *Ibidem.*
[191] *Ibidem.*

If the stipend had been paid in full enabling the author to employ a copyist to help with transcriptions and engage the services of an artist to take charge of illustrations, then the work might have made better progress. Unfortunately by the time he came to write the "Notice" Le Grand had received only 1,250 livres, and this amount in paper, of the thirty-eight months then due to him, thirty-eight months during which the project had been modified and expanded so as to be beyond recognition. This was the real problem. Even without financial assistance Le Grand would probably have been able to complete and publish the *Histoire de la Poësie française*, a formidable and yet feasible task. Now he was committed to three separate major works. We know already of the addition of a history of the French language. By 1799 the "projet de gravures" has been abandoned in favour of a comprehensive *Histoire des Usages, des Arts et des Sciences en France*, for the principal concern is no longer simply the poetry of France but the whole of French literature "dans toute son étendue et avec toutes ses parties."[192] Le Grand had earlier feared to modify the plan he had submitted to Bénézech:

... la peur de me jeter dans une entreprise à laquelle ma vie ne suffirait peut-être pas, m'empêchait d'y rien changer.[193]

Clearly his fears had been well justified:

... j'ignore, et ne puis même entrevoir, quand finiront mes recherches, et quand il me sera permis d'appeller le Goût à mon aide pour rédiger ce que j'aurai amassé et pour en tirer parti.[194]

What was to be the last of the three studies, the *Histoire des Usages, des Arts et des Sciences en France*, would seem to represent a fresh attempt at the *Histoire de la Vie Privée des Français* of which only the first section, a disappointment to the author, had appeared in 1782:

Il formera une histoire de France, d'un nouveau genre, et totalement différente de celles que nous avons; et nous fera connaître nos ayeux sous des rapports jusqu'à présent inconnus.[195]

Of encyclopedic proportions, the work would treat everything from architecture to music, costumes to recreations, Le Grand not shrinking from detail. The article on warfare alone would comprise twenty-six subdivisions dealing with such varied aspects as sieges, weapons and

192 Fol. 72.
193 *Ibidem.*
194 Fol. 70.
195 Fol. 72.

even the breeds of horses used in battle. All quotations and extracts were to be taken from authors of the period in question, all illustrations copied from miniatures found in contemporary manuscripts. Quite apart from anything else, the work, it seemed, would be a boon to modern artists and playwrights:

On ne verra plus de Dessinateurs donner aux Rois et aux Guerriers de la troisième Race le costume et l'armure des Grecs et des Romains ... Enfin l'auteur tragique connaîtra, pour chaque siècle et pour chaque condition, les habits et les ornements qui leur étaient propres; et l'illusion du théâtre en sera plus complette.[196]

The *Histoire de la Langue française*, to precede the general history of French literature, was to be equally comprehensive, tracing the development of the language in five stages from its origins, the time of the Roman conquest, to its eventual perfection in the works of authors like Fénélon, Boileau and Voltaire. The subject had been treated many times before but never to the satisfaction of Le Grand who intended that nothing of relevance should be omitted:

... jusqu'ici personne n'en a entrepris une histoire complette et détaillée ... je crois qu'en applaudissant au zèle de tous et aux recherches de quelques-uns d'entre eux, on peut se flatter de dire sur cet objet quelque chose de neuf encore.[197]

Already by the time he came to write the "Notice sommaire sur les trois ouvrages auxquels je travaille" he had completed a considerable proportion of the work, having gathered enough material for a substantial volume in-8. If only peace would come to restore new life and order to the disrupted book-trade, then it seemed this volume might soon appear.

But of course it was the centre-piece of the project, the *Histoire de la Littérature française*, which would make the greatest demands upon Le Grand's time and energy. Even before he might approach the subject proper he felt he must accustom his readers to the "strange ideas," the ignorance and superstition to be found in the works that were to be his concern:

... je crois devoir tracer, dans un avant-propos, un tableau abrégé de l'état

---

[196] Ff. 74–75.
[197] Fol. 77. Originally Le Grand had even intended to include here a brief historical account of the written language as a science, treating everything from the profession and materials of the copyist to the arts of printing and book-binding. He eventually decided that such information might best be included in the *Histoire des Usages, des Arts et des Sciences en France*.

où en étaient les lumières en France, quand sa langue commença d'avoir des écrivains.[198]

In what way did the feudal system affect France's earliest poets? To what extent were they influenced by contemporary religious beliefs? What effect did the growth of commerce and industry have upon the progress of French literature? Why was it that the nation which had supplied the literary models of Europe in the twelfth and thirteenth centuries suddenly lost all rank, only regaining its position of pre-eminence under Louis XIV? Surely a whole volume would not suffice to contain the answers to these questions.

The work itself would be divided into six main sections, "Histoires rimées," "Romans," "Fabliaux ou Contes," "Contes dévots," "Pièces dramatiques" and "Poëmes moraux," each comprising numerous sub-divisions. In the second section, for example, all the various kinds of romances would be treated separately and in some detail. In addition, Le Grand proposed not only to list all those romances preserved for posterity in manuscript form but to give an account of each one and extracts of the best amongst them. Other sections were hardly less ambitious. That concerning the drama would deal with the three main periods of the early French theatre from its origins at the time of the "fabliers" through the fourteenth and fifteenth centuries to the literary renaissance under François I, and would be subdivided thus:

Pièces à plusieurs personnages parlant l'un après l'autre telles que les *Discours de Charlatans.*

Pièces avec une action, à plusieurs personnages, et dialoguées.

Pièces dévotes, telles que les *Miracles*, les *Mistères* &c.

Pièces comiques, telles que les *Sotties.*

Pièces pastorales dramatiques.

Pièces pantomimes à grand spectacle, entremêlées de quelque dialogue et d'action.[199]

It seems the author's enthusiasm had caused him to lose all sense of proportion.

It is perhaps not so surprising that Le Grand should be thus inspired by a project which after all not only entailed the kind of work in which he was most experienced, the detailed manuscript researches which had been the foundation for his earliest publications, which not only involved him as a man of letters, but at the same time obliged him to exploit to the full his many other talents, at the same time involved Le

[198] Fol. 78.
[199] Ff. 79–80.

Grand the archeologist, the scientist, the historian. If the first two sections of the project would easily accommodate his passion for French
language and literature, then the third would allow him ample scope
for his interests in other fields. Indeed he would add even greater variety to the work by collecting material for all three sections at one and
the same time as each manuscript passed through his hands, thereby
finally removing the threat of monotony. And as if this were not encouragement enough, Le Grand was also much inspired by the thought
that his researches would be of considerable benefit to the Bibliothèque
Nationale itself. A detailed catalogue, arranged in order of subjects, of
the manuscripts held in this library had already begun to appear, but
until this time there had been no mention of those in French, the basis
of the new project for which Le Grand would require a precise account
of each and every one:

... j'amasse ainsi, chemin faisant, des matériaux pour le catalogue; je fais
partiellement le catalogue, sans néanmoins m'en occuper directement; et ce
résultat est tel que quand enfin je les aurai tous, il me suffira de les rédiger et
de les classer pour être en état de publier le catalogue.[200]

Le Grand's researches must surely have been facilitated by a decree
issued in 1794 authorizing the Keeper of Manuscripts at the Bibliothèque Nationale to take from other collections whatever manuscripts
he wished. On the 23rd fructidor an IV (1796) the Minister of the
Interior, Bénézech, wrote the following letter to Le Grand:

Je vous autorise, citoyen, à vous concerter avec le citoyen Ameilhon, conservateur du dépôt littéraire, rue Louis-la-Culture, pour la remise des manuscrits réunis dans le dépôt qui lui est confié. Je viens de lui écrire pour
l'autoriser définitivement à les remettre à la Bibliothèque nationale de la rue
de la Loi.[201]

This was surely the kind of freedom of which Le Grand had earlier
dreamed. The drawback, of course, was that these new powers could
only add to his task, time, not the availability of material, now being
the important factor.

Clearly there was more work than could be managed by one pair of
hands, and yet Le Grand, refusing to entrust others with his researches,
would engage only the services of copyists:

Eh! comment oserais – je garantir à mes lecteurs l'authenticité de tout ce que

---

[200] Fol. 70.
[201] *Ms. Paris, Arsenal 6499*, fol. 159. H. Martin discusses the powers given to the Bibliothèque Nationale and quotes Bénézech's letter to Le Grand in his *Histoire de la Bibliothèque de
l'Arsenal*, p. 431.

j'avance et de tout ce que je cite, quand je n'aurai pas vu par moi-même et que je parlerai sur la foi d'autrui? Je suis donc réduit à travailler seul et à n'avoir que des Copistes. Aussi ne puis – je prévoir quand finira mon travail . . . .[202]

But he would do his utmost to complete the project, of which different parts were to appear successively, and promised that in the event of his death he would leave all the necessary materials for anyone who might care to finish the task. Le Grand could not have known, of course, but this fatal interruption would come within the space of two years in which time, it seems, he could not hope to complete even one of the three major histories.[203] A move to publish at least part of the project posthumously appears to have been without outcome.[204] But the fruits of these great efforts were not entirely lost to the reading public. Realizing the hopelessness of his task, Le Grand used materials collected for his project to contribute several lengthy papers to the *Mémoires de l'Institut National*, of which he had the honour of being elected a member on May 24th 1798,[205] and, from the same source, furnished a large number of articles to the fifth volume of the *Notices et Extraits*.[206]

It is one of the ironies of history that the most ambitious amongst men should be granted the least time in which to reach their goals. Le Grand was only sixty-three years of age when he died and in his prime as a scholar. If he had lived but a short time longer then perhaps the medievalists of today would have better cause to remember the debt of gratitude owed to him. Here was a man who, though obviously gifted

---

[202] "Notice," fol. 80.

[203] Le Grand died on the 6th December 1800 after a brief illness which appeared to give no cause for concern.

[204] Cf. an examination of the *Histoire de la Langue et de l'ancienne Littérature françaises, des Sciences, des Arts et des Usages* in a "Notice sur les ouvrages de Le Grand d'Aussy" opening a volume of Le Grand's manuscript papers, *Ms. Paris, B.N.n.a.f. 10859*, ff. 30ro–54ro: "Faut-il conserver l'espoir de faire la publication totale de cet ouvrage? Ou doit-on y renoncer? Ne pourrait-on pas, au moins, essayer un prospectus ou spécimen, d'une ou deux feuilles, avec une Notice biographique?" (Fol. 31vo.)

Cf. a similar notice, by the same hand, introducing a rough draft of Le Grand's *Essai sur la Langue, les Sciences et la Littérature françaises* which was to preface the main opus, *Ms. Paris, B.N.n.a.f.10858*, ff. 2vo–llro.

[205] Cf. *Magasin Encyclopédique*, 4e an, 1798, vol. I, p. 553: "Le citoyen Le Grand d'Aussi, auteur de la 'Vie privée des Français' et d'un 'Voyage en Auvergne,' a été nommé membre de la seconde classe de l'Institut, celle des sciences morales et politiques dans la section de l'histoire, dans la séance générale du 9 prairial."

It should be noted that the journal makes no mention of the *Fabliaux ou Contes* here. Le Grand succeeded Gaillard at the Institut and, two years after his death, was replaced by Dom Poirier. Two of his papers were published posthumously. See bibliography.

[206] Cf. the "Notice sommaire sur les trois ouvrages auxquels je travaille," fol. 70: "En attendant, j'ai mis à profit une partie des extraits que j'avais faits. Nommé par l'Institut membre de la Commission pour l'impression du volume de la *notice des manuscrits*, j'ai fourni au volume 42 articles, dont la plupart sont des examens raisonnés de poëmes ou d'ouvrages curieux et ont été rédigés d'après douze ou quinze manuscrits et plus." See bibliography.

in many other fields, had devoted almost his entire life to the study and popularization of the Middle Ages and its literature, his enthusiasm for this work only increasing as he grew older. The mass of material Le Grand d'Aussy left behind, including a considerable amount relating to the last major project, bears ample testimony to his life of industry, to his unfailing determination and energy.

Not all this work would in fact go unappreciated. Although known to only a few, to his friend and colleague Lebreton for example, Le Grand had left amongst other things the manuscript of a *Vie d'Apollonius de Tyane*, found worthy of publication in 1807.[207] More important, he had prepared a third edition of the *Fabliaux ou Contes* and this too would eventually be made available to the general reading public.

It is clear that Le Grand had begun work on this even before his first excursion into the provinces in 1787 for in the earlier edition of the *Voyage d'Auvergne* he speaks of searching through the manuscripts held in the library at Clermont in the hope of finding relevant material:

... comme depuis quelque tems je m'occupe d'une troisième édition des Fabliaux, je voulais savoir si parmi ces manuscrits je trouverais d'anciennes Poésies françaises.[208]

It may even have been that preparations were completed shortly after his return to the capital, the fluctuations in literary fashion brought about by the Revolution making him reluctant to publish. But we know at least that in its earlier editions the collection had been loudly applauded by contemporary French critics and we shall in fact see that it had enjoyed considerable success in English translation. Surely of all his works and unpublished projects this was the one Le Grand himself favoured most. Many tributes had been paid to him during his lifetime and others would follow after his death, but surely he himself would have regarded the re-edition of the *Fabliaux ou Contes* by Antoine-Augustin Renouard nearly thirty years after his death, a full fifty years after its first appearance, as the greatest tribute of all.[209]

---

[207] Paris (L. Collin) 2 vols.

[208] P. 30.

[209] *Fabliaux ou Contes, Fables et Romans du XIIe et du XIIIe siècle, traduits ou extraits par Legrand d'Aussy, troisième édition, considérablement augmentée*, Paris (Jules Renouard) 1829, 5 vols. in-8. In the editor's preface Renouard acknowledges that Le Grand himself had made all the necessary preparations for a third edition (vol. I, p. i). These preparations appear to have taken the form of an annotated second edition. Cf. *Catalogue d'une précieuse collection de livres, manuscrits, autographes, dessins et gravures composant la Bibliothèque de feu M. Antoine-Augustin Renouard... dont la vente aura lieu le Lundi 20 novembre et les trente jours suivants...*, Paris (L. Potier) 1854, p. 371, no. 3632: "*Fabliaux ou Contes du XIIe et du XIIIe siècle, traduits ou extraits par Le Grand d'Aussy*, Paris 1781, 5 vol. in-18 br. Exemplaire préparé pour une nouvelle édition avec notes, corrections et additions de la main de Le Grand d'Aussy. Le tome 1er manque."

PART TWO

THE *FABLIAUX OU CONTES*

INTRODUCTION TO PART TWO

Le Grand did not enter lightly into the *Fabliaux ou Contes*. When first challenged by that circle of detractors to justify his regard for the literature of the Middle Ages he had set out to prove that certain of the poets of these "siècles d'ignorance" were not altogether without merit and still worthy of some attention. If on a small scale this could be achieved relatively easily with a few hurried translations, then what success might be anticipated with a lengthy collection wherein it would be possible actually to exploit the appeal of these poets and thereby establish the justice of the cause beyond all doubt. Clearly the *Fabliaux ou Contes* would represent an extension of the response to that first challenge:

Je pris la liberté de dire que, pour le style, le goût, la critique, pour tout ce qui tient à l'art, il ne falloit point le chercher dans les ouvrages de ce temps; mais que si l'on vouloit se contenter d'esprit et d'imagination, on pourroit, à une certaine époque, en trouver chez nos vieux poètes; et j'ajoutai qu'il nous restoit d'eux, en ce genre, des choses fort agréables qui méritoient d'être connues.[1]

Equally, of course, the collection would be an elaboration of this response. If Le Grand was anxious to obtain recognition for certain of the poets of medieval France, then this was not simply, nor even primarily, because he found them to possess a certain wit and some imagination. For their apologist the forerunners of Molière, Racine and Voltaire merited both the attention and admiration of the eighteenth century for other equally if not more valid reasons and, of course, it would have been foolish, even, as we shall see, foolhardy, not to make this apparent in the collection. Needless to say, Le Grand did not fail to exploit an opportunity to clarify and consolidate his position.

Quite apart from any literary merit which they might possess, the

[1] *Observations sur les Troubadours*, pp. 4–5.

poets of medieval France, insisted Le Grand, should be of interest to
the eighteenth century for the picture of contemporary society, manners and customs, arts and sciences, which they present in their works.
The historian who refuses to seek his material anywhere but in the
pages of other historians is guilty of ignoring the most abundant store
of information available to him:

Quand même la Littérature de ce tems ne serait rien à ses yeux, ne sait-il pas
que ces manuscrits, si déraisonnablement dédaignés par lui, peuvent ajouter
un prix immense à son travail, autant par le tableau des moeurs & des
usages qu'ils offrent, plus que tout autre Ouvrage quelconque, que par les
anecdotes particulières & la multitude de détails curieux qu'ils contiennent
sur les Duels, les Tournois, les Armes, les Monnaies, sur le Gouvernement, la
Chronologie, la Jurisprudence du tems, l'Art de la Guerre, l'Administration
de la Justice, &c. &c. &c., & sur l'Histoire même.[2]

A few well-chosen examples would have sufficed to demonstrate the
validity of this view, of course, but Le Grand was not only intent to
establish the historical relevance of Old French literature, he was in
fact most anxious to set before his readers a relatively complete picture
of medieval society as represented here, to dispel something at least
of the ignorance and prejudice with which the "Siècle des Lumières"
looked back to the "nuits de ténèbres" of the Middle Ages.[3] No excuse
would be made for the multitude of notes employed to this purpose:

Si elles apprennent quelque chose, elles ne sont pas trop nombreuses.[4]

The notes in fact become as important as the pieces which give rise to
them.

Equally important is the question of the contribution made by
France to the literary renaissance in medieval Europe. Le Grand was
something of a patriot and genuinely grieved to think that his countrymen, so eager to boast of their language, their theatre and even their
fashions as the admiration and inspiration of the western world, should
be ignorant of a far greater distinction enjoyed by their homeland but a
few short centuries ago:

... que c'est à elle qu'on doit les premiers Poëtes, & le renouvellement de la

---

[2] *Fabliaux ou Contes*, vol. IV, pp. iv–v.

[3] Cf. Voltaire, *OEuvres Complètes*, (Paris, Garnier Frères, 1877–85, 52 vols.) vol. XXVIII,
Mélanges VII, p. 565: "Défions-nous de tout ce qu'on a écrit dans ces temps d'ignorance et
de barbarie. Comparons un moment ces nuits de ténèbres à nos beaux jours; comparons la
multitude de nos florissantes villes avec ces prisons qu'on appelait fertés, châtels, roches,
basties, bastilles; nos arts perfectionnés à la disette de tous les arts; la politesse à la grossièreté...".

[4] *Fabliaux ou Contes*, vol. I, preface, p. xcvi.

Poésie; que sa Musique fut recherchée, ses Contes, ses Romans admirés, imités ou traduits chez toutes les Nations....[5]

Some might find such a revelation of scant interest but those with any degree of concern for the honour of French literature would surely not fail to see its import. For Le Grand himself this question touched upon the glory of France, not a matter about which to remain indifferent:

L'amour-propre trouvait peu d'aliment dans un Ouvrage qui ne demandait que beaucoup de lecture & quelque goût; mais cet Ouvrage tenait en quelque sorte à la gloire de ma Patrie; il renfermait nos titres d'aînesse littéraire; & dès-lors il m'est devenu précieux.[6]

It was precisely in defence of what he saw as the nation's birthright that Le Grand would feel obliged to pass those fateful remarks upon the troubadours.

Though perhaps accidental in origin, the collection was clearly not of haphazard construction without design or purpose. But if the most careful consideration had been given to the ends it should achieve, then equally it was not without considerable forethought that Le Grand chose the genre of "fabliaux ou contes" as the means to these ends. It had not been by accident that when first challenged to produce sample pieces from the Middle Ages still readable in the eighteenth century he had turned immediately to the fabliaux. It must be remembered that Le Grand had served his apprenticeship as a medievalist under some of the most distinguished masters of his day and thereby acquired a thorough knowledge of Old French literature. Briefly, he was in a position to judge for himself. Clearly he had learnt much by collaborating with men like Paulmy on the *Mélanges tirés d'une grande Bibliothèque* and the *Bibliothèque des Romans*, and it was not only the "fabliaux ou contes" which he had come to appreciate through his association with Sainte-Palaye:

The sources of the Glossary were immensely rich and varied. Manuscript romances, 'fabliaux' and 'coutumier,' legal documents, historical works, and chronicles in private and public collections in France, Switzerland, and Italy were drawn upon as were also early printed editions and the dictionaries and compilations of Borel, Bourgoing, Corneille, Du Cange, Laurière, La Martinière, Ménage, Monet, Nicot, Pasquier, Oudin, and Trippault. No stone was left unturned.[7]

Le Grand may well insist that he was literally "blackmailed" into publishing these *Fabliaux ou Contes*, but we can feel certain that he would

---

[5] *Idem*, p. xliii.
[6] *Idem*, p. c.
[7] L. Gossman, *Medievalism*, p. 191.

not have hesitated to replace them with some other genre, the romances for example, had he thought it better suited to his purposes.

Our purpose has been to outline the three aims envisaged in the *Fabliaux ou Contes*. We have treated these individually while taking care to avoid suggesting that they were unrelated. The contrary is true. From the preface to the first volume of the collection it is clear that each forms an integral part of the author's one fundamental purpose, which at this time might best be described as the defence and popularization of Old French literature. To establish the justice and make plain the implications of this definition we must now set the *Fabliaux ou Contes* in its true context. Le Grand was not working in a vacuum. Not only does he bear the mark of his time, he put his own mark upon that time.

CHAPTER I

LITERARY TEXTS OR HISTORICAL DOCUMENTS?
THE MIRROR OF MEDIEVAL SOCIETY

Paradoxical as it may at first appear, La Curne de Sainte-Palaye, whilst foremost amongst the medievalists of his century, ranks equally amongst those of his day least appreciative of the literary merits of the "anciens rimeurs." Whether or not he in fact gave whole-hearted support to the charges of coarseness and barbarity levied unceasingly against them, it was certainly never his intention to establish himself as the apologist of those whose productions had, he felt, been justly overshadowed by subsequent literary achievement:

Que les Partisans des Siècles qu'ils n'ont ni vus ni connus nous vantent l'heureuse simplicité de nos Aieux. Que leur mauvaise humeur s'exhale en vaines déclamations contre la subtilité de nos Ecrivains modernes. Pardonnons à ceux-ci leurs écarts peut-être trop ingénieux et trop raffinés; mais ne regrettons pas ceux qui les ont précédés. Comparons les Ecrits de ces temps barbares avec ceux que l'Imprimerie depuis 200 ans environ a mis entre nos mains. Soyons pénétrés de reconnoissance sur-tout pour ces hommes respectables qui, vers le milieu du siècle dernier ont achevé d'épurer notre langue.[1]

In fact this was a view not altogether uncommon amongst those who, in opposition to the "Anciens," to men like Rigoley de Juvigny whose plea was for a return to the models of classical antiquity,[2] like Sainte-Palaye

---

[1] *Ms. Paris, B.N. fonds Bréquigny 154*, fol. 26. These lines are quoted by L. Gossman (*Medievalism*, p. 255) who does much both to demonstrate and to account for what will emerge as the eighteenth century's predominantly historical interest in medieval literature. In particular, cf. pp. 247–253.

[2] Cf. "Discours sur le progrès des lettres en France," vol. I, p. 66. We know that La Curne himself did not value too highly the art of France's medieval poets, but it is clear from the severity of Rigoley de Juvigny's indictment of the Middle Ages and its literature that here all similarity ends: "On avoit entièrement oublié l'usage de la langue Latine, & l'on ne parloit, on n'écrivoit plus qu'en langue Romance, ou rustique; c'est-à-dire, dans un idiome barbare, mêlé d'un Latin corrompu. Aussi quels écrits vit-on éclore? Comme le goût tient à la vérité, & qu'il étoit perdu depuis long-temps, le faux prit la place du vrai. L'Histoire

himself turned a generally sympathetic eye towards the Middle Ages. For if the eighteenth century can be regarded as the period when medieval studies became a viable alternative, perhaps, as it would appear, even a serious threat to classical scholarship, then it was most decidedly not a time at which the careful editing of medieval literary texts was generally regarded as a worthwhile occupation.

This is not to suggest that the eighteenth century disdained altogether to treat the literature of these centuries past as literature. Evidence to the contrary abounds. Indeed, an immense amount of vital research was undertaken at this time by scholars like Sallier with his papers on Charles d'Orléans and Jean Lemaire des Belges, or Le Beuf with his work on Guillaume de Machaut, a poet who would also draw the attention of Caylus, this latter perhaps best remembered for his observations on the fabliaux. It is significant to note, however, that all the aforementioned items appeared in the *Mémoires de l'Académie des Inscriptions et Belles-Lettres*, this institution alone, it would seem, providing those interested with the opportunity of publishing such material.[3] Even more significant is the fact that we are dealing here with studies of authors and their works and not with editions of literary texts, a clear indication of the attitude adopted by the scholars themselves:

Quelques analyses de ces fabliaux, & des citations fidelement extraites, mettront le lecteur à portée de juger du mérite de ces ouvrages ....[4]

It seems never to have been La Curne's intention to bring before the public in the form of scholarly editions the fruits of the immense efforts

---

travestie perdit son exactitude & sa sévérité; les Romans, digne nourriture des esprits vides & inappliqués, pleins d'un merveilleux absurde, firent les délices d'une imbécille oisiveté. Le succès de ce nouveau genre d'écrits, dont la durée fut longue, n'a rien qui doive étonner." (*Idem*, pp. 35–36.)

[3] L'Abbé Claude Sallier: "Observations sur un recueil manuscrit des poésies de Charles d'Orléans," *Mém. Acad. Inscr.*, vol. XII, pp. 580–592. "Recherches sur la vie et les ouvrages de Jean le Maire," *idem*, pp. 593–624.

L'Abbé Jean le Beuf: "Notice sommaire de deux volumes de poésies françoises et latines conservés dans la Bibliothèque des Carmes-Déchaux de Paris," *Mém. Acad. Inscr.*, vol. XX, pp. 377–398.

Le Comte de Caylus: "Deux Mémoires sur Guillaume de Machaut, poète et musicien dans le XIVe siècle, avec une notice de ses principaux ouvrages," *idem*, pp. 399–439. "Mémoire sur les Fabliaux," *idem*, pp. 352–376.

Bimard de La Bastie, Lévesque de La Ravalière and, of course, La Curne de Sainte-Palaye are also names which, amongst others, are worthy of mention here. Cf. Madeleine Jouglard: "La connaissance de l'ancienne littérature française au XVIIIe siècle" in *Mélanges offerts par ses amis et ses élèves à M. Gustave Lanson*, Paris (Hachette) 1922, pp. 272–273.

[4] Caylus, "Mémoire sur les Fabliaux," p. 361.

he devoted to copying and annotating medieval pieces from the manu-script originals.[5]

To some extent at least this common aversion can be attributed to the lack of enthusiasm with which the public at large received such editions, although when we come to define more precisely the manner in which La Curne and his colleagues approached the literature of the Middle Ages it will become clear that this was indeed no more than a contributory factor. It is nevertheless useful to take account of the tastes of the contemporary reading public in so far as these are indicative of the attitude of the eighteenth century in general towards its literary heritage, this attitude well represented in a remark appearing in September 1747 in the *Mercure* which, it will be remembered, refused to publish the poetry of the "anciens rimeurs" more than one item at a time:

... nos anciens poètes ne sont que des enfans et vous sçavez que les enfans peuvent amuser un quart d'heure, mais qu'à la longue ils se rendroient insupportables.[6]

Although numerous friends had done what they could to convince him of the necessity of translation, Etienne Barbazan refused to present those pieces to appear in his *Fabliaux et Contes* in anything but their original form:

... on espère ... que le Vocabulaire qu'on y joint donnera quelque facilité de les entendre; & qu'une fois accoutumés à leur langage, on ne les trouvera plus ni si barbares, ni si obscurs. En effet quand on verra & quand on sera convaincu que ce langage, tout barbare qu'il paroît, n'est autre chose que la langue latine un peu changée, on ne le trouvera pas plus extraordinaire que celui d'aujourd'hui.[7]

Unfortunately the poor reception of Barbazan's undertaking would appear to indicate that the public did not share his views. A full two decades later the *Journal Encyclopédique* would suggest that the compilers of the *Annales Poétiques* had done well to end their search for ma-

---

[5] L. Gossman, *Medievalism*, p. 264: "There is no reason to believe that he at any time planned to publish the texts which he studied with such care and zeal."
Gossman also quotes La Bastie as writing to Mazauges: "Ce seroit abuser de la presse que de la faire rouler sur les morceaux grossiers de nos ancêtres." (*Idem*, p. 343.)

[6] See above, p. 9, note 25.

[7] *Fabliaux et Contes des Poëtes françois des XII, XIII, XIV & XVes siècles, tirés des meilleurs auteurs* (Paris, Vincent, and Amsterdam, Arkstée et Merkus, 1756, 3 vols.) vol. I, preface, pp. xlvi–xlvii. Cf. also Barbazan's *L'Ordène de Chevalerie* (Paris, Chaubert & Hérissant, 1759) Avertissement, p. x: "Un lecteur, qui pour entendre un ouvrage ancien aura recours à une traduction, ne s'instruira jamais à fond; d'ailleurs les traductions ne nous rendent pas toujours les beautés qui sont dans les originaux."

terial with Villon, since anything earlier would have proven unintelligible to readers, and go on to praise Le Grand d'Aussy for his decision to both translate and abridge the fabliaux:

L'homme de lettres qui donne aujourd'hui au public trois volumes des anciens fabliaux, fait mieux encore: il les traduit, prend la liberté de les abréger, liberté nécessaire pour les faire lire, supprime quelques détails licencieux ou impies (car nos dévots aieux n'étoient point sans reproche à ces deux égards); enfin, il n'a rien négligé pour que des richesses si long-terms enfouies ne fussent pas perdues pour nous.[8]

Le Grand himself, with an understanding of contemporary tastes perhaps out of reach of his provincial predecessor, Barbazan, could speak only disparagingly of the attitude adopted by this latter:

De bonne foi, peut-on se flatter qu'il se trouvera des gens assez courageux pour entreprendre une lecture, dans laquelle, dix fois à chaque phrase, il leur faudra consulter un Vocabulaire. Ce n'est pas connaître les Lecteurs Français, que de leur présenter un pareil travail.[9]

If anything Le Grand's remarks are something of an understatement, for not only did the public fail to show any enthusiasm for works such as that of Barbazan, contemporary readers appear for the most part to have been quite unconcerned as to whether those pieces presented to them in translation, more or less complete or in extract form, were genuinely medieval texts carefully composed after the originals, later and much corrupted versions, reconstructions or adaptations of these, or even quite simply pure inventions. We are not concerned here with those highly successful authors who, like Mme de Tencin with *Le Siège de Calais*,[10] Mlle Ihéritier and *La Tour Ténébreuse*[11] or La Dixmerie with his *Cléomir et Dalia*,[12] to a greater or lesser extent and with varying degrees of integrity and accuracy as it were adopt the Middle Ages for their own purposes, for example, by employing the colours, the atmosphere of these centuries, often more specifically some well-known historical event, as the backdrop to their narrative. It is not our purpose to catalogue the many varied and successful ways in which

---

[8] *Journal Encyclopédique*, 1780, vol. II, pt. I, p. 73.

[9] *Fabliaux ou Contes*, vol. I, preface, p. lxxxvii. G. Ellis refers to Barbazan's collection in his preface to G. L. Way's translation of Le Grand's work: "A collection of Fabliaux was printed in 1756, from the manuscripts, in three small volumes, with a glossary to each; but even with this assistance they are so little intelligible to a modern Frenchman, that the work is said to be scarcely known, even among the learned, at Paris." (*Fabliaux or Tales, abridged from French manuscripts of the XIIth and XIIIth centuries*, London, R. Faulder, 1796, vol. I, preface, p. i.)

[10] La Haye (J. Neaulme) 1739, 2 vols.

[11] Paris (Vve de C. Barbin) 1705.

[12] Paris, 1763.

eighteenth-century writers adapted the Middle Ages to their own ends. From "romans historiques" to verse composed in the "style marotique," the permutations seem almost endless.[13] Our concern here is rather with what might best be described as pseudo-medieval texts, a justifiable description when we pause for one moment to compare them with the results obtained by "editors" of more serious intent.

By far the most popular form employed by these editors was, understandably enough, the extract in modern translation, perhaps, as Le Grand would have it, the only method by which one might hope to reach the public:

Il n'est pas possible de faire lire les Fabliaux autrement, que dans une traduction où l'on se permettra certaines libertés.[14]

The success of this form is perhaps most clearly attested by the contemporary periodical press and more specifically by those "Bibliothèques" which, in response to public demand, began to abound in the 1770's, particularly in the latter half of the decade. In 1778 the *Annales Poétiques* commenced publication with the poetry of Thibaut de Champagne, the editors stating their position in the "Avertissement" to the first volume:

... pour adoucir la fatigue de cette Lecture ... nous nous sommes permis d'élaguer et même de corriger quelquefois le style des Pièces que nous avons recueillies.[15]

In the following year alone at least three similar collections were to appear, the *Bibliothèque d'un Homme de goût*,[16] the *Nouvelle Bibliothèque de Campagne*[17] and the *Mélanges tirés d'une grande Bibliothèque*, and this was by no means the end of the series.[18] But the most significant and the most popular of all such enterprises was undoubtedly the *Bibliothèque universelle des Romans* which had begun to appear in July 1775 at the rate of one or two volumes per month, few of which did not include extracts of the old romances. To its editors, who first exhausted the Marquis de Paulmy's own library and then set to work on La Curne's, the authors of later collections clearly owed an immense debt of gratitude:

---

[13] Cf. H. Jacoubet, *Le Comte de Tressan*, pp. 84–114.
[14] *Fabliaux ou Contes*, vol. I, preface, p. lxxxvii.
[15] P. vi. Cited by L. Grossman, *Medievalism*, p. 260.
[16] Avignon and Paris, 2 vols.
[17] Amsterdam and Paris.
[18] Cf. H. Jacoubet, *Le Comte de Tressan*, pp. 192–193.

Il semble que le succès de la 'Bibliothèque des Romans' ait inspiré à plusieurs gens de lettres le désir & le courage de revenir à l'étude de notre ancienne littérature françoise, presque entièrement négligée de nos jours. C'est depuis la publication de cet ouvrage qu'on a tenté de ressusciter nos vieux poëtes ....[19]

Amongst those contributing to the restoration were indeed some who, as we shall see, might justifiably pretend to a certain degree of integrity in their approach to source material and to the extract form. But the success enjoyed by such undertakings as those listed above was not entirely nor even primarily due to their efforts. A. G. Contant d'Orville, disciple of the Comte de Tressan, co-editor with the Marquis de Paulmy of the *Mélanges tirés d'une grande Bibliothèque* upon which, as we know, Le Grand had collaborated, makes clear his own particular conception of this kind of work in the preface to his *Gérard d'Euphrate*, extracted from a sixteenth-century chronicle:

Il ne suffisait pas de réformer le style du roman de 'Gérard d'Euphrate,' il fallait en changer entièrement la marche, en adoucir les incidents, en créer de nouveaux et se préparer de la matière pour composer d'imagination un second volume que le premier auteur promettait et qu'il n'a pas donné.[20]

But the undisputed master of the art is Tressan himself. He would eventually take over the direction of the *Bibliothèque des Romans*,[21] seriously altering its course.

The Marquis de Paulmy had been concerned with fidelity and exactitude in a properly ordered sequence of extracts, his translations essentially concise, unembellished, almost hurried:

Le reste du roman, c'est-à-dire la majeure partie de l'Ouvrage, ne contient plus guère que des récits de combats ou d'aventures incroyables lesquelles n'ont, la plupart, qu'un rapport excessivement éloigné avec 'Percefor-est' ....[22]

He may, as here, have had reason to make omissions, but he would be scrupulously careful not to add gratuitously to the original, his purpose being to convey a concise yet complete impression of this latter, as for example in the case of "Hughes Capet":

---

[19] *Journal Encyclopédique*, 1780, vol. II, pt. I, p. 72.

[20] *Ancienne chronique de Gérard d'Euphrate, duc de Bourgogne, traitant pour la plupart son origine, jeunesse, amours et chevaleureux faits d'armes, avec rencontres et aventures merveilleuses de plusieurs chevaliers de son temps, extrait de l'édition de Paris de 1559 in-folio, remise en français moderne et augmentée de la conclusion de ce roman*, Paris, 1783, 2 vols. Cf. H. Jacoubet, *Le Comte de Tressan*, pp. 325-329, who cites these lines.

[21] In January, 1779.

[22] *Bibliothèque des Romans*, January 1776, p. 61.

Nous allons en donner l'extrait suivi sans interruption, & sans aucun mélange, ni de réflexions, ni de remarques, ni de citations de vers dans le langage ancien ....[23]

Tressan was of a different breed. His earlier extracts did display the influence of the first director of the *Bibliothèque des Romans*, of Paulmy, but as his success continued and increased so he availed himself more and more of his independence. Expositions and conclusions, lengthy interpolated episodes would be reduced to a minimum to provide the original with a greater unity, Tressan's principal concern being the essential subject of the romance in question, now to be elaborated and dramatized. Furthermore, the "originals" from which Tressan composed his extracts were in fact late corrupted versions, more often than not the most recent edition available, "L'histoire amoureuse de Florès & de Blanche-Fleur"[24] even taken from a sixteenth-century translation of a Spanish romance, much to Le Grand d'Aussy's dismay:

Lorsqu'on donna dans la 'Bibliothèque des Romans' l'extrait de 'Florès & de Blanche-Fleur,' l'Homme illustre, l'Ecrivain charmant qui avait composé ce morceau, l'avait travaillé sur une traduction faite ainsi d'après l'Espagnol. Il ignorait que 'Florès & Blanche-Fleur' était dans l'origine un Roman français. J'en prévins, mais trop tard : l'extrait était déjà imprimé en partie.[25]

Whether or not the author of the extract had been aware of this could surely have made little difference.

In his later extracts Tressan would not hesitate to omit whole chapters without warning to his readers. No longer would he be content simply to précis those expositions and conclusions he found unfitting in respect of length or tone, now rewriting them entirely to his own liking. Even character and circumstance were not considered sacred but remodelled to his own requirements:

Il s'y employa avec un zèle dont les résultats tantôt nous font sourire et tantôt nous scandalisent ... Il bouscula sans gêne aucune les récits des anciens conteurs, il intervertit l'ordre des faits, il ajouta au besoin des épisodes de son crû. Il ne prétendait pas faire oeuvre de science ... Mais qu'est-ce qui pouvait bien subsister de l'esprit du XIIe ou du XIIIe siècle sous la plume d'un ancien habitué du Temple ou d'un courtisan de Lunéville?[26]

---

[23] *Bibliothèque des Romans*, January 1778, p. 10. On Paulmy's approach, cf. H. Jacoubet, *Le Comte de Tressan*, pp. 316–322.

[24] *Bibliothèque des Romans*, February 1777, pp. 151–225.

[25] *Fabliaux ou Contes*, vol. IV, Avertissement to "Parténopex," p. 258.

[26] Edmond Estève: "Le Moyen âge dans la littérature du XVIIIe siècle," a lecture given on the 12th May 1923 at the Institut des Hautes Etudes de Belgique and published in the *Revue de l'Université de Bruxelles* for that year (pp. 352–382) p. 379.

But we should in fact be neither amused nor shocked even by "false" extracts such as "Ursino":[27]

Je ne saurais certifier que l'original d' 'Ursino le Navarin' existe en entier tel qu'il devrait être pour m'avoir mis en état de faire cet extrait.[28]

That little or nothing remained of the true spirit of the Middle Ages appears to have been a matter of indifference to the public which, indeed, proved most enthusiastic about this particular piece. Quite simply, Tressan and his disciples were responding to contemporary tastes, supplying a definite need which they themselves had clearly helped to create. Their efforts should not be disdained. Readers were given just what they wanted and showed their gratitude accordingly:

On comprend par l'extrait de 'Pierre de Provence'[29] que l'oeuvre originale devient de moins en moins nécessaire au traducteur et à l'adaptateur et qu'il se sent assez assoupli à ce travail pour pouvoir tirer bientôt de son propre fonds quelque soi-disant extrait dans le goût de ceux qu'il a faits jusqu'ici d'après des modèles, quitte à mystifier un public tout acquis et prêt à pardonner une fraude commise pour lui plaire.[30]

This attempt to define more precisely the true nature of eighteenth-century tastes in "medieval" literary texts has so far involved consideration only of the two extremes in the whole range of publications meant to reply to these tastes, Barbazan's scholarly enterprise, the *Fabliaux et Contes*, as courageous and admirable as it was impracticable, and those pseudo-medieval pieces produced by Tressan, Contant d'Orville and their like. Somewhere between the two extremes, however, there is what has been seen as an area of compromise, a convenient although, as we shall hazard to suggest, misleading way of denoting that particular point in the scale, to which only scant reference has so far been made, perhaps most worthy of our attention. If few of the medieval poets were published in their original form in the eighteenth century

---

[27] *Bibliothèque des Romans*, January 1779, vol II, pp. 47–142, February 1779, pp. 3–106.

[28] By far the finest example of what Henri Jacoubet aptly terms "l'admirable désinvolture de Tressan en matière d'érudition" is that notorious "Chanson de Roland" which appeared in the *Bibliothèque des Romans* in December 1777, pp. 210–216: "Sans nous amuser à déterrer dans la poussière des Bibliothèques, quelques fragments imparfaits & barbares de cette Chanson: sans recourir à la supposition d'un Manuscrit, dans lequel cette Chanson se trouveroit transcrite dans son langage original, imaginons plutôt quel pouvoient en être le sens et le goût... Enfin, voici ce que nous croyons que chantoient nos soldats, il y a sept ou huit cents ans en allant au combat."

Jacoubet provides us with a very thorough account of Tressan's work and clearly defines the various stages in his development as an author of extracts. Cf. *Le Comte de Tressan*, pp. 232–315.

[29] *Bibliothèque des Romans*, August 1779, pp. 91–160.

[30] H. Jacoubet, *Le Comte de Tressan*, p. 249.

whilst many were successfully exploited by the unselfconscious "adapt-
ateurs," then Le Grand's collection, a highly popular and yet by no
means frivolous piece of work, proves well enough that a serious attempt to bring literary texts of the Middle Ages before a contemporary
reading public was not necessarily predestined to failure. Extracts of
the "anciens rimeurs" presented in such a way as to be immediately
accessible to readers and yet composed against a background of the
most solid erudition and scholarship in fact enjoyed some considerable
success at the time, a point which does not escape the attention of Albert Pauphilet who explains the situation thus:

C'est le XVIIIe siècle qui a véritablement redécouvert le Moyen Age, et il
l'a d'emblée rendu non à une poignée d'érudits ou d'amateurs de singularité,
mais à un vaste public. Car la science de ce temps ne se tient pas à l'écart du
monde; elle en recherche au contraire la faveur, et malgré la nouveauté de
ses objets, se souvient de la grande règle classique, qui est de plaire.[31]

Pauphilet's explanation is undoubtedly a valid one and Le Grand
d'Aussy himself clearly defines his own purpose as "plaire et instruire."[32] But the question is, did this search for public favour really
call for any great sacrifice from the majority of these scholars? Even
had they been able actually to predetermine the tastes of the reading
public, would they in fact, given this free choice, have preferred to
present their texts in any fundamentally different way? With scholars
and "uninitiated" readers equally unenthusiastic about texts published
in their original form, was it not to be expected that they would eventually meet quite naturally upon common ground? Such a meeting,
perhaps the first of its kind, took place in La Curne de Sainte-Palaye's
Aucassin et Nicolette[33] which might be said to represent the happy medium between Barbazan's ill-fated efforts and Tressan's later, more
imaginative extracts, an honest translation with great care taken to
preserve the essential tone of the original[34] yet, as the subtitle "Les
Amours du bon vieux temps" would suggest, thoroughly in keeping
with the public's obvious literary preferences:

---

[31] Albert Pauphilet, *Le Legs du Moyen Age*, Melun (Librairie d'Argences) 1950, p. 37.
[32] *Fabliaux ou Contes*, vol. I, preface, p. ii.
[33] The "Romance d'Aucassin et de Nicolette" was first published in the *Mercure* for
February 1752 (pp. 10–64) and later with "La Châtelaine de Saint Gilles" as *Les Amours du
bon vieux temps*, Vaucluse and Paris (Duchesne) 1756.
[34] "Le Traducteur n'a fait que mettre dans un françois intelligible le texte original qui ne
pourroit être entendu que d'un petit nombre de personnes qui ont pris la peine de se rendre
ce langage familier. Il a rendu scrupuleusement dans la Prose la simplicité & la naiveté du
dialogue; mais à l'égard de la versification, il n'en a pas toujours conservé aussi exactement
la mesure & les rimes." (Avertissement, pp. 6–7.)

En somme on ne saurait mettre trop haut la publication de Lacurne. Vulgarisateur de cette science de nos antiquités qu'il avait acquise avec tant de peine, il faisait confiance au public et lui soumettait une oeuvre du vrai moyen âge. Le succès qui l'accueillera, la vogue dont elle jouira mise à la scène, l'adaptation qu'en donnera en 1784 la Bibliothèque des Romans montrent qu'il n'avait pas surestimé la compréhension de ses contemporains.[35]

If we reflect for one moment it will become clear that this was in fact the only possible way in which medieval literature could be brought before the uninstructed mass of the eighteenth-century reading public. It is very probably true to say that the most relevant and valid work undertaken on medieval literature at this time was indeed that done by those in whom we find that same quality attributed above to La Curne de Sainte-Palaye, the harmonious combination of scholar and "vulgarisateur," men like Le Grand d'Aussy himself who, as we shall later see, in this respect bears a striking resemblance to his former master.

The Marquis de Paulmy, with a far more careful, more studied approach to the extract form than his immediate successor, Tressan, must undoubtedly rank as ". . . l'un de ceux qui ont contribué le plus à vulgariser le moyen âge . . .".[36] Paulmy had an affection for romances of every kind and of every era but a particular passion for the romances of chivalry, a passion which he would enable his contemporaries to share through the Bibliothèque des Romans and the Mélanges tirés d'une grande Bibliothèque, creating a new enthusiasm for a genre he felt to have been unjustly neglected hitherto:

Cette classe n'a point de modèle dans l'antiquité. Elle est due au génie des François; & tout ce qui a paru, de ce genre, chez les autres peuples de l'Europe, a été postérieur aux premiers Romans que la France a produits, & n'en a été pour ainsi dire qu'une imitation.[37]

But difficult as it would be to overestimate the value of Paulmy's work, both the standpoint of such authors and the immediate validity of their contribution are perhaps most effectively demonstrated by the Mémoires sur l'ancienne Chevalerie[38] where few critics have failed to note the

---

[35] H. Jacoubet, Le Comte de Tressan, pp. 172–173.
[36] Idem, p. 317.
[37] Bibliothèque des Romans, July 1775, Discours préliminaire, p. 14.
[38] The five "Mémoires sur l'ancienne Chevalerie considérée comme un établissement politique et militaire," read at the Académie des Inscriptions between November 1746 and August 1750 and first published in volume XX of the Académie's Mémoires (pp. 597–847), appeared separately in 1759 in two volumes with a third companion volume, Mémoires historiques sur la Chasse, added in 1781 (Paris, Duchesne). A second, three-volume edition was published in this same year and in 1826 appeared a new edition by A. P. Barginet with an introduction and notes by Charles Nodier (Paris, Girard, 2 vols). References are to this latter.

facility with which La Curne is able to fuse his considerable talents as a scholar with his most enviable awareness of contemporary tastes, those tastes which he himself can be said to have shared and which it was his obvious intention to satisfy:

En ménageant moins l'érudition, j'aurois sans doute satisfait davantage la curiosité des amateurs de l'antiquité; mais aurois – je également plu à cette partie aimable de la société à laquelle cet ouvrage est principalement consacré? Puissent les Dames accueillir avec bienveillance ce dernier fruit d'une Plume qui s'est toujours exercée de préférence dans un genre de littérature dont elles font leur plus cher amusement.[39]

What was essentially a very scholarly piece of work was thus presented in such a way that the public found little difficulty but great pleasure in reading it and indeed became filled with a new curiosity for the subject. The *Mercure*, for example, in an account of the first of the "Mémoires," proved highly appreciative of La Curne's approach and did not conceal the enthusiasm with which it looked forward to the remainder of these "dissertations intéressantes & curieuses":

... l'Auteur a fait disparoître l'immense amas d'érudition qui fait la base de son discours, pour ne laisser voir que la méthode, la clarté, l'élégance d'un écrivain qui sçait approfondir sa matière sans s'appesantir, & trouve le moyen de plaire & d'intéresser dans un sujet qui ne sembloit destiné qu'à instruire.[40]

Yet a moment's reflection will once more reveal that this was in fact the only possible way of presenting this kind of material to a public such as La Curne's. There can surely be no doubt about the immense value of publications like *Aucassin et Nicolette* and the *Mémoires sur l'ancienne Chevalerie*, the value of the contribution made by individuals like La Curne de Sainte-Palaye, scholar turned popularizer. Paradoxically, it was only because these scholars themselves had no blind faith in the Middle Ages or its literature that they could make such efforts to bring both before the contemporary reading public. La Curne, with his

---

[39] *Mémoires sur l'ancienne Chevalerie*, vol. I, preface, pp. vii–viii. These lines are reproduced by L. Gossman (*Medievalism*, p. 279) who devotes a chapter to the "Mémoires sur l'ancienne Chevalerie" and the "Mémoires historiques sur la Chasse."

[40] *Mercure*, December 1746, p. 103. A more recent critic, Edmond Estève, expresses a similar view: "...pour tout ce qui regarde la partie descriptive et pittoresque, il réussit par l'abondance et la précision des détails à nous donner, sans recherche ostentoire, l'impression de la couleur. Les tableaux qu'il nous fait de l'education donnée aux pages, des tournois, du voeu de paon, des funérailles des chevaliers sont des morceaux pleins d'animation et de poésie." ("Le Moyen âge dans la littérature du XVIIIe siècle," p. 368.)

views,[41] had no qualms about opening his library to the editors of the *Bibliothèque des Romans*:

... M. de Sainte-Palaie, à qui l'histoire de la Chevalerie, & même celle de la langue Françoise, ont de si grandes obligations, a voulu que nous lui en eussions de particulières. Il nous a ouvert les trésors de son cabinet, & nous a procuré le moyen d'en tirer parti.[42]

This leads us directly to the one question which has so far been avoided but which is clearly central to our purposes here. Why, in view of their generally poor opinion of the literary merits of the "anciens rimeurs," did the most distinguished medievalists of the eighteenth century devote so much time and effort to collecting and establishing literary texts of the Middle Ages? Those brilliant scholars of the following century, to be blessed with a far more sympathetic atmosphere in which to work, would in fact owe much to the advances made in the field of textual criticism by their less fortunate predecessors, of whose efforts the dis-interested public remained largely ignorant.[43] It was not only Le Grand d'Aussy who would draw profitably upon the immense fund of annotated manuscript copies executed for or actually by La Curne de Sainte-Palaye,[44] La Curne who, claiming for medieval French texts the same scholarly respect with which were approached the productions of classical antiquity and yet at the same time warning against the un-reliability not only of early printed editions but equally of late manu-script versions, must surely rank amongst the greatest innovators of his time.[45] But again we must ask the purpose of such industry, for we know that scholarly editions of medieval texts were but rarely the ob-ject envisaged. Were the fruits of these labours to be reaped only by a later generation of medievalists? In a way, of course, those "oeuvres de vulgarisation" produced by scholars like La Curne can be seen as an immediate return for the work done collecting, annotating and estab-lishing texts. But clearly they alone do not explain the volume and precision of this work. What then was the true nature of scholarly in-terest in medieval literature at this time?

---

[41] *Mémoires sur l'ancienne Chevalerie*, vol. I, pp. 337–338: "...en lisant tout ce que nous avons dit à l'honneur de la Chevalerie, on se sera rappelé que les siècles dans lesquels elle étoit la plus florissante, furent des siècles de débauche, de brigandage, de barbarie et d'hor-reur...".

[42] *Bibliothèque des Romans*, February 1777, p. 45.

[43] Cf. Madelaine Jouglard's "Les études d'histoire littéraire en France au XVIIIe siècle" in *La Revue du Mois*, 10th April, 1915, pp. 440–441: "...Le zèle des chercheurs n'est point refroidi par ces appréciations. Inconnus du public, raillés des journalistes, ils s'en consolent par le plaisir des découvertes qui leur montrent l'excellence de leurs méthodes."

[44] Cf. L. Gossman, *Medievalism*, pp. 264–267.

[45] *Idem*, pp. 225–226.

The answer to our question is indicated by the frequently obvious bias of these same "oeuvres de vulgarisation," of the celebrated *Aucassin et Nicolette*, for example, where the translator states quite emphatically that he is concerned to demonstrate not the literary but rather the historical value of the piece:

Il ne s'agit pas de donner un ouvrage sans défaut, celui-ci en a beaucoup qu'on ne prétend pas dissimuler; il est question de faire connoître au vrai nos anciennes moeurs . . . .[46]

The "Mémoire concernant la lecture des anciens Romans de Chevalerie" can leave us in no doubt as to La Curne de Sainte-Palaye's predominantly historical approach to the productions of the "anciens rimeurs."[47] If he felt significant works of literature could be published in extract form only to their detriment,[48] then it was most decidedly not his considered opinion that the "romans de chevalerie" suffered unduly from this method of presentation:

. . . ceux qui les ont composés, sont souvent fastidieux par leurs fictions, leur composition, le tour de leur esprit, & la grossièreté de leur style: & c'est peut-être une raison de plus pour désirer qu'on les fît bien connoître par des extraits.[49]

The "Mémoire" indeed includes a plea for a "bibliothèque générale & complète de tous nos anciens Romans de Chevalerie" where La Curne defines for us the nature of his approach, indicating the only manner in which he believed such a work could be presented, that is as a uniform series of extracts, and making plain what he himself considered should be the primary concern of its authors:

On s'attacheroit par préférence à tout ce qui paroîtroit de quelque usage pour l'Histoire, pour les Généalogies, pour les Antiquités françoises & pour la Géographie: sans rien omettre de ce qui donneroit quelques lumières sur les progrès des Arts & des Sciences.[50]

The suggestion that those compiling the collection might also wish to preserve ". . . ce qu'il y auroit de remarquable du côté de l'esprit & de

---

[46] Edition of 1756, Avertissement, p. 7.

[47] "Mémoire concernant la lecture des anciens Romans de Chevalerie" read before the Académie des Inscriptions on December 13th 1743 and published in vol. XVII of the Académie's *Mémoires*, pp. 787–799.

[48] *Idem*, p. 797: "Les bons livres perdent toûjours à être abrégés. Les beautés principales sont anéanties ou défigurées dans l'extrait le mieux fait: & d'ailleurs nous savons combien il est dangereux de faire des abrégés des bons livres; puisque de tels abrégés ont causé la perte d'un nombre infini des meilleurs ouvrages de l'antiquité."

[49] *Ibidem*.

[50] *P*. 798.

l'invention; quelques tours délicats & naïfs, quelques traits de morale & quelques pensées ingénieuses ...",[51] this suggestion again comes almost as an after-thought. Thirty years later, when writing the "Discours préliminaire" to the first volume of the *Bibliothèque des Romans*, a collection bringing La Curne's proposals to some kind of fruition at least, the Marquis de Paulmy would be similarly unequivocal about the purpose of the enterprise and the nature of his own interest in the romance:

Il offre une chaîne de livres qui forment presque une histoire complette de plusieurs siècles. Elle ne sera point interrompue dans la Bibliothèque que nous allons offrir au Public.[52]

It is not in fact in the eighteenth century that such a lively interest in the national past is to be witnessed for the first time. Two hundred years earlier scholars, while often at the same time decrying the literature of the Middle Ages, were already engaging upon major historical researches into this period. Etienne Pasquier devoted more than half a century to his *Recherches de la France*, inquiring into the manners and customs, the laws and institutions, the language and literature of these times, and declared:

Je pense avoir esté le premier des nostres qui ay défriché plusieurs anciennetez obscures de ceste France.[53]

A contemporary, the celebrated Claude Fauchet, proved equally industrious with his dissertations on French magistrates and dignitaries, on chivalry and heraldry,[54] his *Recueil de l'origine de la langue et poësie francoise*[55] and, most important, the *Recueil des antiquitez gauloises et françoises*,[56] all of which, in the opinion of Albert Pauphilet

... montrent en lui un vrai savant, qui recherche bien les documents et aime à remonter, en toutes choses, aux faits initiaux.[57]

National and regional pride assured Pasquier and Fauchet of a throng

[51] *Ibidem.*

[52] *Bibliothèque des Romans*, July 1775, Discours préliminaire, p. 15.

[53] *Les Recherches de la France, revues et augmentées de quatre livres*, Paris, (J. Mettayer & P. L'huillier) 1596. Cited by A. Pauphilet, *Le Legs du Moyen Age*, p. 26.

[54] *Origines des dignitez et magistrats de France, recueillies par Claude Fauchet – Origines des chavaliers, armoiries et héraux, ensemble de l'ordonnance, armes et instruments desquels les François ont anciennement usé en leurs guerres. Recueillies par Claude Fauchet*, Paris (J. Périer) 1600.

[55] *Recueil de l'origine de la langue et poësie françoise, ryme et romans. Plus les noms et sommaire des oeuvres de CXXVII poetes françois, vivans avant l'an M.CCC*, Paris (M. Patisson) 1581.

[56] Paris (J. du Puys) 1579.

[57] Albert Pauphilet, *Le Legs du Moyen Age*, p. 27.

of followers.[58] In 1609 appeared André Duchesne's *Antiquitez et recherches des villes, chasteaux et places plus remarquables de toute la France,*[59] this succeeded by a number of works dealing more specifically with particular towns or areas amongst which Paris was an obvious favourite.[60]

At the same time there were those sections of society with perhaps a rather more personal interest in the Nation's past. While Vulson de la Colombière's *Théâtre d'Honneur et de Chevalerie* was, at least in part, an attempt to "... remettre la noblesse dans son ancien lustre ..."[61] and Jean Le Laboureur undertook his *Histoire de la Pairie de France et du Parlement de Paris*[62] at the request of certain nobles, others like Jacques de Cassan and Théodore Godefroy looked to the interests of the monarchy.[63] The Church was by no means a disinterested party and an immense amount of research on ecclesiastical history was undertaken at this time, Jean Mabillon and the Benedictine scholars of Saint-Maur being particularly worthy of note for such productions as the *Acta Sanctorum,* the *Vetera Analecta* and the *Annales Ordinis Sancti Benedicti.* But it would be unfair to suggest that all such scholars had ulterior motives or indeed that the work of those who clearly did was in any way inferior. In any event their researches provided a later generation with a most solid foundation upon which to build, a foundation composed

[58] La Curne de Sainte-Palaye was to consult both for his proposed *Dictionnaire des Antiquités françoises.* Cf. L. Gossman, *Medievalism,* p. 268.

[59] *Les Antiquitez et recherches des villes, chasteaux et places plus remarquables de toute la France, divisées en huict livres selon l'ordre et ressort des huict Parlemens,* Paris (J. Petit-Pas) 1609.

[60] Cf. Nathan Edelman, *Attitudes of Seventeenth-Century France toward the Middle Ages,* New York (King's Crown Press) 1946, p. 49. Edelman deals at some length with the vast researches undertaken by sixteenth and seventeenth-century historians on the Middle Ages.

[61] *Le Vray théâtre d'Honneur et de Chevalerie ou le Miroir Héroique de la Noblesse,* Paris (Augustin Courbé) 1648, 2 vols. in-folio. The quotation is taken from vol. I, ch. VIII, "Des anciens chevaliers errans et des choses plus remarquables qu'on trouve touchant les Chevaliers de la Table Ronde, avec leur nom & leurs armes, & de plusieurs autres choses divertissans," p. 131.

[62] London (S. Harding) 1740.

[63] Jacques de Cassan: *La Recherche des droits du roy et de la couronne de France, sur les royaumes, duchez, comtez, villes et pays occupez par les princes estrangers, appartenant aux rois très chrestiens, par conquestes, successions, achapts, donations, et autres titres légitimes,* Paris (F. Paneray) 1632.

Théodore Godefroy: *Traitez touchant les droits du roy très chrestien sur plusieurs estats et seigneuries possédées par divers princes voisins, et pour prouver qu'il tient à juste titre plusieurs provinces contestées par les princes estrangers,* published by Jacques Dupuy, Paris (A. Courbé) 1655.

Nathan Edelman mentions one amusing but perhaps inevitable result of this increase in historical research inspired by personal interest: "Bourgeois were interested in discovering a long lineage for themselves, and many noblemen, in a desire to maintain their more ancient prestige, also claimed an imposing but fabulous ancestry... In the reign of Louis XIII, the vogue of fanciful and fancy genealogies began in earnest, and inspired the novelist Charles Sorel to ordain in 1632 that no one might trace back his ancestry to more than three thousand years before the deluge, except those, of course, who could produce authentic claims drawn up before a royal notary!" (*Attitudes of Seventeenth-Century France,* p. 51).

not only of historical studies, such as have been listed above, but of compilations of documents and of etymological dictionaries and glossaries intended to facilitate comprehension of these documents. Important advances in the field of medieval philology were made at this time by Ménage,[64] Borel[65] and, most important of all, by Du Cange whose *Glossarium ad Scriptores Mediae et Infimae Latinitatis*[66] and *Glossarium ad Scriptores Mediae et Infimae Graecitatis*,[67] in addition to prefaces describing in the first case the transformation of Latin and in the second the evolution of Greek, in addition to the definitions and etymologies, also contained numerous valuable historical essays. The glossaries have perhaps justifiably been termed "encyclopedias of medieval civilization".[68]

That the eighteenth century, which for the most part could speak only disparagingly of the literary merits of the "anciens rimeurs," should in its turn display a lively historical interest in the Middle Ages is thus not a matter for surprise. A tradition, as it were, had been established and, far from breaking with this latter, the Age of Enlightenment would ensure that it continued to flourish. Towards the end of the seventeenth century appeared Brice's highly successful *Description de la ville de Paris* in which readers are taken on what might be termed a voyage of architectural and archeological discovery through the capital and thereby acquainted with "... nos anciennes lois, coutumes, moeurs, le caractère et le génie de notre nation ...".[69] More than half a century later Saint Foix would publish his equally successful *Essais historiques sur Paris*, similarly defining his purpose as "... faire connaître quelles ont été en différents temps les moeurs et les coutumes de la nation ...".[70] In his *Monuments de la Monarchie françoise* the celebrated Benedictine scholar Bernard de Montfaucon set out to compose, with the help of illustrations, what must be regarded as a general history of French civilisation, treating everything from the Monarchy and the Church to furniture and fashion.[71] The results he obtained may have been disappointing but the work was certainly valid in its time

---

[64] Gilles Ménage: *Les Origines de la langue francoise*, Paris (A. Courbé) 1650.
[65] Pierre Borel: *Trésor de recherches et antiquitez gauloises et françoises*, Paris (A. Courbé) 1655.
[66] Paris ((L. Billaine) 1678, 3 vols.
[67] Lyon (Anisson, J. Posuel et C. Rigaud) 1688, 2 vols.
[68] Cf. N. Edelman, *Attitudes of Seventeenth-Century France*, p. 65.
[69] *Description nouvelle de ce qu'il y a de plus remarquable dans la ville de Paris*, Paris (N. Legras) 1684. Cf. H. Jacoubet, *Le Comte de Tressan*, pp. 78–79.
[70] *Essais historiques sur Paris*, London, 1754–1755. Cf. H. Jacoubet, *loc. cit.*
[71] *Monuments de la Monarchie françoise*, Paris (J.-M. Gandouin et P.-F. Giffart) 1729–1733, 5 vols.

and must have been of considerable use to Montfaucon's contemporaries. Indeed, the Benedictines as a whole were responsible for immense and invaluable efforts in the field of historical scholarship with collections like the *Recueil des Historiens des Gaules et de la France*, the *Gallia Christiana* and the projected *Recueil des Historiens des Croisades*.

Clearly the Middle Ages had become an extremely popular area of study amongst contemporary scholars. In his *De l'Esprit des Lois* Montesquieu had much to say about the manners and customs of the period[72] and Voltaire, however much he may have despised "... ces temps de grossièreté, de rapines et de meurtres ...",[73] nevertheless found them worthy of study and comment. Not the least responsible for this interest were the members of the Académie des Inscriptions et Belles-Lettres, the institution which perhaps did most to promote and advance research on the national past. The Académie had at first, as its name suggests, been preoccupied with composing those devices or inscriptions to be carved on monuments erected by the King, but in 1701 it was reorganized by Louis XIV and given as its purpose the study of the history and antiquities of the Nation. Members were not slow to realize that a concerted effort would be required if this purpose was to be fulfilled and in January 1727 Camille Falconet read a paper which, claiming for French history that same respect with which scholars approached the study of classical antiquity, called for just such an effort.[74] Principal driving-force at the Académie, Falconet set before his colleagues a detailed programme of the researches which in his view required their earliest attention, a programme proposing, for example, histories of weights and measures, of the coinage, of literature, arts and sciences, manners and customs, and, what is more important, insisting heavily upon the need for a glossary of the French language, a geographical dictionary and a comprehensive bibliography of French writings, the basic tools of historical research. La Curne de Sainte-Palaye, only twenty-seven years of age when elected to the Académie, would reiterate these ideas in his own "Plan de travail pour l'Acadé-

---

[72] L. Gossman notes a striking similarity between Montesquieu and Sainte-Palaye historian. The two were apparently acquainted and knew each other's work. Cf. *Medievalism*, pp. 279–280.

[73] *Essai sur les Moeurs* (*OEuvres Complètes*, vol. XII) ch. LXXXII, "Sciences et beaux arts aux treizième et quatorzième siècles," p. 66: "La Comparaison de ces siècles avec le nôtre (quelques perversités et quelques malheurs que nous puissions éprouver) doit nous faire sentir notre bonheur, malgré ce penchant presque invincible que nous avons à louer le passé aux dépens du présent."

[74] "Sur nos premiers traducteurs françois avec un Essay de bibliothèque françoise," of which a summary is to be found in the "partie historique" of the Académie's *Mémoires*, vol. VII, pp. 292–300. Cf. L. Gossman, *Medievalism*, pp. 163–167.

mie des Belles-Lettres"[75] and perhaps do more than any other to put into execution the proposals made in Falconet's paper.

While La Curne did play a not altogether insignificant part in collections like the *Recueil des Historiens des Gaules et de la France*, the *Histoire littéraire de la France* and the *Recueil des Historiens des Croisades*, the scale and indeed the value of his efforts in the field of historical scholarship are best demonstrated by those major projects with which he thought to fulfil what in his own and in Falconet's opinion was the real purpose of the Académie. Falconet himself may have collaborated with his immediate successor on the *Dictionnaire géographique* but it was La Curne who had principal responsibility for the proposed glossary of Old French and who, in his *Projet d'un Glossaire françois*,[76] stressed its importance to researches on medieval history generally, at the same time testifying to the immense popularity of these latter:

Il n'y a pas de temps à perdre: des Recueils précieux, toujours protégés par le Gouvernement, tels que le 'Gallia Christiana,' les Ordonnances de nos Rois, nos anciens Historiens, l'Histoire littéraire de la France, et l'Histoire de la Diplomatique, sont continués avec une ardeur toute nouvelle: d'autres non moins importants sont entrepris avec le même zèle et le même courage: une Description historique, géographique et diplomatique de la France, un Traité des Monnoies, une Histoire de toutes les branches du Droit public François, des Histoires particulières de plusieurs provinces de France: tous ces Ouvrages réclament unanimement le secours d'un Glossaire François . . . .[77]

Most important of all, the editors of the *Recueil des Historiens* were approaching the stage where much of their source material was in the vernacular so that a glossary had become indispensable if that same degree of exactitude and fidelity achieved in earlier volumes of the collection was to be maintained.[78] Unfortunately, despite his own unfailing efforts, continued even after 1762 when discussions with Falconet, Foncemagne, Bréquigny and d'Alembert had led to serious modifications, despite the efforts of his numerous assistants, amongst them Le Grand d'Aussy, La Curne would never see publication of his work. Contemporary scholars eagerly awaited its appearance[79] but a full cen-

---

[75] Cf. L. Gossman, *Medievalism*, pp. 167–168.

[76] Paris (H.-L. Guérin & L.-F. Delatour) 1756. The *Projet* is included by Favre in his edition of La Curne's *Glossaire*, vol. I, pp. iv–xii. References are to this latter.

[77] *Projet d'un Glossaire françois*, p. vii.

[78] *Ibidem.*

[79] The *Journal Encyclopédique* saw that La Curne brought to this work: ". . .un esprit singulier pour des savants, cet esprit de justesse qui écartera la superfluité des citations, qui rapprochera les termes anciens des nouveaux avec la gradation de leurs métamorphoses, qui ne rassemblera que des expressions lumineuses pour développer le génie de la langue.

tury would elapse after the author's death before the true value of the
Glossaire, unequalled in its day, could be appreciated.[80]

If the purpose of the glossary was to facilitate the historian's understanding of vernacular sources,[81] then La Curne was equally concerned
with both cataloguing and publishing these sources. We know already
that he was involved in the work undertaken for the *Recueil des Historiens des Gaules et de la France,* apparently a member of the committee appointed by d'Aguesseau to supervise the efforts of the Benedictines,[82]
and his interest in medieval chronicles is evidenced by the numerous
papers concerning these latter which he published in the *Mémoires de
l'Académie des Inscriptions.*[83] Further to this, La Curne, together with
Secousse, Bréquigny and Foncemagne, engaged upon a *Table chronologique des diplômes, chartes, titres et actes imprimés concernant l'histoire de
France,*[84] a catalogue of all the relevant material already available in
print. Bréquigny emphasized the value of such a collection in the preface to the second volume:

Si on examine avec soin les Chartes dont nous ne pouvons indiquer que le
sujet principal, on n'en trouvera presque aucune qui ne renferme incidem-
ment des traits propres à répandre du jour, soit sur les parties essentielles de
l'Histoire générale, la Chronologie, la Géographie, les Généalogies; soit sur
les parties les plus intéressantes de l'Histoire particulière, les Loix, les
Usages et les Moeurs de nos ancêtres.[85]

When it came to cataloguing manuscript sources, La Curne, if anything, proved more industrious still. Convinced that the earlier manuscripts provide the historian with his richest and most reliable store of
information on the national past, he set out to write detailed accounts

Souvent il nous fera voir dans un mot l'origine d'un usage ou d'une loi: un autre terme
amènera la description d'une fête, et l'art qu'il aura de réduire toutes ses connaissances à
un but doit faire qu'on apprenne l'histoire d'une nation en croyant n'étudier que sa langue."
(August 1758, p. 123.)

[80] Reference has already been made to L. Gossman's article on the *Glossaire* in *French
Studies,* vol. XII, pp. 346–358.

[81] Further to the *Glossaire* La Curne's work on language includes an attempt to trace the
origins of French in his "Remarques sur la Langue Françoise des XIIe et XIIIe siècles comparée avec les Langues Provençale, Italienne et Espagnole, dans les mêmes siècles," published in the *Mém. Acad. Inscr.,* vol. XXIV, pp. 671–686 and in Favre's edition of the *Glossaire,*
vol. X, pp. 377–382: "Ce seroit retrancher un des principaux objets sur lesquels l'esprit
philosophique doit s'exercer, que de négliger l'étude des Langues, et de mépriser la recherche
des étymologies, qui en fait une partie des plus essentielles." (P. 377.)

[82] Cf. L. Gossman, *Medievalism,* p. 235.

[83] Gossman devotes a chapter (pt. III, ch. V) to La Curne's work on the chronicle sources
of medieval history and lists the relevent "Mémoires" in his bibliography (Appendix I, pp.
359–361).

[84] Paris, 1769–1876, 8 vols.

[85] P. iii.

of all those specimens he could trace, in the major Italian libraries as well as in private and public collections in his own capital, an undertaking which coincided with the need for a comprehensive catalogue of the French manuscripts held in the Bibliothèque du Roi. La Curne became involved in yet another project whose completion he could not possibly hope to see. In fact he would not even live long enough to be gratified by a far more immediate but hardly less significant outcome of his endeavours, the appearance in 1787 of the first volume of the *Notices et extraits des manuscrits de la Bibliothèque du Roi*, that most excellent of scholarly publications which can be said to have evolved from his work.

If it would be improper, even in such a brief survey of La Curne's work on the history and antiquities of France, not to mention the celebrated *Mémoires sur l'ancienne Chevalerie*, according to Madelaine Jouglard "... une histoire suivie et excellente de l'institution ...",[86] then equally such a survey could not be regarded as truly representative without some reference to the *Dictionnaire des antiquités françoises* and to the *Histoire littéraire des Troubadours*. The dissertations on chivalry were in fact extracted from the former, an ambitious compilation covering the many and varied aspects of French society, its history and development over a period of centuries. Little escaped La Curne's attention or failed to arouse his interest:

Its articles deal with the government, administration, and finances of the realm, with ecclesiastical antiquities and the relations and spheres of influence of Church and State, with the social classes and their changing relationships, with commerce and the national economy, with the laws and their administration, with the ideas and attitudes of different classes of society at different times, with education, the arts, and sciences, with medieval customs, royal and ecclesiastical cere monial, methods of warfare, architecture, clothing and dress, furnishing – in short, with everything from medieval communications or fish merchants to the origins of the monarchy and to the wool trade in the fourteenth century.[87]

Regrettably only those who knew or worked with the author or who might consult his manuscript, sold to the Bibliothèque du Roi, would ever benefit from the vast researches undertaken for the *Dictionnaire des antiquités francoises*, destined to remain unpublished. In fact the *Histoire littéraire des Troubadours*, implementing yet another of Falconet's proposals, came near to suffering the same tragic fate and it was only thanks to the assistance given by Foncemagne and the efforts of a suc-

---

[86] "Les études d'histoire littéraire en France au XVIIIe siècle," p. 430.
[87] L. Gossman, *Medievalism*, pp. 269–270.

cession of editors that the three volume collection appeared in La Curne's own lifetime.[88]

La Curne de Sainte-Palaye is clearly something of an exception and yet his unfailing passion for the Middle Ages and the massive efforts he devoted to unveiling this period can surely be regarded quite simply, not as symptomatic of a revival of interest in the national past, but rather as an expression of the continued, although much increased enthusiasm with which his countrymen in general looked to this latter:

M. de Sainte-Palaye, si célèbre par ses Mémoires sur l'ancienne Chevalerie, a fait aussi les recherches les plus savantes sur l'Histoire des troubadours. Il y a employé plusieurs années d'une vie infiniment active et laborieuse. Il a voyagé exprès en Italie et en Provence et s'y est donné des soins et des peines incroyables pour ramasser tout ce qui pouvait répandre quelque lumière sur une partie si intéressante et si peu connue de notre littérature. Le travail qu'il a fait sur cet objet est immense.[89]

If there was nothing really new or surprising about the interest shown by La Curne and his contemporaries in the history and antiquities of the nation, then the idea that fictional texts of the Middle Ages could provide an invaluable fund of information relevant to these latter, an idea clearly fundamental to *Aucassin et Nicolette* and, according to Paulmy's "Discours préliminaire," to the *Bibliothèque des Romans*, this idea again was equally well-rooted in the past. As we know already, the scholars of the sixteenth and seventeenth centuries, like their successors, showed little respect for medieval literature as such, Montaigne's impression of the old romances indicative of the disdain with which the artistic abilities of the "anciens rimeurs" were generally viewed:

... des 'Lancelots du Lac', des 'Amadis', des 'Huons de Bordeaux' et tel fatras de livres à quoy l'enfance s'amuse, je n'en connoissois pas seulement le nom, ny ne fais encore le corps, tant exacte estoit ma discipline.[90]

Not all, of course, were quite as severe as Montaigne and it is true, for example, that a summary history of French poetry from its origins to the sixteenth century is included by Pasquier in his *Recherches de la*

---

[88] *Histoire littéraire des Troubadours, contenant leurs vies, les extraits de leurs pièces, & plusieurs particularités sur les moeurs, les usages, & l'histoire du douzième & du treizième siècles*, Paris(Durand neveu) 1774, 3 vols. This edition was reproduced by *Slatkine Reprints* in 1967.

[89] Grimm, *Correspondance littéraire*, ed. Tourneux (Paris, Garnier frères, 1877–1882, 16 vols.) vol. X, p. 488. Cited by L. Gossman, *Medievalism*, p. 322, note 101.

[90] *Essais*, Livre premier, ch. XXVI, "De l'Institution des Enfants." Text presented by Jean Plattard, Paris (Les Belles Lettres) 1946 (Les Textes Français) vol. II, p. 51.

France.[91] But Pasquier's again is a predominantly historical approach, concerned as he is more with questions relative to the origins and development of rhyme than with true critical appreciation of the works themselves. More interesting, however, is that he should not altogether neglect these early productions in his researches on the manners and customs, the laws and institutions of medieval France, that he should both realize and exploit the historical value of Old French literature:

> Etienne Pasquier dans ses 'Recherches de la France' … est amené plus d'une fois, en remontant aux origines soit d'une expression ancienne, soit d'une institution, à trouver dans notre vieille littérature non seulement un renseignement nouveau mais un trait de couleur locale, et même une véritable impression d'art. Ainsi, à propos des chirurgiens et chirurgiennes dont la profession est réglementée par un édit, il rappelle l'habitude qu'avaient jadis les femmes de soigner les chevaliers blessés et nous renvoie, à fin de preuves, aux romans, 'images de nos coutumes anciennes.'[92]

Fauchet's is a similar case. He may view the efforts of France's earliest poets with an eye far more enthusiastic and appreciative than that of Pasquier, compiling a unique collection of romances which his predecessors have exploited and then rejected "… ainsi que des Esclaves malades abandonnez pour leurs dangereuses maladies, par de mauspiteux maistres …" and which he might now consider his own,[93] but in his *Recueil de l'Origine de la Langue & Poësie Françoise* he fails to make plain to his contemporaries the reasons for his enthusiasm, fails to make plain to them the true literary merits of the numerous poets upon whom he comments.[94] What is evident from Fauchet's writings is that these same poets can be of some considerable service to those concerned with unearthing the past. What he does make plain is his own firm belief in the value of medieval literary texts as historical sources. In the

---

[91] Livre VII. Cf. N. Edelman, *Attitudes of Seventeenth-Century France toward the Middle Ages*, p. 307.

[92] H. Jacoubet, *Le Comte de Tressan*, p. 6.

[93] *Origines des Dignitez et Magistrats de France*, Epitre au Lecteur.

[94] Cf. *Changing attitudes towards medieval French literature*, an inaugural lecture delivered in the University of Hull, 15th February 1966, by Professor C. E. Pickford (University of Hull Publications, 1966) p. 8: "Despite his vast erudition, his love for his subject, the desire which he had to enable others to share the texts which he had read, Fauchet's writings did little to change the attitude of the majority of writers and critics who either knew nothing whatsoever of medieval literature or else despised it and declared it to be worthless… He nowhere devotes sufficient attention to the great medieval texts… Fauchet was following in the tradition of La Croix du Maine, who, in his 'Bibliothèques Francoises,' published 1583–4, collected much information together, but, by concentrating on the antiquarian and biographical aspects, failed to convey the literary merits of medieval texts. The prison of oblivion in which medieval literature was, according to Fauchet, incarcerated, was not, in fact, unlocked by those who had the key."

Origines des Dignitez et Magistrats de France he pays homage to those who
"... sous des sujets fabuleux ne laissent d'avoir representé plusieurs
façons & manières de vivre de leur siècle ...",[95] those whose works will
frequently serve to document this study. While Fauchet's account of
the functions of the "sénéchal" will be supported by evidence from
Raoul de Cambrai, the *Roman de la Charrette* and *Guillaume de Dôle*, his explanation of the office of "chambrier" by reference to, amongst other
things, *Doon de Nanteuil*, *Le Tournoiement d'Antichrist* and *Aubry le Bourgoing*, quotations from the *Roman des sept Sages*, *Ciperis de Vignevaux*, *Judas
Machabée* and the *Roman de Troie* will help clarify the meaning of the
term "connétable."[96] Similarly with the *Origines des Chevaliers*, *Armoiries et Héraux* where once again this "vray & fidelle Historiographe"
frequently draws for documentary evidence upon medieval literary
texts, the *Roman du Nouveau Renart*, the *Roman de la Chasse* and so on.[97]
As Fauchet himself explains:

... des choses mesprisees peuvent encores estre utiles & profitables avec le
temps & par occasion.[98]

Amongst the many who, as we saw earlier, were to follow in the footsteps of the great sixteenth-century scholars and, for whatever reasons,
turn their attention to the Middle Ages, were not a few who clearly
shared Fauchet's belief that non-historical, fictional texts dating from
the period could greatly facilitate their researches, at the very least
serve to corroborate their findings. Numerous such works, the *Roman des
ducs de Normandie*, the *Roman des Royaux Lignages*, the *Roman de Florimond*,
are interspersed amongst the more traditional sources which André
Duchesne consults for his genealogies of noble families, of the house of
Montmorency, for example.[99] While Jean Le Laboureur, author of the
Histoire de la Pairie de France, agrees that the old romances are not fit
reading matter for the uninstructed masses, he nevertheless insists that
"... il y a de la honte à un savant de ne les avoir pas lus, ou de les
avoir lus sans profit."[100] Establishing himself as the apologist of these
productions which, he claims, quite simply present "un portrait du

[95] Dédicace au duc de Bouillon.
[96] Cf. J. G. Espiner-Scott: *Claude Fauchet: sa vie, son oeuvre*, Paris (Droz) 1938, pp. 329–349.
Cf. also H. Jacoubet, *Le Comte de Tressan*, pp. 6–7.
[97] Cf. Espiner-Scott, *Claude Fauchet*, pp. 350–358. Cf. also C. E. Pickford, *Changing attitudes
towards medieval French literature*, p. 5.
[98] *Origines des Dignitez et Magistrats de France*, Epitre au Lecteur.
[99] *Histoire généalogique de la Maison de Montmorency*, Paris (R. Cramoisy) 1624. Cf. H.
Jacoubet, *Le Comte de Tressan*, p. 7.
[100] Cited by H. Jacoubet, *Le Comte de Tressan*, pp. 8–9.

vieux temps" and should therefore shock us no more than do those naked figures of ancient statuary, he explains why he himself felt obliged to take up their defence:

Je devais cette apologie à nos vieux romans de chevaliers errants pour le service que j'en ai tiré, pour faire valoir leur autorité en matière de chevalerie et même pour la pairie de France dont quelques-uns nous représentent les droits et prérogatives telles qu'elles étaient du temps de leurs auteurs.[101]

There are those who would criticize him for citing the "romanciers" as authorities when at the same time he is drawing for evidence upon works composed by true historians, but these latter fail to treat the manners and customs of their time:

... il en faut chercher le portrait dans ces vieux romans qui nous en ont conservé l'idée avec des mots qui servent à découvrir l'origine des choses.[102]

It is not at all difficult to imagine what would have been the fate of the old romances had they been obliged in the sixteenth and seventeenth centuries to stand or fall by their literary merits alone. As it is, if they held little appeal as works of literature, then their popularity amongst historians at least was assured. The position is made abundantly clear in the interesting dialogue *De la Lecture des vieux Romans*,[103] where Ménage, Sarazin and the author, Jean Chapelain, discuss the *Lancelot*. Chapelain may have had his own collection of medieval romances and have enjoyed reading them, but he shows himself hardly less severe than Ménage, who appears as their most ardent detractor, when it comes to a literary appreciation:

L'auteur est barbare, qui a écrit durant la barbarie et pour des barbares seulement ... il est toujours sur une même figure et chante toujours sur un même ton; il est dur, il est raboteux, il est l'antipode des grâces ... on n'en saurait lire une seule page sans bâiller et sans avoir mal à la tête.[104]

As historian, however, and this is Chapelain's true standpoint, he finds such a piece as the *Lancelot* comparable with the writings of Livy. Certainly the romance was not intended as a book of history, presenting only fabulous events in the lives of mythical characters. But it was written in an unenlightened age when the only valid work of reference upon which the author might draw for the backdrop to these imagin-

---

[101] *Ibidem.*
[102] *Ibidem.*
[103] First published in 1728 in *Continuation des Mémoires de littérature et d'histoire de M. Salengre*, vol. VI, pp. 281–342. References are to A. C. Hunter's edition, *Opuscules Critiques* (E. Droz) 1936, pp. 205–241.
[104] P. 221.

nary events and fictitious characters was in fact "le livre du monde," when anything but the manners and customs, the everyday behaviour of the poet's own time would have been completely alien to those encountering the tale. While Livy carefully describes the "moeurs et coutumes" of an earlier time, the romance accurately mirrors those of the period in which it was composed, and the *Lancelot* is for Chapelain ". . . une représentation naïve, et, s'il faut ainsi dire, une histoire certaine et exacte des moeurs qui régnoient dans les Cours d'alors."[105]

In the dialogue Chapelain makes reference to two of his contemporaries who equally did not fail to realize but indeed exploited the historical utility of the old romances. Chantereau-Lefebvre was not afraid to admit that he had found the *Lancelot* of invaluable assistance when writing his treatise on fiefs:

I'ay autrefois leu dans le Roman de 'Lancelot du Lac,' l'interprétation du droict des Fiefs . . . et ie puis assurer que ie n'ay rien vue de si clair, et de si précis sur ce sujet, en quelque Feudiste que ce soit.[106]

When Vulson de la Colombière compiled his *Théatre d'Honneur et de Chevalerie* with the intention ". . . faire connoître à la noblesse la vertu de ses ayeuls et luy faire voir qu'ils apprenoient l'art de bien vivre dans les divertissemens de leurs tournois . . .",[107] this is in the hope, as we recall, of restoring the nobility to its past glory, he did not confine his researches to medieval chronicles. The literature contemporary with these tournaments he found to be of considerable service to him, Arthurian and other romances providing a wealth of documentation:

. . . livres desquels nous pouvons tirer la façon et la véritable manière des principales choses qui se pratiquoient de leur temps: par exemple si dans leurs livres ils vouloient descrire un festin; une entrée de ville; une bataille ou un Tournoy, ils le faisoient purement et simplement de la mesme sorte que l'on pratiquoit ces choses de leur temps.[108]

---

[105] P. 219. Sarazin compares the old romances to old paintings, tapestries and statues: ". . .comme ces reliques nous représentent les modes d'alors, on peut dire ce que dit M. Chapelain, que ces vieux romans nous peignent au naturel les moeurs et les coutumes de ces mêmes siècles." (P. 220.)

[106] *Traité des Fiefs et de leur Origine. Avec les preuves tirées de divers autheurs anciens et modernes*, Paris (L. Billaine) 1662, pp. 87–88. Cf. N. Edelman, *Attitudes of seventeenth-century France toward the Middle Ages*, pp. 321–322.

[107] Vol. I, Préface servant d'avertissement à la noblesse.

[108] *Idem*, p. 42. The documentation clearly also served the moral purpose of the composition: "La description de tous les combats, soit à la jouste, soit à l'espée, qui se firent dans cet admirable Tournoy, est charmante, & je ne trouve point de Lecture plus divertissante, ny qui allume avec plus d'ardeur le courage aux jeunes gens, & qui leur donne plus d'envie d'acquérir de l'honneur, & se pousser avec affection aux pénibles & dangereuses entreprises." (*Idem*, p. 292.)

Clearly the idea that the scholar might justifiably exploit the historical potential of medieval fictional pieces while at the same time, given that he ever considered them as such, disdaining these as works of literature, this idea had been widely acknowledged well before La Curne de Sainte-Palaye came to publish *Aucassin et Nicolette* or the Marquis de Paulmy to inaugurate the *Bibliothèque des Romans*:

> La plus grande part des Antiquailles se tire des Anciens Romans tant en Prose, qu'en Vers, comme les Perles des fumiers d'Ennuis.[109]

"Tout le monde," wrote Sainte-Palaye, "sent assez que chaque siècle se peint dans les ouvrages d'esprit et d'imagination qu'il a produits ou qu'il a fait revivre." Few can be said to have done more to encourage exploitation of this knowledge than he himself. When this same scholar had emphasized the need for a "bibliothèque générale & complète de tous nos anciens Romans de Chevalerie," stating clearly the kind of information to be gleaned from these latter, he had in fact been calling for a serious methodical study of the literary sources of medieval history:

> ... Qu'il me soit permis de souhaiter que quelques gens de Lettres se partagent entre eux le pénible travail de lire ces sortes d'ouvrages, dont le temps détruit tous les jours quelques morceaux, d'en faire des extraits, qu'ils rapporteront à un systême général & uniforme; afin que cessant de prendre des routes différentes, on ne soit point obligé de recommencer souvent les mêmes lectures.[110]

We know already something of the immense and careful labours which Sainte-Palaye devoted to the study of the chronicle and documentary sources of medieval history. If anything he proved even more industrious, more painstaking in his work on fictional material, and in his efforts to unearth and catalogue all those manuscripts of some relevance for scholars interested in the period of the Middle Ages, from which were later to evolve the *Notices et Extraits*, in these efforts we find literary sources now approached with the same method, the same care and attention hitherto reserved only for the study of traditional historical documentation:

> Sainte-Palaye's notices are full, detailed, well-ordered, and models of their kind ... First, he gives a complete physical description of the codex, then, with the aid of palaeography, language, information available in the text and references to it in other texts, the manuscript is dated, miniatures and

---

[109] André Favyn: *Le Théatre d'Honneur et de Chevalerie* (Paris, 1620, 2 vols.) vol. I, p. 91.
[110] "Mémoire concernant la lecture des anciens Romans de Chevalerie," p. 798.

vignettes are described with care, and an attempt is made to identify the original owner and subsequent history of the manuscript. The contents are described with the help of generous quotations which marginal notes suggest Sainte-Palaye hoped to extend still further. Finally the manuscript is compared with others of the same work where these exist.[111]

The systematic study of the old romances which Sainte-Palaye advocated was meant by him to be a work marked by similar attention to detail – an ordered series of extracts, taken from the manuscript versions as much as from the printed editions, wherein the emphasis would be upon details relevant to the history and antiquities of the nation, to genealogy and geography, to the progress made in the arts and sciences, and yet where, although the literary merits of any text be of only slight interest, exact information on both composition and author would be furnished. "Le moyen de donner une sorte de valeur et d'attirer quelque considération à nos anciens poètes," wrote Caylus, "c'est de recueillir tous les faits historiques que leurs ouvrages renferment ...".[112] Sainte-Palaye would do much to obtain true scholarly respect for the poets of the Middle Ages.

Such respect marks the attitude adopted by the Marquis de Paulmy and is precisely that which distinguishes him from Tressan, his collaborator on the *Bibliothèque des Romans*, that periodical which, in its early days at least, can be said to have brought Sainte-Palaye's proposals for a systematic study of the old romances to some kind of fruition. In fact, the two principal collaborators would argue bitterly over the direction to be taken in the collection, Tressan making serious modifications, imprinting his own personality upon it when he eventually took charge in January 1779. Paulmy, at least in the eyes of his colleague, already in his seventies by this time, was a difficult man to please, constantly rejecting extracts submitted by Tressan until they had been remoulded to his own liking, exercising his prerogative as director to make additions where he thought fit and to suppress those excessive "gaîtés," as he put it.[113] Matters eventually came to a head in 1778 when Tressan,

[111] L. Gossman, *Medievalism*, p. 220. For the collection of notices, cf. *Mss. Paris, B.N. fonds Moreau 1654–61* (8 vols. in-folio), *1662–76* (15 vols. in-quarto, a second version).

[112] "Premier mémoire sur Guillaume de Machault," *Mém. Acad. Inscr.*, vol. XX, pp. 399–400.

[113] Cf. *Ms. Paris, Arsenal 6408*, ff. 78–80, "Pièces relatives au différénd survenu entre M. de Paulmy, le comte de Tressan et M. de Bastide, à propos de la 'Bibliothèque des romans'": "Si j'ay quelquefois ajouté quelque chose du mien, j'ay cru bien faire, et je n'ay pas imaginé que cela pût m'être reproché par l'auteur du reste de l'extrait. Si j'ay adouci, ou supprimé des gaîtés, c'est parce que je les ay cru trop fortes pour être imprimées, non comme étant de moi, car elles ne pouvoient jamais m'être imputées; mais comme étant de M. le Cte de

no longer able to tolerate this incessant interference from the Marquis, took his work on the first books of the *Amadis* to the publisher Pissot without a word to his superior. The anger of this latter, despite Jean-François de Bastide's gallant attempts to bring about a reconciliation,[114] could not be assuaged:

... mon party est pris de ne plus m'immiscer dans le travail de la 'Bibliothèque des Romans' que tout-au plus jusques au mois de Juin prochain inclusivement.[115]

By this time he would have completed four years as director of the publication and would have finished dealing with the romances of the Charlemagne cycle. By this time too Tressan's translation of the first parts of the *Amadis* would have been published by Pissot. Whether or not he then continued this work would be a matter of some indifference to Paulmy:

Pour moy, je ne me mêleray plus ni de cet article ni de rien qui concerne la 'Bibliothèque des Romans.' Je n'y fourniray plus ni livres, ni secours, ni extraits, et j'auray grand soin d'avertir que je n'y prens plus aucune part. Le propriétaire du Privilège continuera si bon luy semble avec tels coopérateurs que bon luy semblera.[116]

When we recall what we know already of the Tressan "manner" as it was later to evolve, then it becomes clear that the two men, at opposite poles as it were, could not possibly have continued working together. Using wherever possible the manuscripts or the earliest printed models, the Marquis was concerned to publish accurate extracts in ordered sequence. More important in this context, he intended to ensure that his readers were made properly aware of what he himself considered perhaps the most interesting and attractive quality of his favourite genre:

Il offre une chaîne de livres qui forment presque une histoire complète de plusieurs siècles. Elle ne sera pas interrompue dans la Bibliothèque que nous allons offrir au public.

Tressan. Ma délicatesse ne pouvoit regarder que luy, puisque les extraits paroissoient sous son nom." (Fol. 79 rovo.)

Henry Martin gives an account of this dispute in his *Histoire de la Bibliothèque de l'Arsenal*, pp. 37–41.

[114] The Marquis de Paulmy did not appear openly in the collection. M. de Bastide lent his name to the *Bibliothèque des Romans* and held the "privilège."

[115] *Ms. Paris, Arsenal 6408*, ff. 79vo–80ro.

[116] *Ibidem.* The Marquis in fact ceased to collaborate upon the collection as early as December 1778, closing his library to those who might wish to continue publication. Cf. H. Martin, *Histoire de la Bibliothèque de l'Arsenal*, p. 41.

In theory at least the collection would not fall too far short of the recommendations made by the demanding La Curne de Sainte-Palaye, his proposals closely matched in the title of the new *Bibliothèque universelle des Romans, ouvrage périodique dans lequel on donne l'analyse raisonnée des romans anciens et modernes, français ou traduits dans notre langue, avec des anecdotes et des notices historiques et critiques concernant les auteurs ou leurs ouvrages, ainsi que les moeurs, les usages du temps, les circonstances particulières et relatives et les personnages connus, déguisés ou emblématiques*. The historical potential of the old romances was to be approached with at least something of the method and attention to detail called for in the "Mémoires concernant la lecture des anciens Romans de Chevalerie," that genuine scholarly respect later altogether absent from the works of the unselfconscious although highly successful "adaptateur" Tressan. In fact, we might note that those extracts appearing in the earlier volumes of the *Bibliothèque des Romans* did not go entirely unapplauded, the *Mercure*, in a survey of the results obtained during the first year of publication,[117] praising them highly and going to some lengths to underline the great interest and value of the historical insights which they afforded, the romances a true mirror of the period in which they were composed:

Nous avons en ce genre, une richesse nationale qui est telle qu'aucun autre peuple n'en possède et peut-être n'en soupçonne une semblable.[118]

If we have said that Sainte-Palaye did much to encourage consideration of the literary texts of the Middle Ages as valid historical sources, then it is evident from his own scholarly undertakings on the medieval period that he was one to practise what he preached. Few in his time can have made greater use of the historical relevance of Old French literature. When discussing the extent of Le Grand d'Aussy's familiarity with his literary heritage, we mentioned in particular the invaluable experience he must surely have gained while engaged upon Sainte-Palaye's *Glossaire de l'ancienne langue françoise*, a project involving, in addition of course to the study of earlier dictionaries and glossaries, the meticulous examination not only of medieval chronicles, legal and historical documents, but equally of the fictional productions of the period, the romances, more important for Le Grand, the fabliaux.[119]

[117] June 1776, pp. 108–136.
[118] Cf. H. Jacoubet, *Le Comte de Tressan*, p. 189.
[119] It is important to note in passing that the *Glossaire*, intended as an instrument of historical research we remember, was to prove more than a simple dictionary of Old French, finally comprising numerous short historical essays which Sainte-Palaye considered highly relevant in such an undertaking and whose eventual value to those consulting the glossary did not escape the *Journal Encyclopédique*: "Souvent il nous fera voir dans un mot l'origine

These latter featured again amongst the equally varied sources of the proposed *Dictionnaire des antiquités françoises*, an encyclopedic survey of French society over a period of four centuries, comprising articles upon almost every conceivable aspect of this, the arts and sciences, commerce, education, government and administration, furniture and clothing, this information drawn without distinction from historical and non-historical texts alike:

Completely disparate works like the histories of Jean de Venette or of Glaber, the Provençal poets, Eustache Deschamps, the two 'Gérard de Roussillon,' the Chevalier de la Tour's 'Instructions à ses filles,' the 'Arbre des batailles,' the medieval versions of Ovid's 'Ars amandi,' and Bouteiller's 'Somme rurale' were conceived as complementary sources, cutting across distinctions of genre. Once a source had been dated, and its reliability and documentary possibilities determined, there was no reason – in Sainte-Palaye's view – why it should be handled in isolation from other sources of a different type.[120]

The essence of La Curne's approach is seized by Edmond Estève in his analysis of the *Mémoires sur l'ancienne chevalerie*, considered in its own time as now a most excellent history of the institution,[121] a work where once again poets and chroniclers of the Middle Ages are called without distinction to give testimony:

Suivant une méthode qui a été après lui reprise plus d'une fois, il donne la littérature en apparence la plus légère pour base à l'érudition la plus solide, et il fait de la poésie l'auxiliaire de la science.[122]

One need only glance at the annotations with which Sainte-Palaye filled the margins of his manuscript copies to see precisely what the efforts of the "anciens rimeurs" represented for him, what he sought in

d'un usage ou d'une loi: un autre terme amènera la description d'une fête, et l'art qu'il aura de réduire toutes ses connaissances à un but doit faire qu'on apprenne l'histoire d'une nation en croyant n'étudier que sa langue." (August 1758, p. 123.)

[120] L. Gossman, p. 269. Two manuscript versions of the *Dictionnaire des antiquités françoises* are preserved in Paris, the first, *B.N. fonds Moreau 1511–23*, of 13 volumes in-folio, and the second, *Arsenal 4277–4353*, of 77 volumes in-quarto. The Arsenal catalogue of manuscripts lists at least two supplements to the *Dictionnaire*, a further 23 volumes of material.

[121] Cf. Madeleine Jouglard's appraisal as cited above, p. 78; also *Mercure*, December 1746, pp. 89–103, February 1749, pp. 3–16.

[122] "Le Moyen âge dans la littérature du XVIIIe siècle," p. 368. It is interesting to compare the opinion expressed by Geoffroy writing in the *Journal de Monsieur* in 1781: "Les mémoires de M. de Sainte-Palaye sur la chevalerie et les divers morceaux qu'on y a joints réunissent à l'utilité de l'histoire les agrémens du roman; l'auteur instruit et amuse à la fois; il nous fait bien connaître l'esprit, le caractère et les moeurs de nos ancêtres; il est vrai qu'il s'appuie souvent sur le témoignage des romanciers; mais pour ce qui regarde les usages du temps, les romanciers ont presque la même autorité que les historiens." (Vol. IV, p. 3.)

them. In their importance to Le Grand d'Aussy's collection the copies of the fabliaux manuscripts have yet to be dealt with in some detail, of course. But since this genre has already been mentioned in relation to Sainte-Palaye's historical researches, let us simply note that in these copies his attention is reserved almost exclusively for points of language and for "ce qui paroîtroit de quelque usage pour l'Histoire, pour les Généalogies, pour les Antiquités françoises et pour la Géographie." He may indicate variants to be found in other manuscripts, his own copies of these and printed editions, often giving the readings where these differ significantly. But it is evident from his exhaustive coverage of those items of linguistic and historical interest, the manner indeed in which these latter are signalized, that he is preoccupied with the search for the kind of material relevant to such projects as the *Glossaire* or the *Dictionnaire des antiquités*. Annotating a copy of *Li Jugement d'amors* taken from *ms. 7615* of the then Bibliothèque du Roi,[123] Sainte-Palaye suddenly realizes that he possesses another copy of the same tale after a different manuscript, a copy already bearing all relevant notes and indications:

Je ne continuerai pas d'extraire cette piece: je m'apercoi que c'est la même dont j'ai une autre copie faite sur le ms. des Fabliaux de la Biblioth. de S. Germain des Prez No 1830 au fol. 41 où elle est intitulée 'de Florance et de Blanchefleur' et dont j'ai fait les Extraits de Mots, antiq., Géogr. &c.[124]

On those very rare occasions when he does give his attention to the literary value of a particular fabliau, Sainte-Palaye invariably confines himself to such brief remarks as "pièce à remarquer pour la versification," or the quite non-committal "jolie pièce," remarks which go almost unnoticed in the mass of other annotations more relevant to the researcher's purposes.

It may be interesting to note finally that the overriding historical bias of La Curne's interest in medieval literature in fact explains in part the very failure of one of his own major projects, the *Histoire littéraire des Troubadours*, which Le Grand d'Aussy was actually to cite in evidence in his case against the "provençalistes" during the protracted "querelle des trouvères et des troubadours":

Leur histoire existe; ouvrez-la, qu'y trouverez-vous? Des Sirventes, des Tensons, d'éternelles & ennuyeuses Chansons d'amour, sans couleur, sans images, sans aucun intérêt; en un mot, une assoupissante monotonie, à laquelle tout l'art de l'Editeur & l'élégance de son style n'ont pu remédier.[125]

[123] Present *B.N. f. fr. 1593.*
[124] *Ms. Paris, Arsenal 2768*, fol. 198 vo.
[125] *Fabliaux ou Contes*, vol. I, preface, p. xlviii.

Were the Provençal writers really devoid of all poetic talent? Or was it rather that their historian did not quite do them justice? Though it was Sainte-Palaye himself who, in response to Falconet's plea for just such a history,[126] undertook the groundwork for the project, twice visiting Italy in the search for manuscripts of Provençal poetry, copying and translating these before finally, with Foncemagne's help, compiling from them the extracts which would form the basis of the composition, the task of preparing these same extracts for publication was in fact to fall to the Abbé Millot.[127]

To judge from certain remarks made in the "Discours préliminaire," this already celebrated historian seemed to consider his purpose in the three-volume collection to draw attention to and obtain proper respect for the troubadours, then almost lost to memory and at best viewed "comme des aventuriers sans état; comme des écrivains sans lumière et sans goût, dont les fades galanteries méritent un oubli éternel, et dont les ouvrages n'ont rien d'intéressant que pour les amateurs d'antiquités qui passent inutilement leur vie à dérouiller de misérables monumens gothiques."[128] But if it had in fact been Millot's intention properly to acquaint his readers with Provençal poetry in order to ensure a just appreciation of this latter, then he can be said largely to have failed in this intention. In any event the opinion which he himself formed of the literary merits of the troubadours, an opinion voiced again and again in the collection, was hardly one to stimulate greater interest in their works:

... je l'avoue, les fades lieux communs de galanterie, les répétitions fréquentes des mêmes pensées & des mêmes expressions, les longueurs & le mauvais goût rendroient insupportable un recueil complet de leurs ouvrages. Il a fallu supprimer, élaguer beaucoup, & ces sacrifices ne méritent aucun regret.[129]

What the Abbé did do was to stress repeatedly the immense value of the historical insights which these same productions afford. Poets and

---

[126] In the paper he had read before the Académie des Inscriptions in 1727. See above, p. 75.

[127] Sainte-Palaye had failed to obtain satisfaction from numerous other editors before he finally handed his extracts to Millot, who was compelled to rely entirely upon these, being unacquainted with Provençal. All credit for the composition was given to the original researcher: "Le mérite de cet ouvrage appartient spécialement à M. de Sainte-Palaie. Je n'ai fait que mettre en oeuvre avec plaisir les matériaux qu'il a rassemblez avec tont de peines..." (Vol. 1, Avertissement, p. x). L. Gossman deals at some length and in most interesting detail with the *Histoire littéraire des Troubadours* in chapter 10 of part III of his book. His fourth appendix presents the amazing list of Sainte-Palaye's copies of Provençal "chansonniers."

[128] Vol. I, p. xiii.

[129] Discours préliminaire, vol. I, p. liv.

not chroniclers, he says, were quite naturally "les peintres de la socié-té," taking simply as the backdrop to their works what they them-selves saw and heard, the customs and fashions, the ideas and opinions of their own time, the resultant tableaux never more reliable than when the brushwork is that of the troubadours. Typical of Millot's ap-proach are the remarks he makes upon the merits of the "tensons":

Ces jeux d'esprit devoient donner plus de ressort aux talens; mais comme les talens médiocres ne peuvent franchir les bornes de la médiocrité, parmi un très-grand nombre de tensons il y'en a peu d'un rare mérite ... Elles ont néanmoins l'avantage, celles mêmes dont la traduction paroîtroit la plus in-sipide, de nous instruire sur les opinions & les sentimens de leurs auteurs, & sur l'esprit de leur siècle.[130]

The lasting impression is that Provençal poetry is by far more useful to know than pleasant to read, precisely the opinion which the *Mercure* formed of the *Histoire littéraire des Troubadours* itself.[131]

If critics were disappointed by this lack of any real literary apprecia-tion of the troubadours, then it was simply that Millot, unacquainted with Provençal and thus relying entirely upon the material provided by the original researcher, had given the collection the same emphasis he himself must surely have noted in this material. Sainte-Palaye can-not be said to have been particularly interested in, let alone inspired by the artistic abilities of the Provençal poets and he approached their writings entirely in accordance with what we have observed to be his predominantly historical interest in medieval literature generally:

... he had carefully annotated his copies with historical observations, he had begun a *Dictionnaire des antiquités des troubadours* from the information he found in the poems, and he had composed an historical introduction, a 'Ta-bleau historique des siècles où régna la poésie provençale,' in which he tried to outline the political and intellectual background of Provençal poetry ... Millot, finally, despite his promises, discerned no more than this in the volu-minous extracts and notes Sainte-Palaye put at his disposal, no more than a mass of data on the political and social history of the Middle Ages ....[132]

Thus it was that Le Grand d'Aussy could effectively employ the col-lection to his own ends, ends which would seem to make a mockery of the *Histoire littéraire des Troubadours*. But Le Grand himself, we know, was to engage upon just such a project. Was there no possibility of a

[130] *Idem*, p. lxvi.
[131] July 1774, pp. 125–132.
[132] L. Gossman, *Medievalism*, p. 318.

danger similar to that which thwarted Sainte-Palaye presenting itself here?

Knowing Le Grand d'Aussy to have worked under the close supervision of the Marquis de Paulmy on the *Bibliothèque des Romans*[133] and the *Mélanges tirés d'une grande Bibliothèque* and of La Curne de Sainte-Palaye on the proposed *Glossaire de l'ancienne langue françoise*, we naturally expect to rediscover something at least of these two most distinguished scholars in him. In fact, the particular attitude which Le Grand adopted towards the Middle Ages and its literature, his personal understanding of and approach to medieval studies were clearly very much determined by his former employers, particularly striking being the resemblance which the author of the *Fabliaux ou Contes* bears, understandably enough, to his "premier maître," his friend and benefactor, to Sainte-Palaye.[134]

If Le Grand devoted a lifetime of industry to the study of the medieval period, then, like his former master, he rarely allowed his enthusiasm as a scholar to blind him to even the most harsh of realities. He too realized and willingly acknowledged that this was a time of superstition and ignorance.[135] More important, he was hardly less severe than his illustrious predecessor in his appreciation of the literature produced under such conditions:

Malheureusement ces temps . . . n'étoient pas ceux des lumières. Cette caste guerrière, qui donnoit à la France des chevaliers sans peur et sans reproche, ne savoit être que guerrière encore, et elle s'en glorifioit. Ses livres, si par hasard elle lisoit ou se faisoit lire, ses livres étoient les ouvrages futiles du temps; des vers, des chansons, des contes, et surtout ces romans de chevalerie qui, par les incroyables prouesses qu'ils contenoient, la tenoient sans cesse en exaltation."[136]

He did, as we shall later attempt to establish, display a certain sympathy, even a definite liking, for one or two of the medieval genres, but for the most part he can be said to have concurred with his highly critical contemporaries. For Le Grand too the greater part of medieval fiction had been justly overshadowed by the efforts of later authors,

---

[133] Extracts composed by Le Grand for the *Bibliothèque des Romans* can be found, for example, in *Ms. Arsenal 6608*, ff. 1–22.

[134] Cf. *ms. Paris, Arsenal 6588*, fol. 84 ro.

[135] *Fabliaux ou Contes*, vol. IV, Discours préliminaire to the "Contes dévots" p. xxxv: "Mon intention. . . n'est pas, à beaucoup près, d'entreprendre l'apologie des siècles d'ignorance. Je ne crois pas mériter assez de mépris pour être soupçonné d'une démense pareille."

[136] Quotation taken from the "notice" announcing the *Voyage d'outre-mer* which lack of time prevented Le Grand from reading at the Institut national but which was reproduced in the *Magasin Encyclopédique*, 6e Année (1800) vol. III, pp. 482–489.

particularly those romances, a genre ". . . qu'heureusement pour nous, de meilleurs Ouvrages ont anéanti."[137] But if this was indeed the case, then why this immense industry and unfailing enthusiasm? Why the *Fabliaux ou Contes*? One answer to our question, but not the only answer, as we shall see, is obvious from what has already been said of the purpose of this collection and more especially of Sainte-Palaye. Like Sainte-Palaye's, Le Grand's interest in the Middle Ages and medieval literature is very much, though not exclusively as is perhaps the case with his teacher, that of the historian.

The nature of Le Grand's interest in the national past is perhaps most accurately indicated by the *Voyage d'Auvergne*, which work would seem to comply with the recommendations made by the "new historians" of the eighteenth century, those who called, not for biographies of kings and noblemen, but for the study of man, his manners and customs, his laws and institutions, those who ". . . sought the causes of historical change in the ambitions of men and in the force of institutions, of geography, of climate, of technical and economic conditions."[138] In 1784 the *Mercure*, praising Papon's *Histoire générale de Provence*,[139] defines what it now considers the "good historian" as one who speaks little of courts and princes but much, for example, of peoples, of climate, soil and plants, of customs and laws, commerce and cartography.[140] These, as we know, were precisely Le Grand's concern in the *Voyage d'Auvergne*, a work treating ". . . ce qui regarde la nature du sol, les révolutions qu'il a éprouvées, ses productions, climat, météores, produits de volcanisation, mines, carrières, lacs, eaux minérales, moeurs des habitans, constitution physique, population, arts, commerce, manufactures, industrie, etc., etc.".[141]

Strictly speaking, of course, this latter was not a book of history. The *Histoire de la Vie Privée des Français* was intended as such. But here again Le Grand made it clear that this was a different kind of history, one not dealing exclusively with major events and therefore admitting only of Kings and Ministers of State or great generals, but taking as its principals "le Bourgeois dans sa ville, le Paysan dans sa chaumière, le Gentil-homme dans son château, le Français enfin au milieu de ses

---

[137] *Fabliaux ou Contes*, vol. I, preface, p. xxxvii.
[138] Cf. L. Gossman, *Medievalism*, pp. 107–112.
[139] Paris, (Moutard) 1776–1786, 4 vols.
[140] *Mercure*, December 2nd, 1784.
[141] Sub-title to the second edition. It might be remembered that Le Grand also helped to complete Levaillant's *Second voyage dans l'intérieur de l'Afrique*, a very similar kind of enterprise.

travaux & de ses enfans.''[142] An ardent patriot, Le Grand was genuinely dismayed to think that his compatriots should deem the intimate, everyday life of the Romans worthy of such a study while altogether neglecting that of their own ancestors. Surely here was a subject far more worthy of the French scholar's attention and one clearly of much greater appeal than those more traditional histories of France:

Ce tableau ... est celui de nos Pères; c'est pour nous en quelque sorte une galerie de portraits de famille; & cette collection, si je ne me trompe, doit nous intéresser plus que l'autre encore.[143]

Much has already been said of the *Histoire de la Vie Privée des Français* and of the eventual disappointment it brought both the author and those who had impatiently awaited its appearance.[144] The idea for this historical survey of French manners and customs through the ages came originally, as we know, from Paulmy, who clearly set great store by the project to judge from the vicious quarrel which ensued from Le Grand's failure to give the Marquis what he considered proper recognition for his part in the work. In fact, the enterprise seemed destined to fail from the very outset, Contant d'Orville, the original compiler, producing most unsatisfactory results during the eighteen months he spent engaged upon it. Le Grand never completed the collection and even J. B. B. de Roquefort, who re-edited the first three volumes in the early nineteenth century, could not keep his promise to do so. Yet if the project did prove something of a disaster, then this had nothing whatever to do with Le Grand's enthusiasm or ability as historical researcher, and this is what particularly interests us here.

The scale of the researches called for by the plan which Paulmy had drawn up was immense, Le Grand devoting ten or more hours a day over a period of between twelve and fifteen months to the meticulous search for relevant information. At the end of this time he found himself in possession of well over a thousand "bulletins," individual short notices, the longest comprising no more than three or four lines, covering an enormous variety of topics from "abbayes" to "tournois," from

---

[142] Vol. I, Avertissement préliminaire, p. v. We should recall here Le Grand's observations on that rare but most admirable of societies in the *Lettre sur la communauté des Guittard-Pinon.*

[143] *Histoire de la Vie Privée des Français,* vol. I, Avertissement préliminaire, pp. v–vi. Le Grand thought little of Montfaucon's *Monuments de la Monarchie Française:* "On sait qu'il n'y a que ce qui concerne les Rois, les Princes de leur sang, les grands officiers de la couronne et ceux de leur maison. Il semble que la nation y soit comptée pour rien." (*Ms. Paris, B.N. n.a.f. 6228,* fol. 75.)

[144] See above, pp. 23–25.

"architecture" to "repas."[145] Under the letter "P," for example, we find notices concerning, amongst many other things, "papyrus,""pèlerinages," "perruques," "pillards," "poésie," "politique," "pourpoint," "prédicateurs" and "privilèges." In all, the collection of "bulletins" can be said to represent an encyclopaedic work of reference on things medieval, and there is an obvious comparison to be drawn with Sainte-Palaye's *Dictionnaire des antiquités françoises.* Although this latter was never published, Le Grand, disciple, friend and admirer of its author, would most certainly have had access to the manuscript even if this had not eventually been sold to the Bibliothèque du Roi. We cannot be certain that he actually made use of its contents, but clearly it had some considerable influence upon the manner in which he approached the researches basic to the *Histoire de la Vie Privée des Français.*[146]

Since Le Grand was to complete only the first part of this collection, then would the greater part of his researches be left unexploited? Of course, we know already that the *Histoire de la Vie Privée des Français* was not in fact the only significant historical enterprise upon which this enthusiastic scholar was to engage. The many hundreds of "bulletins" would, it seems, provide an excellent, a most solid foundation for the ambitious *Histoires des Usages, des Arts et des Sciences en France,* born out of the proposals for a history of French poetry from its origins to modern times. It will be remembered that the latter project had soon developed in Le Grand's mind to become a history of French literature "dans toute son étendue et avec toutes ses parties," to be complemented by a history of the language and by a number of illustrations showing costumes, architecture, musical instruments, armaments and so forth, these illustrations eventually forming only part of the plan for a comprehensive history of manners and customs, arts and sciences,[147] again a new kind of history:

Je me suis donc résolu à en séparer tout ce qui tient aux arts, aux sciences et aux usages, et d'en faire un traité à part, qui joint aux deux autres, mais distinct et séparé, en deviendra le complément. Il formera une histoire de France, d'un nouveau genre, et totalement différente de celles que nous

---

[145] Cf. *Histoire de la Vie Privée des Français,* vol. I, Avertissement préliminaire, pp. viii–ix. The collection of "bulletins," catalogued alphabetically, is contained in *mss. Paris, B.N. n.a.f. 10855* (A – D, 387 folios), *10856* (E – N, 423 folios), *10857* (O – V, 375 folios).

[146] It would be interesting to compare Le Grand's "bulletins" with corresponding articles in the manuscript *Dictionnaire.*

[147] See above, pp. 44-47.

avons; et nous fera connaître nos ayeux sous des rapports jusqu'à présent inconnus.[148]

It is clear from Le Grand's manuscript papers[149] that this was to be a work on similar lines to the *Histoire de la Vie Privée des Français* and yet of far greater scope and much wider appeal, a work perhaps more in keeping with what Falconet had had in mind when calling for this kind of study.[150]

Unfortunately the enormous three-part history, as it will be remembered, was never to appear in its entirety, the author realizing and freely acknowledging that he had once again been not a little over-ambitious.[151] Le Grand did, however, find an outlet for at least some of the material collected for the project in the *Notices et Extraits* and in the "mémoires" which he read before the Institut national as a member of its second class, "Sciences morales et politiques."[152] These latter, including such titles as "Mémoires sur les voyageurs français antérieurs au quinzième siècle," "Histoire de l'établissement du droit coutumier en France," "Mémoire sur l'établissement des dixmes en faveur du clergé," are the work of an accomplished historian with a profound interest in all aspects of the national past. In a study of early legislation in France Le Grand sets out to compare Salic law with that of the Bourguignons and that of the Visigoths, tracing the history of each,

[148] *Ms. Paris, B.N. n.a.f. 6228,* "Notice sommaire sur les trois ouvrages auxquels je travaille," ff. 70–80.

[149] In particular the "Notice sommaire sur les trois ouvrages auxquels je travaille" and the "Essai sur la langue, les sciences et la littérature françaises."

[150] It is interesting to note in passing that just as Sainte-Palaye had composed a "Tableau historiques des siècles où régna la poésie provençale" as an introduction to the *Histoire littéraire des troubadours,* so Le Grand considered it essential, despite his proposals for a comprehensive history of usages, arts and sciences, that his *Histoire de la littérature française* be prefaced with a similar historical exposé: "La plupart des ouvrages que j'aurai à faire connaître offrent des idées si étrangères, ils montrent tant d'ignorance et de superstition, que pour empêcher mes lecteurs d'en être sans cesse étonnés, je crois devoir tracer, dans un avant-propos, un tableau abrégé de l'état où en étaient les lumières en France, quand sa langue commença d'avoir des écrivains." (*Ms. Paris, B.N. n.a.f. 6228,* ff. 77–78.)

[151] See above, pp. 50–51. Le Grand had promised his readers that the remaining sections of the *Histoire de la Vie Privée des Français* would not compare in volume with the first. (Vol. I, Avertissement préliminaire, p. xii.)

[152] Cf. *Bibliographie des travaux historiques et archéologiques publiés par les sociétés savantes de la France,* vol. III, 1re livraison (Paris, Imprimerie nationale, 1896) p. 184: "L'acte constitutionnel du 5 fructidor au III (22 août 1795) décida la création d'un 'Institut national des sciences et des arts.' L'Institut fut organisé par la loi du 3 brumaire an IV (25 octobre 1795), qui jeta les bases de l'enseignement public en France. Il fut divisé en trois classes ainsi réparties: 1re classe, 'Sciences physiques et mathématiques'; 2e classe, 'Sciences morales et politiques'; 3e classe, 'Littérature et beaux-arts.'"
Many years earlier La Curne de Sainte-Palaye had proposed the division of the Académie des Inscriptions into various classes. (Cf. L. Gossman, *Medievalism,* p. 168.) He had similarly presented material collected for the uncompleted *Dictionnaire des antiquités* to this Academy in the form of "mémoires." (*Idem,* p. 273.)

analysing them and examining their relative merits and shortcomings. An interesting "Mémoire sur les anciennes sépultures" not only contains a rich fund of information on ancient burial rites, the construction and decoration of tombs through the ages, but includes a plea for properly organized archeological excavations both in the capital, and particularly in Saint-Germain des Prés, and in the provinces, together with detailed instructions as to how these should be carried out.[153] The "mémoire" concludes with a recommendation that the Musée des Monuments français be furnished with a properly representative collection so as to be worthy of the name, that it contain tombs and sarcophagi of the many varied kinds, menhirs, even barrows, and all these carefully exhibited to their greatest advantage:

> Puissent se réaliser bientôt les vues diverses que je viens de hasarder en faveur de cet établissement! C'est alors vraiment qu'il aura le droit de se dire le Musée des monumens français, puisqu'alors seulement sa collection sera complète et qu'à remonter aux temps les plus reculés, aucune espèce ne lui manquera. Quel autre en Europe présentera un spectacle aussi singulier, aussi piquant et aussi nouveau? et quel est le Français ou l'étranger qui, voyant réuni là ce que nulle part encore on n'a même projeté de recueillir, ne s'empressera de le connoître, et n'accourra y étudier cette partie de notre histoire primitive, qui d'ailleurs est l'histoire commune de toute l'Europe?[154]

We might pause for one moment to note that Le Grand's historical enterprises did bring him a certain amount of recognition at least. J. B. B. de Roquefort was not alone in realizing the value of such a work as the *Histoire de la Vie Privée des Français* which would inspire a sequel, the *Vie publique et privée des François*, many years after the original author's death. The history of fruit-growing extracted from this study of French manners and customs through the ages and published in Frankfurt in 1800 appears to have been the only source of information on this subject then available to the German people:

> ... inzwischen bleibt doch das Büchlein als Hülfsmittel zu einer künftigen vollständigern Geschichte des Obstbaues, und bis dahin, als das Einzige, was wir über diesen Gegenstand besitzen, sehr schätzbar.[155]

In 1824 de Roquefort republished the treatise on France's ancient sepultures, claiming it to be amongst the most complete and most en-

---

[153] Excavations were undertaken in Saint Germain des Prés according to Le Grand's request, but the find proved a little disappointing since the tomb in question had been rifled. Cf. *ms. Paris, Arsenal 6588*, note to fol. 61 ro.

[154] *Mémoire sur les anciennes sépultures nationales*, Paris (Baudouin) an VII, p. 272.

[155] *Verscuh einer Geschichte des Obstbaues*, Vorrede des Ubersetzers.

lightening of its kind.[156] The *Magasin Encyclopédique* had much to say in praise of the "mémoires" which Le Grand presented before the Institut national, and deeply regretted that death should have prevented him from completing his major historical undertaking:

Ce sont de savans résultats de l'étude qu'il avoit faite pendant quarante années, du langage, des moeurs, de la littérature et des arts de nos ancêtres: ce sont de précieux échantillons, capables de faire regretter le grand ouvrage dont il s'occupoit, et que la mort, encore trop prompte, quand elle l'auroit frappé beaucoup plus tard, ne lui a pas permis de terminer.[157]

In fact, this regret was obviously shared by others and, as we know, there was at least one suggestion that it might be possible to publish this work in part, a clear indication of the respect Le Grand had earned himself as historical researcher:

Faut-il conserver l'espoir de faire la publication totale de cet ouvrage? ou doit-on y renoncer? Ne pourrait-on pas, au moins, essayer un prospectus ou spécimen, de une ou deux feuilles? avec une Notice biographique?[158]

To return to what is the real purpose of our discussion, it is important to remember the value which Le Grand as a student of the Middle Ages attached to the manuscripts of the period. A former pupil of Sainte-Palaue, he was perhaps more keenly aware of their historical utility than were many of his contemporaries, more capable of exploiting this and therefore more eager to do so. Like his old master, he saw important sources where others might not have thought or cared to look. The "Notice sur l'état de la marine en France au commencement du XIVe siècle, et sur la tactique navale usitée alors dans les combats de mer" is taken from Guiart's *Branche aux royaux lignages* which contains the detailed account of an important naval battle in which the French and Flemish fleets engaged in 1304. If historians hitherto have placed insufficient emphasis upon this encounter or reported it inaccurately, remarks Le Grand, then it is because they have relied exclusively on Villani's account, unwilling to go to Guiart's commentary which, written but a few short years after the event, is superior in every re-

---

[156] *Des Sépultures nationales*, preface, p. 5: "L'un des membres les plus distingués de l'Institut, M. Legrand d'Aussy, connu par de savantes recherches sur les Gaulois et les Francs, avait composé, sous la forme d'un Mémoire, le plus complet, le plus lumineux 'Traité des Sépultures nationales.' Nous publions aujourd'hui cet ouvrage, où l'on retrouve toute l'érudition et la sage méthode de l'auteur."

[157] The remarks were made in reference to the "Mémoire sur l'établissement des dixmes en faveur du clergé" and the "Mémoire sur les pèlerinages en France," 6e an, 1801, vol. V, p. 376.

[158] *Ms. Paris, B.N. n.a.f. 10859*, fol. 31 vo.

spect.[159] And of what special relevance is this latter? The answer is that Le Grand is able to extract from it a wealth of most interesting and detailed information upon everything from the manner in which a fleet would be convoked, the types of vessel this would comprise and their relative efficiency, to the tactics employed for attack or defence and even the music peculiar to the navy at the time:

De tous les monumens que j'ai été à portée de connoître et de recueillir sur notre ancienne marine, je n'en sais aucun qui ait l'étendue de celui-ci et qui remonte aussi haut.[160]

The "Voyage d'outre-mer et retour de Jérusalem en France par la voie de terre pendant le cours des années 1432 et 1433, par Bertrandon de la Brocquière," which Le Grand extracted and translated into modern French from a manuscript in the Bibliothèque nationale, was deemed worthy of a place in the *Mémoires de l'Institut national* for very similar reasons. Here historians, geographers and antiquaries alike would find much to interest them in the details which La Brocquière gives of the route he followed, the towns and countries through which he travelled and the princes who governed these, of the ports of Syria then still in use, of the fireworks he came upon in Damascus, and of many other such objects "... d'autant plus curieux à connoitre pour nous qu'ils sont, ou à peine indiqués dans l'histoire du temps, ou totalement omis."[161]

But, of course, it is not only in his understanding of the historical utility of such pieces as those mentioned above that Le Grand proves himself a true disciple of Sainte-Palaye. Far more significant, obviously, is the respect with which he, as a serious student of all aspects of medieval life and society, treats the fictional productions, more specifically the literary manuscripts, of the period. His firm belief in the validity of these as historical sources is evidenced, for example, in his contributions to the *Notices et Extraits*, which collection, we might stress once again, can be said to have evolved from the enormous efforts

---

[159] *Notice sur l'état de la marine en France au commencement du XIVe siècle et sur la tactique navale usitée alors dans les combats de mer*, Paris (Baudouin) n.d., pp. 19–22.

[160] *Idem*, p. 2.

[161] Cf. *Magasin Encyclopédique, loc. cit.* Cf. also the "Discours préliminaire" to the "Voyage d'outre-mer," *Mémoires de l'Institut national des Sciences et Arts: Sciences morales et politiques*, vol. V, Paris (Baudouin) fructidor an XII, p. 466: "Sa relation n'est qu'un itinéraire qui souvent, et surtout dans la description du pays et des villes, présente un peu de monotonie et des formes peu variées; mais cet itinéraire est intéressant pour l'histoire et la géographie du temps. Elles y trouveront des matériaux très précieux, et quelquefois même des tableaux et des aperçus qui ne sont pas sans mérite."

which Sainte-Palaye devoted to cataloguing and preparing notices of
all manuscripts of some historical relevance. The Institut national
made perfectly clear what was to be the nature of the work submitted
for publication here in a "Programme sur la continuation de la Notice
des Manuscrits de la Bibliothèque nationale et autres bibliothèques"
distributed at an open meeting in 1798. Although the choice of manuscripts would be left free, one single but very significant recommendation was made to those who might care to participate, that they take
in preference the most interesting of manuscripts, that is those dealing
with useful sciences or containing facts and information hitherto largely
or altogether ignored:

A ce double titre, les manuscrits Arabes et Persans qui traitent de l'astro-
nomie, de la géographie, de l'histoire du moyen âge; les recueils originaux
sur l'histoire, particulièrement sur l'histoire de France, seront ceux dont les
extraits piqueront davantage la curiosité des savans.[162]

The "notices" contributed by Le Grand were in keeping with what
was after all, for a publication of the Institut national, a quite natural
bias. A quotation from the "notice" on "Le Jeu spirituel de la Paume
ou de l'Eteuf" will suffice in evidence:

Que me suis-je proposé en donnant la notice de cet insipide manuscrit? Est-
ce de jeter quelque intérêt sur une production absurde qui ne m'a procuré
à moi-même que du dégoût? Non, certes: l'homme de lettres et le savant
n'ont rien à chercher dans ces fruits de l'ignorance et de la superstition;
mais peut-être qu'en voyant ce qu'elles imaginoient 'pour expier leurs
péchés,' le philosophe y trouvera un fait de plus pour l'histoire de l'esprit
humain.[163]

These "notices," as we know, were compiled from material collected
for the histories of language, literature and the arts and sciences,[164] the
major enterprise to which Le Grand devoted all his energies after his
nomination as Keeper of Manuscripts at the Bibliothèque nationale.[165]
It is clear that for the third part of this work he intended to make no
distinction between the literary and the more traditional sources of
French history. Not just some but all the French manuscripts held in
this library were to be thoroughly scoured for information relevant to
any or all of the three sections:

---

[162] The "Programme" appears at the head of the fifth volume of the *Notices et Extraits*
Paris (Imprimerie de la République) an VII, pp. 1–4.
[163] *Idem*, p. 157.
[164] See above, p. 51.
[165] See above, p. 44.

Du reste, en ce moment, je les fais marcher toutes trois de front dans mon travail; et ce que je ne dois pas oublier de dire, c'est que l'une ne nuit en rien aux autres; parce qu'à mesure qu'un manuscrit me passe sous les yeux et que j'y trouve quelques passages qui concernent l'une des trois, je les transcris et les dépose dans celui de mes cahiers qui leur est destiné . . . .[166]

Equally, of course, he would not discriminate between the manuscripts from which were to be taken the quotations, extracts and illustrations he considered essential to a history of usages, arts and sciences through the ages:

Mes citations et mes extraits seront faits avec la plus grande exactitude d'après les auteurs du tems. Les gravures que j'y joindrai pour en faciliter l'intelligence, ne seront point des ouvrages d'imagination. Toutes auront été copiées très scrupuleusement ou calquées d'après les miniatures des mss.[167]

Le Grand certainly knew the value of the well-chosen illustration[168] and thus of the miniatures he came upon in his researches,[169] compiling alphabetical lists of "objets de gravures"[170] with detailed references to the manuscripts in which appear the miniatures featuring these objects.[171] The literary manuscripts of the Middle Ages are well represented here.

In addition to the material which he was to amass after his appointment to the Bibliothèque nationale, Le Grand, as we know, already had an excellent basis for his history of usages, arts and sciences in that collection of "bulletins" he had originally compiled for use in the *Histoire de la Vie Privée des Français*. We noted earlier that it is possible to draw a comparison between this collection and the researches undertaken by La Curne de Sainte-Palaye for his *Dictionnaire des antiquités françoises*. But there is more than a similarity of purpose here, each scholar attempting an exhaustive survey of life and society in the France of centuries past, and the comparison is rendered even more valid by the variety of sources exploited without distinction in each

---

[166] "Notice sommaire sur les trois ouvrages auxquels je travaille," fol. 72. We might remember that, just as had been the case with Sainte-Palaye, Le Grand's own comprehensive researches fell in with the need for a good catalogue of French manuscripts held in the Bibliothèque nationale. See above, p. 50. Cf. also L. Gossman, *Medievalism*, pp. 219–222.

[167] "Notice sommaire sur les trois ouvrages auxquels je travaille," fol. 74.

[168] The *Voyage d'Auvergne*, for example, was originally to contain a number of illustrations. See above, pp. 37–38.

[169] "Notice," fol. 71: "Ces manuscrits dont la lecture est si dégoutante contiennent, la plupart, une grande quantité de miniatures, qui toutes grossières qu'elles sont ordinairement, deviennent extrêmement précieuses par les objets qu'elles représentent."

[170] The third volume of the second edition of the *Voyage d'Auvergne* contains a list of those subjects Le Grand considered worthy of illustration for anyone who might care to undertake the work. See above, *loc. cit.*

[171] *Ms. Paris, B.N. n.a.f. 10859*, ff. 69ro – 128ro.

case. Like Sainte-Palaye, Le Grand draws as much upon the romances and the fabliaux for his "bulletins" as he does upon medieval works of history, the chronicles for example:

Chemises.

Après yssirent quarante demoiselles montées sur noirs pallefrois et vestues de blanches canises rozetées de vermeilles taches qui merveilleusement affiéroient sur le blanc.

Percef. vol. 2. fol. 118 R⁰ c.l.[172]

Methodically searching through the manuscripts of the Bibliothèque nationale for material relevant to the proposed *Histoire des Usages, des Arts et des Sciences en France*, Le Grand was engaged upon something very much akin to the systematic study of the fictional sources of medieval history called for in the "Mémoire concernant la lecture des anciens Romans de Chevalerie." Clearly he was just as keenly aware as the author of this paper of the historical relevance of Old French literature. "Quiconque a un peu lu, & s'est accoutumé à lire avec attention," he wrote, echoing his teacher and benefactor, in the preface to the *Fabliaux ou Contes*, "sait que non-seulement chaque peuple a son style propre & sa façon de conter, mais encore, que dans les ouvrages de pure imagination, tels que les Romans, & dans ceux même des Romans qui ne sont composés que des fictions les plus extravagantes, on voit les moeurs, le caractère, l'esprit d'une Nation peints d'une manière aussi vraie, & souvent plus saillante que dans son Histoire même."[173] More important, Le Grand was equally concerned to make the fullest possible use of this by now common knowledge and to encourage others to do so, complaining bitterly of the disdain shown by contemporary historians for the literary manuscripts of the Middle Ages. His first objection was not that this precluded all possibility of a just appreciation of the artistic abilities of the "anciens rimeurs" on their part, rather that by their total rejection of anything but the efforts of other historians they remained ignorant of the mass of interesting and vital detail which the works of the Nation's earliest poets offer upon every aspect of life and society in medieval France,

... sur les Duels, les Tournois, les Armes, les Monnaies, sur le Gouvernement, la Chronologie, la Jurisprudence du tems, l'Art de la Guerre, l'Administration de la Justice, &c. &c. &c., & sur l'Histoire même.[174]

---

[172] *Ms. Paris, B.N. n.a.f. 10855,* fol. 234 ro.
[173] Pp. lxv–lxvi.
[174] *Fabliaux ou Contes,* vol. IV, Discours préliminaire to the "Contes dévots." pp. iv–v.

Clearly these convictions went a long way towards determining the nature of Le Grand's approach to his first major enterprise which, as we have attempted to establish, was in essence an elaboration of the response he had made when first challenged to justify his regard for the "anciens rimeurs."[175] If Le Grand was to take up their defence, then obviously this defence would be based largely upon the historical utility of medieval French literature, and just as Sainte-Palaye stressed as the purpose of his *Aucassin et Nicolette* "faire connoître au vrai nos anciennes moeurs,"[176] so his disciple in the preface to the *Fabliaux ou Contes* requested his readers to pay particular attention to the picture of medieval society which they would find here, "une des clés principales de l'Ouvrage qu'on va lire."[177] This being so, what better medium for the apology than the "conte," of all the medieval genres that, in Le Grand's view, presenting the most accurate, the most interesting and the most complete picture of life in these centuries past:

En effet, un Conte n'étant ordinairement que le récit d'une action bourgoise, il est aisé de concevoir que ce récit doit contenir mille détails concernant la vie privée de nos Pères. Qu'on me cite un seul ouvrage du tems où les moeurs de tous les états soient représentées avec autant de vérité, d'agrément & d'étendue que dans les fabliaux.[178]

It is interesting to note that, when discussing or actually exploiting the historical relevance of the literary productions of the Middle Ages, many of Le Grand's predecessors, Pasquier, Fauchet, Duchesne, Chapelain, Le Laboureur, Vulson de la Colombière, appear to have turned first and foremost to the romances.[179] It was precisely these latter which Paulmy signalized as offering "presque une histoire complète de plusieurs siècles" and it will be remembered that Sainte-Palaye's proposals for a systematic study of the fictional sources of medieval history called specifically for "une bibliothèque générale et complète de tous nos anciens Romans de Chevalerie." Certainly Le Grand himself would have much to say of the utility of this genre, but was he to be the first to express this view of the fabliaux as the most valid of all the literary sources available to the historian, since neither Caylus in his "Mémoire sur les Fabliaux" nor indeed Barbazan in his *Fabliaux et Contes* had cared to give too much attention to this aspect of the tales?

---

[175] See above, pp. 7–8.
[176] *Les Amours du bon vieux temps*, Vaucluse and Paris (Duchesne) 1756, Avertissement, p. 7.
[177] P. xix.
[178] *Observations sur les Troubadours*, pp. 139–140.
[179] See above, pp. 80–84.

In fact, we know already that Sainte-Palaye, though perhaps at one time preoccupied with his researches on chivalry and therefore quite naturally with the romances, was by no means blind to the value of the medieval "conte,"[180] extracting an immense volume of information upon every aspect of medieval society from the countless folios of his copies of manuscript fabliaux. These same carefully annotated copies were quite obviously the foundation for Le Grand's own faith in the historical utility of this genre, the very inspiration for his *Fabliaux ou Contes* of which they formed the basis:

Je dois à M. de Sainte-Palaye les premiers matériaux avec lesquels j'ai commencé cet Ouvrage, & qui m'en ont même inspiré le projet.[181]

Whatever the origin of the particularly high regard which Le Grand as historian had for the fabliaux, he had clearly given the whole question of fictional sources a great deal of thought and went to some lengths in his collection to justify his position. It is important to remember the kind of historical detail which particularly fascinated Le Grand and which he considered most important. When Papon, attempting to establish the superiority of the troubadours over the "trouvères," pointed out that the works of the Southern poets contain not only a fund of interesting detail on the great events and great personages of France's history but also innumerable anecdotes concerning the Nation's oldest families,[182] the argument appeared irrelevant to the author of the *Fabliaux ou Contes*. Accounts of battles and biographies of princes and politicians did not alone compose the substance of history in his view.[183] Nor was it proper, in his opinion, for the historian to concern himself with anecdotes regarding ancient noble families, which could only be

---

[180] It is interesting to note that a translation of the "Dit des trois chevaliers et del canise" was to appear in the third volume of the *Mémoires sur l'ancienne chevalerie*, Paris (Ameilhon) 1781, pp. 138–164. "Lorsque les Mémoires de la Chevalerie parurent en 1759," runs the preamble to the final manuscript draft of the translation, "l'Auteur ne connoissoit pas encore un grand nombre de Poësies et d'autres pièces françoises conservées dans plusieurs Bibliothèques tant de France que des pays étrangers. Ayant continué depuis ses recherches, il a encore découvert des monumens précieux qui jettent un nouveau jour sur cette partie intéressante de nos antiquités françoises." (*Ms. Paris, B.N. fonds Moreau 1653*, fol. 39 ro.) In a "notice" following this translation appears the remark: "Rien n'est plus propre à faire connoître le caractère des Nations dont nous sommes issus que la lecture de nos anciens Romanciers et particulièrement de nos fabliaux." (*Idem*, fol. 50 ro.)

[181] *Fabliaux ou Contes*, vol. I, preface, p. lxxxix.

[182] In the last of the five "Lettres sur les Trouvères & les Troubadours" contained in his *Voyage littéraire de Provence*.

[183] *Fabliaux ou Contes*, vol. IV, Discours préliminaire to the "Contes dévots," p. v.: "L'Histoire en effet n'est pas seulement le récit des événemens politiques & guerriers qu'a pu éprouver successivement une Nation: c'est le tableau de ses différens âges. Or ce tableau, pour être intéressant, exige d'autres couleurs que celles des simples faits historiques."

of interest to those who might discover there the names of their ancestors. For Le Grand the historical work should be of wider, far more general appeal, containing, as was the case in the *Voyage d'Auvergne* and as he had intended it should be in both the *Histoire de la Vie Privée des Français* and the proposed *Histoire des Usages, des Arts et des Sciences en en France*,[184] details of interest to all readers:

... car tel est le grand art, l'art secret de l'Historien. Veut-il être lu? Il doit alors, si je ne me trompe, écrire, non pour sa Province, non même pour sa Nation seule, mais pour tous les peuples qui sont cultivés & qui lisent.[185]

Although the *Fabliaux ou Contes* was not a work of history in the strictest sense, nevertheless the historical detail it contained would be of interest not simply to the members of one social class or the inhabitants of one province but to all Frenchmen alike, the author drawing for his insights into medieval society upon those works which in his view afforded the most representative picture of the Nation as it then was. All literature, said Le Grand, reflects the environment in which it was composed:

Cette observation paraîtra fondée en raison, si l'on réfléchit que l'Ecrivain, au milieu de toutes les folies qu'enfante son cerveau, est obligé d'employer des hommes, & que les hommes qu'il emploie sont ceux qu'il voit autour de lui.[186]

But this being the case, it was clearly essential, he claimed, for the historian making any use of fictional sources to ensure that the details he found there were truly representative of the period which concerned him. It particularly dismayed Le Grand to see that even quite celebrated historians had often thought to discover a true impression of medieval society in the "contes dévots" or "miracles." This impression was invariably one of ignorance and superstition:

... soyons convaincus que des gens enfermés toute leur vie dans un Monastêre, mal instruits par conséquent de ce qui se passait, mal placés pour bien voir, & d'ailleurs remplis de préjugés, ne sont pas les gens qu'il faut consulter lorsqu'on vent connaître les moeurs d'un siècle.[187]

What could be ascertained from these tales was some idea of the spirit which dictated them and this in itself was of value.[188] However, it was

184 See above, p. 47.
185 *Observations sur les Troubadours*, p. 138.
186 *Fabliaux ou Contes*, vol. I, preface, p. lxvi.
187 *Fabliaux ou Contes*, vol. IV, Discours préliminaire to the "Contes dévots," pp. xxxiii–xxxiv.
188 *Idem*, pp. xlv–xlvi: "Présentés sous ce point de vue, ils ne seront plus, à nos yeux, comme ci-devant, des monumens d'ignorance, de bêtise & de mauvais goût: ce seront des

wrong, Le Grand held, to judge the whole of medieval society after them. He would not himself defend that society, but it was only proper that credit should be given where credit was due:

> ... il faudrait assez respecter nos Pères, pour ne leur faire au moins que les seuls reproches qu'ils méritent.[189]

It was not to the "contes dévots" then but rather to the romances and the fabliaux that Le Grand insisted one must look to obtain a just impression of life in these centuries past. Their authors shared all the prejudices common to the Nation at the time whilst having none of those peculiar to the clergy. More important, since they composed their works for the enjoyment of society as a whole, they quite naturally presented in them the manners and customs of that society, the only ones their public could have recognized.[190] The "fabliers" and the "romanciers" might wel be found inaccurate when it came to points of geography, of history or chronology, but the utility of their works did not reside in such details.[191] What was to be exploited was the particular relation which these works bear to the society in which they were composed, the fabliaux, whose very purpose, one might say, was to expose society to itself, the most faithful mirror of all:

> Opinions, préjugés, superstitions, coutumes, ton des conversations, manière de faire l'amour, tout se trouve là, & beaucoup de choses ne se trouvent que là. J'ose même croire que quand on les aura lus, on connaîtra mieux les Français du treizième siècle, que si on lisait toutes nos Histoires modernes.[192]

In the preface to the first volume of the *Fabliaux ou Contes* Le Grand makes it abundantly clear that his readers are to treat the notes contained in his collection with the same deference as the extracts giving rise to them. These notes are not only essential to a proper understanding of the texts but valid in their own right for the light they shed upon the manners and customs of the period in which the original pieces were composed:

---

pièces curieuses, dignes d'être recueillies, parce qu'elles offrent en raccourci ce que furent pendant long-tems chez une partie des français la Religion & la Morale; & à ce titre peut-être mériteront-ils de fixer l'attention."

[189] *Idem*, p. xxxv. In this Discours préliminaire Le Grand gives examples of the kind of misinterpretations of which historians can be and indeed have been guilty.

[190] *Idem*, p. xxxviii.

[191] Cf. *Fabliaux ou Contes*, vol. IV, p. 254, note (a): "Mais la Géographie, la Chronologie, l'Histoire sont des objets sur lesquels il ne faut pas chicaner nos vieux Rimeurs. Si quelquefois on reproche aux Poëtes modernes d'être ignorans, que sera-ce des Poëtes du XIIIe siecle?"

[192] *Idem*, vol. I, preface, p. lxviii.

Au reste, ce sera l'utilité de ces notes, qui fera mon excuse. Si elles apprennent quelque chose, elles ne sont pas trop nombreuses. On reproche tant à notre Histoire sa sécheresse & sa monotonie; on est si las de voir toujours les Rois avec quelques Grands sur la scène, & jamais la Nation, que peut-être aura-t-on quelque indulgence pour un Auteur dont les recherches n'ont pour objet que la Nation seule, & qui la fait connaître jusques dans les plus petits détails de sa vie domestique.[193]

Despite their utility, however, the notes did prove something of a problem for Le Grand. How might he incorporate them in his collection without detriment to the narratives which would scarcely be enhanced by constant interruptions of this kind? He finally realized that the only solution was to bring the notes together at the end of each tale, a method which clearly had its disadvantages and which he would later reject when composing his general history of French literature, adding instead, it will be remembered, the comprehensive *Histoire des Usages, des Arts et des Sciences en France*:

Si je n'explique les articles qu'à mesure qu'ils se présenteront, une instruction, ainsi morcelée, disséminée dans les notes qui sans cesse seront coupées par d'autres de nature différente, sera perdue et devra être regardée comme nulle.[194]

Although Le Grand himself acknowledged that the *Fabliaux ou Contes* would demand a second reading to be properly understood and appreciated,[195] it becomes evident that this was indeed the only method of approach possible here when we see that, in the first three volumes at least,[196] the notes to individual extracts may comprise as many as ten full sides and more of small print, even proving longer than the extracts themselves.[197] It may even occur that a particular note will give rise to yet another point of interest which, though of little or no relevance to the tale in question, is nevertheless deemed worthy of our attention.[198] To help the reader there is included in the third volume of

---

[193] *Idem*, p. xcvi.

[194] "Notice sommaire sur les trois ouvrages auxquels je travaille," fol. 72.

[195] Vol. I, preface, p. xcvii: "...il contient une infinité de choses, que l'on ne comprendra bien qu'à une seconde lecture; parce qu'elles tiennent à l'ensemble des moeurs du tems, & que les traits qui peignent ces moeurs, se trouvent, par la forme indispensable de l'Ouvrage, dispersés & épars."

[196] In the fourth volume, "Contes dévots, Fables et Romans anciens," the problem becomes negligible, a large number of the most important points of interest having already been discussed. Cf. vol. IV, p. 114, note (a), and p. 287, note (a): "La plupart des usages dont il sera fait mention dans ce volume, ont déjà été expliqués dans les volumes précédens, comme je l'ai remarqué plus haut."

[197] For example, cf. "Huéline et Eglantine," vol. I, p. 230.

[198] For example, cf. vol. II, p. 26, note (d).

the *Fabliaux ou Contes* a lengthy alphabetical list of those points the author considers of particular interest together with references to the tales in which they occur.[199]

It is not only in the volume and variety of his notes that we see the importance Le Grand attached to his particular aspect of his work. In the preface to the first volume of his collection he announces that certain of the more impious or licentious tales, those he feels he need not suppress entirely, are to be presented only in expurgated versions or in the briefest of summaries, which procedure he considers altogether justifiable:

Ce n'est point là dépouiller un Auteur, c'est le mettre en état d'entrer chez les honnêtes gens.[200]

On the other hand, he refuses to censor the manners and customs depicted in the tales. They should, he says, be viewed with the same eye as those ancient statues which, though everywhere exposed to public regard, fail to shock us with their nudity because they are accepted by one and all quite simply as monuments to artistic alibity:

Quelqu'étranges que soient les moeurs des Fabliaux, il est de mon devoir de les représenter telles qu'elles sont, puisqu'elles peignent leur siècle.[201]

Equally Le Grand feels himself obliged to omit nothing that has any bearing upon life and society in these centuries past. A certain "morceau impie" which Sainte-Palaye excludes from his translation of *Aucassin et Nicolette* is summarized by Le Grand in a note to his extract of the tale. He would, he says, have followed Sainte-Palaye's example and omitted the passage altogether.

... si je ne m'étais fait une loi de ne rien omettre de tout ce qui sert à peindre les moeurs. Joint à ceux du même genre qu'on a vus précédemment, il fera connaître la façon de penser qui se répandait déjà, & chez les beaux esprits d'alors, & chez une partie de la nation.[202]

Although he finds it necessary to interrupt the tale of "Boivin de Provins" because of the further modifications he feels he would need to

[199] Pp. 449–468. In the second edition this "table générale" occupies pp. 427–468 of the fifth volume, pp. 389–411 of the fifth volume in the third edition. The "table" thus covers the whole five volumes in these two later editions.
[200] P. lxxiii.
[201] P. lxxii. Cf. also a note to "Aucassin et Nicolette": "De pareilles moeurs nous paraîtront bien étranges, & je n'entreprends pas de les excuser; mais mon devoir est de les représenter telles qu'elles sont." (Vol. II, p. 213, note (f).)
[202] Vol. II, p. 210, note (a).

make in order to render the piece acceptable to his readers, he nevertheless feels obliged at least to summarize that which remains

... ne fût-ce que pour montrer quelles furent les moeurs d'un siècle dans
lequel la partie la plus distinguée de la nation était amusée par des grossièretés aussi révoltantes.[203]

More important, passages which would normally be rejected as adding
nothing to or actually detracting from the effect of a particular extract
are retained when seen by Le Grand to have some historical interest,
as in the case of the tourney which features in "Parténopex," for example.[204]
    But what perhaps above all else proves the value which the author of
the *Fabliaux ou Contes* attached to the picture of medieval society presented in his collection, what perhaps above all else firmly establishes
Le Grand within what we have seen to be the long tradition of historically oriented medievalism, a tradition dating from the sixteenth century, is that he should include in the collection pieces whose only merit
is that they shed light upon the manners and customs of the period in
which they were composed, pieces which indeed, in his own view, actually detract from the literary reputation of the "anciens rimeurs."
Such a tale is "L'Indigestion du Villain"[205] or "De la Vieille qui sé-
duisit la jeune Femme":

Toute ridicule que nous paraîtra cette fiction, je la crois digne de remarque,
en ce qu'elle représente les moeurs.[206]

As Le Grand explained in his preface,

... ce sont-là les moeurs du tems auxquelles je prie mes Lecteurs de faire
attention, parce que c'est une des clés principales de l'ouvrage qu'on va lire.

---

[203] Vol. III, p. 320. In the "Notes pour la nouvelle édition des Fabliaux" there is a
translation of "Jouglet" similarly interrupted: "Ce qui suit... offre des images si dégoûtantes qu'on ne peut plus le présenter qu'en extrait. Je crois devoir publier ce fabliau, pour faire
connaître l'esprit d'un siècle qui s'amusait de pareilles grossièretés." (*Ms. Paris, B.N. n.a.f.
6227*, fol. 17.)
    These notes contain translations of a number of the more dubious fabliaux under the
heading "Extraits de Fabliaux licencieux." Cf. also Le Grand's remarks on "Audigier" in
Ms. Paris, B.N. n.a.f. 6226, fol. 13.
[204] Vol. IV, p. 376, note (a): "J'ai cru ne devoir rien supprimer de tous ces détails, parce
qu'ils nous peignent très-bien ce que c'était que ces Tournois si fameux, & la manière dont
on s'y battait."
    Earlier in this romance such a passage is summarized in a note: "J'ai supprimé dans le
récit ces circonstances qui n'ajoutent rien à l'intérêt; mais j'en préviens ici parce qu'elles
peignent les moeurs." (P. 330, note (a).)
[205] Cf. vol. II, p. 113, note (a).
[206] Vol. III, p. 152, note (a).

Here then for Le Grand was at least one very good reason why the efforts of France's earliest poets were still worthy of attention even in the eighteenth century. He had said in the preface to his collection that any success the *Fabliaux ou Contes* might obtain would primarily be attributable to the tableau of past manners and customs found there,[207] and contemporary periodicals confirmed this:

> ... on croit ne lire que des Contes, & l'on fait un cours d'antiquité; on apprend les moeurs, & les usages des siècles passés; par le moyen des notes savantes qui accompagnent les Fabliaux, on trouve dans ces jeux d'une imagination Romanesque un fonds prodigieux de Doctrine, & l'on peut reitrer autant de fruit de ces petits Romans, que de la lecture du Glossaire de Ducange, avec cette différence que l'érudition qu'ils nous procurent, n'est point achetée par l'ennui.[208]

Those who were to present the collection to the English nation would not fail to stress the value of this instruction,[209] one such edition bearing the most apt of titles: *The Feudal Period: illustrated by a series of tales romantic and humorous.*[210]

But just as the author of the *Fabliaux ou Contes* was not the first, nor would he, of course, be the last to realize the particular historical utility of the fabliaux. B. de Roquefort-Flaméricourt, who consulted Le Grand's work for his dissertation *De l'Etat de la Poésie françoise dans les XIIe et XIIIe siècles*,[211] said of these tales:

> Ce genre de poésie peignoit les actions ordinaires de la vie et les moeurs générales; c'est un miroir fidèle et véritable de l'Histoire civile et privée des François.[212]

Alcius Ledieu expressed a similar view in a work entitled *Les Vilains dans les oeuvres des Trouvères*[213] and eight years previous to this A. Joly had inserted in the *Mémoires de l'Académie nationale des Sciences, Arts et*

---

[207] Vol. I, pp. lxvii–lxviii.

[208] *Année littéraire*, 1782, vol. IV, p. 327. Cf. *Journal de Littérature, des Sciences et des Arts*, 1779, vol. VI, pp. 102–103; *Journal Encyclopédique*, 1780, vol. II, pt. 1, pp. 78–79. By 1781 Le Grand had seen how right he was. Cf. *Observations sur les Troubadours*, p. 140.

[209] For example, cf. *Fabliaux or Tales abridged from French manuscripts of the XIIth and XIIIth centuries*, London (R. Faulder) 1796, preface, p. ii: "Works of fancy, written in remote ages, are the most authentick historical documents with respect to the manners and customs of the times in which they are composed."

[210] Wm. Carew Hazlitt, London (Reeves and Turner) 1873.

[211] Paris (Fournier) 1815.

[212] P. 188.

[213] Paris (J. Maisonneuve, editor) 1890, p. 8: "Les fictions les plus invraisemblables ont presque toujours une base qui repose sur un fait réel. A ce titre, les fabliaux sont une source précieuse pour la reconstitution de la physionomie de la société." Cf. also the Avant-propos, pp. v–vi. Ledieu makes reference to Le Grand's collection.

Belles-Lettres de Caen a most interesting paper headed "De la condition des vilains au moyen âge d'après les Fabliaux."[214] When Louis Brandin published his *Lais et Fabliaux du treizième siècle* in 1932[215] he too gave voice to that conviction which was the very basis of the *Fabliaux ou Contes.* Le Grand's appreciation of the fabliau as a valid social and historical document was clearly most just.[216] But Brandin, in the introduction to his collection, stressed equally the literary merits of this genre. Not only does the fabliau enable us to reconstruct a detailed picture of life in these centuries past, but ". . . la naïveté, la vivacité, le vivant des conversations qu'il met en scène parachèvent l'illusion."[217] The question is, with what impression of the artistic abilities of the "fabliers" would Le Grand's own readers be left?

---

[214] 1882, pp. 445–492.

[215] No. 15 in the series "Poèmes et récits de la vieille France," Paris (E. de Boccard, editor).

[216] Apart from those already mentioned, a great many other scholars have discussed and actually exploited the historical utility of the fabliaux. A. Méray, for example, published in 1876 *La vie au temps des cours d'amour; croyances, usages et moeurs intimes des XIe, XIIe et XIIIe siècles, d'après les chroniques, gestes, jeux partis et fabliaux.* Numerous such works are included by Per Nykrog in the second and third parts of his bibliography to *Les Fabliaux* (pp. 298–308).

[217] P. xxiv.

CHAPTER II

FRANCE AND THE LITERARY RENAISSANCE IN MEDIEVAL EUROPE. THE VINDICATION OF THE "TROUVÈRES."

If Le Grand d'Aussy's interest in medieval French literature was very much that of the historian, then it was that of the historian moved essentially by patriotism. Almost invariably the object of his researches was "la Nation" and he was never afraid to show his feelings for his homeland:

Oui, j'aime mon pays avec transport, il est vrai; je me glorifie d'être Fran-çois, et ne vois sur la terre aucune nation chez laquelle je désirerois de préfé-rence que la nature eût placé mon berceau.[1]

It was therefore quite to be expected that he should prove enthusiastic about something be found to shed a new and interesting light upon a subject very close to his heart. But for the author of the *Fabliaux ou Contes* the efforts of France's earliest poets merited the attention of the patriot for one other very important reason.

Although Le Grand himself spoke frequently of the Middle Ages as a time of superstition and ignorance and, generally speaking, would never have thought to compare with those of a more enlightened age like his own the literary productions of that period,[2] nevertheless he had no mean opinion of the rôle his native land had earlier played in the development of western civilization, especially proud of what he considered her contribution to the restoration of European letters. At the origin of that restoration, he held, were the works of the "trouvères" who hailed from the northern provinces of France, the poets of the "langue d'oïl" or "romane françoise":

Telles que sont enfin ces productions, elles ont été le premier fruit que les Lettres renaissantes aient donné à l'Europe depuis l'invasion des Barbares;

[1] *Observations sur les Troubadours*, p. 6.
[2] "... bien loin assurément de pouvoir entrer en parallèle avec nos chef-d'oeuvres moder-nes ..." (*Fabliaux ou Contes*, vol. IV, Discours préliminaire, p. ii).

& si les Ouvrages du dernier siècle & du nôtre peuvent se glorifier d'avoir
procuré à la France la supériorité de talent sur tous les peuples qui l'en-
tourent, les Ouvrages dont je parle ont ... le mérite de prouver encore l'an-
tériorité de ce talent.[3]

There were those, Le Grand knew, who would consider this a matter
of little consequence, but true Frenchmen could surely not think it so.
As for him, the idea that he might add to the Nation's glory by proving
the West grateful to France for the revival of poetic invention in that
hemisphere, precisely this idea, he insists, not only sustained him during
the four long and arduous years he spent engaged upon the *Fabliaux ou
Contes*,[4] but actually inspired in him the courage to undertake the collection in the first place. He had realized full well that the work involved would frequently bring boredom and even at times prove dis-
tasteful to him:

Mais d'un autre côté, à travers cette longue route d'épines, j'entrevoyois un
but bien consolant pour moi, la gloire de ma patrie ... j'allois être à portée
de prouver que l'Occident doit aux François la renaissance de la poésie, et
surtout celle du genre des contes, et cette seule idée m'inspiroit un courage
infatigable.[5]

It saddened Le Grand to think that his countrymen, while very much
aware and even boastful of the prominent rôle played by France in the
cultural life of eighteenth-century Europe, should remain largely ignorant of the Nation's former literary pre-eminence on that continent.
His researches, he says, had proven beyond all doubt that this distinction indeed belonged to her, and it angered him therefore that such an
important fact should have found no place in French history books:

... tout Français aimant naturellement sa Patrie, il doit connaître tout ce
qui peut la lui faire estimer davantage. Pour l'Auteur qui s'en fait l'Historien, c'est un devoir rigoureux de la louer lorsqu'elle y a droit.[6]

In itself the omission might have been excusable, but ignorance of the

---

[3] *Idem*, p. iii.
[4] *Idem*, vol. I, preface, pp. xcix-c.
[5] *Observations sur les Troubadours*, p. 6. Cf. also *Fabliaux ou Contes*, vol. IV, Avertissement
préliminaire, p. 251 : "Lorsque je me dévouai au long défrichement de notre Poésie ancienne,
toute mon ambition, je l'avoue, mon seul but & mon unique consolation dans ce triste &
pénible travail, furent de contribuer à la gloire de ma patrie ...".
   In the "Notice sommaire sur les trois ouvrages auxquels je travaille" Le Grand remarks
on the need for a history of French poetry such as that he proposes: "Elle importe même à
la gloire de la Nation française; puisque ce sont les Français qui les premiers, comme je l'ai
dit et prouvé ailleurs, ont, dans le XIIe et le XIIIe siècle, servi de modéle à l'Europe pour
les Romans, les Contes, les Pièces Dramatiques et autres ouvrages en vers." (Fol. 70.)
[6] *Fabliaux ou Contes*, vol. IV, Discours préliminaire, p. xii.

truth had eventually led to the acceptance of a falsehood in that the poets of the "langue d'oc" or "romane provençale" from the territories south of the Loire,[7] the troubadours, had come to be generally regarded as the fathers of modern European literature:

> ... il n'en est aucun qui ne les croie les pères de toute notre Littérature moderne, & qui ne regarde la Provence comme le point heureux de l'horison, où après une longue nuit de barbarie & d'ignorance, se leva enfin l'aurore de ces jours d'éclat & de gloire dont nous nous enorgueillissons.[8]

Time had lent this totally unwarranted prepossession the appearance of historical fact, explains Le Grand, and so firmly established had it become that he would never have thought to contest the notion had it not been for his association with Sainte-Palaye. Working with this great scholar, foremost amongst students of Old French and Old Provençal literature, he was eventually able to judge for himself the relative merits of the "trouvères" and the troubadours, finding to his surprise that while the productions of the former were filled with gaiety, wit and imagination, the latter could only offer ". . . des poésies tristes, monotones, insipides & illisibles . . .".[9] Even then he was loath to speak out, suspecting that poor taste might perhaps be responsible for such controversial findings. The failure of the *Histoire littéraire des Troubadours*, seeming to confirm these findings, convinced him that, as a patriot, he must finally challenge the pretensions of the Midi. This he made one of his primary goals in the *Fabliaux ou Contes*, striking the first really significant blow in the great "querelle des trouvères et des troubadours." The purpose of the preface to the first volume of his collection Le Grand explains in the *Observations sur les Troubadours*:

> Ma dissertation, puisque c'est ainsi qu'on l'a nommée, avoit pour but de prouver que les troubadours ne méritent pas à beaucoup près la renommée dont ils jouissent, et qu'au contraire, les trouveurs qui ont écrit en romane françoise n'ont pas obtenu toute celle qu'ils méritent. Pour la seconde partie de ce procès, c'étoit à moi de la prouver, et c'est ce que j'ai tâché de faire en publiant les fabliaux.[10]

We know already, of course, that Le Grand was simply bringing into the open a question in which national and regional pride had ensured lively and continued interest for some considerable time. The *Fabliaux ou Contes* did perhaps bring about the first major confrontation, but it

---

[7] Le Grand explains that there was in fact no rigorous geographical boundary separating the two languages. Cf. *Fabliaux ou Contes*, vol. I, preface, note to p. lii.

[8] *Idem*, p. v.

[9] *Observations sur les Troubadours*, p. 2.

[10] *Idem*, pp. 9–10.

cannot be said to have initiated the dispute. Two hundred years earlier, for example, Claude Fauchet had published his *Recueil de l'Origine de la Langue et Poësie Françoise*, written, he says, ". . . pour la gloire du nom François . . .",[11] and included in this a chapter headed:

Quand la Ryme, telle que nous l'avons, commença: & que les Espagnols & Italiens l'ont prise des François.[12]

Here he dismissed the claim that the "Provençaux" were the true "autheurs de la ryme" and challenged them to provide evidence to the contrary.[13] For the troubadours, whose memory was preserved in Jean de Nostredame's *Les Vies des plus célèbres et anciens poètes provensaux,*"[14] ". . . this mass of fiction and fraud . . ." as Nathan Edelman describes it,[15] there was, as we know, no lack of willing defenders. Highly praised by Pasquier in his *Recherches*, their poetry would continue to be extolled throughout the seventeenth century by those who, like Pierre de Caseneuve, considered them the models of European letters, the South the birthplace of rhyme.[16] Towards the turn of the century Pierre de Chasteuil, representing the third generation of a family of "Provençalistes," the Galaup de Chasteuil, spoke out against the denigrators of Old Provençal poetry and the language in which this had been composed to remind them that this language had been the delight of the finest minds for two centuries and more, studied and written by scholars and princes, and

. . . que les poètes provençaux ont été les inventeurs des rimes ou pour le moins qu'ils ont perfectionné l'art de rimer, et qu'ils l'ont appris aux Italiens et aux Espagnols; que le Dante et le Pétrarque ont imité et souvent copié les poètes provençaux et qu'ils ont pris de ceux-ci une partie des beautés qu'on admire dans leurs écrits.[17]

The same Pierre de Chasteuil published an *Apologie des anciens Historiens et des Troubadours ou Poëtes Provençaux*[18] which, in addition to dialogues

---

[11] *Les Oeuvres de Feu M. Claude Fauchet*, Paris (David Leclerc et Jean de Hugueville) 1610, *Recueil de l'Origine de la Langue et poësie Françoise* (f. 533 ro), "Dédicace au Roy de France et de Pologne".
[12] Ch. VII, f. 548vo.
[13] F. 550ro.
[14] Lyon (A. Marsilii) 1575.
[15] *Attitudes of Seventeenth-Century France towards the Middle Ages*, p. 344. Edelman deals at some length with the precursors of the eighteenth-century "Provensalistes." (Pp. 338–361.)
[16] Cf. N. Edelman, *loc. cit.*
[17] Reported in the *Mercure*, February 1726, p. 326. Quotation taken from H. Jacoubet, *Le Comte de Tressan*, p. 73.
[18] Avignon (J. Du Périer) 1704. He was also responsible for a history of the troubadours, which remained unpublished and is now lost.

defending the Provençal poets, contained a rondeau and a virelay composed after their fashion, the latter with the refrain:

Rendons graces aux Troubadours.[19]

Two years later appeared Mervesin's *Histoire de la Poësie françoise*[20]
which hailed the troubadours as "... ces agréables génies qui tirèrent
les Muses de l'assoupissement où elles étoient depuis longtemps en
France ..." and proclaimed that, while they were not to be regarded
as the inventors of rhyme, "... on doit leur attribuer la gloire d'avoir
les premiers fait sentir à l'oreille le véritable agrément de la rime."[21]
Noblot de la Clayette criticised Juvenal de Carlencas for failing to establish the true originators of French poetry in his *Essai sur l'Histoire des
Belles-Lettres*:[22]

Pourquoi passer sous silence les Troubadours de Provence qui en sont sans
contredit les premiers Auteurs.[23]

The view expressed here was that of La Curne de Sainte-Palaye himself,[24] perhaps to be honoured as the first serious defender of Provençal
literature.

While others had done little more than express their belief in the
superiority of the troubadours, Sainte-Palaye undertook to bring their
poetry before his contemporaries in order that they might properly appreciate it for themselves. Millot made it clear in his "Discours préliminaire" that this was indeed the purpose of the *Histoire littéraire des
Troubadours*[25] and stressed the importance of the collection. The true
origins of modern European literature, he said, were to be sought in the
southern provinces of France. The troubadours had breathed life into
a Europe hitherto seemingly dead, inspiring in her poets a new creative
urge and, by their own example, setting them upon the path of reason,
even perfection:

---

[19] Cf. N. Edelman, *Attitudes of Seventeenth-Century France towards the Middle Ages*, pp. 351–
352.
[20] Paris (Pierre Giffart) 1706.
[21] Pp. 62–63. In his own *Histoire de la Poësie françoise* the Abbé Guillaume Massieu expressed a similar view: "Nous avons dit que la Province fut comme son berceau. C'est aux
Peuples de cette Province qu'elle est principalement redevable de sa naissance." (Pp. 91–92.)
[22] Lyon (Duplain) 1740–1744, 2 vols.
[23] *L'Origine et les progrès des Arts et des Sciences*, Paris (H. L. Guétrin) 1740. Quoted in the
Mercure, April 1741, pp. 735–736; also by L. Gossman, *Medievalism*, p. 302, note 11.
[24] The troubadours, he said, were the founders of both French and Italian literature. Cf.
his "Projet d'étude sur l'Histoire de France," *Ms. Paris, B. N. Bréquigny 62*, fol. 212. Again
quoted by L. Gossman, *Medievalism*, p. 303.
[25] Vol. I, pp. xiii-xiv.

... tel est l'enchaînement des choses humaines, qu'à cette première cause presque inconnue on peut attribuer les plus grands effets. Toute révolution dans l'eprit humain mérite d'exercer une curiosité attentive; & les principes de la révolution le méritent pour le moins autant que ses progrès. A cet égard combien les troubadours ne doivent-ils pas intéresser?[26]

But the *Histoire littéraire des Troubadours* can be said largely to have failed in its essential purpose and by so doing the work undoubtedly jeopardized the reputation of the Old Provençal poets. Those who, if indeed they ever gave medieval literature any thought, had earlier been content to dismiss the troubadours as unenlightened vagabonds with little or no taste, their writings of interest only to the eccentric antiquary,[27] but who, given proper encouragement, might perhaps have been induced to alter their opinion, such people could have found in the collection little reason to question the justice of that opinion. More significantly, Millot's own personal disenchantment with Provençal poetry can be said to have reinforced and actually furthered the cause of the "trouvères" in the matter of the "querelle," consolidating the position of those already sympathetic to the North. Millot's "reassurance" was all Le Grand needed to speak out against the pretensions of the southern provinces and issue what was perhaps the most serious challenge the "Provençalistes" had yet had to meet. Neither Lévesque de la Ravalière nor the Abbé Goujet drew opposition as fierce as did the author of the *Fabliaux ou Contes* by their own efforts to reinstate the North as the birthplace of the first French poets.[28] Le Grand's collection, it seemed, represented a grave threat to the fame and glory attached, rightly or wrongly, to the name of troubadour.

In the preface to the "Contes dévots" Le Grand goes to considerable lengths to point out the grave consequences of the disdain shown by the Nation's historians for medieval French literature. It was enough that what he himself considered one of the most rich and vital sources of information available on the Middle Ages in France should be lost to them, but in the ignorance ensuing from their refusal to take into con-

---

[26] *Idem*, pp. lxxv-lxxvi.

[27] *Idem*, p. xiv.

[28] On Goujet and Lévesque, cf. H. Jacoubet, *Le Comte de Tressan*, pp. 75–77. Jacoubet quotes from the preface to Lévesque's *Poésies du Roi de Navarre* (Paris, 1742, 2 vols): "On avait été jusqu'à présent dans la persuasion que nous tenions notre poésie des Provençaux, qu'ils avaient été les inventeurs de nos chansons, dont on faisait remonter la naissance jusqu'au règne de Philippe 1er, mais on verra que c'est à la Normandie que nous sommes redevables des premiers poèmes français que l'on connaisse et qu'il y a eu parmi nous des chansons en langue vulgaire, avant celles que la Provence nous a montrées et qu'elles ont paru plus tard que le règne de Philippe 1er."

sideration anything but the work of other historians they could, of course, have no notion of the honour and distinction which the earliest French poets had brought their homeland. The celebrated authors of the seventeenth and eighteenth centuries had ensured a place for literature in the great histories of France, which now listed their names amongst those of famous generals, princes and politicians. Voltaire did not omit to mention the contribution made by men of letters to the glory of the age of Louis XIV and rightly so for the French naturally took pride in two centuries of literary pre-eminence. But it was all the more regrettable therefore that the Nation should be denied knowledge of a much earlier period in its literary history when the achievement had been hardly less glorious than that of the last two hundred years, equally flattering to the national vanity. The French could simply not suspect that already in the Middle Ages their literature had been the admiration and inspiration of the western world, that in fact France herself had been primarily responsible for the renaissance of letters in medieval Europe:

De pareils titres assurément étaient assez flatteurs pour mériter que la mémoire en fût consacrée dans l'Histoire de la Nation; & tout Français qui, comme moi, s'intéressera vraiment à l'honneur de sa Patrie, s'attendra toujours à les y trouver déposés. Quelle sera donc sa surprise, ou plutôt quelle sera son indignation, lorsqu'il verra que jusqu'à présent le fait ne se trouve dans aucun de nos Historiens . . . . [29]

Lamentable as the omission was, Le Grand continues, little harm could have been done if historians like Velly and Villaret[30] had been prepared to remain silent on a subject about which they were dangerously uninformed. Sooner or later others would have made good their deficiency. The trouble was that they had simply not been content to say nothing and in their ignorance had expounded some wildly erroneous notions about medieval French literature, inconsequential perhaps in the mouths of lesser men but seriously damaging when voiced by those widely respected for their instruction. Their errors had in fact become public errors and it was high time therefore that the truth be made known.[31]

---

[29] *Fabliaux ou Contes*, vol. IV, Discours préliminaire to the "Contes dévots," pp. iii-iv.

[30] Paul François Velly was responsible for vols. 1–7, Claude Villaret for vols. 8–17 and J. J. Garnier for vols. 18–30 of the *Histoire de France, depuis l'établissement de la monarchie jusqu'au règne de Louis XIV*, Paris, 1769 – an VII (1799) 33 vols.

[31] Cf. also *Fabliaux ou Contes*, vol. I, preface, note to p. iii: ". . . je cite de préférence cet Historien estimable, parce que les erreurs qu'accrédite un Ecrivain de son mérite, deviennent bientôt les erreurs de toute la Nation."

Velly is censured by Le Grand for knowing so little about the poets who first established French literary supremacy in Europe as to proclaim their finest achievement to be an absurd collection of "contes dévots" in fact composed in Italy. It is true, he says, that France produced similar collections hardly more worthy of praise, but Velly should at least have cited these if he had wished to belittle the efforts of the "anciens rimeurs." Ideally, of course, he should have made it clear that despite the ignorance and barbarity of the Middle Ages the Nation at this time was also producing works filled with gaiety, wit and imagination, of which a number have been preserved. By some strange quirk of fate, however, those productions in which the French might justifiably take pride have been lost to memory while the "contes dévots," though meriting no better end, have acquired a certain renown. Yet just as it is improper for the historian to cite some strange anecdote he might encounter in these tales, some detail ". . . curieux à force de bêtise & de simplicité . . .",[32] as indicative of the state of medieval French society generally, so he is altogether unjustified in condemning the whole of the literature produced in France during the period of the Middle Ages after the "contes dévots." These latter never enjoyed the popularity of the romances or the fabliaux, composed as they were in the shadows of the monastery by men set apart from the rest of their fellows:

. . . juger le XIIIe siècle par ces seules productions, ce serait une injustice, égale à-peu-près à celle que commettraient nos neveux, si un jour ils allaient apprécier le nôtre par nos cantiques de Mission, par nos Noëls populaires, ou par la vie de Marie Alacoque.[33]

For Le Grand the injustice is already sufficient but even the "contes dévots," he feels, have not received fair treatment from modern historians. Not content to mislead the public by proclaiming them representative of medieval French literature generally, they have done all they could to present them in the worst possible light.[34] Yet quite apart from the value of the insight which these tales provide into a particular section of society in medieval France,[35] several examples of the genre are not without a certain literary merit, which point has rarely been given due emphasis. The majority of critics have taken their ideas on

---

[32] Discours préliminaire to the "Contes dévots," p. xxviii.
[33] *Fabliaux ou Contes*, vol. III, p. 440.
[34] Cf. a note to "Du Moine qui fut sauvé par l'intercession de Notre-Dame," *idem*, vol. IV, p. 11.
[35] Discours préliminaire to the "Contes dévots," p. xlvi: ". . . elles offrent en raccourci ce que furent pendant longtems chez une partie des Français la Religion & la Morale . . .".

the "contes dévots" from Velly or from a paper on Gautier de Coincy's *Miracles de Notre-Dame* published in the *Mémoires de l'Académie des Inscriptions et Belles-Lettres* by the younger Racine.[36] The latter, while he finds that certain of the pieces included here are written with elegance, simplicity and grace, deals only with the most insipid of the "miracles" and can speak only disparagingly of the collection as a whole, too absurd, he says, to bear reading in full. Le Grand, hastening to remark that he himself feels obliged to have a thorough knowledge of any manuscript upon which he is to pass judgement, admits that he sees even less than Racine in Coincy's work:

Comsi m'a paru simple & naturel; mais niais, plat, sans imagination & sans aucun charme.[37]

But he points out that another collection of "contes dévots" has been preserved, one which is in fact far superior to the *Miracles de Notre-Dame*. It would have been more fitting for Racine to concern himself with the *Vies des Pères* where there is a better choice of subjects in tales more skilfully narrated. Unfortunately, while Coincy has been translated and cited over the years to become in modern times and object of ridicule, the author of the *Vies des Pères* has been condemned to oblivion:

... car il semble, encore une fois, qu'un mauvais Génie, ennemi de la France, se soit fait pendant long-tems un plaisir malin d'engloutir successivement dans l'oubli les meilleures productions de notre antique Littérature, pour ne laisser surnager & arriver vers nous que ce qui méritait le plus d'être oublié.[38]

If only those historians who had felt obliged to make some comment upon the efforts of France's earliest poets had gone to the manuscripts instead of sheepishly reiterating the opinions of their equally uninformed predecessors, then the influence of this "mauvais Génie," argues Le Grand, would have been nullified. It dismays him to think that even those responsible for histories of French literature have failed to take this trouble, so that he might fill a volume with the errors of which they have been guilty on the subject of the "anciens rimeurs." Through the negligence of scholars like Massieu the Nation still lacks an accurate history of its poetry:

---

[36] Vol. XVIII. Cf. *Fabliaux ou Contes*, vol. III, p. 440, note (a).
[37] Discours préliminaire to the "Contes dévots," p. xix.
[38] *Idem*, p. xxi.

L'histoire de notre Poèsie Française reste encore à faire; & j'exhorte à cette laborieuse entreprise ceux de nos Gens de Lettres qui se sentent du courage & du goût. Ils ne croiront pas sans doutre remplir un parail titre, en nous donnant quelques analyses erronnées ou tronquées, & quelques noms ou vers pris au hazard dans Pasquier, dans Fauchet, &c. Ils voudront apprécier nos Poëtes d'après leurs Poésies mêmes; ils compulseront, ils étudieront les manuscrits du tems; & je les préviens que ce ne sera point là le travail d'un jour.[39]

Although it is not Le Grand's purpose to supply this need,[40] he does regard the *Fabliaux ou Contes* as ". . . des Mémoires faits pour servir à l'Histoire de notre ancienne Littérature . . ."[41] and, as part of this attempt to make good at least some of the damage done by scholars less conscientious then himself, includes in his collection several examples of superior "contes dévots":[42]

Ils suffiront pour modifier au moins le mépris, que jusqu'à présent on leur a prodiqué à tous en général.[43]

But Le Grand's task is not simply one of establishing that medieval French literature has been grossly misrepresented by modern critics. Amongst these are not a few who, he considers, have been guilty of a crime far worse than that of either Velly or Racine, who have added insult to injury by not only seriously underrating the efforts of the "anciens rimeurs" but actually attributing to others the great distinctions which the Nation's earliest poets earned for themselves. It is enough for Villaret to refer to these as "nos insipides Versificateurs", but that he should announce that while the French were hardly beginning to stammer their first crude attempts at poetry the Italians were already producing verse of considerable merit, this for Le Grand is altogether inexcusable.[44] A learned historian like Villaret should know that

---

[39] *Fabliaux ou Contes*, vol. III, pp. 93–94. Le Grand would later have no difficulty in justifying his own proposals for a history of French poetry: "A la vérité, ı'abbé de Massieu, en 1721, a publié sur notre ancienne Poësie un petit Traité, qu'on peut même dire écrit purement et avec goût. Mais, ce qui est inconcevable! cet homme qui entreprenait de nous faire connaître nos vieux Poëtes, n'en avait pas lu un seul en manuscrit. Tous les Romanciers, Chansonniers, Fabliers, Dramatistes et autres Rimeurs des trois siècles antérieurs à la découverte de l'Imperimerie (et ce nombre est immense) lui étaient totalement inconnus. Le peu qu'il en dit est copié d'après les notices erronées ou trez imparfaites qu'a publiées Fauchet sur quelques-uns d'entre-eux; et l'histoire de notre Poësie reste encore à faire en entier." ("Notice sommaire sur les trois ouvrages auxquels je travaille," fol. 70.)

[40] Cf. *Fabliaux ou Contes*, vol. I, preface, p. xxvii.

[41] *Idem*, p. xcv.

[42] One in each of the first three volumes and "two or three" more in the fourth. He admits that the remainder of those appearing in volume IV are of little value.

[43] *Discours préliminaire* to the "Contes dévots," pp. xxxix.

[44] Cf. *idem*, pp. xi–xii.

France had poets of some worth composing in the vernacular before any of her European neighbours, that these same poets were responsible for the revival of literary activity in the West, that even the Italians sang their praises and sought inspiration in their works. Every French writer, as a patriot, should be aware of this, and particularly the historian whose duty it is to honour the Nation whenever honour is due to her:

Que sera-ce donc, quant au lieu des éloges qu'elle mérite, il l'humiliera injustement pour couvrir d'autres peuples d'une gloire qui, légitimement, n'appartient qu'à elle![45]

Villaret's eulogy of early Italian poetry probably incenses Le Grand even more than do the claims made for the troubadours, although he undoubtedly considers the "Provençalistes" his most serious adversaries. If he can prove the pretensions of the Midi unfounded and establish the "trouvères" of the northern provinces of France as the true fathers of modern European literature, then Villaret is clearly discredited in the process.

In the preface to the first volume of the *Fabliaux ou Contes* Le Grand argues that the reputation of the troubadours rests not upon outstanding literary achievement but essentially upon the simple fact that they were acclaimed in Italy. An affinity of language rendered them easily accessible to the Italians in whom they could boast of having inspired a taste for poetry, and it is the gratitude shown to them by two or three celebrated Italian writers which has saved them from oblivion. Because Petrarch and Dante applaud them it has been taken for granted that the troubadours must surely have been great poets and they have gone down in history as such without anyone thinking to verify their right to do so.[46] On the other hand, the "trouvères" and their compositions have been almost entirely lost to memory. Modern critics and historians who have recalled them to mind have done so usually in a tone so patronizing or disdainful as to discourage anyone from seeking further acquaintance with them. It is time then, insists Le Grand, that the "trouvères" and the troubadours be properly judged according to their

---

[45] *Idem*, pp. xii-xiii.
[46] Cf. A. Jeanroy, *La Poésie lyrique des Troubadours* (Paris, 1934, 2 vols.) vol. I, p. 2: "Si les troubadours sont enfin, au début du XVIe siècle ,sortis de l'oubli, c'est à leurs grands imitateurs italiens qu'ils le doivent. Quand les poésies de Dante et de Pétrarque, quoique bien vivantes encore, devinrent des objects d'étude, on fut amené à rechercher leurs sources, à s'enquérir de leurs modèles, et l'on rencontra sur sa route les troubadours, dont ils avaient été, l'un et l'autre, de fervents admirateurs."

merits. He proposes therefore briefly to survey the literary revival which took place in medieval France and to examine the respective contributions of the northern and southern provinces to this:

La question intéresse l'histoire de notre Littérature, & elle n'est point étrangère à mon sujet.[47]

Since numerous modern writers, as Le Grand claims, have failed to realize precisely what the Nation's historians understood by "provençal," the discussion opens with a definition of terms and of territories. As a result of the Roman and then barbarian invasions, it is explained, two new languages developed in France, each having the idiom of the first conquerors as its basis and therefore retaining the name "Romaine" or "Romane" despite a separate evolution in accordance with later influences. Gradually the Latin tongue was ousted and the two new languages became predominant dividing the country between them, the "Langue d'Oïl" to the north of the Loire and to the south the "Langue d'Oc." This latter, however, was also to be styled "Langue Provençale":

Raimond IV, de Saint-Gilles, Comte de Provence, possédent en même-tems une grande partie de la Gothie & de l'Aquitaine, on s'accoutuma à nommer simplement 'Provence' tous ses Etats; 'Provençaux,' ses différens Sujets; & langue 'Provençale,' la langue commune qu'ils parlaient.[48]

Since this eventually became established practice throughout the Nation it should be realized that when historians discuss "Provençal" poetry they refer to the verse produced not only in Provence proper but in all the southern provinces of France, or rather to all that composed in "Romane Provençale" for there were poets in Catalonia, Aragon and Italy who adopted this idiom:

De cent quarante Troubadours environ dont la patrie est connue, il n'y en a que vingt-six qui soient de la Provence proprement dite.[49]

Having thus dismissed one fundamental though apparently not infrequent misconception, Le Grand now proceeds to compare with the

---

[47] *Fabliaux ou Contes*, vol. I, preface, p. v.

[48] *Idem*, p. vii.

[49] *Idem*, p. viii. To avoid confusion Le Grand will later employ the term "Provençals" when referring to the compatriots of the troubadours generally, as opposed to the inhabitants of Provence in particular. Cf. *Observations sur les Troubadours*, note to p. 21. The *Journal des Sçavans* considers this procedure unworthy of a man of taste like the author of the *Fabliaux ou Contes*: "M. Legrand sait bien qu'il n'est jamais permis d'avoir recours au barbarisme pour distinguer des objects, quand deux mots d'explication peuvent faire le même effet." (November, 1782, pp. 742–743.)

few who rhymed in "Romane Provençale" the countless poets who expressed themselves in "Romane Française." And yet, though numbers do have some bearing on the comparison to be drawn, he is quite obviously concerned principally with the quality of the production rather than the quantity. For, as it is explained, rhyming was an art as yet without rules and the whole Nation seems to have wished to indulge itself. Although almost everything was set down in verse, only a fraction of the poetry dating from the period has any real value. Le Grand in fact recognizes only three genres as valid, and it is these with which he will primarily be concerned in weighing the efforts of the troubadours against those of the "trouvères":

... au milieu de toute cette écume grossière d'un tems d'ignorance, on doit distinguer trois espèces de Poésies, qui, destinées spécialement à l'amusement de la Noblesse & des Princes, formaient en quelque façon une classe à part: ce sont les Romans, les Chansons & les Contes.[50]

First to be treated is the medieval "chanson" and in particular the "chanson militaire" on which Le Grand allows himself only a few general and altogether non-committal remarks. He comments briefly upon the origins of the genre, as old as the Nation itself, its purpose and its popularity, noting Charlemagne's singular affection for such verse and the success enjoyed for so long a time by the *Chanson de Roland*. His only regret is that this, along with so many later examples of the type, should be lost to his century. He is clearly better acquainted with the "chansons d'amour" of which rather more have been preserved, although here again he is content to be brief, remarking upon their former abundance and yet mentioning only three poets, Saint Bernard, Abélard and Thibaut de Champagne, by name. But he does at least express an opinion on medieval love-songs, one based upon first-hand experience painstakingly acquired in the capital's great libraries:

Ce ne sont la plûpart que des lieux communs d'une fade galanterie, de tristes supplications à leur maîtresse pour l'attendrir, des plaintes éternelles contre les médisans, un début trivial qu'on croirait avoir été d'usage, tant il est souvent employé: 'la verdure renaît, le rossignol chante, je veux chanter aussi.'[51]

Now and then, Le Grand admits, one may come upon lines written with simplicity and feeling, but this is all that can be expected. Medieval poets would appear to have been wanting in gaiety for they have

---

[50] *Fabliaux ou Contes*, vol. I, preface, p. x.
[51] *Idem*, p. xvi.

left none of those songs inspired by pleasure and enjoyment of life, not even "chansons de table."

Of the two varieties of "chanson" which remain to be discussed according to Le Grand's understanding of the genre, he defers treatment of the "pastourelle" and passes immediately to the "jeu parti."[52] The form of the latter is explained and its popularity accounted for. It was not only the respect shown to the lady which, giving weight to all matters of love, made of this "badinage galant" a serious preoccupation, but also the effects of the great passion which scholars of the period shared for dialectics:

> ... il arriva qu'on le fit consister en une métaphysique de sentiment, ridicule à force d'être déliée.[53]

Numerous examples of the kind of questions debated in the "jeu-parti" are given and these lead Le Grand quite naturally into a brief discourse on the Courts of Love whose origins, he believes, are to be sought in Southern France where they proved particularly successful. Here then for the first time in the discussion proper North and South are openly juxtaposed, although we are not as yet concerned with purely literary achievement, for we are simply not informed whether the songs of the "trouvères" are superior to those of the troubadours or indeed if the reverse is the case. Perhaps Le Grand finds "trouvères" and troubadours equally skilled in the genre or, as it would appear, considers this the least of the three to be discussed, the question of where the medieval "chanson" first flourished or was first perfected a matter of no great consequence bearing little relation to the honours due to a particular province. In any event we should not be surprised to see him readily proclaim the "Provençaux" to be the originators of the Courts of Love. It is enough, he feels, that these "risibles procès" should have been deemed worthy of serious attention:

> Il fallait encore que les 'Cours d'amour' ... eussent une telle sanction que personne n'osât en appeler. C'est-là un prodige dont on ne doit gueres se flatter pour les décisions humaines.[54]

---

[52] Le Grand does not distinguish between the "jeu-parti" and the "tenson": "Ces derniers sont ce que les Troubadours nommaient 'Tenson,' c'est-à-dire, des questions de jurisprudence amoureuse." (*Idem*, p. xviii.)

[53] *Idem*, p. xix.

[54] *Idem*, p. xxii. Cf. also a note to "Huéline et Eglantine" concerning the Courts of Love: "Voici l'une des institutions les plus bizarres & les plus incroyables peut-être qu'ait jamais imaginées l'esprit humanin. Avec son inutilité réelle & l'importance qu'on y mit, elle nous paraîtra doublement ridicule; & cependant il en est peu qui ait été reçue avec autant de

Rather more space is given to the romance, a genre apparently closer to Le Grand's heart than the "chanson"[55] and in any event one more useful to his purposes here. Neither gallantry nor love, he tells us, lies at the origin of the romance, but the same kind of distorted religious fervour which brought about the crusades. And it is the fanatical concern with the fight against the infidel, he continues, that underlies the three earliest "ouvrages Romanesques" known to him. All three feature Charlemagne as the great adversary of the Saracens and have him embarking upon some expedition, into Palestine,[56] Spain,[57] or Languedoc.[58] More significantly, all three were composed by monks and, employed by them in part as a means of glorifying their orders, their abbeys or particular miraculous relics, bear the unmistakable stamp of monasticism. But a kind of fiction so obviously suited to the wild, unchecked imagination was quickly seized upon by poets who adopted the genre, and frequently the same hero, Charlemagne, although rejecting the subject matter, depicting not some great defender of the faith but instead the knight-errant preoccupied with slaying giants, rescuing fair damsels, winning tourneys and performing feats of great valour for his lady:

La Chevalerie venait de naître; ils la transportèrent dans leurs poëmes avec sa bravoure inquiète, avec son ardeur pour les exploits merveilleux, & cette galanterie fameuse dont elle était devenue l'origine.[59]

Having conjectured upon the origins of the romances[60] and spoken

respect, qui se soit maintenue avec moins de moyens, & puisse se glorifier d'avoir autant influé sur les moeurs." (*Fabliaux ou Contes*, vol. I, p. 244, note (K).)

What Le Grand has to say here about the Courts of Love, their origins and importance, is dismissed by J. Lafitte-Houssat as a "... dissertation toute de fantasiie et d'imagination ...". (*Troubadours et Cours d'Amour*, "Que sais-je", no. 422, 1966, pp. 30–31.)

It is interesting to note that in the third edition of the *Fabliaux ou Contes* the "jeux-partis" are said to have originated in southern France, the Courts of Love in the North: "Je me contenterai de remarquer ici qu'il est parlé de ces établissements dans nos fabliaux, et qu'il n'en est pas dit un seul mot dans les poésies des troubadours. D'où résulte une observation importante qui peint les moeurs des deux moitiés de la France; c'est que les 'tensons' ou 'jeux-partis,' c'est-à-dire les chansons de controverse amoureuse, furent imaginés par la galanterie troubadouresque, et que les cours-d'amour sont dues à la galanterie françoise." (*Fabliaux ou Contes*, 1829, vol. I, preface, pp. 18–19.)

[55] It should remembered that Le Grand had earlier collaborated on the *Bibliothèque des Romans*.

[56] *Le pèlerinage de Charlemagne.*

[57] *La Chronique de Turpin.*

[58] *Philomena.*

[59] *Fabliaux ou Contes*, vol. I, preface, p. xxv.

[60] In notes prepared for the proposed histories of French language and literature, usages, arts and sciences Le Grand freely admits to knowing little more than his contemporaries about the true origins of the romance: "Au reste l'incertitude où ils nous laissent sur ce point d'histoire et de critique est excusable. Quelque important qu'il soit pour la littérature, je suis

briefly of the three types, "Romans de Chevalerie," "Romans d'A-mour" and "Romans de Férie," Le Grand can now turn to the question of the popularity and value of this genre, a question of far greater relevance to the primary object of his discussion. For the romances, he tells us, were enormously successful not only in France but also abroad. Indeed, a number of those translated into Italian and Spanish enjoyed such a reputation for so long a time that eventually, when they had been altogether forgotten by the French, they were rendered back into their original tongue by translators who genuinely believed them to be of foreign invention:

Il y a sur ce fait plusieurs exemples connus: il me serait aisé d'en ajouter plusieurs autres.[61]

The English, too, welcomed the romance but, envious of their neighbours across the Channel, created a new hero to set at its centre, King Arthur, and even had the audacity to list part of France amongst his conquests. Loathsome as this whole notion might be to eighteenth-century France,[62] the legend of Arthur, an element of magic enhancing the chivalrous exploits described, so appealed to French poets that numerous "romanciers" exploited it and took as their central figure some supposed paladin of this hero of heroes. And similarly the "conteurs" whose tales will open the present collection.

The romances, then, enjoyed great favour and particularly the romances of chivalry.[63] Francois I, who found enormous pleasure in these, had the *Amadis*, ". . . Romans originairement Français . . .",[64]

forcé de convenir qu'en effet les preuves décisives manquent; et que moi-même, malgré toutes les recherches que j'ai pu faire, je ne puis, comme eux, qu'offrir des semi-preuves et proposer des conjectures."
    He can only hope that his own ideas on the subject, essentially those of the preface to the *Fabliaux ou Contes*, will prove more convincing and probable than those which have already been put forward by others: "Elles me paraissent au moins développer si naturellement le motif qui donna naissance aux ouvrages primitifs; elles en expliquent si bien l'esprit par les époques où ils parurent qu'elles équivalent presque à une preuve directe et à des témoignages originaux." (*Ms. Paris, B.N. n.a.f. 6627*, ff. 165–167.)
    [61] *Fabliaux ou Contes*, vol. I, preface, p. xxviii.
    [62] Le Grand would appear to have been no friend of the English: ". . . si l'on se rappelle qu'au tems où s'écrivaient ces fictions mensongères, l'Angleterre conquise obéissait à des Princes Français, on conviendra qu'aux yeux de Lecteurs attentifs, il en est des Nations dans leurs écrits, comme des individus: toujours le caractère y perce par quelque endroit." (*Idem*, p. xxix.)
    [63] Four classes are specifically mentioned: "Romans d'Artus," "Romans de Charlemagne," "Romans des Amadis" and those ". . . dont les Héros n'étaient ni Chevaliers de Charles ou d'Artus, ni descendans du Gaulois Amadis; mais des Paladins, ou des Princes que le Poëte fait vivre dans d'autres tems, ou dans d'autres Cours; tels que Perceforêt, Alexandre, &c. &c. &c." (*Idem*, p. xxx.)
    [64] Later scholars will not share this certainty. Cf. G. S. Williams, *The Amadis Question*, New York and Paris, 1909.

translated from the Spanish and the series was so widely applauded, especially during the reign of Henri II, we are told, that according to La Noue it would have seemed sacrilegious for anyone to speak ill of it. La Noue's own indictment of this kind of literature in his *Discours Politiques et Militaires*[65] clearly fails to impress Le Grand who insists that, if the romances of chivalry did have some baneful influence in the sixteenth century, then for four hundred years previous to this they had done much to dissipate ignorance, to foster the advance of poetry, to encourage the nobility to read and, above all, to instil into the Nation a spirit of high-mindedness and that thirst for honour which makes heroes of men:

> Quelques Auteurs respectables ont reproché à Cervantes, d'avoir par son Dom-Quichotte anéanti en Espagne l'esprit de Chevalerie. Je ne serais pas surpris que quelqu'un chez nous regrettât les Romans qui inspiraient cet esprit; sur-tout quand il se rappellera quels livres en ce genre on leur a fait succéder.[66]

Young or old we are all enthralled by these stories of incredible exploits at once terrifying and uplifting, and by only applying a little more skill in tales of a greater variety the "romanciers" could surely have produced truly memorable results. As it is they have sunk into oblivion for they lacked the genius of poets like Homer and Ariosto who worked from similar basic materials but will always be remembered and admired. All the same, this is no reason to decry those who first acclaimed the romances for at the time there was no branch of literature more worthy of their praises. And if this is not ample pretext, then Le Grand would have it known that amongst the romances are not a few which have a real interest:

> Je dirai plus, c'est que même dans la plûpart des autres on trouvera, malgré tous leurs défauts, (& j'en atteste quiconque aura le courage de les lire), des morceaux très-agréables, & sur-tout un talent particulier pour exciter la curiosité & l'admiration. Ceux dont la veuve Oudot a composé sa bibliothèque bleue, ne font-ils pas encore les délices du peuple, tout étrangère qu'est pour lui une pareille lecture?[67]

Is it not strange then, Le Grand now asks, that the romances, a genre which not only proved most popular but actually merited the applause

---

[65] *Discours Politiques et Militaires*, Geneva (Droz) 1967 (Textes Littéraires Français) pp. 160–176: "Que la lecture des livres d'Amadis n'est moins pernicieuse aux jeunes gens, que celle des livres de Machiavel aux vieux."
[66] *Fabliaux ou Contes*, vol. I, preface, p. xxxiii.
[67] *Idem*, pp. xxxiv-xxxv.

it received, should have flourished in the northern provinces of France alone? He knows of only four romances originating in the South and all of them "Romans dévots."[68] Here, then, is just one more of those points to which the panegyrists of the troubadours have paid no mind. These southerners are renowned for their lively imagination and their gallantry and yet their sun-drenched regions did not produce one single "Roman de Férie" or "Roman d'Amour." More important still, not one romance of chivalry was composed here, although at the time the mood of the Nation as a whole was one clearly favouring poets who dealt in stories of great exploits. Not that Le Grand, with all his experience of the genre, sets any great store by the romances of chivalry when he views them in the light of subsequent literary achievement. But, he insists, they were the epics of the period and if one remembers that in their day they were in fact unparalleled and extraordinarily successful both at home and abroad, then it is tempting to ask if the troubadours were simply incapable of thinking on the epic scale.

Already the cause of the "Provençalistes" is seriously discredited and Le Grand has hardly begun his campaign. For there is a branch of medieval French literature even more appealing than the romance in its variety where the "trouvères" again proved themselves superior by far to their southern counterparts, the short story, the "conte" or fabliau. Once again the reader is treated to a brief discourse on the origins of the genre, universally popular, which in France would appear, according to Le Grand, to have evolved from the need to find something rather less substantial then the romances with which to entertain the country's nobles on those infrequent occasions when they came together for particular feasts and ceremonies. The length of these sagas, and perhaps also their tone, made them unsuitable for such gatherings and so shorter, more lighthearted tales were devised, fabliaux. On the other hand, the possibility that these latter originated in Asia is not altogether discounted. Quite the contrary, for it is true, remarks Le Grand, that a number of those pieces appearing in the collection were taken from the Arabic and it is well known that the genre had enjoyed great favour in the East from the earliest times.

But again the question of origins is of only secondary importance. We are concerned to know who rendered the fabliau so popular a genre

---

[68] *Honorat de Lérins, Gérard de Roussillon, Guillaume au Court-nés* and *Philomena* which Le Grand reluctantly cites as one of the first three "Ouvrages Romanesques" composed in France, ". . . de peur qu'on ne me soupçonne de vouloir diminuer en quelque chose la gloire des Provençaux." (*Fabliaux ou Contes*, vol. I, preface, note to pp. xxxv-xxxvi).

in medieval France, for popular it was. The revival of poetry and the encouragement this received from the nobility, we are informed, brought forth a whole army of histrions whose sole function was to travel from province to province reciting the work of the Nation's poets, which they put to music and sang while accompanying themselves on various instruments. Often they were joined by versifiers and almost invariably their retinue included "Jongleurs" to entertain with sleight of hand or trained animals, and so they would go from town to town and from manor to manor delighting commoner and nobleman alike. It is true that they were despised for their vagabond existence, for their greed and immorality, but their talents more than compensated for this and it was not only in France that they were made welcome. Richard I of England offered them great rewards to appear at his court and there is evidence that by the thirteenth century they had penetrated into Italy. And who was it brought such honour to the Nation? All credit must go to the "trouvères," claims Le Grand, for their colleagues in the South would appear according to the *Histoire littéraire des Troubadours* to have been responsible for only two real "contes," both appearing at a time when the majority of those originating in the North were already in circulation.[69]

France, we are told, has no notion of the glory that was formerly hers:

... que c'est à elle qu'on doit les premiers poëtes, & le renouvellement de la Poésie; que sa Musique fut recherchée, ses Contes, ses Romans admirés, imités ou traduits chez toutes les Nations; sa Chevalerie enfin, & sesTournois adoptés depuis la Baltique jusqu'à la Méditerranée. Il n'y eut pas jusqu'à sa Langue, toute barbare qu'elle paraît à nos yeux, qui eut une fortune prodigieuse.[70]

What are we to understand by this if not that in Le Grand's view it is time the northern provinces were given proper recognition for the distinctions they won for the Nation. The "trouvères" were responsible

---

[69] One by Arnaud de Carcassès (cf. *Histoire littéraire des Troubadours*, vol. II, pp. 390–395), the other by Raimond Vidal (*idem*, vol. III, pp. 296–308). Le Grand gives them both in extract (*Fabliaux ou Contes*, vol. I, preface, pp. xlv–xlviii) for purposes of comparison and clearly thinks little of either. Four others included in the *Histoire littéraire des Troubadours*, another by Raimond Vidal (*Histoire littéraire des Troubadours*, vol. III, pp. 277–296), two by Pierre Vidal (*idem*, vol. II, pp. 266–309) and one by Cigala (*idem*, vol. II, pp. 153–173), he discounts: "On sent qu'aucune de ces fictions ne doit être regardée comme un conte. Les deux de Pierre Vidal ne sont que des cadres adroits pour amener quelque instruction; celle de Raimond, un jugement dans le goût des Sentences des Cours d'amour; & celle de Cigala, une Tenson ou Jeu-parti." (*Fabliaux ou Contes*, vol. I, preface, note to pp. xlv-xlvi.)

[70] *Fabliaux ou Contes*, vol. I, preface, p. xliii.

for the revival of poetry in France, in Europe. The "trouvères" were the authors of the romances and the fabliaux. And it was their idiom, the idiom of the northern provinces, "la Romane Française," that was acclaimed above all other European tongues. The Normans took it with them to Naples and to Sicily,[71] the Crusaders into the East and William the Conqueror to England where it was so highly esteemed that children were sent to France to learn it. On one occasion Brunetto Latini even employed it in preference to his own tongue:

Ce triomphe de la Langue, quel qu'il soit, n'est encore que le triomphe de la Romane Française. Dans tout ce qu'on vient de lire, il ne s'agit aucunement de la Provençale.[72]

What then of the glorious reputation of the troubadours and of the prestige enjoyed by the southern provinces of France?

As Le Grand suggests, the reader might well care to consult Millot's collection and judge for himself of the talents of the troubadours. He should prepare for the unexpected:

Leur histoire existe; ouvrez-la, qu'y trouverez-vous? Des Sirventes, des Tensons, d'éternelles & ennuyeuses Chansons d'amour, sans couleur, sans images, sans aucun intérêt; en un mot, une assoupissante monotonie, à laquelle tout l'art de l'Editeur & l'élégance de son style n'ont pu remédier.[73]

Despite all the advantages they had over the "trouvères," a melodious language, a favourable climate, idyllic surroundings, the troubadours with their "gai saber" could produce only mournful songs of love. Why did they neglect the "conte," most light-hearted of all the genres and undoubtedly amongst the most popular? Is it not strange that their humour should have found its most frequent expression in satire, that

---

[71] Here le Grand adds a significant note: "Ce sont eux probablement qui y portèrent l'usage de la rime: car Pétrarque dit au commencement de ses Epîtres, que c'est de la Sicile que l'Italie l'a tirée. Si ce fait était prouvé ,il diminuerait beaucoup la gloire des Provençaux, qu'on regarde comme les premiers maîtres des Italiens." (*Idem*, p. xliii.)

[72] *Idem*, p. xliv. Compare an earlier view, that of Pierre Daniel Huet, *Traité de l'Origine des Romans* (Faksimiledrucke nach der Erstausgabe von 1670 und der Happelschen Ubersetzung von 1682) Stuttgart (J. B. Metzlersche) 1966, pp. 69–70: "Les Troubadours, les Chanterres, le Conteurs, & les Jongleurs de Provence, & enfin ceux de ce pays qui exerçoient ce qu'on y appelloit 'la science guaye,' commencerent dès le temps de Heu Capet à romaniser tout de bon, & à courir la France, débitant leurs Romans, & leurs 'Fabliaux' composez en langage Romain: car alors les Provençaux avoient plus d'usage des lettres & de la Poësie que tout le reste des François."

Cf. also *idem*, p. 89: "Mais pour revenir aux Troubadours ou Trouverres de Provence, qui furent en France les Princes de la Romancerie dès la fin du dixiesme siecle, leur mestier plut à tant de gens, que toutes les Provinces de France, comme j'ay dit, eurent aussi leurs Trouverres."

[73] *Fabliaux ou Contes*, vol. I, preface, p. xlviii.

they should have thought so highly of the "sirvente" as to make it their speciality:

Quelles réflexions douloureuses présenterait ce fait si on osait l'approfondir![74]

Although it is now more or less left to the reader to weigh for himself the value of the contributions made by "trouvère" and troubadour to the medieval literary revival, Le Grand would secure a decision favouring the North with one or two additional remarks. Firstly, the collection will establish beyond all doubt that the "trouvères" are the fathers of modern French theatre. As tasteless and absurd as they might now appear, the morality- and mystery-plays, the farces and "sotties" of the thirteenth century were the beginnings of the drama in France, and all originated in the North. To the troubadours the French stage owes nothing. Secondly, it is time someone remarked upon the curious fact that those provinces which in the twelfth and thirteenth centuries produced the authors of the romances and the fabliaux are precisely those which in the seventeenth and eighteenth centuries again produced the Nation's most distinguished names, Molière, Racine, Voltaire, Condé, Descartes, Vauban, etc. Twice, then, Nature would appear to have bestowed the gift of genius far more liberally in the North. This phenomenon Le Grand cannot explain:

Mais je ne puis m'empêcher de remarquer que déja elle commençait à douer nos Provinces septentrionales de cette vertu créative, de cette vigueur & fécondité de production, qui depuis, pour la seconde fois, mais à plus juste titre, a rendu nos bons Evrivains le modèle&l'admiration de l'Europe.[75]

Before the discussion is brought to a close, the exaggerated reputation of the poets of the Midi is accounted for. It is attributable, says Le Grand, to the simple fact that the term troubadour survived while that of "trouvère" was quickly lost to memory. Originally applied only to the Provençal poets, the former eventually came to be used in place of "Provençaux," which meant equally the inhabitants of Provence proper, to distinguish the rhymers of the southern provinces generally. The term troubadour was necessary to avoid confusion and was therefore retained, unlike "trouvère" which soon fell from memory and with it the poets who had been so named. The Italians, too, helped to keep the troubadours fresh in mind and to elevate them, and soon scholars were making no mention of their northern counterparts:

[74] *Idem*, p. 1.
[75] *Idem*, preface, p. liii.

... de-là est résulté une erreur: c'est que les passages concernant les 'Trouveurs,' leur furent indistinctement appliqués; qu'on leur fit honneur de la
plupart des faits qui regardent ceux-ci, & qu'insensiblement ils finirent ainsi
par être regardés comme les seuls pères des Lettres Françaises.[76]

When it is read that a "Ménétrier"[77] appeared at the court of some
prince, it is taken for granted that he entertained with Provençal verse
and no thought is given to the fact that this would have been understood only in certain provinces:[78]

Si un Musicien des bords de la Garonne venait aujourd'hui dans les villes &
châteaux de Normandie ou de l'Isle-de-France, nous chanter du Goudoulin,
je le demande, quelle fortune ferait-il?[79]

There may be evidence to suggest that Provençal poetry occasionally
penetrated into the North, but then singers from Germany and Italy
have once or twice ventured into France and it would be absurd for
some compatriot of theirs to come along in two or three hundred years
time and cite this fact as proof of the great popularity German or Italian music enjoyed here in the eighteenth century.

To conclude this section of his preface Le Grand again recommends
that the reader now decide for himself where credit is most due. The
evidence is there for him to view in Millot's collection and to this Le
Grand would refer the many who will undoubtedly think to challenge
his own particular views. If it should happen that the public find for
the "trouvères" then he would like to think that the poets of the South
would not be too dismayed at losing the position of pre-eminence they
have enjoyed until now. Nature has favoured them in so many other
things and at least one glorious distinction would remain theirs:

Il leur restera au moins d'avoir inspiré à l'Italie le goût de la Poésie, d'avoir
formé, & pour ainsi dire nourri de leur lait, Pétrarque, le Dante &c; & une
pareille gloire a de quoi flatter encore.[80]

We have said that the lasting impression of the *Histoire littéraire des
Troubadours* was hardly one to stimulate greater interest in the works of

---

[76] *Idem*, pp. lv-lvi. In a note to these pages Le Grand insists that the two songs of Richard
I were originally composed by him in French and not Provençal as the *Histoire littéraire des
Troubadours* would have it (vol. I, p. 55).

[77] *Idem*, p. xcii: "J'appelle ... 'Ménétriers,' les Musiciens, dont le métier était de chanter
& de jouer des instrumens ...".

[78] In a note to pp. lvii-lix of the preface examples of the two idioms are furnished for comparison by the reader.

[79] *Fabliaux ou Contes*, vol. I, pp. lviii-lix.

[80] *Idem*, pp. lxi.

the southern poets, that the collection failed in its essential purpose if it had indeed been intended properly to acquaint the public with Proven-çal verse and ensure a just appreciation of this. Whether Le Grand him-self privately attributed the poor success of the three volumes to Sainte-Palaye and Millot or genuinely felt that all that could be done had been done, as he will later insist in reply to those who would set all blame squarely upon the translator's or the editor's shoulders,[81] he ex-ploited the public's disappointment with the collection to the full.[82] Le Grand's own purpose was two-fold:

... prouver que les Troubadours ne méritent pas à beaucoup près la renom-mée dont ils jouissent; & qu'au contraire les Trouveurs qui ont écrit en Romane française, n'ont pas obtenu toute celle qu'ils méritent.[83]

He knew full well that he himself would be obliged to furnish the evi-dence necessary to uphold this latter cause and, for reasons that have yet to be discussed, this evidence would consist principally in the fabliaux. On the other hand, he considered the case against the trou-badours already quite sufficiently substantiated:

... ce qu'on nous a donné des Poésies provençales avoit été regardé un-animement comme très-médiocre; sur cela il n'y a qu'une voix, et je ne crains pas d'être contredit.[84]

Not only did the failure of the *Histoire littéraire des Troubadours* give Le Grand the courage to speak out against the "Provençalistes" once a literary career, as he would have it, had been thrust upon him, it pro-vided in fact his most powerful weapon in the campaign to deflate the reputation of the poets of the "Midi." Surely neither Sainte-Palaye nor Millot could have suspected to what ends their efforts would eventually be turned.

If none could deny that Millot's collection left but a poor impression of the poetic abilities of the troubadours, then there were those, Le Grand knew, who would simply refuse to accept the work as valid evidence in the case against the South. Then again, Le Grand realized

[81] Le Grand knew, of course, that other scholars employed by Sainte-Palaye had failed to do the enterprise justice before Millot finally undertook the work of editor. Cf. *Observations sur les Troubadours*, pp. 2–3.

[82] On the reception of the *Histoire littéraire des Troubadours*, cf. L. Gossman, *Medievalism*, pp. 321–323. In 1784 Cambry could still write in the Avertissement to a "Notice sur les Troubadours" contained in his *Contes et Proverbes* (Amsterdam, 1784): "Il seroit intéressant d'avoir une histoire détaillée de la vie & des écrits des Troubadours." (P. 76.)

[83] *Observations sur les Troubadours*, pp. 9–10.

[84] *Ibidem.*

that those remarks with which he had introduced this evidence in the preface to the first volume of the *Fabliaux ou Contes* could not fail to provoke some reaction. He was well aware that however much he protest his impartiality[85] he would not go uncriticized:

Au reste, il m'étoit aisé de prévoir que mon insurrection trouveroit des contradicteurs; & je devois m'y attendre. Il est des têtes où toute opinion qui entre la première, jette de telles racines, que tout ce qui vient ensuite la contredrire n'est regardé d'abord que comme une erreur.[86]

What Le Grand did not anticipate was the vehemence of the criticism levied against him, and perhaps also its volume.[87] We know that he had at first thought to make no reply to Papon's attack in the *Voyage littéraire de Provence*, deeming the "Cinq lettres sur les Trouvères et les Troubadours" unworthy of serious consideration. But Papon was quickly joined by others equally concerned to preserve untarnished the name of troubadour and Le Grand had not completed his collection before he saw himself obliged to enter the lists.[88] In 1781 he published the *Observations sur les Troubadours* not only to defend the statements made in the preface to the first volume of the *Fabliaux ou Contes* but equally to establish the validity of the evidence he had cited in support of his cause, the *Histoire littéraire des Troubadours*. The *Observations* were meant to put an end to all argument, but since we know already that the "querelle des trouvères et des troubadours" would continue to rage for some considerable time after their publication, we might review them as they appear in the third edition of the *Fabliaux ou Contes* published in 1829. A. A. Renouard considered it important to include here

---

[85] Numerous remarks Le Grand makes in the course of the collection are clearly meant to give an impression of impartiality. Cf. for example, vol. I, preface, pp. lx-lxi; vol. IV, the Avertissement following the preface to the "Contes dévots"; *Observations sur les Troubadours*, p. 31, pp. 165-166.

The *Mercure* was later to accuse Le Grand of partisanship but he firmly denied this: "Lorsque j'entrepris d'examiner la question des Troubadours, je cherchais la vérité. A force de recherches je crus l'avoir trouvée, et alors je publiai mes remarques, qui par la faiblesse des réponses qui m'ont été faites jusqu'ici me paraissent aujourd'hui démontrées. Mais je déclare sur mon honneur que si, au lieu d'être né Picard, je fusse né Languedocien ou Provençal, je ne les eusse pas moins publiées." (*Ms. Paris, B.N. n.a.f. 6227*, fol. 24.)

[86] *Observations sur les Troubadours*, p. 7.

[87] Cf. *Année Littéraire*, 1782, vol. IV, pp. 329-330: "... ce jugement de M. le Grand, quelque motivé, quelqu'équitable qu'il soit, a excité une espece de querre littéraire: on sait que les têtes méridionales s'échauffent facilement. Les partisans & les compatriotes des Troubadours, ont sonné le tocsin sur celui qui leur enlevoit leur gloire ...".

[88] It is in the Avertissement following the preface to the "Contes dévots" in vol. IV that Le Grand asks his readers not to condemn him before he has had time to defend himself. At this stage, of course, he was still hoping to add to the collection a supplement containing the remaining three out of the four romances he had wished to include in volume IV.

all those additions which Le Grand himself had prepared for a third edition of his collection:

Mais attaqué, il s'est très bien défendu, et réimprimer les dissertations sans leurs nouveaux développements eût été priver l'auteur des avantages d'une légitime défense, et passer condamnation sur des reproches dont il démontre l'injustice.[89]

Since the case against the troubadours rests almost entirely upon the Sainte-Palaye – Millot collection, it is only to be expected that Le Grand first concern himself with those who claim this presents no true picture of Provençal poetry. Papon, for example, insists that if the pieces contained in the *Histoire littéraire des Troubadours* appear insufferably boring, then the fault lies with the translator, for the eternal theme of the troubadours, love, is enhanced in the original Provençal with a wide variety of images and turns of phrase, whereas in the modern French version there is no such diversity.[90] This objection, raised also by the Abbé de Fontenay,[91] fails to impress Le Grand who scorns Papon's efforts to demonstrate with quotations the "beauties" of the poetry composed by the much maligned rhymers of the South:

Pour moi, je puis me tromper; mais de bonne foi je doute fort que celles-ci ajoutent beaucoup à l'idée qu'on a d'eux.[92]

Although modern critics would agree that the love lyrics of the troubadours can prove monotonous reading,[93] it would seem that the translations appearing in the *Histoire littéreraire des Troubadours* could have been more skilfully executed. Sainte-Palaye himself was largely responsible for these, Millot, unacquainted with the Provençal originals, making only slight modifications in respect of style,[94] and we know already that this great scholar appeared to be little concerned with the poetic abilities of the troubadours:

[89] *Fabliaux ou Contes* (1829) vol. I, avis de l'Editeur, p. vii.
[90] *Voyage littéraire de Provence*, Paris (Moutard) 1787, vol. II, pp. 259–260.
[91] *Affiches de Province*, 1780, no. 8.
[92] *Observation sur les Troubadours*, p. 11. Le Grand notes here that of all his critics Papon is alone in "daring" to cite examples of troubadour verse.
[93] Cf. E. Hoepffner: *Les Troubadours dans leur Vie et dans leurs Oeuvres*, Paris (Armand Colin) 1955, p. 18: "Comme partout, dans une foule pareille, la médiocrité domine. A première vue, à les lire d'affilée, les chansons occitanes, notamment les chansons d'amour, produisent l'effet d'une grande monotonie. On a pu dire autrefois qu'après avoir lu un de ces poètes, on les connaît tous."
[94] Cf. *Histoire littéraire des Troubadours*, Avertissement, vol. I, pp. x-xi: "Quoi qu'il en soit, le mérite de cet ouvrage appartient spécialement à M. de Sainte-Palaie. Je n'ai fait que mettre en oeuvre avec plaisir les matériaux qu'il a rassemblés avec tant de peines. J'ai suivi ses traductions, en donnant au style une tournure plus libre & plus variée. Ses remarques & celles de ses premiers coopérateurs m'ont épargné l'ennui des recherches."

The dull, monotonous translations were substantially his, as were too the literary judgements and comments. He himself had shown his lack of feeling for the literary value of the poems and had pointed the way to an external exploitation of them as source material for the historian, or, at best, elements of a picturesque décor.[95]

Nevertheless, the *Journal de Littérature, des Sciences et des Arts* seconds Le Grand in refusing to allow any blame on the part of the translators:

Il est certain que le Traducteur d'un Ouvrage peut le faire lire avec plus ou moins de plaisir; mais dès qu'on suppose qu'il le comprend, il ne peut nous en cacher le sens, le plan, l'invention, &c. & rien de tout cela n'est agréable dans les Poësies monotones des Troubadours.

Moreover, had not this verse been translated by the most learned of men, perhaps the only ones capable of an accurate rendering.[96]

Less justified perhaps is Fontenay's suggestion that Sainte-Palaye's initial researches left much to be desired, that a good deal of Provençal poetry still lies buried in the archives and libraries of southern France and of Italy so that any attempt at a critical appreciation of this must for the moment be subject to question.[97] The argument is ill-founded as Le Grand makes plain. He had worked with Sainte-Palaye and knew him to be the most careful and meticulous of scholars. He is certain that his former master left no stone unturned in his search for manuscript sources. Further investigation is not warranted:

... je conseille aux curieux qui voudroient se dévouer à ces fouilles ingrates de ne point les entreprendre s'ils sont jaloux d'employer utilement et leur temps et leurs peines.[98]

How can Fontenay believe that scholars may yet make vital new discoveries when one remembers that Sainte-Palaye's own researches

[95] L. Gossman, *Medievalism*, p. 321.
[96] *Journal de Littéraire des Sciences et des Arts*, 1782, vol. IV, p. 53. Cf. L. Gossman, *Medievalism*, p. 313: "The reduction of his [Sainte-Palayes's] material into a few volumes of extracts could not be left to others, since it demanded an ability to read the texts which few besides himself possessed."
[97] Cf. also Mayer's "Observations critiques sur les 'Fabliaux ou Contes'" in the *Mercure*, April, 1780, pp. 151–152.
[98] *Observations sur les Troubadours*, p. 12. L. Grossman remarks upon the thoroughness of Sainte-Palaye's survey of the manuscript sources of Old Provençal poetry and cites part of a letter written in 1742 where the great scholar himself expresses the desire to make his study a definitive one: "Si l'ouvrage est par lui mesme très ingrat, j'espère le rendre si complet que personne après moi ne sera plus tenté d'y perdre son tems." (L. Gossman, *Medievalism*, pp. 303–307.)
In his fourth appendix Gossman lists Sainte-Palaye's copies of Provençal "chansonniers" (pp. 365–366) and in his fifth those troubadours mentioned or discussed for the first time in the *Histoire littéraire des Troubadours* (pp. 367–368).

produced fifteen volumes in-folio, embracing four thousand individual items, twelve hundred fragments.[99] Then again, Millot had quite naturally included in the *Histoire littéraire des Troubadours* only the finest of these pieces:

> Or l'on conviendra qu'il y a là de quoi asseoir un jugement, et que par conséquent on peut sans scrupule après cela prononcer sur le talent des troubadours.[100]

There is, of course, the consideration, and Le Grand does not take this into account, that Millot's choice of poems had in fact been dictated by that historical bias, so obvious in his preface to the collection, which he shared with Sainte-Palaye.[101] If anyone, then, it is the editor who is at fault here, certainly not the researcher.

Papon's own efforts to prove the *Histoire littéraire des Troubadours* unrepresentative of Old Provençal poetry do not end with his indictment of the translator. There is, he says, a great deal of evidence to suggest that the troubadours were responsible for a large number of romances and "contes" which have simply not survived to be viewed by eighteenth-century scholars.[102] But Le Grand demands to see the original texts and points out that the few titles cited, "... n'offrant qu'un nom ...", prove nothing and in any case include "dits," moralities and "sirventes." Nor will he accept the perfection of the Provençal language as proof that the troubadours produced works far superior to those which have been preserved.[103] For a language, he insists, is not brought to perfection by the great authors who use it. Indeed, a nation cannot hope to produce writers of any merit until her language is fixed and has already attained a certain degree of perfection. It follows

---

[99] Cf. *Histoire littéraire des Troubadours*, Avertissement, vol. I, p. cviii: "Quinze volumes 'in-folio,' contenant les pièces provençales, avec les variantes des différents manuscrits; huit autres volumes d'extraits, où ces pièces sont en partie traduits, où chacune est désignée dans l'ordre alphabétique des auteurs; sans parler du glossaire, des tables, & d'une infinité de notes: voilà un des nmonumens les plus extraordinaires du courage que peut inspirer à l'homme de Lettres, non l'ambition ou l'intérêt, mais le seul désir d'acquérir des connoissances & les communiquer."

[100] *Observations sur les Troubadours*, p. 13.

[101] Cf. L. Gossman, *Medievalism*, p. 318: "The works which he judged worthy of reproduction in full or at length were those which threw light not so much on the literature of the troubadours as on the religious and political controversies and on the social conditions of their age".

[102] *Voyage littéraire de Provence*, vol. II, pp. 224–225. Cf. also Bérenger's *Porte-feuille d'un Troubadour*, note to p. 81: "Les guerres qui, durant trois cents ans dévastèrent la Provence, ont dévoré des Manuscrits précieux, les seuls peut-être d'après les quels on eût pu juger du mérite des Troubadours d'une manière irréfragable ...".

[103] *Voyage littéraire de Provence*, vol. II, pp. 228–230.

therefore that a rich and harmonious idiom like Provençal can exist without there being any great literary genius to exploit it:

... et prétendre que la romane provençale a eu beaucoup de bons ouvrages, parce qu'elle étoit supérieure à la romane françoise, c'est avancer que l'agriculture a nécessairement été florissante dans un pays parce que le sol y étoit de bonne qualité.[104]

Although Le Grand accepts that a number of troubadour productions must have been lost or destroyed during the five or six hundred years separating the eighteenth century from the period of their composition, he would point out that time has most certainly treated the works of the "trouvères" with no greater respect. How is it that what remains of these latter includes a number of pieces of some considerable merit whereas dismal "sirventes" and mournful songs of love are almost all that is left of Provençal poetry? Can it be that time delighted in obliterating only the finest examples of this, or that copyists all came to some agreement whereby they would set down only the most mediocre compositions of the troubadours? If these latter had produced either romances or fabliaux then surely specimens of them would have been preserved, for it is to be remembered that the poets of the southern provinces have enjoyed one important advantage over their colleagues in the North, that of having not only their names and biographies but also a number of their works recalled to mind by historians both in France and in Italy.[105] The "trouvères" have had no such good fortune:

Les ouvrages de ceux-ci, ainsi que leurs noms, sont restés dans le plus profond oubli jusqu'à Fauchet, qui le premier enfin a réveillé leur mémoire, mais qui assurément n'a pas réveillé le désir de les connoître.[106]

Determined to establish the former literary pre-eminence of the trou-

---

[104] *Observations sur les Troubadours*, p. 15. In the first chapter of *La Poésie lyrique des Troubadours* Alfred Jeanroy asks why lyric poetry should have originated in the southern province of France and remarks: "... alléguer la formation précoce d'une langue 'riche e sonore,' c'est commettre un véritable paralogisme. C'est précisément la poésie qui perfectionne la langue et au prix de longs efforts; et tous les dialectes de l'Europe méridionale fournissaient des ressources équivalentes à celles qui furent utilisées uniquement par nos compatriotes du Midi." (Vol. I, p. 64.)

[105] A considerable amount of attention was indeed given to the troubadours in the 16th, 17th and early 18th centuries, but very few texts were published. Cf. A. Jeanroy, *La Poésie lyrique des Troubadours*, vol. I, pp. 2–24. Jeanroy points out that the Sainte-Palaye-Millot collection was in fact the first literary history of the troubadours to appear. The thrid section of the introduction to *La Poésie lyrique des Troubadours* opens with the remark: "Ce qui manquait encore, à la fin du XVIIIe siècle, c'était l'instrument essentiel, unique, de tout travail sérieux, un recueil de textes soigneusement publiés." (Vol. I, p. 13.)

[106] *Observations sur les Troubadours*, p. 17.

badours despite the absence of documentary evidence, Papon points to the glorious reputation once enjoyed by the poets of the South, celebrated not only in Italy but in France in England and in Spain.[107] The author of the *Voyage littéraire de Provence* is by no means the first to argue thus[108] and we might remember that in the preface to the first volume of the *Fabliaux ou Contes* Le Grand in fact sees the exaggerated renown of the Provençal poets to be primarily attributable to the blind acceptance by the French of the Italians' "panégyriques trompeurs":

On les a crus de grands hommes, parce que Pétrarque & le Dante les chantèrent ....[109]

Papon's remarks now provide him with an opportunity to examine in greater detail the whole question of the popularity of Provençal poetry in medieval Europe.

It is only natural, says Le Grand, that the Italians should have acclaimed the troubadours for their idiom greatly resembled Provençal and at the time they could boast no poets of their own. This no doubt also explains the spread of the language and poetry of the troubadours into Aragon and Catalonia, ". . . lorsque les rois d'Aragon, comtes de Barcelonne, devinrent, par un mariage, comtes de Provence."[110] A knowledge of the songs composed by the poets of France's southern provinces became a matter of pride as much as of pleasure amongst the nobles in these lands and for this reason they set themselves to learning the language of the troubadours. But it should be emphasized that the nobility alone is concerned here, for it is to be noted that when those territories beyond the Alps and the Pyrenees once began producing

---

[107] *Voyage littéraire de Provence*, vol. II, p. 210.

[108] Cf. N. Edelman, *Attitudes of seventeenth-century France toward the Middle Ages*, p. 346: "What need is there of proving the high rank they reached in poetry? Have not the Italians themselves amply demonstrated their admiration for Provençal literature and have they not learned much from it? Read Speroni, Bembo, Equicola, Dante, and especially Petrarch, who begins his list of Provençal poets in the 'Trionfi' with the troubadour Arnaut Daniel. Thus boasts Pasquier." The reference is to the fourth chapter of Book VII of Pasquier's *Recherches*.

[109] Pp. iv-v. A critic of Le Grand's views writing in the *Mercure* for April 1780 refuses to waste his time proving what is already established beyond all doubt: "Vous croyez peut-être que mon projet est de combattre cette opinion [i.e. Le Grand's view that Old French literature owes little to Provence and the troubadours]. Point du tout, Messieurs; je n'ai ni assez de temps, ni assez de courage pour me livrer à la recherche des Monumens qui pourroient faire triompher le sentiment contraire, déjà suffisamment appuyé sur la croyance de plusieurs siècles, & sur le témoignage des Italiens, qui avouent sans détour les nombreux services dont leur poésie ... est redevable à la Poésie Provençale." (P. 103.)

[110] *Observations sur les Troubadours*, p. 21. Cf. A. Jeanroy, *La Poésie lyrique des Troubadours*, vol. I, pp. 186–188.

verse in imitation of the Provençal, all but one of the poets involved were of the upper classes:

.. quant au corps de la nation dans ces contrées, je soutiens qu'il n'entendoit et ne pouvoit entendre les poésies provencales.[111]

When the Italian language became fashionable in Paris in the seventeenth century a large number of courtiers and ladies boasted a knowledge of it, writers frequently cited their Italian colleagues and some even composed verse in their tongue. But for all this Italian remained for the Nation as a whole foreign and altogether unintelligible:

Telle est, dans la plus exacte verité, l'histoire de ce qui arriva en Italie au temps des troubadours. Voilà ce qu'auroient dû savoir leurs panégyristes; et voilà ce qu'ils n'ont pas dit.[112]

Although Le Grand will agree that Provençal poetry may well have penetrated into England, he will not accept that it ever became popular there, and this, he says, is all that matters. In the first place the English spoke the language introduced by William the Conqueror, French, and could not understand Provençal.[113] And in the second, they were totally enraptured by the romances of chivalry:

... et l'on conviendra que les héros de la 'Table-ronde,' avec leurs exploits fameux et la magie de leur protecteur Merlin, étoient bien plus faits pour intéresser, que de fades chansons et des sirventes.[114]

Had the troubadours been celebrated in England, as is suggested, then surely some English poet would have been tempted to distinguish himself in their idiom. The *Histoire littéraire des Troubadours* lists one hundred and forty troubadours whose countries of origin are known, but only one is said to hail from England and that one is Richard I. And what has been said of England can be applied equally to the northern provinces of France. Far from being sought after, the Provençal poets were no better known here than they were across the Channel, for the two halves of the country simply spoke different languages. Le Grand admits that he himself would have found it most difficult to understand the original Provençal had it not been for Sainte-Palaye's commentaries.[115] Moreover, he cannot recall one single passage where a trou-

---

[111] *Observations sur les Troubadours*, p. 24.
[112] *Ibidem.*
[113] Cf. a note to "Des deux Anglais," *Fabliaux ou Contes*, vol. II, pp. 108–109.
[114] *Observations sur les Troubadours*, p. 25.
[115] The *Journal de Monsieur* insists that for this reason Le Grand must be declared incompetent to judge: "Il est donc très-probable que M. le Grand s'est trompé en jugeant des Ouvrages qu'il a tant de peine à comprendre, & en appellant au secours de son opinion les

badour makes reference to the "trouvères" or a "trouvère" to the troubadours.[116]

What now, asks Le Grand, of the dazzling reputation which the troubadours are supposed once to have enjoyed? We have seen that they were in fact unknown not only to a large part of Europe but to the finest half of France, that preferred by the Nation's rulers. And even if their past fame has in no way been exaggerated, this can prove nothing. We are not concerned to know if Provençal poets were applauded, rather if they merited this applause. No work has received greater praise over the centuries than the *Roman de la Rose*, and yet France has produced no more boring or mediocre a composition:

> ... c'est ce mauvais poème qui, en introduisant chez nous les insipides personnages de 'Bel-accueil,' de 'Bon-vouloir,' de 'Male-bouche,' et autres pareils, a gâté le goût des François, ou plutôt a introduit chez eux, pour plusieurs siècles, le mauvais goût ... à l'exception de cinq ou six vers qu'on a retenus, il n'a absolument d'autre mérite pour plaire, que l'allégorie libertine qu'il présente.[117]

It is in the light of such a phenomenon that we begin to see the true value of the compliments paid to the troubadours by the Italians. And if there are those who would yet deny the insignificance of these, let them turn to the *Histoire littéraire des Troubadonrs*, where we are inform-

---

traductions insipides de l'Historien des Troubadours. Enfin il est impossible de décider du mérite de leur poésie, sans une intelligence parfaite de la Romane Provençale, comme il n'est pas possible de bien apprécier les vers de Pétrarque, si l'on ne connoît pas supérieurement toutes les délicatesses de la langue Italienne." (1782, vol. III, pp. 293–294).

It would be interesting to know just how well versed in Old Provençal Le Grand was. In the *Observations sur les Troubadours* he remarks that through his association with Sainte-Palaye "... je me vis enfin à portée d'apprécier les poètes des deux langues." (P. 2). We can probably assume that he exaggerates the difficulty he had with the language in order to give added weight to his argument.

[116] Cf. A. Jeanroy, *La Poésie lyrique des Troubadours*, vol. I, ch. VI, "La poésie provençale dans la France du nord et en Allemagne," p. 267: "Très peu de troubadours nous sont connus pour avoir visité les pays de langue d'oïl ...".

We might note that Jeanroy sees the adoption of courtly poetry in Germany and northern France to have been prompted by a kind of "snobisme aristocratique" (p. 275) which is how Le Grand explains in part the popularity of Provençal verse in Italy and Spain.

[117] *Observations sur les Troubadours*, p. 27. N. Edelman discusses at some length the popularity of the *Roman de la Rose* in seventeenth-century France: "If we consider not only the frequency but the intensity of praise, the 'Roman de la Rose' stood uppermost in renown." (*Attitudes of Seventeenth-Century France toward the Middle Ages*, pp. 383–394.)

An edition of the *Roman de la Rose* published in Amsterdam and Paris in 1735 by Lenglet du Fresnoy was reprinted in Paris in 1798 by Jean-Fréd.-Bernard and revised by J. B. Lantin de Damerey. An extract of the *Roman de la Rose* appears in Tressan's "Corps d'extraits de Romans de Chevalerie" which forms volumes VII-X of the *Oeuvres choisies du Comte Tressan* (Paris, 1787–1791) vol. VII, Paris, 1788, pp. 318–345. On this latter, cf. H. Jacoubet, *Le Comte de Tressan*, pp. 250–251.

ed that Arnaut Daniel's reputation is a gross exaggeration for which Dante and Petrarch are primarily responsible.[118]

If Le Grand insists that little importance is to be attached to the Italians' panegyrics, he is most willing to acknowledge that those territories beyond the Alps owe an immense debt of gratitude to the Provençal poets and had every reason to sing their praises. For the troubadours can boast the most honourable distinction of having inspired Italy with a taste for lyric poetry in the vernacular and of having provided her first models in the genre. Concerned only, as he says, to ensure that credit is given where credit is due, Le Grand will continue to attribute this distinction to the troubadours until the Italians can furnish sufficient evidence to prove him in error. Bartoli's argument[119] he finds unconvincing:

> Pour moi, qui ai cru pouvoir disputer à ces rimeurs un mérite qu'ils n'ont pas, mais qui me fais un devoir de reconnoître celui qu'ils ont réellement, j'avoue avec impartialité que si parmi les arguments du savant antiquaire il en est beaucoup qui m'ont paru concluants, il en est aussi qui ne m'ont point convaincu, et sur lesquels j'attends les preuves nouvelles qu'il promet.[120]

These remarks are not to be misconstrued as indicating some partial capitulation on Le Grand's part. Already in the preface to the first volume of the *Fabliaux ou Contes* he had credited the troubadours with this most significant contribution to the advancement of letters. And this remains Le Grand's only concession, for he would point out that once the Italian poets began composing verse in their own idiom, and not one of those who rhymed in Provençal is worth remembering, they quickly surpassed their former teachers who, despite a glorious reputation, were soon no longer deemed worthy of mention, a point which the editor of the *Histoire littéraire des Troubadours* himself acknowledges.[121] Those essentially responsible for the decline of Provençal poetry, Petrarch and Dante, were in fact those who did most to ensure that the names of the troubadours would not be entirely forgotten. But

---

[118] *Histoire littéraire des Troubadours*, vol. II, p. 481 : "De pareilles autorités ont paru comme infaillibles aux Italiens des siècles suivans, occupés du même sujet: ils ont fait d'Arnaud le prince du Parnasse provençal."

[119] *Observations sur les Troubadours*, p. 30: "Loin que leurs troubadours aient été les premiers à faire renaître au-delà des Alpes le goût des lettres, il avance au contraire que les études y furent antérieures au siècle où ceux-ci commencèrent à rimer."

[120] *Idem*, p. 31.

[121] Discours préliminaire, vol. I, p. lxxiv: "En effet, le Dante, à la fin du treizième siècle, donna l'essor du génie à la langue italienne. Dès ce moment, on la vit fort supérieure au provençal. Pétrarque parut, l'amour l'inspira, & sous le ciel même de Provence, il fit enten-

despite all their efforts an amazingly short period of time elapsed before these names were indeed lost to mind.

If the troubadours fell rapidly from favour, objects the *Journal de Monsieur*, then it is simply that lyric poetry does not fare quite so well in translation as the genre of the "conte," and once the two "romanes" used by the poets of the northern and southern provinces of France had become unintelligible to the greater part of the Nation it was only in translation that their works could be appreciated.[122] The "trouvères" had everything to gain by appearing in a far superior, more polished idiom for it is the naivety and interest of the narrative that constitutes their greatest appeal. The troubadours, on the other hand, could only lose by any such "metamorphosis":

> L'intérêt de cette sorte de poésie est tout entier dans les images, les sentimens, l'harmonie, & les tournures propres à un certain idiôme. Tout cela ne peut se conserver dans un autre.[123]

And whereas the "conte" loses nothing of its appeal in prose, the lyric poem is stripped of all its charm. The argument is reasoned and Le Grand's reply here is perhaps not altogether satisfactory. He would agree with the *Journal de Monsieur* in principle but adds:

> ... quand un morceau lyrique offrira une fiction agréable; quand, à la grâce de l'expression, il joindra encore la séduction du sentiment et le charme de la volupté, alors peut-être il pourra conserver, dans une langue étrangère, une partie de sa beauté.[124]

The qualification "peut-être il pourra" would suggest that Le Grand sees the value of the objection raised, and surely the "fiction agréable" is, as the *Journal de Monsieur* points out, far more essential to the "conte" than to the lyric poem. Then again, Le Grand insists that if Boccaccio

---

dre des sons si mélodieux, des vers si élégans; en un mot, il éclipsa tellement les troubadours, que leur nom, leur langage & leurs poésies disparurent presque entièrement aux yeux de l'Europe."

These lines are cited by Le Grand in the *Observations sur les Troubadours*, pp. 33–34. A. Jeanroy examines the fortunes of Provençal poetry in Italy in the fifth chapter of his *Poésie lyrique des Troubadours*, vol. I, pp. 229–265.

[122] "J'ignorois," remarks Le Grand, "que les rimeurs dont nous parlons eussent été traduits; et je croyois que leur mémoire avoit péri, avant que le temps eût procuré en France cet honneur à aucun d'eux." (*Observations sur les Troubadours*, p. 34.)

[123] *Journal de Monsieur*, 1782, vol. III, pp. 292–293. Cf. also L. P. Bérenger, *Porte-feuille d'un Troubadour*, pp. 90–91: "... ce sont des Contes, & cela se traduit dans toutes les langues; le noeud, les situations restent; mais il est un peu plus difficile de traduire nos chansons, pleines de ces finesses & de ces grâces qui tiennent au génie d'un idiôme délicat & poli ...".

[124] *Observations sur les Troubadours*, p. 35.

remains enjoyable in translation while Petrarch tends to bore, it is not for the reasons adduced by his opponent. Neither poet nor prose-writer gains anything when rendered into a foreign tongue, but Petrarch is devoid of ideas, ". . . il n'a guère que de l'harmonie et du style . . .".[125] and therefore suffers more than Boccaccio whose artistry and diversity are preserved despite the translator. Surely this is in essence the argument of the *Journal de Monsieur*, that by its very nature the lyric poem must lose far more than the "conte" when translated into foreign prose.[126] But even if this were true, adds Le Grand, one fundamental objection would still remain valid:

... et je demanderois, comme je l'ai déjà fait, pourquoi donc les troubadours n'ont pas composé de contes.[127]

Le Grand is quite prepared to acknowledge that, as the *Journal de Monsieur* notes, the "trouvères" themselves were eventually to be eclipsed, to suffer the same fate as the Provençal poets.[128] Already in the preface to the first volume of his collection he had had occasion to remark upon this most regrettable fact:

... nos Poëtes, oubliés tout-à-coup avec leurs compositions, n'ont laissé d'eux aucunes traces.[129]

But he would remind his critic that the literary world had every reason to continue to honour the name of "troubadour":

... les troubadours tant vantés par les beaux-esprits d'Italie, et qui jouirent d'une réputation 'si étonnante,' comment, avec ces éloges, cette renommée, ce mérite, ont-ils donc été tout-à-coup si complètement oubliés?[130]

In Le Grand's opinion no satisfactory reply has yet been made to this question.

Papon is amongst those who insist that if the trouvères had shown any talent they would most certainly have been acclaimed in Italy,

---

[125] *Ibidem.*

[126] It would have been impossible for us to construe Le Grand's argument this way if he had simply stated that, as he believes, Petrarch is inferior to Boccaccio.

[127] *Observations sur les Troubadours*, p. 36. Perhaps this question, first posed in the preface to the first volume of the *Fabliaux ou Contes*, is a valid one. But from the preceding remarks here it is almost as if Le Grand is suggesting that the troubadours should have agreed among themselves to cultivate only those genres which fare well in translation.

[128] *Journal de Monsieur*, 1782, vol. III, pp. 293–294.

[129] P. cvi.

[130] *Observations sur les Troubadours*, p. 36.

whereas this nation reserved its applause solely for the troubadours.[131] But were it true that the Italians had no words of praise for the poets of France's northern provinces, then this silence, claims the author of the *Fabliaux ou Contes*, could prove nothing. It would be only natural for the inhabitants of those territories beyond the Alps to show no knowledge of the productions of the "trouvères" since they did not understand the language in which they were composed.[132] The "trouvères" for their part say nothing of the Italian poets, but this does not mean that the latter were without ability. In any event, both Dante and Petrarch cite and commend works originating in northern France,[133] and are not the numerous verse romances which have appeared in Italy over the last two or three centuries simply imitations, translations, or supplements of those of the "trouvères"? Papon himself admits to having found manuscripts of French romances in Italian libraries.[134] Finally the present collection will prove beyond all doubt that the great Boccaccio himself owes his reputation to the "conteurs" of France's northern provinces:

Postérieur d'un siècle environ à la plupart d'entre eux, il les a copiés: le recueil que je publie en offrira la preuve; et cette preuve il est impossible de la détruire.[135]

For Le Grand, then, the position is this, that whereas the Italians owe

---

[131] *Voyage littéraire de Provence*, vol. II, p. 193: "Si c'est la France, Monsieur, qui a fourni aux Italiens les premiers modèles de la Poésie moderne, il faut avouer qu'elle a obligé des ingrats."

[132] This would appear contradictory to remarks made in the preface to the first volume of the *Fabliaux ou Contes* to the effect that the idiom of the trouvères penetrated to Naples and into Sicily with the Normans. Papon raises the point but the *Observations sur les Troubadours* as they appear in the third edition of Le Grand's collection include the following explanatory note: "... si les d'Hauteville 'portèrent' leur langue dans le royaume qu'ils conquirent, si peut-être elle y fut celle du gouvernement, je n'ai eu garde de dire qu'elle y devint pour cela la langue de la nation. D'ailleurs, y eût-elle été, comme en Angleterre, établie par la force, Naples et la Sicile ne font qu'une foible portion de l'Italie: on eût pu y parler la romane, sans que, pour cela, le reste des Italiens l'eût entendue." (P. 37.)

[133] *Observations sur les Troubadours*, pp. 37–39. Le Grand accurately notes that Dante knows Thibaut de Champagne and the *Lancelot*, mentions Charlemagne and *Roland* and considers that the domain of the "langue d'oïl" embraces "... all that has been composed and set down in prose." Cf. H. Hauvette, *La France et la Provence dans l'oeuvre de Dante*, Paris (Boivin) 1930 (Bibliothèque de la Revue des Cours et Conférences) pp. 147–170. Hauvette examines at some length Dante's acquaintance with medieval French literature, his knowledge of the prose versions of the romances and of the "chansons de geste." Hauvette also devotes a short section of his introduction to "La langue et la littérature françaises en Italie" (pp. 13–18).

[134] *Voyage littéraire de Provence*, vol. II, note to p. 224. Papon claims to have found manuscripts of romances but no collections of "contes". Le Grand remarks that few such collections exist but insists that if Papon had been more meticulous in his researches he would most certainly have come upon examples of the "conte" genre in those manuscripts of which he speaks. (*Observations sur les Troubadours*, pp. 19–20.)

[135] *Observations sur les Troubadours*, p. 40.

their taste for lyric poetry to the troubadours, they are thankful to the "trouvères" for their romances and their "contes." Yet there are those amongst the "Provençalistes" who, not content to deny the contribution made by the poets of France's northern provinces, claim that not only Italy but the whole of Europe first sought all literary inspiration in those territories south of the Loire. Indeed, they have been so bold as to proclaim the "trouvères" grateful to the South for their very language, for when Mayer published his "Observations critiques sur les Fabliaux ou Contes" in the Mercure for April 1780[136] his purpose was to prove Provençal literature "la mère de la Littérature françoise," the French language as it were the "daughter" of Provençal.[137]

In the preface to the first volume of his collection Le Grand had dealt only briefly with the question of language and had little to add when first replying to Mayer in the earlier edition of the *Observations sur les Troubadours*.[138] As they appear in the third edition of the *Fabliaux ou Contes*, however, these latter include a lengthy and most detailed treatise on the two "romanes," occupying well over a third of the dissertation.[139] Its purpose is to establish that the two idioms were not in fact "mother and daughter":

Les deux romanes sont des soeurs qui, pour employer la même façon de parler, ayant eu une même mère, mais un père différent, conservèrent pendant leur enfance quelques traits d'une origine commune, mais dont la res-

---

[136] Pp. 147–160.

[137] Mayer does not actually refer to Old Provençal as "la mère de la romance françoise," as Le Grand states in his *Observations* (p. 40), only to Provençal literature as the "mother" of French literature. But he does use the term "daughter" and seems to base his whole argument upon the belief that as a poetic idiom Provençal is much older than French: "Nous n'avons point de Pièces de Poésies en Romane Françoise avant le milieu du douzième siècle, & nous en avons en Romane Provençale depuis le commencement du onzième." ("Observations critiques sur les 'Fabliaux ou Contes'", p. 149.)

[138] *Fabliaux ou Contes*, second edition (1781) vol. II, pp. 48–50.

[139] It will be remembered that in his later years Le Grand was to undertake a history of the French language from its origins to modern times. Of the three major histories he planned this would appear to have been the only one ever to near completion. Early in 1799 he could remark of it: "Celle-ci est fort avancée. Déjà même ce qui en est la partie la plus difficile est fait en entier, puisque je l'ai conduite jusqu'au XIVe siècle et rédigée de premier jet. Ce travail, en l'état où il est, formerait un assez fort volume in-8°; et peut-être même, si la paix venait rendre au commerce de la librairie quelque activité, pourrais-je le publier l'an prochain; tandis que je continuerai de travailler pour en donner la suite." ("Notice sommaire sur les trois ouvrages auxquels je travaille," fol. 75.)

Amongst other manuscripts in Le Grand's hand the Arsenal library holds one containing just such a work: *Ms. Paris, Arsenal 6588*, ff. 1ro-30vo: "Histoire de la langue française, depuis son origine jusqu'à nos jours; ouvrage entrepris et fait en grande partie d'après les manuscrits de la Bibliothèque nationale." The additions made to that section of the *Observations sur les Troubadours* concerned with language were drawn from the researches undertaken for this projected history of the French language.

semblance s'altéra enfin tellement avec les années, qu'au temps de nos fabliers il étoit difficile de reconnoître en elles une même naissance.[140]
Following this discussion the history of Old French is continued to the
period of the "conteurs" and finally the reader is asked to compare the
extracts included here with the specimens of Old Provençal provided
for this purpose. For Le Grand this juxtaposition will demonstrate just
how dissimilar the two "romanes" had become by the twelfth century
and from this it will be clear ". . . qu'il est impossible que les troubadours aient pu devenir les instituteurs de notre nation et les maîtres de
nos poètes."[141]
It is at this point that Le Grand turns his attention to the criticism
levied against the evidence he presents in support of his second cause,
to prove the "trouvères" of France's northern provinces worthy of a
reputation far greater than that which they have so far enjoyed, to
criticism relating specifically to the fabliaux, his "pièces justificatives."[142] However, we must defer examination of the replies made here
since we have yet to discover precisely why, of all the genres cultivated
by the "trouvères," Le Grand should find the merit and ability of these
latter best evidenced in the "fabliaux ou contes." Thus, forgetting for
one moment the case for the "trouvères," let us further consider that
against the troubadours. Le Grand is clearly anxious to put an end to
all debate and having, as he believes, justified his preface and, as we
shall see, successfully upheld the fabliaux as irrefutable proof of the
former excellence of these poets of the North, he concerns himself in the
final section of the *Observations* with the various efforts made by his op-

---

[140] *Observations sur les Troubadours*, p. 41. Fauchet perhaps first introduced the idea that
Provençal had once been spoken throughout France before being relegated to the South. Cf.
Fauchet's *Recueil de l'Origine de la Langue et Poësie Françoise, Oeuvres*, ff. 539vo–540ro. L. Grossman notes that the idea was still enjoying considerable favour when Sainte-Palaye came to
question it in a paper read before the Académie des Inscriptions in March 1751: "Remarques sur la Langue Françoise des XIIe et XIIIe siècles comparée avec les Langues Provençale Italienne et Espagnole, dans les mêmes siècles. (*Mém. Acad. Inscr.*, vol. XXIV, pp.
671–686; also reprinted by J. M. C. Leber, *Collection des meilleures dissertations*, Paris 1826–
1838, vol. XIV, pp. 278–300 and by L. Favre in vol. X of his edition of Sainte-Palaye's
Glossaire, pp. 377–382.) Sainte-Palaye saw the similarity of the languages of northern and
southern France in the early stages of their development but considered that they ". . . began
to assume their distinctive characteristics at about the same time. His rejection of Provençal
as the mother of Old French was patent to his contemporaries." (L. Grossman, *Medievalism*,
pp. 207–209.)
[141] *Observations sur les Troubadours*, p. 106. "Les Francs, qui n'étoient que des Barbares,"
claims Mayer, "confièrent aux Troubadours le soin pénible de polir leur langue & leur
génie . . . ils devinrent les Précepteurs & les oracles des François." ("Observations critiques
sur les Fabliaux ou Contes," *Mercure*, April 1780, p. 148.)
[142] Cf. *Journal Encyclopédique*, 1780, vol. II, pt. I, p. 73: "Cette préface & la publication
des fabliaux qui servent comme des pièces justificatives pour ce qu'il contient fera tomber
plusieurs préjugés littéraires, & plusieurs opinions universellement répandues."

ponents to extol or at least exonerate the name of "troubadour" in the face of so much adverse publicity.

Just as in the preface to the first volume of the *Fabliaux ou Contes* Le Grand had thought to consolidate his position by noting other distinctions earned by the North, so the "Provençalistes" would sway public opinion by citing "additional" evidence of the former literary preeminence of the South. Both Papon and Mayer insist that the troubadours were not, as suggested, unpractised in dramatic composition, Mayer that they were in fact the originators of French theatre.[143] In reply Le Grand finds it sufficient to quote the *Histoire littéraire des Troubadours*:

... l'art dramatique fut toujours ignoré des troubadours.[144]

One other merit, in Papon's view, raises the troubadours far above their rivals in the North, that their works not only present "une peinture vraie & naturelle" of the manners and customs of the thirteenth century, but contain innumerable anecdotes concerning the private affairs of princes and other great personages, reveal hitherto unknown facts about important events like the crusades, offer a fund of the most interesting detail on private wars, on the clergy, on the Nation's oldest and most distinguished families.[145] We know already that for Le Grand such "minuties" were not the historian's primary concern:

[143] Cf. Papon, *Voyage littéraire de Provence*, vol. II, note to p. 251; also Mayer, "Observations critiques sur les Fabliaux ou Contes," p. 154: "Il n'est que trop vrai que les Drames des Troubadours n'existent plus: il est cependant bien plus vrai qu'ils sont les inventeurs du genre Dramatique. Jean & César Nostradamus, Bastero (dans la Crusca Provençale) leur en attribuent l'invention."

[144] Vol. I, p. 443. Le Grand also quotes from the Discours préliminaire to the *Histoire littéraire des Troubadours* where it is noted that Nostredame, cited in evidence by Papon as well as Mayer, helped to spread this erroneous notion. (Discours préliminaire, vol. I, pp. lxviii-lxix.) Cf. N. Edelman, *Attitudes of Seventeenth Century France toward the Middle Ages*, p. 344: "... noticing the lack of dramatic literature in the troubadours' output, he [Nostredame] converted 'tensons' into comedies." Nostredame's *Les Vies des plus célèbres et anciens poètes provençaux* is most severely criticized by Millot: "Ce qu'il y a de très-sur, c'est que les vies de Nostradamus, comparées à celles-ci, ne doivent passer que pour un recueil de fables, aussi défectueux par le fond que par la forme." (Discours préliminaire, vol. I, p. lxxvii.)

On Nostredame's influence in the 16th, 17th, 18th and 19th centuries, cf. the Chabaneau-Anglade edition of the *Vies*, Paris (Champion) 1913, ch. V, pp. 145-176.

[145] *Voyage littéraire de Provence*, vol. II, p. 255: "... les ouvrages des Troubadours forment un tableau, qui, malgré ses défauts, est précieux pour quiconque veut connoître l'homme, l'histoire, les familles, les usages & les moeurs."

This, of course, was one argument Le Grand could not refute by simply quoting the *Histoire littéraire des Troubadours*. Papon later suggests that the troubadours are to be read primarily for their "peinture vraie & naturelle des moeurs" and not for their poetic merits: "En général il ne faut pas chercher dans leurs ouvrages la richesse de l'invention, le choix & l'heureux enchaînement des pensées, l'art délicat des bienséances, ni enfin ce discernement qui présente les choses avec les différentes nuances que le goût & la nature assignent à chaque objet. Quoiqu'on y trouve quelquefois de ces morceaux que les siècles brillants de la littéra-

... il doit ... écrire non pour sa province, non même pour sa nation seule, mais pour tous les peuples qui sont cultivés, et qui lisent.[146]

And it is, he remarks, unjust of Papon to oppose the whole of Provençal poetry to what is in fact only a fraction of the output of the "trouvères," the fabliaux.[147] If the troubadours offer "une teinte de chevalerie,"[148] then the romances composed by their colleagues in the North present chivalry in its entirety:

J'ose même assurer, sans crainte d'être contredit, que si nous étions réduits, pour la connoître, aux seules lumières que peuvent nous fournir nos historiens anciens nous n'en aurions aujourd'hui que des notions très imparfaites: encore une fois, c'est dans nos romans que réside le véritable esprit de la chevalerie.[149]

But if what is sought is in fact "une peinture vraie & naturelle des moeurs," then Le Grand refuses to accept that one could do better than turn to the fabliaux. Indeed, it is to their socio-historical relevance that the success of his collection is largely to be attributed:

Qu'on me cite un seul ouvrage du temps où les moeurs de tous les états soient représentés avec autant de vérité, d'agrément et d'étendue que dans les fabliaux![150]

It becomes evident that the troubadours were destined to excel as poets, claims the Abbé de Fontenay, when one considers the enormous advantages they enjoyed. Imagination, sensibility, idyllic surroundings, a most favourable climate and a rich and harmonious idiom, surely these also help explain the great poetic masterpieces produced in ancient Greece and Rome. How can Le Grand seriously compare with the troubadours those insensitive poets of the foggy and frozen North with their clumsy, barbarian tongue so ridiculed by foreigners even in modern times.[151] But the comparison is a serious one and Le Grand would point out that the "trouvères" reigned supreme despite the pro-

---

ture ne désavoueroient pas, on ne doit considérer les Troubadours que comme peintres des moeurs d'une nation, qui, sans être entièrement civilisée, cessoit pourtant d'être barbare." (*Voyage littéraire de Provence*, vol. II, p. 262.) This was, of course, Millot's conclusion.

[146] *Observations sur les Troubadours*, p. 138.

[147] *Voyage littéraire de Provence*, vol. II, pp. 257–258: "Les fabliaux ,monsieur, ne présentent aucun de ces avantages ni pour l'histoire générale, ni pour celle des familles. La nation y est absolument muette."

[148] *Idem*, vol. II, p. 254: "Il y règne une teinte de chevalerie qui fait plaisir , & que n'ont pas les Ouvrages des Trouvères."

[149] *Observations sur les Troubadours*, p. 139.

[150] *Idem*, p. 140.

[151] *Affiches de Province*, 1780, no. 8.

blems posed by a language which, in fact, despite its imperfections, was then as it remains the most celebrated in Europe:

Elle n'a, ni la pompe majestueuse de l'espagnol, ni la force énergique de l'anglois, ni la douceur, l'accent, la flexibilité de l'italien; et cependant ses écrivains l'ont rendue la plus célèbre et la première des langues modernes.[152]

And quite apart from the fact that the skies of northern France are not, as Fontenay and Bérenger suggest, invariably overcast, climate has in any case little bearing upon the question. If weather and temperature did seriously influence poetic output and ancient Greece had these to thank for her glorious reputation, then those countries most favoured by the sun would produce the world's foremost men of letters, and surely modern Greece would be amongst the most fertile. Colder climes are not devoid of men of imagination and sensibility, for is it not the case that in the last century and a half English poets have far outnumbered the Italian. It may generally be true, as the *Journal de Monsieur* observes, that genius best flowers in those regions subject neither to enfeebling excessive heat nor numbing extreme cold,[153] but there are numerous significant exceptions to the rule. The Arabs live under a burning sun and yet no nation has had more glorious a history. Climate, like language, is not, then, the important factor:

... pour faire éclore et pour perfectionner chez un peuple les talents du génie, il faut plusieurs causes, tant physiques que morales, combinées ensemble, et ... si, dans ce nombre, on peut compter le climat, il est peut-être une des moins nécessaires.[154]

These remarks lead Le Grand quite naturally to a re-examination of that most curious of phenomenon, noted in the preface to the first volume of the *Fabliaux ou Contes*, whereby Nature would appear to have bestowed the gift of genius far more liberally in the North of France than in the South. The observation had brought forth a storm of protest, all the more vehement perhaps as Le Grand had not been able to

---

[152] *Observations sur les Troubadours*, pp. 143–144.
[153] *Journal de Monsieur*, 1782, vol. III, p. 302.
[154] *Observations sur les Troubadours*, p. 152. This is, in fact, very much akin to the conclusion drawn by the *Journal de Monsieur*: "Nous disons que, même à génie égal, les plus grands Poëtes doivent se trouver dans les climats ou l'instrument de la poésie est susceptible de plus grandes beautés, où la langue est plus favorable & plus docile à l'imagination. Mais ce n'est pas une raison pour que ces mêmes climats produisent toujours de grands Ecrivains. D'autres causes plus puissantes encore, les moeurs & le gouvernement influent sur le génie d'une Nation. Que sert un terrain fertile au peuple paresseux qui ne daigne pas le cultiver? Que sert la plus belle langue du monde à celui dont l'esclavage étouffe l'imagination & avilit l'âme?" (1782, vol. III, pp. 302–303.)

account for this odd state of affairs.[155] He now feels that he can offer some explanation, for it is not simply a matter of chance:

> Il paroît tenir à un autre fait qu'on ne peut contester: c'est la différence extrême qui subsiste entre les divers cantons de la France, non-seulement au physique, mais encore au moral.[156]

To see the justice of this one need only compare the inhabitants of contiguous provinces, those of Languedoc with those of Provence, the Picard with the Norman, the Norman with the Breton. They are all French but all have their own distinctive features, their own particular stamp, witness the innumerable proverbs in which these are caricatured. They differ even in the food they eat, the games they play and the work they choose to do. This variety is in itself inexplicable but perhaps not so very surprising when one considers that even the soil of France varies from province to province in the degree of its fertility, that even those regions equally blessed never produce exactly the same fruits:

> Et quand on voit une si grande différence entre les vins de Bordeaux et de Champagne, et ceux de Bourgogne ou de Roussillon, doit-on s'étonner que le Bourguignon, le Champenois, le Gascon et le Roussillonnois puissent différer en talents?[157]

Le Grand's arguments might appear a little more relevant if he could now proceed to demonstrate that France's southern provinces, though perhaps sadly lacking in literary talent, have produced the Nation's greatest minds in other spheres of activity. In fact, he cannot. All he can do is point once more to "the unequal distribution of genius":

> Il me semble au moins que, dans la plupart des arts et des sciences, ceux des François qui font époque, ceux qui les premiers les ont poussés à un degré de perfection inconnu avant eux, sont les compatriotes des trouveurs.[158]

When Le Grand had first declared these findings he had been rebuked in that letter which appeared in the *Mercure* for April 1780 attacking the *Journal de Paris* for approving the preface to the first volume of the *Fabliaux ou Contes*. In the letter it is observed that it is not talent which has lacked in the southern provinces but the atmosphere necessary to enable this to flourish. For centuries now gifted people here have been

---

[155] *Fabliaux ou Cintes*, vol. I, preface, pp. lii-liii: "J'ignore les causes de ce phénomène, & laisse à d'autres l'honneur de les découvrir."
[156] *Observations sur les Troubadours*, pp. 153–154.
[157] *Idem*, p. 156.
[158] Examples are provided for the various branches of the arts and sciences.

deprived of the benefits enjoyed by those who inhabit that part of the country honoured by the presence of the Court:

Ici, depuis le règne de Louis IX, la puissance de nos Rois a rassemblé autour du Trône tout ce qui lui prête de l'éclat, & en relève la majesté; ici, ont commencé les établissements utiles, les institutions honorables; ici, le désir de s'illustrer, auguillonné par la présence plus prochaine du Souverain, par l'appât des faveurs qu'il dispense, & par la vue de ceux qui, les premiers, les ont recueillies, a développé des talens dont le germe est par-tout, mais qui ne peuvent éclore que sous une influence favorable.[159]

In the capital there is great enthusiasm for the arts and for the poet or the painter this enthusiasm is both rewarding and inspiring. In the South a man considers that fate has dealt him an evil blow if his son takes up the pen or the brush:

L'esprit d'invention ressemble à l'Art de la déclamation. Ayez des Spectateurs, vous aurez bientôt des Acteurs. Créez des regards qui les admirent, & les hommes de génie vont naître.[160]

The explanation would appear more plausible than that offered by Le Grand himself, but it is dismissed without ceremony by this latter. In the first place he would object that, while Paris can bring talents to perfection, neither the capital nor the Court can help those without ability. The city itself has produced few great men of letters despite the many benefits which aspiring authors there enjoy. Secondly, these benefits are available to all Frenchmen and are not reserved for Parisians alone. Corneille hailed from Rouen, Bossuet from Dijon: the only advantage these had over Fléchier, who came to Paris from Avignon,[161] and Campistron, who was born in Toulouse, was the talent with which they were born. Finally, we are not concerned to know whether or not poetry was encouraged and patronized in the southern provinces of France, for genius will out:

... quand la nature accorde à quelqu'un qu'elle favorise un talent réel, elle lui donne en même temps cette impulsion irrésistible qui, malgré tous les obstacles, le ramène bientôt à sa vocation primitive, et le force de s'y livrer ... .[162]

---

[159] *Mercure*, April 1780, p. 105. For Mayer this explains why Provence has produced no great dramatists. Cf. Mayer's "Observations critiques sur les Fabliaux ou Contes," *idem*, p. 159.

[160] *Idem*, p. 109.

[161] Fléchier was born in Pernes in the former Comtat Venaissin (Vaucluse).

[162] *Observations sur les Troubadours*, p. 160.

The question is whether or not the South can boast any great authors, and the answer is that it cannot.

This last remark, Le Grand knows, will arouse some indignation. But he would point out that his sole object is to set down the facts as they appear to him, that he has no wish to belittle the efforts of any living author. On the contrary, those who, in the last quarter of the eighteenth century, are contributing most to France's literary prestige, are in fact the compatriots of the troubadours, not a few of whom manage to retain a certain modesty despite their obvious abilities. Such humility, however, is rare indeed in the South where people generally consider themselves naturally far more imaginative than all other Frenchmen. The Abbé de Fontenay sees them as "doués d'une sensibilité profonde, d'une imagination vive et brillante," and even this is scant praise when compared to Bérenger's eulogy of his Provençal compatriots:

Chez ces peuples aimables, l'activité est un privilège national; la gaîté, un héritage commun; le talent poétique ou le don de l'éloquence, une ressource ... Nul peuple n'est plus facile à émouvoir par des idées accessoires. Sa mobile imagination, sa prompte sagacité saisit toutes les relations des objets, franchit, supplée tous les intermédiaires ...163

And yet, though the southern provinces can now boast poets of some merit, they have not produced one who can be said to have led the way in his own particular genre, to match Corneille or Racine, Molière or Marivaux, Régnier or Boileau, Rousseau or Piron.164

This, then, is the case against the troubadours.165 In conclusion Le Grand would only reaffirm his own neutrality:

Eh! que m'importe à moi encore une fois le mérite des troubadours et celui de leurs neveux! Que les uns et les autres soient en poésie bien au-dessous de

---

163 Cited by Le Grand, *idem*, p. 162.

164 The *Journal de Monsieur* considers this "failure" to be largely attributable to the southerner's impetuosity: "On remarque dans nos meilleurs poètes plus de raison que d'enthousiasme, et le goût, la raison, le bon sens n'est pas ce qui domine dans les têtes provençales ... Il paroît que les poètes qui nous arrivent des provinces méridionales ont plus d'imagination et d'enthousiasme que nos autres poètes; mais cet enthousiasme ne sert qu'à augmenter les excès du mauvais goût, dont ils n'ont pu se préserver au milieu d'une contagion universelle." (1782, vol. III, p. 307.)

Le Grand, who feels that the periodical is here confusing imagination with impetuosity, points out that he himself, most ardent critic of the descendants of the troubadours, would not question their reason and good taste. (*Observations sur les Troubadours*, pp. 164–165.)

165 Our purpose has been only to survey the criticism levied against the author of the *Fabliaux ou Contes* for his insistence "... que les troubadours ne méritent pas à beaucoup près la renommée dont ils jouissent ...", and to note Le Grand's replies. In fact, numerous other objections raised by the "Provençalistes" in respect of this insistence are not answered in the *Observations sur les Troubadours*. However, a detailed examination of these would be of little relevance to our purposes here.

leur réputation, comme j'en suis convaincu, et comme je crois l'avoir prouvé, qu'en résultera-t-il pour ma gloire littéraire?[166]

He would have published these observations had he himself been of the South and would like to believe that men of letters here will view them with the same impartial eye. Their honour remains intact for the writer does not depend for his reputation upon those who have gone before him. If his homeland has thus far produced few great names, then it falls to him to render her name glorious:

... telle est la gloire à laquelle il doit prétendre, ou plutôt il ne doit être que François, ne connoître que la gloire de la France, et n'être jaloux que de celle-là seule.[167]

Although a considerable amount of space is given to the case against the troubadours, we have seen that the greater part of this is devoted to a justification of the proofs cited and not to the presentation of evidence, already abundant, in Le Grand's view, in the *Histoire littéraire des Troubadours* which his readers might consult for themselves. In the case for the "trouvères," however, the reverse is true. One or two pages, of the *Observations sur les Troubadours*, which have yet to be discussed, are seen as sufficient to demonstrate the validity of the "pièces justificatives" offered, these in fact accounting for the remainder of the collection, that is to say the full complement of extracts. This last remark may appear curious since we have indicated already that it was with the fabliaux that Le Grand would attempt to establish the former literary pre-eminence of northern France, and we know that his collection contains examples of numerous other genres, including fables, romances and "contes dévots." It could be argued that these latter are of only secondary importance, being relegated for the most part to the fourth volume. Yet a supplement was promised and we can assume that this was not without purpose. Admittedly it is not only the fabliaux

---

[166] *Observations sur les Troubadours*, pp. 165–166.

[167] *Idem*, p. 166. The *Mercure* for May 1782 considers that the *Observations* may well prove of service to modern writers in the South: "Que chacun ajoute ses observations à celles de M. le Grand: si elles confirmoient les siennes, il auroit rendu le service le plus éminent aux Provinces méridionales, en détruisant le préjugé qui engageoit peut-être leur jeunesse à se livrer à des ouvrages d'imagination, & à négliger le genre plus grave de la morale & de la philosophie, auquel leur génie paroît être plus propre. Il est beau d'être Racine ou Boileau, Chaulieu ou La Fontaine; mais les noms de Montaigne & de Montesquieu, de l'Hôpital & de Gassendi, ne se font pas entendre avec moins de plaisir." (P. 133.)

Bérenger thinks otherwise: "Il est certain que l'effet de la nouvelle brochure, je n'ose dire son but, pourroit être comme vous le remarquez très-bien, Monsieur, non-seulement d'armer la France contre elle-même, mais encore de nous jetter dans une erreur de vocation dont les suites seroient aussi funestes qu'irréparables." (*Porte-feuille d'un Troubadour*, p. 108.)

which Le Grand sees to be of great historical relevance, but the few notes occasioned by the extracts of other genres could not alone justify their inclusion in the collection. It is as we have said. The fables, "pastourelles," romances, even the "contes dévots" are as essential as the fabliaux to Le Grand's object, to prove the "trouvères" worthy of far greater esteem that they have hitherto enjoyed.

The position becomes clear when we recall how, in the preface to the fourth volume of the *Fabliaux ou Contes*, Le Grand bemoans the fate which medieval French literature has suffered at the hands of scholars less diligent than himself. These latter are seen to have committed a double crime by their abject refusal to go to the manuscripts in order to judge for themselves of the merits of France's earliest poets. Most regrettable of all, of course, is that in their ignorance they should have attributed to others the great honours won by their own forbears. Villaret might have been excused if, unaware that once before his homeland had been the admiration and inspiration of Europe in matters of literature, that the French could claim responsibility for the revival of poetic activity in the West, he had been content to remain silent on the subject of the Nation's literary heritage. But for Villaret to crown the Italians with these distinctions while denigrating those to whom they should rightly be given, this is an unpardonable sin in the eyes of a patriot such as Le Grand, who considers it his duty to remove all blemish from the honour of France:

Or, l'ouvrage que j'allois entreprendre me paroissoit tenir à la gloire de la France: j'allois être à portée de prouver que l'Occident doit aux François la renaissance de la poésie ... et cette seule idée m'inspiroit un courage infatigable.[168]

This, then, is Le Grand's primary concern here, to set before his countrymen the evidence necessary to correct the insulting notion propounded by Villaret and his like. But it is not his sole concern.

Villaret's crime is no more than an exaggerated extension of that perpetrated by the majority of his colleagues. His is the grossest form of misrepresentation in Le Grand's view, but others are condemned for failing, through this same rejection of manuscripts, in what is seen as a patriotic duty, for doing the Nation a great injustice without actually detracting from her international literary prestige. Velly may not declare the Italians to have been the poetic masters of medieval Europe but he displays such an ignorance of Old French literature as to de-

---

[168] *Observations sur les Troubadours*, p. 6.

scribe a ridiculous collection of Italian "contes dévots" as the finest remnant of this. The consequences of such an error are unthinkable. Already it would have been quite sufficiently irresponsible for him to cite collections of such tales genuinely composed in France as representing the limit of the abilities of the "anciens rimeurs." To be just, of course, he should have noted that these latter composed works which, considering the coarseness and stupidity of the age, must be applauded for their wit and imagination. But there would appear to have been a conspiracy on the part of historians to present the efforts of the Nation's first poets in the most unflattering, in the worst possible light. Even the "contes dévots" have suffered, for Racine, hailed by other critics as an authority whose instruction renders superfluous any first-hand knowledge of the texts, paints an altogether false picture of them in his paper on Coincy's *Miracles de Notre-Dame.* Just as the "contes dévots" are not to be thought representative of medieval Franch literature generally, so Racine's "Mémoire," dwelling upon the most inane examples of Coincy's work, must be dismissed as conveying no true impression of the "contes dévots." Although Le Grand himself insists that there is no comparison to be drawn between the "siècles d'ignorance" and the Century of Light, he nevertheless considers it unjust of the historian to condemn the whole of medieval society after some odd "anecdote monacale." Similarly in matters if literature, where all that is asked is justice for the "anciens rimeurs":

... je pense ... qu'il faudrait assez respecter nos Pères, pour ne leur faire au moins que les seuls reproches qu'ils méritent.[169]

Le Grand declares that he would quickly fill a whole volume were it his aim to draw attention to the many erroneous notions propounded by scholars on the subject of "nos vieux Poëtes." But this is not his object in the *Fabliaux ou Contes.* Nor is the collection envisaged as a history of French poetry, although such a study is still sadly lacking. It is, however, an integral part of Le Grand's purpose here to make good at least some of the damage done by Velly, Racine and even Massieu. If the extracts of the fabliaux will prove the "trouvères" of northern France to have been pre-eminent in medieval Europe, then those of other genres will testify to what, in view of the period, are the often considerable abilities of the "anciens rimeurs." These latter are perhaps not always worthy of loud applause, but neither do they invariably merit the contempt with which, more often than not, they are treated:

[169] *Fabliaux ou Contes,* vol. IV, Discours préliminaire to the "Contes dévots," p. xxxv.

On trouvera insérées parmi les Fabliaux, certains Pièces qui ne sont point des Contes: mais je regarde le recueil que je donne ici, comme des Mémoires faits pour servir à l'Histoire de notre ancienne Littérature, jusqu'à présent si peu connue. Quelques morceaux curieux, choisis dans différens genres, m'ont paru remplir ce projet; sur-tout quand je les ai trouvés instructifs & qu'ils ne s'éloignaient point trop du sujet principal.[170]

Firstly let us take the "contes dévots." We know that Le Grand sees the value of the particular historical insights which these provide but we know too that the fourth volume of the *Fabliaux ou Contes*, containing the majority of extracts of genres other than the fabliaux, is not explained by the few notes it offers.[171] Thus we can assume that the "contes dévots" are presented not primarily as documents of social history but as literature, although we have seen that Le Grand sets them apart from the rest of medieval French poetry and, generally speaking, has but little regard for them. In fact, it would not occur to him to proffer the "contes dévots" as a testimony to those abilities which, in his view, rendered "nos vieux Poëtes" supreme in medieval Europe:

En publiant les Fabliaux, j'ai cité les imitations qui en avaient été faites, & je l'ai même regardé comme un devoir, parce que ces imitations tenaient à la gloire de la Nation Française. Je ne cite point celles des Contes dévots, parce que ce n'est point là un Ouvrage que la France puisse se faire honneur de revendiquer.[172]

However, he is equally aware that modern critics have been a little too eager to voice their contempt for this genre, several examples of which are not without a certain appeal:

Quoique la plupart des Miracles ne prêtent réellement que trop au ridicule, comme je l'ai déjà dit; quoique le genre lui-même n'en soit pas exempt, on est forcé d'avouer néanmoins, (& ceux qui affectent tant de les mépriser eussent dû en convenir s'ils les avaient lus), qu'il s'y trouve nombre de morceaux agréables qu'on est tout surpris de rencontrer au milieu des platitudes les plus dégoûtantes. Je dirai plus: il se trouve plusieurs de ces Contes qui offrent de l'imagination, de l'esprit, de l'intérêt même, & jusqu'à une sorte d'art dans la narration.[173]

---

[170] *Idem*, vol. I, preface, p. xcv.
[171] Cf. the note to "Parténopex," vol. IV, p. 287, (a): "La plupart des usages dont il sera fait mention dans ce volume, ont déjà été expliqués dans les volumes précédens, comme je l'ai remarqué plus haut."
Earlier, in a note to "De l'Hermite qui mit son âme en plège pour celle d'un orfèvre," Le Grand remarks: "Presque tous les usages dont il est parlé dans les Contes dévots, ont été expliqués dans les Fabliaux." (Vol. IV, p. 114, note (a).)
[172] Note to "De l'Hermite que le diable enivra," vol. IV, p. 70.
[173] Discours préliminaire to the "Contes dévots," pp. xxxviii-xxxix.

For this reason, as we know, three examples of superior "contes dévots" are inserted amongst the "fabliaux ou contes" in the first three volumes of the collection[174] and almost two hundred pages of the fourth are devoted to a treatise on the genre and to additional extracts. The majority of these latter, comments Le Grand, have little more than their originality to recommend them, but one or two match those given earlier[175] and adequately serve his purpose here:

Ils suffiront pour modifier au moins le mépris, que jusqu'à présent on leur a prodigué à tous en général.[176]

A considerable number of fables by Marie de France are given in extract form in the fourth volume of the *Fabliaux ou Contes* since, as the author explains, Marie was perhaps the first French poetess and has so far been denied proper recognition.[177] Yet, however much Le Grand himself may esteem Marie and her work, and clearly he has no mean opinion of either,[178] he declines to list the imitations of more than one of her tales since these are not for the most part of her own invention[179]

---

[174] The collection in fact opens with one of these, "Merlin," of which Le Grand thinks highly. Cf. a note to this tale, vol. I, pp. 8–9: "Il n'est personne qui ne se rappelle ici le Bûcheron d'Esope imité par La Fontaine. Ce serait faire un honneur bien gratuit, peut-être, à l'Auteur de 'Merlin,' que de le supposer capable d' avoir connu le Fabuliste grec; mais au moins, s'il est imitateur, il a, sans le savoir, imité comme les grands maîtres & il faut convenir que la situation de ce père malheureux qui veut mourir parce qu'il va voir périr sa famille sans pouvoir la sauver, est bien autrement intéressante que celle d'un paysan fatigué qui demande la mort parce qu'il a trop de peine."
The second example, "De l'Hermite qu'un ange conduisit dans le siècle," opens the second volume of the collection and is described in a note to page 13 as a "fabliau." We know that Le Grand distinguishes between the fabliaux and the "contes dévots" but must assume that, in order to ensure a just appreciation of these latter, he does not wish to make the distinction clear to his readers at this stage. The third example, "Du Prud'homme qui avait été marchand," occupies pp. 183–190 of vol. III. Only in a note concluding the third volume of the *Fabliaux ou Contes* is it pointed out that these three tales are "contes dévots." (Pp. 439–441.)
[175] "De l'Hermite qui mit son âme en plège pour celle d'un orfèvre" is one of these. Cf. a note to this tale, vol. IV, p. 113. Here Le Grand again remarks upon the merits of "Merlin."
[176] Discours préliminaire to the "Contes dévots," p. xxxix.
[177] Cf. Vol. III, p. 441, note (b): "L'Abbé le Beuf qui nous a donné le nom de quelques femmes savantes de ces tems-là, ne parle point de celle-ci." The reference is to Lebeuf's *L'Etat des sciences en France, depuis la mort du roy Robert . . . jusqu'à celle de Philippe le Bel . . .*, Paris (Lambert et Durand) 1741.
[178] Speaking of Marie's moral purpose, he comments thus: "De pareils sentiments dans une femme de beaucoup de mérite, sont faits pour honorer son sexe; comme dans le tems ses écrits honorèrent son siècle. Marie fut la seule de ce siècle qui se livra au genre de la Fable; ce qui peut-être indique, plus que tout autre chose la solidité de son esprit & la justesse de son goût." (Avertissement préliminaire to the fables, vol. IV, pp. 152–153.)
[179] "Ceux qui, depuis Esope & Phèdre, ont fait des Collections de Fables, ont presque toujours réuni ces deux Auteurs; mais presque toujours aussi ils y en ont ajouté quelques-unes, tirées d'Auteurs étrangers ou plus modernes. C'est ce qu'a fait au XIIIe siècle Marie de France." (*Idem*, p. 158.)

and it matters little therefore how often foreign authors may have sought inspiration in them. The fable in question, "Le Villain et le Loup," is amongst the last to be extracted:

> Cette Fable est la seule de laquelle j'ai cité quelques imitations. Il m'eût été facile de faire la même chose pour le plus grand nombre des précédentes. Mais ces sujets n'étant point la plupart de l'invention de Marie, & par conséquent ne tenant point à l'honneur de la France comme nos Fabliaux, nous sommes moins intéressés à les revendiquer sur ceux qui pourraient les avoir pillés.[180]

Forgetting for one moment "Parténopex," which completes the fourth volume of Le Grand's collection, let us consider the importance of those extracts of other genres inserted amongst the "fabliaux ou contes" in the earlier volumes. In the first, for example, we find a "pastourelle,"[181] a genre much appreciated by Le Grand and one to which he might have devoted more space, even a full collection, had the tales concerned been less "free" and more varied. "Mais qui en lit une," he says, "en a lu mille."[182] Thus only one example is given to acquaint the reader with the type and to convey to him some impression of its merits:

> Cependant pour faire connaître à mes Lecteurs ce genre de poésie, je vais en donner une dont le dénouement est assez plaisant . . . .[183]

In contrast the third volume of the *Fabliaux ou Contes* contains extracts of six "romances" or "lais,"[184] this being a genre whose poor success Le Grand cannot explain and which he himself esteems so highly as to wish to claim it for the North despite the lack of imitators:

---

[180] Vol. IV, p. 241.

[181] This is inserted amongst the notes to "Les deux Ménétriers," vol. I, pp. 309–310. Introducing this extract, Le Grand points out that it is not a "fabliau" but is included for the insight it provides into the functions of the "ménétrier" and ". . . la quantité presque incroyable de talens qu'on verra qu'exigeait une profession décriée." Those for whom the history of Old French poetry holds little interest are advised to omit this piece or to read only the "pastourelle." (*Idem*, p. 299.)

[182] *Idem*, p. 308.

[183] *Idem*, pp. 308–309. In A. A. Renouard's edition of the *Fabliaux ou Contes* four "pastourelles" are included in the notes to "Les deux Ménétriers" (vol. II, pp. 384–390.)

[184] ". . . c'est-à-dire, un petit poöme, composé de stances régulières, & contenant le récit d'une aventure amoureuse, & ordinairement tragique. Le nom que nous lui avons donné annonce une origine ancienne. Cette denomination cependant ne se trouve point dans les manuscrits. Les Romances qu'on va lire, y portent le titre de Lais, ou y sont sans titre comme les Chansons. Je serais fort porté à croire que l'invention de ce genre de poésie est due à Audefroi: au moins des six Romances que j'ai découvertes, il y en a cinq qui lui appartiennent." (P. 168.)

These five are: "Amelot," the "Lai d'Idoine," the "Lai d'Isabeau," the "Lai de Béatrix" and "Argentine." "La Châtelaine de S. Gilles" is given as the sixth "romance." The extracts occupy pages 168–182 of the third volume.

Il est étonnant qu'il ait trouvé aussi peu d'imitateurs, & qu'un poëme où, avec le charme du chant, se trouvaient réunis à la fois la narration animée & l'intérêt dramatique des Fabliaux, n'ait pas été accueilli par la nation, sur-tout dans un tems où elle n'avait que de tristes & monotones chansons ... Mais, au reste, quel qu'ait été le succès de ces différentes compositions, elles n'en sont pas moins un titre pour la gloire de nos Provinces septentrionales, auxquelles la propriété en appartient incontestablement.[185]

It would be strange indeed if Le Grand did not include in the *Fabliaux ou Contes* extracts of what he himself considers to be the earliest monuments of French theatre. These may often be tasteless and chaotic but they paved the way for "les jours brillans de notre Scène" and for this reason alone they merit the attention of a century perhaps too eager in disdaining those to whom it is most indebted. More than this, however, these farces, mystery-plays and moralities are the property of the northern provinces of France and should be claimed for them. The troubadours contributed nothing.

Although Le Grand can think of few pieces quite so badly written as the "Lai de Courtois"[186] the latter is nevertheless presented in the first volume of his collection [187] since this "fabliau" is seen to represent the beginnings of the drama in France. The extract serves in fact to introduce not only a number of remarks which Le Grand is anxious to make upon a question touching upon the glory of France, but also certain interesting though hitherto little known works "... que je vais donner ici comme de monumens précieux pour l'histoire du théâtre & de la poésie française."[188] They were composed, he says, by the "fabliers":

Ce sont eux qui ont ouvert en France la carrière dramatique; & le genre de leurs ouvrages, faits pour être chantés ou déclamés par des Ménétriers, devait naturellement les y conduire; sur-tout quand leurs Contes dialogués, comme ils en ont quelques-uns, offraient le récit alternatif de deux personnages.[189]

This, claims Le Grand, is how Greek tragedy originated. To create a

---

[185] Introduction to "Ammelot," pp. 168–169. In the *Voyage de Provence* Papon proposes that Le Grand translate the love-songs of the "trouvères" in order that they might be compared to those of the troubadours (vol. II, pp. 249–250). The challenge is not accepted: "C'est là un défi que je n'ai garde d'accepter. J'ai déjà déclaré ce que je pensois de ces chansons, qui, à dire le vrai, ne valent pas mieux que celles de leurs rivaux. Les seules en ce genre qui méritent d'être citées sont quelques romances et quelques pastourelles." (*Observations sur les Troubadours*, p. 20.)

[186] *Fabliaux ou Contes*, vol. I, p. 325: "J'en ai peu vues d'aussi mal écrites, & dont la narration fût aussi obscure & aussi diffuse ...".

[187] Pp. 325–328.

[188] Note to the "Lai de Courtois," p. 330.

[189] Pp. 330–331.

drama it was necessary only to increase the number of speakers and provide an action, the procedure adopted for the "Lai de Courtois," very probably the "Adam" of all subsequent mystery-plays, farces, "sotties" and moralities. To these crude beginnings Rutebeuf, Jean Bodel and Adam de Le Hale gave order and form, as the reader might observe for himself in the extracts of "Le Miracle de Théophile," "Le Jeu de S. Nicolas" and "Le Jeu du Berger et de la Bergère"[190] which now follow.[191] These may be found amusing in their clumsiness, but the eighteenth century should moderate its scorn:

Aujourd'hui que l'industrie & les arts nous ont procuré mille commodités superflues, nous nous moquons du tems où nos aïeux marchaient nus pieds. Cependant celui qui le premier alors s'avisa de creuser un morceau de bois pour s'en faire une chaussure, était assurément un homme fort supérieur à ses contemporains.[192]

"Le Mariage, alias le Jeu d'Adam le Bossu d'Arras" and Rutebeuf's "Les Croisades, alias Dispute du Croisé et du Non-croisé" are later presented as further examples of early French theatre and Le Grand mentions that he knows of two other such pieces contained in the La Vallière manuscript from which he has taken "Le Jeu de S. Nicolas," although these latter do not merit attention.[193] Further manuscript researches, he says, would surely produce many similar "Jeux," but those extracted here meet his purpose:

... ceux-ci du moins sont suffisans pour prouver que l'époque de notre Théâtre remonte plus haut qu'on ne l'a cru jusqu'ici, & qu'au treizième siècle nous avions déjà des drames, & même des drames dans plus d'un genre, puisque voilà une pastorale, une farce (le Jeu du Pélerin), deux pièces dévotes, & des pièces morales (le Mariage & les Croisades).[194]

And all this glory for the northern provinces of France.

[190] "Le Jeu de Robin et de Mation."
[191] These extracts occupy pages 333–360 of the first volume.
[192] Note to the "Lai de Courtois," pp. 331–332. While Le Grand thinks little of the "genre absurde" of Rutebeuf and Bodel (note to "Le Jeu du Berger et de la Bergère," p. 358) he praises "Le Jeu du Berger et de la Bergère" despite the improbable sequence of the events: "...cette jolie pastorale avec une marche claire, avec des moeurs antiques, simples & pures, présente d'ailleurs des détails si agréables & une naïveté si exquise, que si on la compare aux mistères & aux sotties que renferment les premiers âges de l'histoire de notre Théâtre, on ne pourra jamais croire à la prodigieuse distance d'une dégénération pareille." (Note to "Le Jeu de S. Nicolas," p. 346.)
[193] Cf. the note to "Le Jeu du Berger et de la Bergère," p. 357. One of the two pieces deemed unworthy of inclusion is "Le Jeu du Pélerin," the other is not named. A note to "De l'Herberie, alias Le Dit de l'Herberie" in the third volume of the collection reads thus: "Cette pièce pourrait fort bien avoir été un de ces Jeux dont il a été parlé dans le premier volume, une sorte de farce dramatique, à deux personnages, ou à trois si l'on y faisait jouer l'homme qui vient se plaindre du mal de dents." (P. 355.)
[194] Note to "Le Jeu du Berger et de la Bergère," p. 358.

Extracts of what are described as two allegorical fabliaux, "La Ba-taille de Charnage et de Carême" and "La Bataille des Vins," are given in the second volume of the *Fabliaux ou Contes*.[195] But these stand alone, similar pieces known to Le Grand being judged so insipid as to be unworthy of even the briefest extracts.[196] Indeed, it is very probably true that the two presented here are included not primiraly as a further testimony to the diverse abilities of the "trouvères" but rather for the notes to which they give rise. In each case these are longer than the extracts themselves.[197] Elsewhere in the collection other genres are only mentioned and perhaps briefly defined, failing, it seems, to serve any of Le Grand's purposes. In a note to "Les deux Ménétriers," for exam-ple, Le Grand insists that he would have liked to cite examples of the "chansons de geste" in order to convey to his readers some better no-tion of their form, content and merits. But those he might have used are "si niaises & si plates" that he felt he must abandon the idea since the extracts he might offer would not be properly representative of the genre as a whole and he would himself be committing that crime for which Villaret, Velly and Racine are censured, misrepresentation.[198] Thus, if Le Grand declines to furnish examples of certain genres it is because these would not help him towards the ends he envisages and, since further discussion of those types to which he devotes no more than a few lines of explanation would be superfluous to our own aims here, we might turn finally to the extract of "Parténopex," this occupying a third of what we know to be a purposeful fourth volume.

It is not only the degree of success achieved by Le Grand in bringing Old French literature before the masses which sets him apart from the

---

[195] Pp. 119–126 and 136–140 respectively.

[196] Cf. a note to "La Bataille des Vins," pp. 140–141.

[197] In this way, as we have seen, the majority of points of interest have been dealt with before the fourth volume of the collection is reached.

[198] *Fabliaux ou Contes*, vol. I, p. 301. Le Grand does not appear to distinguish between "chansons de geste" and other "chansons militaires" or "chansons de soldats." (Cf. Paul Zumthor, *Histoire littéraire de la France médiévale*, Paris, Presses Universitaires de France, 1954, paragraph 278, pp. 143–144.) This is apparent from remarks made both in the preface to the first volume of the collection (pp. x–xiv) and here in the note to "Les deux Ménétriers": "Ces Chansons de geste, distinguées ici des autres chansons ordinaires, sont probablement ce qu'Albéric appelle Heroicae cantilenae, c'est-à-dire, celles qui célébraient les gestes & actions des preux Chevaliers, soit fabuleux, soit véritables. De ce nombre était la chanson de Rolland dont il a été parlée plus haut. Elle n'est point parvenue jusqu'à nous. Mabillon en a publié une en ancien langage Teuton, faite sur Louis III, à l'occasion d'une victoire que ce Prince remporta en 881, sur les Normands, & qui a de grandes beautés. J'en ai trouvé plusieurs autres du même genre chez nos Poëtes, & en particulier une sur la victoire de S. Louis à Taillebourg ...". (P. 310.)

In the notes to "Les deux Ménétriers" as they appear in the third edition of the collection, Schilter's Latin translation of the "Chant de Victoire sur Louis III, fils de Louis-le-Bègue" is given with a rendering in French (vol. II, pp. 372–376).

majority of his fellow medievalists. He is perhaps the first successful
popularizer to give his attention to something other than the romances.
It is clear from the preface to "Parténopex" that he is far from sharing
Paulmy's enthusiasm for the genre:

De toutes les branches de notre vieille Littérature, celle-ci, quoique la plus
abondante, quoique plus abondante même que toutes ensemble, est néanmoins celle de toutes qui aujourd'hui, relativement à sa fécondité prodidi-
euse, nous offre le moins de quoi nous glorifier.[199]

Yet from our acquaintance with the preface to the first volume of the
Fabliaux ou Contes we know that, if Le Grand finds these lengthy tales
monotonous in their uniformity,[200] he does not consider that they are
all equally to be despised. Quite the contrary, for there are those, he
says, which have a real interest:

Je dirai plus, c'est que même dans la plûpart des autres on trouvera, malgré
tous leurs défauts, (& j'en atteste quiconque aura le courage de les lire), des
morceaux très-agréables, & sur-tout un talent particulier pour exciter la curiosité & l'admiration.[201]

The romances, moreover, were extremely popular in their day and for
the very good reason, as he insists, that they were then unmatched. But
of even greater importance for Le Grand is that they were acclaimed
and imitated in both Spain and Italy, having originated in the northern provinces of France, the South failing for some reason to cultivate
the genre despite its popularity.[202] Why is it then that Le Grand does
not choose to devote his attention primarily to the romances since, in
his view, these latter adequately demonstrate not only that, for their
time, the "trouvères" were poets of considerable ability, but also, and

---

[199] *Fabliaux ou Contes*, vol. IV, p. 252.
[200] Vol. I, preface, pp. lxiii, lxxxv.
[201] *Idem*, pp. xxxiv-xxxv.
[202] *Idem*, p. xxxvii. The Marquis de Paulmy, with a passion for romances of every kind
and every era, had a particular affection for the romances of chivalry for similar reasons:
"Cette classe n'a point de modèle dans l'antiquité. Elle est due au génie des Français, et
tout ce qui a paru de ce genre chez les autres peuples de l'Europe a été postérieur aux premiers romans que la France a produits, et n'en a été pour ainsi dire qu'une imitation. Ce
genre ne s'est pas conservé, quoique intéressant pour le coeur et propre à élever l'âme, parce
qu'il était gigantesque et presque hors de nature." (Discours préliminaire to the *Bibliothèque
des Romans*, July, 1775.)
It is interesting to note that the reason Paulmy gives for the decline in popularity of the
genre is almost exactly that which Le Grand alleges for its continued success over the fabliaux,
the romances of chivalry fashionable in translations and adaptations for more than five
hundred years: "Mais la Chevalerie avait répandu dans la Nation l'enthousiasme des hauts
faits; & les Romans, par le merveilleux continuel de leurs aventures, flataient ce goût d'héro-
isme. Les Fabliaux, au contraire, n'offraient dans la trivialité des leurs, que des évènemens
domestiques, peu faits pour intéresser auprès de tous ces monstres & de ces géants terrassés
...". (*Fabliaux ou Contes*, vol. I, preface, p. lxxxv.)

more significantly, that they were not the humble disciples of the troubadours and even led the rest of Europe?

It had in fact originally been Le Grand's intention to do just this, to
extract the most pleasing sections of the more interesting romances and
publish a collection ". . . qui, selon moi, serait devenu comme la juste
balance où l'on aurait pu peser & apprécier ces Trouveurs."[203] But,
quite apart form the fact that he could hope for little success with so
disjointed a compilation, he soon realized that his scales would be im-
properly balanced, that such a collection could not be truly representative of the romances in that it would make obvious only their merits
and never their shortcomings. Le Grand's purpose is to ensure a just
appreciation of the "anciens rimeurs," no more and no less. Anything
conveying a false impression of these, even if it be flattering in its inac-
curacy, is to be condemned. He can make use of the romances but to be
scrupulously fair he must present complete examples of them.[204] This
is how, in the preface to "Parténopex," Le Grand explains his rejection
of the romances as the most useful means to the ends he envisages here.
One wonders if he would be quite so scrupulous if he did not in any
case consider the much imitated fabliaux poetically superior and of
far greater historical relevance. All things considered, it seems unlikely
that he could ever have thought seriously of publishing a collection of
romances with a supplementary volume of fabliaux extracts.

Le Grand's only concern was to find sufficient romances worthy of
translation. Fortunately his researches lead to discoveries far beyond
his expectations and when he comes to write the introduction to that
section of the *Fabliaux ou Contes* headed "Romans"[205] his intention, as
we know, is to present four complete examples representative of the
genre as a whole.[206] These will not, he says, be unknown to his readers,
all but one having already appeared in extract form in the *Bibliothèque
des Romans*. This does not, however, render his own translations superfluous, for one cannot hope to convey an accurate impression of the old
romances through extracts, whatever the skill of their author. A well-
constructed modern piece can be thus dissected, the procedure reveal-
ing to us all the artistry and skill of the intellect behind the written

---

[203] Avertissement préliminaire to "Parténopex," vol. IV, p. 254.
[204] *Idem*, pp. 254–255.
[205] I.e. the Avertissement préliminaire to "Parténopex."
[206] "Dans ce nombre j'en ai choisi quatre: un de Fêrie, un de Chevalerie, un d'amour,
un enfin dans le genre burlesque; car c'est à ces quatre classes qu'on peut les réduire tous,
quoique cependant il n'y en ait peut-être pas un seul sans amour & sans Chevalerie." (Vol.
IV, p. 255.)

word. Those responsible for the old romances do not, however, share the advantages of centuries of learning and experience enjoyed by the great writers of the seventeenth and eighteenth centuries:

Mais pour nos Romanciers, qui ne savaient seulement pas s'il y avait un art & des règles, pour nos Romanciers, dont le plus grand mérite consiste dans les détails & dans des morceaux exquis de sentiment & de naïveté; les présenter par extraits, c'est à la fois les dépouiller de tous leurs agrémens, & ne les montrer qu'avec leurs seuls défauts.[207]

Those who are generally considered to have done most to popularize medieval French literature in eighteenth-century France, the editors of the *Bibliothèque des Romans*, are thus censured as guilty of that crime for which Villaret, Velly and Racine are condemned, gross misrepresentation. For Le Grand this is the first time that the romances presented here will have been shown to the public in their true colours.[208]

We have yet to deal with the question of method but already it is clear that, at least as far as the romances are concerned, Le Grand does not share the views of his former master, Sainte-Palaye, who, when calling for a "bibliothèque générale et complète de tous nos anciens Romans de chevalerie," emphasized, as we know, that this should be a collection of historically oriented extracts:

Great works of art, he argued, cannot be published in extract without suffering grievous damage. Works of mediocre or uneven quality, however, would lose nothing by being published in this way . . . .[209]

Paulmy, first director of the *Bibliothèque des Romans*, went a long way towards implementing La Curne's proposals, of course, but clearly the

---

[207] *Idem*, p. 256.

[208] Le Grand himself, of course, had contributed to the *Bibliothèque des Romans* under Paulmy! In notes clearly prepared for that section of the proposed *Histoire de la Littéraire française* to be devoted to the romances we read: "Tressan, la bibliothèque des Romans, Mayer &c. ont donné des extraits de nos R. de chevalerie; mais ils n'ont travaillé que sur les versions imprimées, c'est à dire sur des imitations; et eux-mêmes, pour rendre leur ouvrage plus agréable à lire, y ont mis tous les embellissemens du rouge et des mouches et s'y sont permis tous les changemens que leur a fournis leur imagination. Ce n'est pas d'après ces extraits infidèles et défigurés qu'on peut prendre une idée de notre poésie ancienne." (*Ms. Paris, B. N, n.a.f. 6227*, fol. 164.)

However, in the "Notice sommaire sur les trois ouvrages auxquels je travaille" Le Grand states that he is to present romances in extract form in this history, moreover that he is to extract only the best: "J'indiquerai tous les Romans que nous ont transmis les manuscrits. Je donnerai une notice de chacun, et un extrait de ceux qui seront les meilleurs." (Fol. 79.)

Surely this is the very method he rejects in the Avertissement préliminaire to "Parténopex," hardly less improper, according to the standards set here, than that of Tressan and his colleagues. The only possible justification is that the remarks made in the "Notice" refer to a history of French literature and that a collection on similar lines to the *Bibliothèque des Romans* is not envisaged.

[209] L. Gossman, *Medievalism*, p. 256.

real target of Le Grand's disdain is that most unscrupulous "remani-
eur," Tressan.[210]

It is bad enough that Tressan should misrepresent the romances by
presenting them in extract form, but that he should take the extract of
"Florès et Blanchefleur"[211] from a sixteenth-century translation of a
Spanish romance[212] with no mention of the true origins of the piece,
this, for Le Grand, is quite intolerable:

Il ignorait que "Florès & Blanche-Fleur" était dans l'origine un Roman
français. J'en prévins, mais trop tard: l'extrait était déjà imprimé en partie.
D'après mon avis cependant on fit une note qui, autant que je puis me le
rappeller, fut placée à la fin du volume.[213]

The problem was, as indicated in the preface to the first volume of the
Fabliaux ou Contes, that those responsible for the prose versions of the
romances neglected most of the finest pieces, which were adopted by
France's more appreciative neighbours and eventually came to be
viewed as of foreign origin. In 1779 Couchu published "Partenuple de
Blois" in the same periodical, the *Bibliothèque des Romans*, and claimed
to have himself translated it from the Old Castilian whereas, we are
told, it is no more Spanish than "Florès et Blanchefleur."[214] Both tales
are amongst those to be translated by Le Grand:

Quels que soient ces deux Ouvrages, je les réclame tous deux au nom de ma
Patrie. Ils sont à elle, ils lui appartiennent; & c'est pour en convaincre mes
Lecteurs, que de préférence j'ai choisi de les traduire tous deux. Je citerai à
chacun le titre original qui nous l'assure. Que ceux qui se les arrogent, produisent dans leur langue un manuscrit plus ancien; & alors je me rétracte.[215]

We know, of course, that there is sufficient space in the fourth volume
of the *Fabliaux ou Contes* for only one romance and that the supplement
promised, containing the remaining three, does not appear. It may

---

[210] We know already that Paulmy and Tressan almost came to blows over the licence
this latter permitted himself in his extracts.

[211] *Bibliothèque des Romans*, February and March 1777, pp. 155–225.

[212] *L'histoire amoureuse de Flores et Blanchefleur samye avec la complainte que fait un amant contre
Amour et sa dame, le tout mis d'espagnol en français*, by Jacques Vincent, Paris, 1554. Cf. H.
Jacoubet, *Le Comte de Tressan*, p. 242: "Tressan en a fait un roman XVIIIe siècle à mettre
entre les 'Lettres Persane' et 'Zadig.' "

[213] Avertissement préliminaire to "Parténopex," vol. IV, p. 258. Although Le Grand
does here refer to Tressan as "l'Homme illustre, L'Ecrivain charmant," it is difficult to
believe that he genuinely respects one he sees guilty of so serious a crime.

[214] The extract of "Partenuple de Blois" appeared in the volume for December. Couchu
claimed to have translated if from a sixteenth-century edition by Alcala de Hénarez.

[215] Avertissement préliminaire to "Parténopex," vol. IV, p. 259.

stand alone but nevertheless "Parténopex," as we have seen, serves Le Grand's purposes well.[216]

Let us turn finally to the main body of extracts, to the "fabliaux ou contes," for we know already that, of all the genres cultivated by the "trouvères," it is here Le Grand finds the once much appreciated abilities of these latter best evidenced. The discussion need not be lengthy. Le Grand makes it abundantly clear in his preface that it is the first three volumes of his collection which contain the necessary "pièces justificatives" to prove that the poets of France's northern provinces were not uncultured barbarians, as they have so often been presented, but deserve recognition for the distinctions they won for the Nation in surpassing all other European poets, including the troubadours of Provence, to become the admiration and inspiration of the West.

That in a barbarian age simple, uncultured, untutored Frenchmen, with no models or fine books to use as a foundation, were composing tales which not only amused their contemporaries but would continue, in one form or another, to bring joy to later centuries, surely this fact alone, says Le Grand, renders the "fabliers" worthy of our attention, makes us curious on their count. But we have reason to be more than just curious:

... Si j'ajoutais que ces mêmes hommes sont les premiers, qui depuis l'invasion des Barbares aient fait paraître des Contes en Europe; que les autres

---

[216] In the third edition of his collection Le Grand intended to add *Blancandin et Orgueilleuse d'amour* and this is included by Renouard in his own edition of the *Fabliaux ou Contes* (vol. V, pp. 319–354). It is neither translated in full nor given in the usual extract form: "...j'ai cru pouvoir me conformer à ce qu'a fait le comte de Caylus dans son extrait non imprimé de la totalité du manuscrit dont je viens de faire mention."

The manuscript in question, from which *Blancandin* is taken, is *Saint-Germain 1830* (present *B.N. 19152*) and in his "extrait" of this Caylus, instead of translating the individual pieces, gives a brief analysis of each one, interspersed with quotations from the original: "Cette méthode, que j'adopte pour cette seule fois, a l'avantage de mettre sous les yeux du lecteur un assez grand nombre de vers agréables, qui sont la principale recommandation de ce roman. C'eût été un travail inutile que de recommencer celui du comte de Caylus, je l'ai donc à-peu-près employé, sauf, plus de retranchements encore sans lesquels cette pièce auroit probablement paru trop longue à beaucoup de mes lecteurs." (*Fabliaux ou Contes*, 1829, vol. V, pp. 200–202.)

Le Grand now has no difficulty in justifying this method of presentation: "J'ai pensé que, présenté sous cette forme inusitée dans tout le reste du recueil, ce roman y jetteroit quelque variété et le termineroit d'une manière satisfaisante." (P. 202.)

Renouard in fact concludes the fifth volume of this third edition with his own translation of *Le Voyage d'outre-mer, du comte de Ponthieu*: "Au reste, qu'il soit plus ou moins complètement inventé, ce petit roman n'est pas sans intérêt; sa naïveté est bien un peu dans le genre des livres de la Bibliothèque bleue, mais cependant j'ai cru ne pas devoir la faire disparaître dans ma traduction." (Note to p. 202.)

The translation occupies pages 355–374. As Renouard points out, the tale was first published in its original form by Méon in the first volume of his *Nouveau Recueil de Fabliaux et Contes*, Paris (Chasseriau) 1823, 2 vols.

Nations n'ont fait que les copier ou les imiter; que l'Italie leur doit ce Bocace dont elle est si fière, & auquel elle attribue l'invention d'un genre charmant: alors on commencerait, je crois, à s'intéresser pour eux.[217]

We know, of course, that Le Grand has a particular affection for the fabliaux and we shall later attempt to establish that he considers certain examples of the genre valid even in the light of all subsequent literary achievement. Here, however, he is applying yesterday's standards. It is enough for his readers to understand that these tales are important for what they represented in their own time.

If extracts would suffice to demonstrate that the "fabliers," given the period in which they practised their art, were men of considerable talent, then extracts alone, of course, could furnish no proof of the debt of gratitude which France's neighbours owed to her. Yet Le Grand's primary object is to establish that, while the genre of the "conte" may well have originated in the East,[218] the French were responsible for its introduction and success in Europe:

C'est chez eux qu'en ce genre agréable, sont venus puiser leurs voisins, & les Italiens sur-tout auxquels il a fait un nom.[219]

The question, then, is important not only for its bearing upon the "querelle des trouvères et des troubadours," these latter having failed to cultivate this particular genre, but also in that it touches upon the glory of France, foreigners having stolen, copied and adapted the fabliaux over centuries without anyone thinking to demand recognition for their true authors.[220] But how to prove this plagiary? The solution is a very simple one. The extracts of particular fabliaux will be followed by lists of imitations and adaptations of the French originals, these usually preceding the notes to points of historical or otherwise non-literary interest. It is by extracting the fabliaux that Le Grand considers he can most effectively dismiss the notion of the "trouvères" as barbarian scribblers, by listing imitations of their fabliaux that he can best demonstrate what respect is owed to them as innovators. In the *Observations sur les Troubadours* Le Grand explains that the purpose of the preface to the first volume of his collection is two-fold, to prove that

---

[217] *Fabliaux ou Contes*, vol. I, preface, pp. lxii-lxiii.
[218] *Idem*, p. xl.
[219] *Idem*, p. xcix.
[220] *Idem*, p. lxxxv: "L'Etranger imite, pille, copie impunément ces derniers [the fabliaux] & personne ne réclame pour l'honneur de la France. On ne songe même ni à les recueillir ni à les imprimer, ni à les traduire en Prose, comme les Romans."

while the troubadours do not deserve a reputation such as they enjoy, the "trouvères" do not enjoy a reputation such as they deserve:

Pour la seconde partie de ce procès, c'étoit à moi de la prouver, et c'est ce que j'ai tâché de faire en publiant les fabliaux.[221]

If we have seen that Le Grand is much criticized for the proofs cited in defence of the first part of his "procès," then it is only to be expected that the "Provençalistes" should not allow those presented in support of this second to go unchallenged. Once again the evidence is declared invalid, Le Grand's opponents insisting that the fabliaux are not in fact owed to the "trouvères" of northern France. The most persistent efforts to prove these latter mere plagiaries are made by Papon who devotes three of the "Cinq Lettres sur les Trouvères & les Troubadours" to the purpose of establishing that they took certain of their finer tales form the Arabs, others from the Italians and yet others, of course, from the troubadours of Provence.[222] The "trouvères" did compose some fabliaux and it is easy to distinguish their work, for the art of writing comedy is one demanding abilities which they simply did not possess:

Ainsi, Monsieur ne faites pas difficulté de leur attribuer les fabliaux où vous trouverez une gaieté sans vivacité & sans saillie; une plaisanterie sans sel & sans agrément. Je vous avertis que vous les distinguerez à ces défauts, qui leur donnent un air de famille auquel on les reconnoît aisément.[223]

Le Grand first replies, of course, that he himself does not claim the invention of the genre for the "trouvères" but rather acknowledges that such tales may well have originated in the East, the poets of France's northern provinces coming to know them during the crusades. In a note to "De Celui qui enferma sa femme dans une tour" in the second volume of his collection he does in fact declare that, while it may at times be difficult for him to distinguish those fabliaux of eastern origin,

---

[221] *Observations sur les Troubadours*, p. 10.
[222] *Voyage littéraire de Provence*, vol. II, Letters II, III and IV, pp. 177–192, 193–209 and 210–244 respectively.
[223] Letter II, pp. 183–184. Poorer tales attributed to the "trouvères" by Papon include, in the first volume of the *Fabliaux ou Contes*: "De Cocagne," "Le Bachelier Normand," "Le Siège prêté et rendu," "... & presque tous ceux qui suivent; je dis presque tous, parce qu'il y en a quelques-uns, où se trouvent des circonstances imitées des auteurs étrangers"; in the second: "La Robe d'écarlate," "Des deux Anglais," "L'Arracheur de dents," "L'Indigestion du Vilain," "Du Prud'homme qui retira de l'eau son compère," "Du curé qui eut une mère malgré lui," "Du Curé et des deux ribauds," "De Dom Argent," "Le grand chemin." None are cited from the third volume of Le Grand's collection: "... car il faut abréger, sans aller chercher dans le troisième volume des exemples que le Lecteur appercevra aisément." (Letter II, pp. 181–183.)

he will invariably give credit to the foreigner when there is the least doubt as to ownership:

Dans ce doute, j'ai pris le parti le plus généreux; celui, comme j'ai dit plus haut, d'attribuer généralement aux Orientaux tous les Fabliaux quelconques que je rencontrerai dans leurs ouvrages.[224]

The "Lai d'Aristote," "De la Dame qui fit accroire à son mari qu'il avait rêvé," "Le Chevalier à la trappe," "Le Chien et le Serpent" and "De la Femme qui voulut éprouver son mari" are amongst those tales which Le Grand willingly attributes to eastern poets.[225] For there is no shame in this. Quite the contrary, since he might well ask why only the soldiers of the supposedly gloomy and lifeless North should have thought to bring these stories back to Europe with them, those "gay" southern provinces being slow to cultivate a genre in which, in any case, they failed to distinguish themselves:

Il est fort étonnant que toutes les fois qu'on s'avise de comparer ensemble ces deux familles d'auteurs, l'avantage soit toujours du côté des septentrionaux.[226]

Regarding Papon's claim that certain of the fabliaux originated in Italy, Le Grand would point out that it is possible to date those examples of the genre still preserved in manuscripts held in the great libraries of France and that the period of their composition can be established as the thirteenth century. But not only did the "fabliers" precede the first Italian "conteur," Boccaccio, by something like a hundred years, it is well known that the latter sought inspiration in the former. Papon is mistaken in believing that the Italians could not consider this last remark without some amusement. Le Duchat pointed to Boccaccio's use of the French tale "Le Parement des Dames" for his "Grisel-

---

[224] *Fabliaux ou Contes*, vol. II, pp. 288–292.

[225] Papon lists a number of those tales which he believes have been translated more or less literally from the "Orientaux": the "Lai d'Aristote," "Huippocrate," "Le Jugement de Salomon," "Le Jugement sur les barrils d'huile mis en dépôt," "Du Marchand qui perdit sa bourse," "Le Chien et le Serpent," "Du Prud,homme qui donna des instructions à son fils" and "Des deux bons amins." The reader is asked to compare these with "Du pauvre Mercier," "Le Tailleur du roi et son sergent," "Du Villain qui vit sa femme avec un ami," "Le Bourgeois d'Abbeville" and the "Lai du palefroi vair," this latter cited ". . . pour vous donner une idée de la manière des Trouvères. Le fond du sujet est intéressant; mais le Conte est ennuyeux, froid, insupportable; parce que l'Auteur, comme les autres Fabliers, ses Contemporains, n'a aucuns détails agréables de poésie, & manque de cette sensibilité qui anime tout." It is interesting to note that, generally speaking, Papon considers those tales which the "trouvères" took from their eastern counterparts inferior to those borrowed elsewhere. (*Voyage de Provence*, letter II, pp. 186–191.)

[226] *Observations sur les Troubadours*, pp. 114–115.

da" and Manni was not mocking him when he restored its ownership to the French.[227] Nor was Fauchet ridiculed for his belief that "... Pétrarque & ses semblables se sont aidez des plus beaux traits des chansons de Thiebaut Roy de Navarre, Gaces Brulez, le Chastelain de Coucy, & autres anciens poëtes François ...".[228] Le Grand may not be able to give Papon precise details as to how and when the fabliaux crossed the Alps, but he does know that France once played host to a great many Italians, refugees from the civil strife in their own land:

Je sais que la plupart des usuriers de nos villes étoient Italiens; que la cour de Rome, pour le maintien de ses droits, pour la perception de ses revenus, y entretenoit beaucoup d'Italiens; que presque tout le commerce intérieur du royaume étoit fait par des Italiens, et que même ils occupoient dans la capitale, une rue qui de leur nom est encore appelée rue des Lombards ....[229]

Brunetto Latini wrote his *Trésor* in Paris, Dante spent some time there, Boccaccio and many others came there to study, and from the early thirteenth century the capital's university was popular with Venetian law students. Papon himself admits to having found manuscripts containing Old French romances in Italian libraries[230] and Muratori will vouch that the deeds of Roland and Oliver were sung on the Milan stage, that French "ménétriers" wandered the streets of Italian towns, since in 1288 the senate of Bologna issued a decree prohibiting them from singing in market-places:[231]

---

[227] Cf. A. C. Lee, *The Decameron. Its Sources and Analogues*, London (David Natt) 1909, Day 10, Novel 10, p. 354: "In France it appeared in the fifteenth century in a poetic form in the 'Parement et triumphe des Dames d'honneur,' by Olivier de la Marche, who lived 1426–1502. This is the version that was formerly by Duchat, Manni, de Sade and Le Grand considered to be the dsource of Boccaccio's tale, as it was not then apparently known that La Marche was the author of this work."

[228] *Recueil de l'Origine de la Langue et Poësie françoise, Oeuvres*, fol. 544vo. Le Grand points out that these lines appear also in the *Histoire littéraire de la France* (vol. VI, p. 15) but does not mention here that Huet uses them in his *Traité de l'Origine des Romans* (p. 80).

[229] *Observations sur les Troubadours*, p. 119.

[230] *Voyage de Provence*, vol. II, note to p. 224: "J'ai vu en Italie beaucoup de manuscrits; j'y ai trouvé quelques Romans fort anciens, écrits en Provençal, & d'autres écrits en François; mais je n'ai trouvé aucun recueil de contes en notre langue."

[231] Le Grand, quoting from Ghirardacci's history of Bologna, is careful to explain the precise implications of the decree which Papon interprets as a testimony to the Italians' disdain for the "trouvères" (*Idem*, pp. 236–237 and notes). Henri Hauvette is amongst those who will later cite the decree in attempting to establish to what extent Italians of the period knew and appreciated Old French language and literature: "Ce qui nous surprend davantage, c'est que le peuple des carrefours, évidemment illettré, ait pu suivre les récitations faites par des 'chanteurs français' – cantores Francigenarum, dit un célèbre document bolonais de 1289 ...". (*La France et la Provence dans l'oeuvre de Dante*, p. 15.)
  It is, of course, one of Le Grand's arguments, repeated here, that the common people could not have understood the poetry of the "trouvères." (*Observations sur les Troubadours*, p. 124.)

Après tant de faits et tant de témoignages multipliés, osera-t-on me demander encore si nos fabliaux ont pu être connus des Italiens?[232]

Le Grand takes particular objection to the reasons Papon gives for attributing certain of the fabliaux to the Italians. The husband's jealousy in "De celui qui enferma sa femme dans une tour" is enough to make the true origins of this tale obvious to the author of the *Voyage de Provence*,[233] as if all Italians and only the Italians, mocks Le Grand, were given to jealousy. In "De l'enfant qui fondit au soleil" the merchant goes to Genoa to sell the child given him by his adulterous wife, from which it is concluded that the tale must be of Italian invention since French merchants rarely travelled to Genoa.[234] But even if this were true, and Le Grand refuses to acknowledge it, is Papon not forgetting that Genoa was a very famous city, that the French obtained most of their silks and spices from the Genoese, that a large number of French crusaders embarked at this port? And it is no argument to claim that "... il faut attribuer aux Italiens l'invention des Contes, où avec du choix dans les détails, des circonstances bien amenées, de la facilité, & un certain agrément dans le tissu de la narration, vous trouverez quelque trait de libertinage, ou la satyre des Moines, des gens d'Eglise & des femmes; avec cette différence pourtant, que ces traits, qui ne sont point rares chez les Fabliers, ont dans les Contes, qui sont originairement Italiens, une tournure subtilement ingénieuse."[235] It is following "des principes aussi incontestables"[236] that Papon would attribute such tales as "Le Manteau mal taillé" to the Italiens.[237]

As Le Grand points out, Papon's fourth letter begins with an astonishing admission considering that his purpose here is to establish that the "fabliers" also robbed the poets of France's southern provinces:[238]

---

[232] *Observations sur les Troubadours*, p. 121.

[233] Letter III, pp. 200–201.

[234] *Idem*, p. 200.

[235] *Idem*, pp. 201–202.

[236] *Observations sur les Troubadours*, p. 126.

[237] Others include "Des trois Larrons," "La culotte des cordeliers," "Les trois Aveugles de Compiègne," "Le Testement de l'âne," "Du Villain et de sa femme" and "De la Dame qui fut corrigée."

[238] Cf. Mayer's "Observations critiques sur les Fabliaux ou Contes," pp. 150–151: "On retrouve même encore dans la bouche des paysans de cette Province [Provence], qui ne savent ni lire, ni écrire, presque tous les Fabliaux des siècles les plus anciens. Les variantes que M. L. G. dit avoir trouvées dans les éditions des Fabliaux, viennent à l'appui de ce fait. Ces Fabliaux des Troubadours perdus aujourd'hui, sont restés gravés dans la mémoire des contemporains, jusqu'à ce que les Fabliers en romance Françoise soient venus s'emparer de ce fonds."

Je sens bien que je n'ai aucun titre authentique pour vous prouver le pla-
giat ....[239]

Once again conjectures are offered where only facts can suffice, certain
of the former being such that Le Grand is embarrassed to report
them.[240] When a fabliau tells of loyalty and pure love as they are found
in many of the love-songs of the troubadours, when these emotions are
described with candour and simplicity, when the scene is clearly set in
France's southern provinces, when the tale closely resembles some
troubadour piece, then for Papon it can safely be assumed that this
fabliau is a translation or at least an adaptation of a Provençal original.
Thus "Grisélidis" and "Aucassin et Nicolette" are attributed to the
"Provençals" since the action of one is set in Saluces, the other in
Beaucaire:[241]

C'est ainsi qu'il attribue aux Italiens le fabliau d'Hippocrate, dont la scène
est à Rome. Mais, avec cette façon de raisonner, les Anglois pourront revendiquer 'Cléveland,' et les Espagnols, 'Gilblas'; 'Zaire' sera due aux Arabes,
'Alzire' aux Péruviens.[242]

As for those tales of loyalty and pure love narrated with a simplicity
and candour unknown to the "trouvères," "misérables bouffons, faits
tout au plus pour amuser la populace,"[243] Le Grand would refer Papon
to Millot's collection:

Quand l'histoire n'attesteroit point les désordres & la licence des moeurs, les
ouvrages des troubadours en fourniroient une foule de preuves incontestables. Parmi quelques exemples d'une galanterie pure, assujettie au frein de
la pudeur & des devoirs, on y trouve mille traits de libertinage & de débauche; on y voit les sens maîtriser le coeur, la foi conjugale impudemment
violée, quelquefois les moeurs outragées avec une indécence cynique, enfin
les mêmes vices qu'aujourd'hui, moins déguisés sous d'honnêtes apparen-
ces.[244]

This, very briefly, is Le Grand's reply to those who would challenge
the "pièces justificatives" presented in defence of the second part of his

---

[239] Page 210.
[240] In particular, Papon's efforts to prove "Guillaume au Faucon" an imitation of "La
Vie du troubadour Rambaud": "Je rougis de rapporter de pareilles objections, et j'en
demande pardon à mes lecteurs. Mais j'ai voulu montrer à quoi en étoient réduits, pour me
répondre, mes adversaires, et où les avoient menés des préventions aveugles, un amour de
patrie mal ordonné et ce risible délire de vouloir exclusivement attribuer aux troubadours
tous les talents, parce qu'on naquit soi-même dans une province troubadouresque." (Observations sur les Troubadours, p. 131.)
[241] Voyage de Provence, vol. II, Letter IV, p. 219.
[242] Observations sur les Troubadours, p. 132.
[243] Voyage de Provence, vol. II, Letter V, p. 253.
[244] Histoire littéraire des Troubadours, Discours préliminaire, pp. xxxvii-xxxviii.

"procès." For the author of the *Fabliaux ou Contes* the discussion is now closed and there is no more to be said on the matter of the "querelle des trouvères et des troubadours." Of course, the very fact that the additions made to the *Observations sur les Troubadours* will still be judged worthy of publication in 1829 proves well enough that he is mistaken in this conviction. The debate remains of interest thirty years after Le Grand's death. In his own lifetime it is a burning issue, filling the journals of the day. There is, it seems, no question of a compromise such as that offered by the *Journal de Monsieur*. Opposing parties, insists the periodical, have failed so far to consider this whole question "sous son véritable point de vue." The position is simply this, that the poets of France's southern provinces naturally preferred and excelled in lyric poetry because of their gentle and melodious language, the harsh, discordant idiom of the North being far better suited to the genre of the "conte," a speciality of the "trouvères." Both "trouvères" and troubadours found imitators in Italy and are to be respected for their own original contributions.[245] For Le Grand this would seem to imply that these early poets deliberated at length over the properties of their respective tongues before deciding to adopt a particular genre, a ridiculous suggestion. Moreover, the "trouvères," like their southern rivals, were responsible for many songs, and despite their harsh, discordant idiom some of their fabliaux and the majority of their romances were sung. The Italians spoke a language even more melodious than Provençal, yet Boccaccio ignored this advantage to become a "conteur." The troubadours might well have imitated him had they not lacked the necessary talent.[246] In the "querelle," it seems, no quarter could be given.

Le Grand does in fact make one concession to the troubadours, attributing to them the not inconsiderable distinction of having inspired Italy with a taste for lyric poetry in the vernacular and provided her

---

[245] *Journal de Monsieur*, 1782, vol. III, p. 290.

[246] *Observations sur les Troubadours*, p. 116. Earlier Le Grand rejects the *Journal de Monsieur's* suggestion that the "trouvères" excelled in the genres of the "conte" and the romance since these "... demandent un plus grand usage de la société, une connoissance plus détaillée des moeurs et des passions, & une certaine complication de vices ou de ridicules qu'on est plus à portée d'étudier dans les Cours & dans les Capitales que dans les Provinces". (1782, vol. III, p. 300.) The "fabliers," says Le Grand, were not philosophical courtiers but simple men, their only resource the gaiety and wit with which they were born. Why should they have been more knowledgeable men of the world than the troubadours who, like them, journeyed from château to château and from town to town reciting their compositions: "Qui empêchoit ces troubadours de composer aussi des fabliaux et des romans? Et pourquoi devoient-ils moins réussir que leurs rivaux? Le critique a cru répondre à mon objection, et elle subsiste encore tout entière." (*Observations sur les Troubadours*, pp. 17–18.)

first models in the genre. Here, however, he is concerned only to prove
the French responsible for the revival of literary activity in the West,
for which purpose, of course, the poets of the "Midi" are hailed as
compatriots of the "trouvères":

Il résulte de tout ceci que, si l'Italie doit aux troubadours le goût des vers et
la poésie lyrique, elle doit à nos provinces septentrionales les contes et les
romans. Ce sont là des obligations réelles, des obligations incontestables
qu'elle ne peut désavouer ....[247]

In contrast, when "trouvère" is weighed against troubadour this latter
is invariably found waiting, Le Grand clearly failing to do justice to the
southern provinces of France. Then what of his protestations of complete impartiality:

Je me flatte que les gens de lettres qu'intéressent ces réflexions daigneront les
lire avec des yeux aussi indifférents que les miens, et qu'ils ne croiront point
leur mérite personnel détruit avec celui des rimeurs de leurs provinces. Je
n'ai point l'honneur d'être leur compatriote; mais l'eussé-je été, je n'en
aurois pas moins publié avec la même impartialité tout ce qu'on vient de
lire, et mon amour-propre n'eût point réclamé un seul instant.[248]

If the *Fabliaux ou Contes* does indeed misrepresent the troubadours, and
for the author of the collection misrepresentation is an unforgivable sin,
then one should not immediately ascribe this to the fact that Le Grand
himself was born in Amiens, and whatever his insistence, was clearly
proud to be a northener. It should be remembered that he came to
know the troubadours through his association with Sainte-Palaye
whose own history of these poets left but a very poor impression of their
literary talents. In the opening pages of the *Observations* Le Grand
claims to have been sufficiently acquainted with Provençal to judge
for himself of the merits of those who rhymed in this idiom,[249] yet he
later admits that without Sainte-Palaye's annotations he would have
found this no simple task.[250] It would seem more than probable that Le
Grand, like Millot, formed his opinion of the troubadours from reading
Sainte-Palaye's translations and literary judgements, and we know already that this great scholar's interest in medieval literature was first
and foremost that of the historian. It is no surprise that Millot should

---

[247] *Observations sur les Troubadours*, p. 40.
[248] *Idem*, p. 166.
[249] P. 2.
[250] *Observations sur les Troubadours*, pp. 25–26: "Moi-même qui sais passablement bien la
romane françoise, j'ai eu beaucoup de peine à comprendre la provençale; et sans les secours
que m'ont procurés les commentaires de M. de Sainte-Palaye, très difficilement, je l'avoue,
je serois parvenu à la lire."

leave us with the impression that Provençal poetry is more instructive than entertaining. It would be no surprise if Le Grand himself genuinely failed to see any reason for the reputation enjoyed by the troubadours:

Leur histoire existe; ouvrez-la, qu'y trouverez-vous? Des Sirventes, des Tensons, d'éternelles & ennuyeuses Chansons d'amour, sans couleur, sans images, sans aucun intérêt; en un mot, une assoupissante monotonie, à laquelle tout l'art de l'Editeur & l'élégance de son style n'ont pu remédier.[251]

One thing must finally be said in Le Grand's favour, that where his numerous opponents offer only conjectures in support of their causes,[252] he himself furnishes concrete evidence to prove the "trouvères" worthy of the attention of the eighteenth century, not only as the true fathers of modern French literature but as the former masters of European letters. In concluding our examination of Le Grand's historical interest in the medieval poets we were concerned to know with what impression of the literary abilities of the "trouvères" his readers might be left. If the extracts of the fabliaux and the notes to which these give rise meet the aims envisaged here then the eighteenth century must finally come to recognize them as innovators at least, however "crude" and dated their novelty.

---

[251] *Fabliaux ou Contes*, vol. I, preface, p. xlviii. Perhaps it was only by seriously misrepresenting the troubadours that Le Grand could hope to redress the balance in favour of the "trouvères" who for centuries, as he explains, had been treated with utter contempt.

[252] Cf. Papon, *Voyage de Provence*, vol. II, Letter 1, pp. 176–177: "Je n'ai aucun des livres & des manuscrits nécessaires pour remonter au temps où les fabliaux, auxquels j'attribue une origine étrangère, ont été connus en France, en Italie & en Provence ... Malgré cela, j'ose me flatter que vous vous rendrez à l'évidence de mes autres preuves, & que mes réflexions pourront faire naître à quelqu'un l'idée de faire la comparaison de l'ancienne Littéraire françoise avec l'italienne & la provençale: ainsi vous ne devez regarder mes observations que comme une ébauche légère d'un ouvrage qui seroit véritablement intéressant, s'il étoit bien fait."

CHAPTER III

MEDIEVAL LITERATURE BY EIGHTEENTH-CENTURY STANDARDS. A DISCERNING APPRECIATION

Of that early definition of Le Grand's purpose as the defence and popularization of medieval French literature we have thus far only examined the first part. The plea has been for the recognition of the historical significance of that literature, to be valued not only for its provision of otherwise unobtainable insights into the national past, but as evidence of an earlier "Golden Age" of French poetry worthy of no lesser boast than the seventeenth and eighteenth centuries, evidence of the anteriority of French literary pre-eminence. It remains for us to examine the latter part of our definition then, to justify that description of the *Fabliaux ou Contes* as an extension of Le Grand's response to that first challenge to prove certain of the medieval writers still worthy of his contemporaries' attention as men of letters:

Je pris la liberté de dire que, pour le style, le goût, la critique, pour tout ce qui tient à l'art, il ne falloit point le chercher dans les ouvrages de ce temps; mais que si l'on vouloit se contenter d'esprit et d'imagination, on pourroit, à une certaine époque, en trouver chez nos vieux poètes; et j'ajoutai qu'il nous restoit d'eux, en ce genre, des choses fort agréables qui méritoit d'être connues.

There was clearly only one way for Le Grand to vindicate this claim. He must render the delights of these "choses fort agréables" readily accessible to the detractor. In the *Fabliaux ou Contes*, too, he is not only apologist but also popularizer.

It was noted earlier that, generally speaking, the Age of Reason was not one which saw the literary merits of the "anciens rimeurs" loudly applauded. The classicist's disdain did not suddenly give way to some revolutionary reappraisal and even the most sympathetic amongst medievalists never allowed their involvement to blind them to the harsh but, as they saw it, undeniable truth, that for the most part the efforts

of the Nation's earliest poets had been justly overshadowed by subsequent achievement:

Comparons les Ecrits de ces temps barbares avec ceux que l'Imprimerie
depuis 200 ans environ a mis entre nos mains. Soyons pénétrés de reconnoissance sur-tout pour ces hommes respectables qui, vers le milieu du siècle
dernier ont achevé d'épurer notre langue.[1]

If even the most devoted student of the Middle Ages and medieval
literature felt this way, then what was to be expected of lesser scholars,
or indeed of the uninstructed, rather uninitiated mass of the eighteenth-
century reading public? Despite our previous analysis of La Curne de
Sainte-Palaye's approach to his life's work, it is nevertheless surprising
to note what little distance appears, at first glance at least, to separate
his own view of, for example, the romances, "... souvent fastidieux
par leurs fictions, leur composition, le tour de leur esprit, & la grossièreté de leur style ...",[2] from that of Rigoley de Juvigny who, leader in
that campaign which called for a return to the models of classical antiquity and amongst the most vehement in his condemnation of the
medieval period, found these tales "... pleins d'un merveilleux absurde ..." and thus "... digne nourriture des esprits vides & inappliqués ...".[3] If the *Histoire littéraire des Troubadours* was marked by a lack
of feeling for Provençal poetry as poetry, then we know that Sainte-
Palaye, with nothing but respect for his "excellent rédacteur,"[4] was
himself largely responsible for this.[5]

In view of what has just been said, it may at first seem paradoxical
that we should now seek to establish the continued existence in the
eighteenth century of a tradition of what might be described as discerning sympathy for medieval literature. The paradox will be resolved
as the discussion progresses, but for the moment let us attempt at least
to temper it by noting that it would indeed be strange if, of the many
who, since the decline of the Middle Ages, had turned their attention,
however fleetingly, to the literary productions of that period, there was
not one who had found something to his liking. There are, in fact, more
than just a few, not the least among them Claude Fauchet:

---

[1] La Curne de Sainte-Palaye, *ms. Paris, B.N.f.Bréquigny 154*, fol. 26. Cited by L. Gossman,
Medievalism, p. 255.
[2] "Mémoire concernant la lecture des anciens Romans de Chevalerie," p. 797.
[3] "Discours sur le progrès des lettres en France" in his re-issue of La Croix du Maine's
and Antoine du Verdier's *Les Bibliothèques Françoises*, vol. I, p. 36.
[4] Cf. L. Gossman, *Medievalism*, p. 321.
[5] See above, p. 91.

... on serait tenté de soupçonner que Fauchet eut pour les oeuvres littéraires du Moyen Age, une espèce de sympathie secrète . . . .[6]

Rarely in the *Recueil de l'Origine de la Langue & Poësie Françoise* do we come upon what could be described as a lengthy critical analysis of a medieval work. For the most part Fauchet restricts himself to the shortest and most stereotyped of literary appraisals, the simple remark "... fut bon poëte ..." being often as far as he is prepared to go in his evaluation of a writer.[7] But there are those who are seen to deserve a little more. Blondiaux de Nesle is an "excellent Poëte" whose songs are "pleines de beaux traits."[8] The *Roman d'Alexandre* is praised at some length, containing as it does numerous "bons mots" which Fauchet would revive, "desrocher," "periller," and "... encores plusieurs autres belles manieres de parler, & des mots, que le studieux de la poesie Françoise pourra imiter, ou refondre ainsi que i'ay dict, se les appropriant, comme Virgile ceux d'Ennuis ...".[9] Other quotations will help him demonstrate to his contemporaries the "beaux traits," the "bons proverbes & sentences" he himself has discerned in the verse of Chrétien de Troyes.[10] It may be true that Fauchet's appreciation of Chrétien is far removed from Gustave Cohen's detailed analysis of the poet and his verse.[11] Certainly it is the case that the quotations taken from the works treated are frequently of far greater value than the literary appraisals of those works. But if singly Fauchet's brief approving remarks fail to impress, then they do have some cumulative effect:

... recurrent as they are, they sound like an obstinate retort to 'barbarous' and 'crude'; indeed, they become a sort of favorable cliché.[12]

The author of the *Recueil* merits some respect at least for his efforts to release the literary productions of the Middle Ages from that "... prison d'oubli, où l'ignorance les tenoit pesle-mesle enfermez ...".[13]

If Fauchet finds one of Thibaut de Champagne's songs "... tres-

---

[6] A. Pauphilet, *Le Legs du Moyen Age*, p. 27.

[7] Cf. the "Second livre du Recueil, contenant les noms et sommaire des oeuvres d'aucuns Poëtes & Rymeurs François, vivans avant l'an M.CCC" in Fauchet, *Oeuvres*, ff. 553vo–591vo. Cf. also J. G. Espiner-Scott, *Claude Fauchet*, pt. II, chapters II-IV; N. Edelman, *Attitudes of Seventeenth-Century France toward the Middle Ages*, pp. 327–329; C. E. Pickford, *Changing attitudes towards medieval French literature*, pp. 4–8.

[8] Fauchet, *Oeuvres*, fol. 568ro.

[9] *Idem*, fol. 555ro.

[10] *Idem*, ff. 558ro–559ro.

[11] Cf. Espiner-Scott, *Claude Fauchet*, p. 178.

[12] N. Edelman, *Attitudes of Seventeenth-Century France toward the Middle Ages*, p. 329.

[13] *Recueil*, Livre I, dedication.

belle, pleine de similitudes & translations ...",[14] then Pasquier considers him a poet of whom "... nous devons faire grand estat ...", his verse containing "... un amas de belles paroles d'amour ...".[15] And if there is praise indeed from Pasquier for the fifteenth-century farce of *Maistre Pierre Pathelin*, "... que je leu et releu avec tel contentement, que j'oppose maintenant cet eschantillon à toutes les Comédies Grecques, Latines, et Italiennes ...",[16] then how much more loudly acclaimed is the *Roman de la Rose* with which this "excellent type d'esprit de la Renaissance"[17] appears unable to find fault. Recalling the prestige and thus the influence which a man like Pasquier must have had in his day, Nathan Edelman considers it worthwhile to cite in full this "startling" judgement of the work.[18] For our part we might content ourselves with Edelman's own subsequent remarks:

This, be it noted, was first published in 1607! Pasquier never plunges into such a lengthy literary appraisal of other medieval works, with the exception of Thibaut de Champagne's 'chansons' and 'Maistre Pathelin.' But these he praises highly within a narrower range of qualities; had he been asked to summarize his enthusiastic comments on the 'Roman,' he would have had to say simply: 'It had practically everything.'[19]

It must be emphasized once more that Pasquier's appraisal of the *Roman de la Rose* is really quite exceptionally enthusiastic, exceptional even for Pasquier. Viewed out of context, as it were, it may well appear to set him apart from his contemporaries and even to place him far in advance of the majority of his successors. But taken as a whole Pasquier's judgements of the literary productions of the Middle Ages prove him to be quite simply a man of his time, an important link in the chain no doubt, but by no means sole continuator of that thriving tradition of discerning sympathy for this early literature. His successors deserve

---

[14] Fauchet, *Oeuvres*, fol. 565ro.

[15] *Recherches de la France* in *Les Œuvres choisies d'Etienne Pasquier* (ed. Léon Feugère) Paris (Firmin Didot) 1849, vol. I, pp. 244–247. Cf. N. Edelamn, *Attitudes of Seventeenth-Century France toward the Middle Ages*, p. 320.

[16] *Recherches, Oeuvres choisies*, vol. II, p. 125. As C. E. Pickford notes in his edition of the *Pathelin* (Paris, Les petits classiques Bordas, 1967, p. 119) Pasquier's opinion of the farce would be echoed in the eighteenth century by the Comte de Tressan writing in the *Encyclopédie*, "Parade," vol. XI, p. 888: "La farce de Pathelin feroit honneur à Molière. Nous avons peu de comédies qui rassemblent des peintures plus vraies, plus d'imagination et de gayeté."

[17] Pauphilet, *Le Legs du Moyen Age*, p. 26.

[18] *Recherches, Œuvres choisies*, vol. I, pp. 243–244.

[19] N. Edelman, *Attitudes of Seventeenth-Century France toward the Middle Ages*, pp. 388–389. Edelman devotes the whole of the sixth chapter of his book, more than a quarter of the work, to a discussion of seventeenth-century "Appreciation of medieval literature".

some mention, however brief. Favyn, too, praises the *Rose*.[20] Chapelain, however poor his opinion of the prose *Lancelot*, does find there "du
bon."[21] Though generally disdainful, Mézeray would agree that the
efforts made by French literature in the twelfth and thirteenth centuries to "se déterrer" were not altogether fruitless,[22] while Le Laboureur would actually recommend the old romances in preference to the
more dangerous productions of his own day ". . . où le poison n'est que
mieux préparé."[23] All this is scant praise indeed, one might be tempted
to think, when one remembers how much the Middle Ages had produced that was of value. But set these guarded statements beside
Boileau's extremist indictment of medieval poetry and they can appear
almost reckless in their commendation of that which had gone before
Villon:[24]

> Boileau, high spokesman of his time though he was, did not in this case speak
> for most of his contemporaries nor certainly for all of his century.[25]

We have said that our purpose here is to demonstrate the survival of
this tradition of discerning sympathy for medieval literature in Le
Grand's time. But already the implications of the epithet "discerning"
are becoming obvious and we need not perhaps dwell at too great a
length here on eighteenth-century manifestations of what was clearly
an altogether natural phenomenon. Other examples of such cautious
literary appraisals as those made by Boileau's contemporaries will need
to be cited before our discussion is complete, but for the moment let us
confine ourselves to a further brief examination of the position of him
who has so often before in this study been hailed as the spokesman of
Enlightenment medievalists.

If we know it to have been Sainte-Palaye's considered opinion that
little time was to be wasted regretting the crude efforts of the "anciens
rimeurs," then we have also noted that his plan for a comprehensive
collection of extracts of the romances of chivalry nevertheless included
the recommendation that its compilers might care to accept certain
extracts on purely literary grounds.[26] Sainte-Palaye did in fact discern

---

[20] André Favyn, *Le Théâtre d'Honneur et de Chevalerie* (Paris, 1620, 2 vols.) vol. I, p. 99. We
have already noted the immense favour enjoyed by the *Roman de la Rose* in seventeenth-century France.

[21] *De la lecture des vieux romans*, p. 240.

[22] François Mézeray, *Histoire de France depuis Pharamond jusqu'au règne de Louis le Juste*, Paris
(D. Thierry) 1685, 3 vols.

[23] *Histoire de la Pairie de France*, p. 281.

[24] Cf. Boileau, *Art poétique*, chant I, vv. 113–118.

[25] N. Edelman, *Attitudes of Seventeenth-Century France toward the Middle Ages*, p. 277.

[26] See above, pp. 71–72.

rare points of light shining through the darkness. However unflattering his judgement of the literary productions of the period as a whole, he had his own especial favourites amongst the medieval writers and for these there was the occasional word of praise. Lionel Gossman notes that Froissart's "pastourelles" and "rondeaux" appear to have been particularly favoured and cites the following passage from the "Notice des poésies de Froissart":

L'invention pour les sujets lui manquoit autant que l'imagination pour les ornemens; du reste le style qu'il employe, moins abondant que diffus, offre seulement la répétition ennuyeuse des mêmes tours et des mêmes phrases pour rendre des idées assez communes: cependant la simplicité et la liberté de sa versification ne sont pas toujours dépourvues de grâces, on y rencontre de tems en tems quelques images et plusieurs vers de suite dont l'expression est assez heureuse.[27]

Once again the temptation is to dismiss as insignificant so limited a recommendation from one who had devoted a lifetime of meticulous industry to the study of the Middle Ages and its literature. But Sainte-Palaye was simply continuing in a tradition now two centuries old. His too was a discerning sympathy, hardly noticeable at all perhaps until set against this background of general hostility. Once again, there was no sudden volte-face of opinion on the poetic abilities of the "anciens rimeurs" in eighteenth-century France. As it had been in the sixteenth and seventeenth centuries, it was simply a case of individual medieval writers appealing to certain scholars who marked their approval accordingly, the applause often clearly audible but rarely quite so loud as to offend the ears of their contemporaries. Like Fauchet and even Pasquier, Sainte-Palaye was a man of his time. His suggestion that the "bibliothèque générale et complète de tous nos anciens Romans de Chevalerie" should preserve "... ce qu'il y auroit de remarquable du côté de l'esprit et de l'invention" was not, it should be remembered, his first recommendation to those who might care to undertake the compilation.

The acid test for these "amateurs," of course, is quite simply to ask how medieval literature might have fared had its survival depended solely upon their faith and interest in it as literature and nothing else. The answer is that the "anciens rimeurs" might only now have been finding their rightful place in French literary histories had scholars of the Renaissance been blind to the possibilities of their exploitation on a

---

[27] L. Gossman, *Medievalism*, p. 252.

purely historical basis. Sainte-Palaye was running true to his line when he made it plain that the preservation of those apparently rare flights of inventive genius made by the authors of the old romances was a matter of only secondary importance.

Fauchet may well have had a certain "sympathie secrète" for medieval literature, charitably offering a good home for the romances, used and then cast aside as sickly slaves abandoned by some insensitive and ungrateful master. [28] But the point is that with careful attention these same slaves could be restored to health and thus to useful service. They rendered invaluable assistance to Fauchet in his "difficiles entreprises & laborieuses conceptions," proving well enough that ". . . des choses mesprisees peuvent encores estre utiles & profitables avec le temps, & par occasion."[29] If Fauchet's first consideration was thus the antiquarian interest of medieval literary texts,[30] then Pasquier, too, was predominantly historian in his approach to this early literature, and not only in his exploitation of the romances as "images de nos coutumes anciennes." Whatever his affection for the *Pathelin* or the *Roman de la Rose*, the *Recherches* show him to have been more concerned with the origins and progress of rhyme than with the merits of individual writers. His appraisal of the *Rose* is the exception which proves the rule:

Pasquier's attention is so fastened on the merits of this work that he fails to do what is usually most satisfying to him: he does not digress into any of those philological or historical discussions which we have learned to expect from him.[31]

Since we have already noted in an earlier part of this study the persistence throughout the seventeenth and into the eighteenth century of this historical bias to medieval researches, the purpose of the present discussion requires no more than that we should here emphasize that when those whom we have recently credited with a discerning sympathy for medieval literature publicly turned their attention to that literature it was rarely with the object of instilling this same sympathy in their readers. And when it was, the achievement generally fell far short of that object. La Croix du Maine's *Bibliothèque françoise* is no

---

[28] *Origines des Dignitez et Magistrats de France*, Epître au Lecteur.
[29] *Ibidem*.
[30] Cf. the conclusion to the second book of the *Recueil*, *Œuvres*, fol. 591 vo: ". . . en partie i'ay esté cause de les conserver à la honte de ceux qui les ont pensé indignes d'estres estimez: combien qu'il n'y aye si pauvre autheur qui ne puisse quelque fois servir, au moins pour le tesmoignage de son temps."
[31] N. Edelman, *Attitudes of Seventeenth-Century France toward the Middle Ages*, p. 389.

more than it purports to be, a "catalogue général de toutes sortes d'autheurs, qui ont escrit en françois depuis cinq cents ans et plus, jusques à
ce jourd'huy" with biographical information on the authors listed but
little or no literary appreciation. Chapelain may well find "du bon" in
the *Lancelot* but he concedes to Ménage that its author was a barbarian
writing for an audience of barbarians, "l'antipode des grâces."[32] Thus
he prefers to set his defence of the romances upon a purely historical
basis, this position apparently acceptable to the hostile Ménage, proclaiming the *Lancelot* comparable to the writings of Livy as a mirror of
the past, and having Sarasin agree "... on peut dire ce que dit M.
Chapelain, que ces vieux romans nous peignent au naturel les moeurs
et les coutumes de ces mêmes siècles."[33] If Le Laboureur feels that the
old romances are less likely to poison minds than modern literature,
then he does not regard the former as suitable reading matter for the
ignorant. It is, however, shameful for the scholar not to have read them
or to have gained nothing from reading them. He himself feels it his
duty to take up the defence of these tales of knights-errant for the assistance they have afforded him in his researches:

> ... pour faire valoir leur autorité en matière de Chevalerie, & même pour
> la Pairie de France, dont quelques-uns nous représentent les droits & les
> prérogatives telles qu'elles étoient du tems de leurs Auteurs ....[34]

When first demonstrating that the great antiquaries of the eighteenth
century, Camille Falconet and his colleagues at the Académie des Inscriptions spring immediately to mind, were not the first to show a
lively curiosity about the national past, we noted that various factors
had earlier prompted such curiosity, the interests of Church or State,
of the Monarchy or some particular social class.[35] We have since shown
that scholars concerned were by no means blind to the fact that the
historical insights afforded by medieval literary texts could be exploited
to serve these interests, Vulson de la Colombière, it will be remembered, drawing for documentary evidence in his efforts to "remettre la
noblesse dans son ancien lustre" not only upon chronicles but romances, entertaining enough but more valuable for their particular utility:

> ... je ne trouve point de Lecture plus divertissante, ny qui allume avec plus
> d'ardeur le courage aux jeunes gens, & qui leur donne plus d'envie d'ac-

---

[32] *De la lecture des vieux romans*, p. 221.
[33] *Idem*, p. 220.
[34] *Histoire de la Pairie de France*, p. 281.
[35] See above, p. 73.

quérir de l'honneur, & se pousser avec affection aux pénibles & dangereuses entreprises.[36]

It now becomes evident that this exploitation was mutually beneficial. There can be little doubt that such works as *Le Vray théâtre d'Honneur et de Chevalerie* did much to help preserve the "anciens rimeurs" from oblivion. The great "querelle des trouvères et des troubadours," we might recall, was essentially only the product of a desire to flatter the national or provincial vanity and we know what the dispute did to keep "trouvère" and troubadour alike in the public eye. It was frequently in the absence of any real sympathy for, and even of any proper acquaintance with, the poets concerned, and thus without any effort made to demonstrate their abilities, that proud patriots and provincials declared the first rhymers of the North or South to have been pre-eminent not only in the France of their day but in the whole of medieval Europe:

He (Nostredame) did not analyse. His praises, like those of Fauchet for the 'trouvères,' were brief and cast in the same mold. But that alone could stamp a sort of favourable formula on the readers' minds. Almost everyone of his troubadours, real or imaginary, was a good or a very good poet.[37]

Le Grand d'Aussy, we remember, was eventually to claim that the reputation of the Provençal poets was founded not upon any real literary achievement but solely upon the applause they received from their Italian disciples.[38]

Medieval literary texts were still popular reading matter at the turn of the seventeenth century then, but the public was a largely scholarly one, overlooking the original intentions of the "anciens rimeurs." Even the most complimentary of those early "Provençalistes" were essentially concerned only to popularize their view of the troubadours as the former masters of European letters. The insistence that they had once, many centuries ago, been acclaimed as great poets may well have pandered to southern pride, but it did little to encourage the reading of Old Provençal poetry as poetry, to cause an outcry for the publication of texts. Popular opinion in the South must surely have run thus: "How gratifying to think that even then our provinces were responsible for the Nation's finest poets. But what a long way we have come since then!" It thus remains true that La Curne de Sainte-Palaye and

---

[36] *Le Vray Théâtre d'Honneur et de Chevalerie ou le Miroir Héroique de la Noblesse*, vol. I, p. 292.

[37] N. Edelman, *Attitudes of Seventeenth-Century France toward the Middle Ages*, p. 344. Edelman devotes several pages to the survival of the troubadours in his sixth chapter, "Appreciation of Medieval Literature."

[38] See above, p. 122 and p. 140.

his contemporaries were heirs to a tradition of historically oriented medievalism, a tradition which for the most part they would continue to uphold.

We have noted already with what enthusiasm Enlightenment medievalists applied themselves to the task of laying open these centuries of darkness. Plans for the most detailed researches into manners and customs, laws and institutions, into the progress made in the arts and sciences during this period were, we know, adopted and set in motion.[39] But if these researches were much facilitated by an ever increasing awareness of the historical utility of medieval literature, prompted largely by Sainte-Palaye himself, if fictional texts of the Middle Ages now came to be treated with that respect hitherto reserved only for traditional documentary sources,[40] then what respect, if any, did this same literature obtain when examined, so to speak, out of its historical context? Was any attempt made to demonstrate the value of these texts simply as works of literature, to prove the "anciens rimeurs" still worthy of attention as poets, irrespective of their particular usefulness to antiquaries or indeed of their former pre-eminence?

It should be evident that scholars like Sallier, Caylus or Lebeuf with their studies of individual authors and their works do not concern us here. In the first place, it will be remembered that they were usually restricted to an erudite public, the readers of the *Mémoires de l'Académie des Inscriptions*. In the second place, and more important, these studies, though often illustrated with numerous quotations and extracts, almost invariably betrayed that omnipresent historical bias, being written very much in that spirit in which the Abbé Goujet looked back to the Middle Ages:

... on aime à connoître ceux qui ont commencé à défricher le champ de la littérature; à savoir comment ils s'y sont pris, les progrès qu'ils ont faits, par qui & par quels moiens les sciences ont été développées & perfectionnées: ce que l'on ne connoîtroit point, si l'on ne s'arrêtoit qu'aux ouvrages qui ont acquis cette perfection.[41]

---

[39] See above, pp. 74–76.

[40] Le Laboureur had felt obliged to justify his use of fictional sources: "Je me suis servi de cette occasion, pour rapporter ces traits, par ce qu'on eût peut-être trouvé mauvais que je les eusse mêlé avec l'autorité des véritables Historiens; mais comme ils ne se sont attachés qu'au récit des affaires générales, sans toucher les Coûtumes & les Usages de leur tems, il en faut chercher le portrait dans ces vieux Romans, qui nous en ont conservé l'idée, avec des mots qui servent à découvrir l'origine des choses." (*Histoire de la Pairie de France*, pp. 283–284.)

Sainte-Palaye, we know, drew his information without distinction from fictional and nonfictional sources alike.

[41] *Bibliothèque Françoise*, vol. I, Discours Préliminaire, p. xxxviii.

There were, of course, those who, like their sixteenth and seventeenth-century predecessors, were prepared to mark cautious approval of individual writers. There were many, we saw, prepared to exploit the "anciens rimeurs" by reshaping their works and adapting them to contemporary tastes prior to setting them before a public which, for its part, cared little what remained of the originals and proved so enthusiastic even, or rather especially, about "false" extracts like Tressan's *Ursino*.[42] But there seems to have been no-one with sufficient faith in medieval literature to embark upon a serious "oeuvre de vulgarisation" that would prove this still viable as literature in the eighteenth century. At least, there appears to have been no-one who combined such faith with that essential understanding of the very real limitations of the reading public.

It is no exaggeration to say that the majority of Enlightenment medievalists had no greater confidence in the ability of the "anciens rimeurs" to stand by their own merits than had Voltaire himself. This latter may eventually have acknowledged the historical potential of the old romances but that is all. Unlike the efforts of the great classical writers, they had simply failed to survive as works of literature, now unworthy of consideration as such:

Les romans de notre moyen âge, écrits dans nos jargons barbares, ne peuvent entrer en comparaison ni avec Apulée et Pétrone, ni avec les anciens romans grecs tels que la 'Cyropédie' de Xénophon ....[43]

Thus, for the Comte de Caylus the only way one could hope to gain any kind of respect for these early poets was to bring together all the historical information they offer,[44] the object of Sainte-Palaye's plan for a "bibliothèque générale et complète de tous nos anciens Romans de Chevalerie." Once again, what Sainte-Palaye was advocating was the systematic study of the fictional sources of medieval history, a significant advance but altogether in keeping with that tradition established by Fauchet, Chapelain, Le Laboureur and the rest. The very fact that this was to be a collection of extracts proves well enough that Sainte-Palaye had not the slightest wish to reinstate the authors of the romances as men of letters:

---

[42] See above, p. 66.

[43] A letter from Voltaire to the editors of the *Bibliothèque des Romans*, dated 15th August, 1775 (Oeuvres Complètes, vol. XLIX, *Correspondance XVII*, pp. 354–357). Cited by H. Jacoubet, *Le Comte de Tressan*, p. 179.

[44] See above, p. 85.

Les bons livres perdent toujours à être abrégés. Les beautés principales sont anéanties ou défigurées dans l'extrait le mieux fait : & d'ailleurs nous savons combien il est dangereux de faire des abrégés des bons livres ; puisque de tels abrégés ont causé la perte d'un nombre infini des meilleurs ouvrages de l'antiquité. On n'aura pas la même crainte pour les mauvais, où il est aisé de faire choix des choses utiles & curieuses qui s'y trouvent, comme par hasard : si l'on recueille avec soin ce qu'ils peuvent avoir de précieux, leur perte, quand ils viendront à disparoître, ne causera aucun regret.[45]

Eighteenth-century medievalists were reluctant to undertake scholarly editions of early texts for their historical let alone their literary value.

We have seen already, of course, that there could have been no public for carefully edited medieval literary texts in eighteenth-century France.[46] But we have also suggested that this and the scholar's corresponding lack of enthusiasm to furnish such editions led quite naturally to the appearance of a number of highly popular and yet serious "oeuvres de vulgarisation" of which Sainte-Palaye's *Aucassin et Nicolette* is an excellent example, an honest translation of a medieval text delighting a wide readership.[47] Sainte-Palaye not only knew and understood the tastes of his public, he shared them, and the popularity of his *Aucassin* might be judged in itself sufficient to disprove the view that at the time the "anciens rimeurs" were given no opportunity to stand by their own merits, had we not already noted the avowed object of this publication :

Il ne s'agit pas de donner un ouvrage sans défauts, celui-ci en a beaucoup qu'on ne prétend pas dissimuler ; il est question de faire connoître au vrai nos anciennes moeurs ; comme rien n'est plus propre à les représenter au naturel que cette composition, on a cru ne pouvoir conserver avec trop de fidélité dans la copie, tous les traits de l'original.[48]

Certainly this is an "oeuvre de vulgarisation," but it is not meant to convey some notion of the original author as a great literary genius, rather only to acquaint the reader with certain of the manners and

---

[45] "Mémoire concernant la lecture des anciens Romans de Chevalerie," p. 797.

[46] However, cf. L. Gossman, *Medievalism*, p. 259 : "Lévesque de la Ravalière's edition of the 'Poésies du Roy de Navarre' was exceptional in aiming at a reasonable standard of textual accuracy and at the same time gaining a place on the bookshelves. Lévesque was helped by the curiosity which the romantic legend of Thibaut's love for Queen Blanche aroused in a public voracious for anecdotes of the loves of princes."
The *Poésies du Roy de Navarre* (Paris, 1742, 2 vols.) is the exception proving the rule. Lévesque's attitude is no different from that of his contemporaries. He respects and admires Thibaut but would not think to set him above modern poets : ". . . il mériteroit une estime sans réserve, si . . . son siècle avoit eu la retenue et la sagesse de celui dans lequel nous vivons. (*Les poésies du Roy de Navarre*, vol. I, preface, pp. xviii-xix).

[47] See above, pp. 67-68.

[48] Edition of 1756, *Les Amours du bon vieux temps*, Avertissement, p. 7.

customs of the period in which he was active. It has exactly the same purpose as the *Mémoires sur l'ancienne Chevalerie*, the only difference being that whereas in these latter we discover pleasure and amusement where we might have thought only to find instruction, in the former we are instructed and educated where we might have expected only to be diverted and entertained.[49] It is in this sense that we must understand the term "vulgarisateur" when applied to Sainte-Palaye.

In more than one way, of course, Sainte-Palaye did hasten the coming of that age when the careful editing of medieval literary texts would be seen as a worthwhile occupation. Not only by his own historical under-takings but by the willingness with which he made his advice and his considerable library available to those highly successful "remanieurs" of his day[50] did he help to keep this literature in the public eye until the appearance in the early nineteenth-century of a new generation of rather less conservative medievalists. And these, again, did not fail to exploit that rich store of annotated manuscript copies which he had left, drawing upon it for their own editions of texts and thus, by modern standards, making far better use of it than had Sainte-Palaye himself. For medieval literature was for him only the means to an end. Para-doxically, his readiness to furnish authors like Tressan and Mlle de Lubert with the materials for new adaptations is symptomatic of his almost complete lack of concern for the eventual fate of those texts upon which he himself lavished so much attention and which served him so well:

... si l'on recueille avec soin ce qu'ils peuvent avoir de précieux, leur perte, quand ils viendront à disparoître, ne causera aucun regret.

The few texts he did publish, then, he approached in a manner alto-gether in keeping with this overriding historical bias:

... il fait de la poésie l'auxiliaire de la science.[51]

In one respect the *Histoire littéraire des Troubadours* was inferior to Nostre-dame's *Vies*. The latter work at least, whatever its omissions, inaccura-cies and downright falsehoods, did leave the reader with a favourable impression of those poets to whom it made reference. The Sainte-Palaye–Millot collection contained hardly one word of praise for the

---

[49] We might recall here the *Mercure's* appreciation of the first of the *Mémoires*. See above, p. 69.

[50] Cf. L. Gossman, *Medievalism*, pp. 327–329.

[51] On the six texts which were to appear in the *Mémoires sur l'ancienne Chevalerie*, cf. L. Gossman, pp. 261–262.

troubadours, unless it be in respect of their particular interest and utility to the antiquary. It was never meant to set the troubadours on a par with their illustrious successors, but Le Grand d'Aussy could actually use it to substantiate his own view that even in their own time the Provençal poets were no better than second-rate:

> ... les fades lieux communs de galanterie, les répétitions fréquentes des mêmes pensées & des mêmes expressions, les longueurs & le mauvais goût rendroient insupportable un recueil complet de leurs ouvrages. Il a fallu supprimer, élaguer beaucoup; & ces sacrifices ne méritent aucun regret.[52]

The fact that Le Grand would take great pains to ensure that his own collection would leave the reader with no mean opinion of what the "anciens rimeurs," this time the "trouvères," had once been worth, this in itself does not imply that his general approach to medieval literature differed significantly from that of his former master. Quite the contrary, it would seem, for thus far our examination of the aims envisaged in the *Fabliaux ou Contes* has proven Le Grand to be a true disciple of Sainte-Palaye. He, too, found the Middle Ages to be a period marked by great ignorance and barbarism. He, too, considered that for the most part the efforts of France's earliest poets were "... bien loin assurément de pouvoir entrer en parallèle avec nos chef-d'oeuvres modernes ...".[53] Was he not simply repeating what Sainte-Palaye had taught him when he stressed of what interest and utility medieval literature, and the fabliaux in particular, could be to the antiquary? And similarly, was it not in fact altogether in keeping with that tradition of historically oriented medievalism brought to its high point by Sainte-Palaye that Le Grand should insist heavily upon the former significance of the "fabliers," should be concerned to establish their right to a place in the Nation's literary annals? But if the author of the *Fabliaux ou Contes* had clearly been a most attentive apprentice, if he rejected nothing of the master's teachings, then what becomes of our purpose to prove that his work was in one very important respect distinct from that of his fellow medievalists?

---

[52] *Histoire littéraire des Troubadours*, vol. I, Discours préliminaire, p. liv.

[53] *Fabliaux ou Contes*, vol. IV, Discours préliminaire, p. ii. Le Grand, like Sainte-Palaye, appears to have been only too willing to help the "remanieurs." Cf. B. Imbert, *Choix de Fabliaux mis en vers*, Geneva and Paris (Prault) 1788, 2 vols.: "L'ouvrage de M. Le Grand étant public, tout le monde avoit, comme moi, le droit d'y puiser. Mais je lui dois un remercîment personnel pour une obligation absolument particulière. Ayant appris que je m'occupois de mettre en vers un choix de nos Fabliaux, il a eu l'honnêteté de m'offrir & de me communiquer quelques autres sujets, qu'il vient de découvrir en faisant des recherches pour une nouvelle édition de son ouvrage; aussi je lui dois l'avantage d'avoir ajouté à mon recueil quelques Fabliaux absolument nouveaux pour mes lecteurs." (Vol. I, Avertissement, p. xi.)

It is surely the duty of the apprentice to use the teachings of the master of the craft in order to improve upon him. This is precisely what Le Grand was doing when, as we shall attempt to establish, he made it one of the primary objectives of the *Fabliaux ou Contes* to prove that certain of the medieval poets were still worthy of consideration as poets even in 1779. In no way did this represent a rejection of Sainte-Palaye's position. Both men abhorred the ignorance and grossness of the Middle Ages, but neither considered that the period was to be rejected and forgotten as having produced nothing of value. On the contrary, certain things remained valid even in the eighteenth century. With no misconceptions as to the horrors it actually produced, Sainte-Palaye admired what chivalry was meant to be in its perfect form:

> Properly reconstituted, therefore, chivalry could be adopted, Sainte-Palaye thought, 'par les plus sages législateurs et par les plus vertueux philosophes' of his own time. The modern French aristocracy, for its part, would welcome a revival of chivalry because of that 'fonds de ressemblance qui ne change jamais,' which Sainte-Palaye had discovered in the ancient Franks and in their modern successors. If anything, in short, the times were more suitable to chivalry than they had been in the past.[54]

Although he himself spoke wistfully of "l'élévation d'âme qu'inspirait la Chevalerie,"[55] Le Grand for his part was usually concerned with the more practical side of things when it came to rendering homage to the Middle Ages. Was it not precisely to this period that eighteenth-century society owed such marvellous inventions as printing, oil-painting, clocks, windmills, engraving, paper, gunpowder, firearms, mirrors, the violin, so many other fine things ". . . dont aujourd'hui s'enorgueillit l'esprit humain . . .".[56] What more creditable invention than the compass:

> C'est encore cet âge de ténèbres et de barbarie, qui nous a donné la Boussole; la Boussole, cette invention inestimable à laquelle nous devons la découverte d'un nouveau monde, le passage aux Indes par le Cap de Bonne-Espérance, l'accroissement immense du commerce de l'Europe, le perfectionnement de la navigation, la connaissance du globe, et toutes les Sciences qui ont été le résultat de celles-ci, ou qui en ont profité.[57]

Amongst those remnants of the Middle Ages which both Sainte-Palaye and Le Grand still valued, of course, were a few specimens of the lit-

---

[54] L. Gossman, *Medievalism*, p. 283.
[55] *Fabliaux ou Contes*, vol. I, preface, p. lxxvii.
[56] *Ms. Paris, B.N.n.a.f. 6226*, fol. 77.
[57] *Ibidem.*

erature of the period. Neither esteemed the whole of that literature, but each quite naturally had his own especial favourites amongst the "anciens rimeurs." Sainte-Palaye, we know, enjoyed Froissart's "pastourelles,"[58] Le Grand a variety of pieces, none more, of course, than the fabliaux. Thus Le Grand's desire to publish his regard for certain of what he considered to be the finer examples of medieval literature by presenting these to his contemporaries as works of literature, this, surely, is only a natural progression from Sainte-Palaye's position of private, one might almost say secretive, appreciation. The author of the *Fabliaux ou Contes* did not attack that tradition of historically oriented medievalism from without, he accepted it wholeheartedly but added something of himself. There was no sudden and violent change of emphasis with his collection, only the beginning of a very gradual process of redirection from within. This may at first appear a meagre distinction, but if the *Fabliaux ou Contes* represented only the next logical step, it does not necessarily follow that this was an easy step to take.

On opening this examination of Le Grand's purposes we had said that his collection would quite obviously represent in part an extension of that response he had made when first pressed to produce specimens of medieval literature which even then "... méritoient d'être connues ...".[59] But if this intention is obvious, then it is only because Le Grand himself makes it so. From what we now know of the earlier inflexibility of medieval studies, it becomes evident that this desire to prove certain of the "anciens rimeurs" still readable in the eighteenth century marks Le Grand as something of an innovator. Certainly their work would be presented in the form of extracts and these extracts would represent only a fraction of medieval literary achievement. Certainly Le Grand would be insured against total failure by the fact that these same extracts were to serve other more acceptable ends, to establish the former pre-eminence of the "trouvères," to stress again the historical utility of medieval literature. But the author of the *Fabliaux ou Contes* was a man of his times. He could not and would not advance further than those times would allow. The progress to be made might appear insignificant to the enlightened medievalist of the twentieth century, but it is only in this century that medieval literature has come to be valued as literature. Hitherto Le Grand has been viewed as only another link in that chain of historically oriented medievalism stretching from the sixteenth century, a minor link since his achievement with-

[58] See above, p. 183.
[59] See above, p. 55.

in the strict confines of this tradition was overshadowed by that of Sainte-Palaye. We must now attempt to establish what recognition he deserves as innovator.

Considering the historical utility of medieval literature best evidenced in the "fabliaux ou contes," Le Grand, we know, did not include those extracts of other genres appearing in his collection for their antiquarian interest alone, the fourth volume offering relatively few notes of such interest. Certainly it was with the "fabliaux ou contes" again that he thought himself best able to establish the former literary pre-eminence of northern France, but those additional extracts, we saw, would similarly help to prove the "trouvères" worthy of far greater esteem than they had so far enjoyed.[60] Clearly, then, the "fabliaux ou contes" were not the only specimens of medieval literature that Le Grand valued, and wished to recall, for what they had once represented. In contrast, when it came to comparing the efforts of the "anciens rimeurs" with those of their enlightened seventeenth and eighteenth-century successors, not only was it this genre alone, it was but a fraction of this genre that Le Grand felt could survive such a comparison. But those few exceptions merited the same consideration from his contemporaries as modern works of literature.

There is nothing to suggest that Molière knew the work of the "anciens rimeurs," says Le Grand, and it is to be regretted that he did not:

Que de perles il eût tirées de ce fumier![61]

This, essentially, is what medieval literature represents for the author of the *Fabliaux ou Contes* when judged by eighteenth-century standards, a morass of mediocrity with only the occasional point of high ground. If there are exceptions, then generally speaking the "contes dévots" are not "un Ouvrage que la France puisse se faire honneur de revendiquer."[62] Allegories like "La Bataille de Charnage et de Carême" and "La Bataille des Vins" are no better than the majority of "chansons de geste" that have survived, "si niaises & si plates."[63] Since rarely do we come upon such a piece as "Le Jeu du Berger et de la Bergère," medieval dramatic achievement is significant and worthy of recall only in

---

[60] See above, pp. 156–168.

[61] Note to "Le Médecin de Brai," *Fabliaux ou Contes*, vol. I, p. 410.

[62] In the Discours préliminaire to the "Contes dévots" a quotation from the preamble to one of the tales in the *Vies des pères* is introduced with the exceptional remark: "On ne ferait pas aujourd'hui des vers plus harmonieux & plus doux." (*Fabliaux ou Contes*, vol. IV, p. xx.)

[63] See above, p. 163.

that it represents the beginnings of French theatre.[64] The love-songs of the "trouvères" are as much to be despised as those of their southern rivals.[65]

The third volume of the *Fabliaux ou Contes* does offer six "romances" or "lais" which are highly recommended by Le Grand.[66] But if he values these enough to wish to claim them for the North, despite the lack of imitations, then there is nothing to suggest that he finds them superior to or even comparable with any modern equivalents. Marie de France is honoured as the earliest known French poetess and as the sole fabulist of her century,[67] but there is no critical appreciation of her work:

Je ne dis rien du mérite littéraire de Marie de France; quoiqu'elle eût beaucoup de goût, ainsi qu'on le verra par cinq ou six corrections qu'elle s'est permis de faire à ses deux originaux: corrections qui, si je ne me trompe, sont toutes heureuses. Je ne dis rien de son stile, qui est, comme le leur, simple, clair, & même élégant pour son temps: elle a bien un autre mérite pour nous.[68]

What does Le Grand consider the most precious feature of Marie? It is the possibility that she may conceivably preserve in her works fables by her Greek and Roman predecessors hitherto regarded as lost.[69] The "pastourelles" have much to delight the reader but their coarseness and complete lack of variety render them unworthy of a collection. As with the romances, to read one is to know them all.[70]

Although of the innumerable manuscript and printed romances which have survived there can be no more than twenty worthy of

---

[64] Cf. the note to "Le Jeu de S. Nicholas" cited above, p. 162, note 192.

[65] See above, p. 161, note 185.

[66] See above, pp. 160–161.

[67] See above, p. 159.

[68] *Fabliaux ou Contes*, vol. IV, Avertissement préliminaire to the "Fables," pp. 161–162.

[69] Cf. *idem*, pp. 162–168. It is quite possible, Le Grand suggests, that a number of works by the great historians, poets and orators of antiquity, though the original manuscripts be lost or destroyed, still exist in the form given them by their early translators. Could not the government, which has after all instigated many less promising undertakings, order a search of these translations, setting in charge some learned and industrious man of letters: "Et d'ailleurs si celle-ci n'avait aucun succès, n'est-il pas assûré d'avance qu'elle produira au moins des découvertes utiles pour notre Histoire, ou glorieuses pour notre Littérature? Mon exemple doit encourager. Moi, Littérateur inconnu, sans avoir été secondé par sa protection si favorable, n'ai-je pas eu le bonheur d'en faire quelques-unes de ce dernier genre."

Was Le Grand offering himself as a candidate for the post? In a similar vein, cf. L. Gossman, *Medievalism*, p. 234, note 28: "Sainte-Palaye had the foresight to see that early printed editions are worth consulting for readings which they may have preserved from MSS subsequently lost."

Finally, Sainte-Palaye's own manuscript copies have not infrequently served modern scholars in a similar way. Cf. L. Gossman, *Medievalism*, pp. 264–267.

[70] See above, p. 160.

note,[71] one could take almost any example of the genre at random, Le Grand acknowledges, and be sure to find oneself enthralled by a story of daring adventures and deeds of great valour. But that one example is enough. We may all be children when it comes to such tales, but even a child becomes restless when the storyteller is so predictable:

... arrêtez-vous au premier. Calqués presque tous sur un même plan, vous retrouveriez dans un autre, & les mêmes prouesses, & le même héros; c'est-à-dire, une monotonie fatigante, au dégoût de laquelle il vous serait impossible de résister long-tems.[72]

There are, of course, those areas, matters of detail, where the romances necessarily differ, and such passages can often be so striking in their originality, admits Le Grand, that he had at first thought to publish them as a collection of extracts, his testimony to the ability of the "anciens rimeurs." But the testimony, he realized, would be a lie, these extracts demonstrating only the merits of a genre whose faults are many.[73] Clearly Le Grand could not in all honesty present such a collection as proof that the medieval poets were men of considerable talent by medieval literary standards, let alone that some of their efforts remain valid even by those of the eighteenth century. The idea is abandoned, but the sacrifice is small. Le Grand has found an ideal medium for his message in the fabliaux.

If we did establish precisely why Le Grand considers the "fabliaux ou contes" the most valuable of all the literary sources of medieval history, then all that we know of his regard for these tales as works of literature is that he must esteem them above all else since, as he himself makes clear, it is the first three volumes of his collection, the "fabliaux ou contes" proper, that contain the evidence necessary to prove his view of the "trouvères" as the former masters of European letters. It has now become essential for us to establish that for Le Grand the "fabliers" are indeed, of all the medieval poets, "... ceux ... dans

---

[71] In the notes prepared for the preface to that section of the proposed *Histoire de la Littérature française* to concern the romances we find the following: "Annoncer que ce n'est point un ouvrage d'agrément, mais un voyage à travers un pays inculte inconnu, où l'on trouve seulement de temps en temps quelques bouquets de verdure agréable qui offrent un lieu de repos." (*Ms. Paris, B.N.n.a.f. 6227*, fol. 164.)

[72] *Fabliaux ou Contes*, vol. IV, Avertissement préliminaire to "Parténopex," p. 253.

[73] See above, p. 165. One of the many things which Le Grand disliked about the "romanciers" was their long-windedness: "L'Alexandriade est beaucoup trop longue; et en général c'est le défaut de tous ces féconds romanciers, qui, sans goût ainsi que sans art, se croyoient de grands hommes quand ils avoient cousu et mis bout à bout, tant bien que mal, douze, quinze, et jusqu'à vingt-cinq mille vers." ("Notice de neuf manuscrits de la Bibliothèque nationale, contenant 'Alexandre,' roman historique et de chevalerie," *Notices et Extraits des Manuscrits de la Bibliothèque Impériale*, vol. V (An VII) pp. 101-131.)

lesquels on trouve le plus de fécondité & de talent ...",[74] to demonstrate precisely why and by how much he considers them superior to their contemporaries, on what grounds he can in fact declare

> ... que plusieurs de ses Contes sont tels que j'ose les donner après Bocace & Lafontaine, & que malgré la perfection qu'a dû nécessairement amener un intervalle de cinq siècles, tous les Conteurs qui les ont suivis n'ont peut-être encore, avec beaucoup plus d'art, plus de poésie, plus de grâces dans le style, ni autant de vérité dans la narration, ni autant d'intérêt & de variété dans les sujets.[75]

Firstly, let us take the question of variety, undoubtedly for Le Grand one of the most endearing features of the fabliaux. The romances, he says, are necessarily almost all identical, generally depicting some knight engaged upon various feats of prowess and thereby admitting of only certain more or less stereotyped events. The fabliaux, on the other hand, being individual short stories, are restricted only in respect of their dimensions, not their content. Hence the diversity of these tales, which, unlike the romances, do not fall easily into obvious categories.[76] Variety of subject-matter then, but equally variety of tone. The "fabliers," Le Grand acknowledges, may have been responsible for a number of most unedifying tales, but they could see beyond the ribald:

> En effet, s'ils ont des Contes libres, ils en ont aussi de nobles, d'intéressans, de gais, d'héroïques: quelques-unes de leurs Pièces même, telles que les 'Deux Amis,' 'Grisélidis,' &c. joignent aux situations les plus touchantes, une morale sublime.[77]

This is much more than can be said for their successors, only Boccaccio proving a true disciple in this respect. For the most part modern "conteurs" appear to have chosen to return to that narrow but by no means straight path first beaten, never so heavily trodden, by the "fabliers," making of it their sole highway:

> ... & qui dit Conte aujourd'hui, dit ouvrage licentieux, ou au moins libre.[78]

A few minor erasures and the Church takes no objection to Boccaccio's "contes," but how little would remain of those of La Fontaine, of

---

[74] *Fabliaux ou Contes*, vol. I, preface, p. lxi.

[75] *Idem*, p. lxiii.

[76] *Idem*, pp. lxiii-lxiv. Cf. Johnston and Owen, *Fabliaux*, Oxford (Blackwell's French Texts) 1957, p. ix: "Classification on any grounds is at best arbitrary and cannot take account of every one of the texts. The categories which we shall propose therefore, though convenient, are by no means rigid, and a single text may have claims to be included in more than one."

[77] *Fabliaux ou Contes*, vol. I, preface, pp. lxxiii-lxxiv.

[78] *Ibidem.*

Piron, Vergier, Grécourt and the like if one were to undertake to render them equally inoffensive. What Le Grand finds particularly objectionable is that these "historiettes ordurières" almost invariably revolve around the occupants of some monastery or convent, as if all religious were given to debauchery. Surely there is good and evil in every society, never the one to the exclusion of the other:

Quelque licencieux que soient parfois les Fabliers, on ne leur reprochera pas au moins d'avoir calomnié à ce point un état respectable & le sexe le plus pudibond ... & il faut convenir que les désordres du Clergé de ce tems rendaient en quelque sorte la satyre excusable ...[79].

Although Le Grand is quite prepared to admit that the octosyllabic line with "rimes plates" does not mark the "fabliers" as the greatest of medieval versifiers,[80] as story-tellers he finds them unrivalled by their contemporaries and even, in some respects, in advance of their successors. The "fablier," for example, addresses his audience, a gathering in a public square or a circle of noblemen, far more frequently than does his more verbose colleague, the "romancier," not only at the outset but throughout the course of his narrative. The effect is to bring his tale much closer to the dialogue than any modern "conte," to give a far greater impression of dramatic action. And how this impression is enhanced when, in opposing characters, the "fablier" avoids the monotonous "dit-il," "reprit-il" etc., this procedure apparently recommended by an unwitting eighteenth-century "conteur" as a desirable innovation, and thus gives their exchanges the speed and veracity usually found only in the theatre:

---

[79] *Idem*, p. lxxi. The *Journal de Monsieur* for 1782 can recommend the "contes dévots" appearing in the fourth volume of Le Grand's collection: "...leur absurdité même a quelque chose de piquant & d'original; on est tout étonné d'y rencontrer quelquefois une narration pleine de mouvement, de dramatique & de sentimens."

But it continues: "Parmi ces Contes dévots on en trouve quelques-uns qui ont fourni des sujets de Contes très-indévots, à Grécourt & à Piron; on sent bien que nous ne pouvons rien citer de ceux-là." (*Journal de Monsieur*, 1782, vol. III, pp. 308–318.)

Le Grand's view of organized religion would alter somewhat with the times, although it is for their bigotry and not for any obvious libertinism that he finds the religious of his own day a justifiable object of criticism: "J'avoue que jusqu'à l'époque de la révolution, il y avoit quelque audace à oser attaquer en France la religion du clergé. Aujourd'hui, ce seroit presque une lâcheté." (*Vie d'Apollonius de Tyane*, vol. I, Avant-propos, p. xxxv.)

[80] The admission costs little since he can now proceed to demonstrate of what the "anciens rimeurs" were capable: "... c'est que pour les différentes mesures de vers, pour la variété de coupe des couplets lyriques, enfin, pour tout le technique de la versification, on n'a presque rien inventé depuis nos vieux Poëtes; qu'il n'existe aujourd'hui que ce qui existait de leur tems, & qu'ils connaissaient même des formes de vers agréables qui sont méconnues". (*Fabliaux ou Contes*, vol. I, preface, pp. cii-ciii.)

C'est même aussi chez eux une manière de dialoguer fort ordinaire.[81]

What will strike Joseph Bédier most about the "fabliaux" is the absence of any literary pretensions:

... le poète ne songe qu'à dire vitement et gaiement son conte, sans prétention, ni recherche, ni vanité littéraire. De là ces défauts: négligence de la versification et du style, platitude, grossièreté. De là aussi des mérites, parfois charmants: élégante brièveté, vérité, naturel.[82]

For Le Grand, too, these tales, though often in bad taste and not without their shortcomings, are appealing in that they have ". . . aucun des défauts du bel esprit . . .".[83] Le Grand, too, admires that "vérité" and "naturel." The "fablier," he says, tells his story simply and sincerely. There is no spurious detail in his work, there are none of those imaginative little digressions so often employed to rekindle the interest of a weary reader. But there is an abundance of those "petits détails accessoires," those titbits which add to and so enhance the main picture. Above all, he so gives one the impression of a simple, good-hearted soul telling an honest tale that it becomes impossible, however improbable that tale, not to accept him as such. He has feeling and can be remarkably acute in his depiction of human emotions. But there is no affectation and there are no inconsistencies. He may now and then offer some wise proverb, but never the trenchant maxim so dear to his pretentious successor. How contemptible, for example, those malicious reflections on womankind which have become a special feature of modern "contes." A licentious fabliau, Le Grand admits, could stir youthful emotions, but the effect was never long-lived. Now the poison is much more carefully prepared:

... ces sortes de maximes satyriques, présentées sous l'apparence séduisante de philosophie & de connaissance des passions humaines, laissent, dans les jeunes esprits sur-tout, un mépris des femmes, un fonds d'inquiétude & de défiance sur leur vertu, qui malheureusement ne trouble que trop dans la suite la paix & le bonheur des mariages.[84]

---

[81] *Idem*, p. civ. Per Nykrog is not alone amongst modern critics in similarly finding that ". . . les poètes des fabliaux savent supérieurement manier le dialogue". (*Les Fabliaux*, p. 152.)

[82] *Les Fabliaux*, Paris (Champion) 1964 (6th edition) p. 347.

[83] *Fabliaux ou Contes*, vol. I, preface, p. lxv.

[84] *Idem*, vol. III, note to "Le Pêcheur de Pont-sur-Siene," pp. 431–432. Cf. Guerlin de Guer's remarks on the licentious fabliaux: "Qu'il me suffise du moins (non pour les justifier, grand Dieu!) d'indiquer que les auteurs de ces vilenies, jusque dans leurs excès, ont conservé je ne sais quelle naïveté (nous sommes au XIIIe siècle, non au XVIIIe) et que leur gauloiserie ne s'est jamais aggravée de sadisme ou d'aucun raffinement." ("Le comique et l'humour à travers les âges. Les fabliaux," *Revue des Cours et Conférences*, 1926–1927, p. 345.)

Le Grand lists what he considers the more positive merits of the fabliaux on pp. lxiii-lxv of his preface.

At its very worst the fabliau merely titillates then, whereas the modern "conte" corrupts.

From an eighteenth-century scholar all this is recommendation indeed. But it is not unqualified recommendation. The fabliaux, Le Grand acknowledges, have "bien des défauts" and not all are worthy of recall. His own collection, he admits, is by no means complete, approximately thirty of those pieces known to him being such, "... si insipides, ou si excessivement licencieux ...",[85] that he feels they are better withheld. Nor, indeed, does he necessarily think highly of all those he does include in the collection, as is evident in an introductory note to "Des deux Anglais":

Ce Conte, dont le fonds, quoique plaisant, manque néanmoins d'intérêt, est, comme beaucoup d'autres de ce Recueil, du nombre de ceux qui demanderaient, pour être lus avec quelque plaisir, des détails de Poésie piquans & agréables. Peut-être sera-t-il supportable en n'en présentant que l'extrait.[86]

Some tales, we know, he admits almost against his better judgement, as it were, finding them altogether worthless as works of literature but highly significant as documents of social history.[87] But if, where this is the case, Le Grand makes no effort to conceal his own contempt for such pieces, if he is quite prepared to concede that some fabliaux are less than mediocre even by medieval literary standards, then, wanting only justice for the "anciens rimeurs," he is equally forthright on those he considers of exceptional merit. "De la Demoiselle qui voulait voler" is just one of those tales upon which even Boccaccio cannot improve:

Ce Conte paraît avoir donné naissance à celui de la 'Jument du compère Pierre,' qu'on lit dans Bocace & dans La Fontaine; & ce qui prouve que nos Poëtes ne sont pas si méprisables, c'est qu'ici, où Bocace s'éloigne de Rutebeuf, il est moins ingénieux que lui.[88]

If, as Le Grand thinks it highly probable, the author of "Le Manteau mal taillé" composed his tale as a subtle means of paying homage to his lord, by flattering the latter's mistress or his wife, then "... l'on conviendra que, malgré l'injustice qu'il y a de blâmer toutes les femmes pour en louer une, nos poésies modernes offriraient peu d'exemples d'une louange aussi délicate & aussi fine."[89]

[85] *Fabliaux ou Contes*, vol. III, concluding note, p. 439.
[86] *Idem*, vol. II, p. 107.
[87] See above, p. 109.
[88] *Fabliaux ou Contes*, vol. III, p. 438. Cf. A .C. Lee, *The Decameron. Its sources and analogues*, Day 9, Novel 10, pp. 291–293. As Lee notes, Fauchet also remarks upon Boccaccio's use of this tale which he similarly attributes to Rutebeuf. Cf. Fauchet, *Œuvres*, fol 578 vo.
[89] *Fabliaux ou Contes*, vol. I, pp, 81–82, note (f).

It is because of these and other such pieces that Le Grand's collection will not only prove instructive but also obey that second great rule of "plaire."[90] For, of course, if there are certain fabliaux which in the opinion of the compiler remain viable as literature even in the eighteenth century, then it is not sufficient for him simply to say so. He must himself popularize them in order to prove them worthy of popularization.

It must not be thought that the paucity of the tales which Le Grand would set on a par with works of polite literature in any way detracts from the novelty of his intentions as "vulgarisateur." It is highly improbable that even the most exaggeratedly sympathetic of twentieth-century medievalists would undertake to defend upon purely literary grounds each and every one of those pieces contained in the first three volumes of the *Fabliaux ou Contes*. Imagine, says Per Nykrog, a comprehensive collection of tragedies from 1635 to 1830 or of lyric poetry from Chénier to Baudelaire, what a labour it would be to read such compilations, whatever one's regard for tragedy or for lyric poetry. It is not in this way that the various literary genres are judged but after their finest specimens:

Ne profitons donc pas trop de notre accès facile à de mauvais fabliaux. Il y en a, certes, et ils sont plus nombreux que les bons; mais qu'ils ne nous retiennent pas trop longtemps. Arrêtons-nous aux meilleurs, comme on fait pour les autres genres littéraires.[91]

At the time Per Nykrog is writing, of course, it is well known that the fabliaux are of uneven quality, many devoid of all literary merit. Le Grand, on the other hand, might easily have misled his unenlightened contemporaries by publishing only the superior tales in a much smaller collection, and it is certainly to his credit that he did not do so. But the really important thing to realize here is that even by modern standards Le Grand would not be expected to endorse the whole of that genre to which he devotes so much time and attention.[92] By eighteenth-century standards, of course, it is most unusual that he should so esteem even a fraction of the tales it embraces as to wish to publish them for their literary value. For as with other branches of medieval literature, so

---

[90] Cf. *idem*, vol. I, preface, p. ii.

[91] Per Nykrog, *Les Fabliaux*, p. 142.

[92] Cf., for example, Guerlin de Guer, "Le comique et l'humour à travers les âges. Les fabliaux," p. 345: "Pour être complet, en effet, j'aurais dû noter, dans la collection des fabliaux, ceux qui se distinguent tristement par une indécence qui n'a même pas l'esprit pour condiment, ceux dont on ne peut énoncer seulement les titres. J'ai cru devoir les passer sous silence, parce qu'à mon sens ni le goût, ni la morale, ni la littérature n'ont à voir en ce 'musée secret'."

with the "fabliaux ou contes." There appears to have been no-one either prior to or contemporary with Le Grand with anything approaching even his limited faith in the genre, at least no one showing himself not only anxious to publicize such faith but at the same time competent to justify it before the masses. There appears to have been no other successful "vulgarisateur."

Fauchet was perhaps the first to give any serious attention to the fabliaux and he did so for almost exactly the same reasons as Le Grand. Both men recalled the fabliaux as part of very similar plans to preserve the "anciens rimeurs" from undeserved oblivion.[93] Both realized and exploited the historical utility of these tales.[94] Both, insisting heavily upon the enormous debt of gratitude which France's neighbours owe to her in matters of literature, stressed Boccaccio's particular obligation to the "fabliers."[95] But, most important, Fauchet appears to have shared with Le Grand a certain appreciation of the literary merits of the genre. Amongst numerous examples of these "contes de plaisir & nouvelles"[96] listed in the second book of his *Recueil*[97] there are one or two which are clearly to his liking:

Sire Jehan Chapelain a faict un fabliau du Secretain de Cluny, fort plaisant & bien meslé d'aventures: lequel commence ....[98]

"Le Sacristain" is, in fact, one of three tales, the others being "Les trois Aveugles de Compiègne" and "La Bourse pleine de sens," which Fauchet reproduces in lengthy extracts,[99] no doubt, says Espiner-Scott, in an effort to interest and amuse his readers and particularly Henri III.[100] But here all similarity with Le Grand ends for, of course, Fauchet has no wish to prove any of these tales still viable as literature in his own time. His remains very much a "sympathie secrète."[101] In-

[93] Fauchet's purpose in the *Recueil*, as outlined in the dedication, has already been noted. See above, p. 180. Le Grand, we know, regarded the *Fabliaux ou Contes* as ". . . des Mémoires faits pour servir à l'Histoire de notre ancienne Littérature, jusqu'à présent si peu connue." See above, p. 158.
[94] For example, both demonstrate after "La Robe vermeille" that knights on occasions served as judges. Cf. *Fabliaux ou Contes*, vol. II, p. 94, note (b); Fauchet, *Œuvres*, fol. 511 ro.
[95] For example, see above, p. 200, note 88.
[96] Fauchet, *Œuvres*, fol. 578 ro.
[97] Cf. Espiner-Scott, *Claude Fauchet*, pp. 195–199.
[98] Fauchet, *Œuvres*, fol. 580 vo.
[99] "Les trois Aveugles de Compiègne," *Œuvres*, fol. 579 rovo; "La Bourse pleine de sens," *idem*, fol. 580 rovo; "Le Sacristain," *idem*, ff. 580 vo-582 vo. Le Grand heads his own versions of these tales with the remark: "Fauchet en a donné l'extrait." (*Fabliaux ou Contes*, vol. II, p. 149; vol. III, p. 87 and p. 380.)
[100] *Claude Fauchet*, p. 196.
[101] See above, pp. 179–180.

deed, he restricts himself for the most part to the briefest résumé or description of the fabliaux, only citing two or three lines from each to identify authors:

Hues de Cambray a fait le fabliau intitulé La male honte: qui est une moquerie faitte contre Henry Roy d'Angleterre: & dit de son ouvrage:

> Hue de Cambray Comte & dit
> Qui de cet oeuvre rime fit.[102]

Moreover, he rarely has even as little to say of the literary merits of a tale as he does in the case of "Le Sacristain." Either he remains silent or, as with other branches of medieval literature, contents himself with short, stereotyped remarks as non-committal as those found in the margins of Sainte-Palaye's fabliaux manuscript copies.[103] For La Curne "jolie pièce" suffices, for Fauchet "assez plaisant."[104] Le Grand's earliest predecessor preserves certain of the "fabliers" from oblivion then, but he contributes little or nothing to their rehabilitation:

Fauchet est le premier, je crois, qui ait renouvellé la mémoire des Fabliaux; mais, il faut l'avouer, l'idée qu'en donnent ses Notices ou Extraits, n'était pas faite pour éveiller sur ce point la curiosité.[105]

More than 150 years elapse before any significant advance is made upon Fauchet, a century and a half during which those who turn their attention to the genre do little more than keep the name fabliau alive. In their separate *Bibliothèques Françoises* La Croix du Maine and du Verdier reproduce Fauchet almost verbatim, occasionally adding snippets of additional information.[106] In his *Dictionnaire étymologique de*

---

[102] *Œuvres*, ff. 583 vo - 584 ro. Cf. also his descriptions of, amongst others, "Sire Hain et Dame Anieuse," "Boivin de Provins," "L.Anneau qui faisait ..." and "Les trois Bossus," *ibidem*.

[103] See above, pp. 88–89.

[104] Cf., for example, "Les trois Aveugles de Compiègne," *Œuvres*, fol. 579 ro. Like Le Grand, Fauchet does not hide his contempt for those pieces he finds worthy of it. Le Grand, we know, finds it necessary to interrupt the tale of "Boivin de Provins" because of its coarseness, but he summarizes the remainder "... pour montrer quelles furent les moeurs d'un siècle dans lequel la partie la plus distinguée de la nation était amusée par des grossièretés aussi'révoltantes." (See above, pp. 108–109). In the second book of his *Recueil* Fauchet only mentions "Le Chevalier qui faisait parler ..." for this reason: "C'est un conte de lourde mensonge, & dont ie fay mention seulement pour monstrer à quoy de ce temps-la on prenoit plaisir, & quelles inventions estoyent estimees, & plus agreables." (*Œuvres*, fol. 583 ro.)

[105] *Fabliaux ou Contes*, vol. I, preface, p. lxxxvi.

[106] François Grudé de La Croix du Maine, *Les Bibliothèques Françoises*, Paris (L'Angelier) 1584; Antoine du Verdier, *Les Bibliothèques Françoises* (Honorat) 1585; re-issued by Rigoley de Juvigny, Paris (Saillant et Nyon) 1772–1773, 6 vols. Compare, for example, the three

la Langue françoise Ménage merely defines the term fabliau,[107] Borel only improving upon this in his *Trésor de Recherches* by a few extracts clarifying his own definition.[108] From here we must go to the beginning of Le Grand's own century to find the next reference to the genre, to Dom Joseph Mervesin who devotes a little less than two pages of his *Histoire de la Poësie françoise* to the "Fabels ou Fabliaux" and cites a few lines from "Sire Hain," Guiart's "L'Art d'aimer" and Rutebeuf's "Le Dit des Règles."[109] In a work of identical title published many years later, and posthumously, in 1739, the Abbé Guillaume Massieu notes that the poets of medieval France were responsible for ". . . une quantité prodigieuse de 'Fabels' ou de 'Fabliaux'; c'est-à-dire, comme nous parlerions aujourd'hui, de Contes & de Nouvelles."[110] Amongst those "fabliers" he mentions are Rutebeuf, Hues de Cambrai, Durand and Jean Chapelain, whose "Sacristain" he commends for exactly the same reasons as Fauchet, with one reservation:

Ce Poëme est un long tissu des avantures de ce bon Sacristain, très-diversi-fiées & assez réjouissantes. Les incidens y sont ménagés avec art, mais l'hon-nêteté n'y est nullement respectée.[111]

But Massieu's indebtedness to his predecessors is far too obvious for Le Grand whom we have seen severely censure those who find it sufficient, in so important an undertaking as a literary history of the Nation, simply to regurgitate all that has been said previously:

. . . ce qui est inconcevable! cet homme qui entreprenait de nous faire con-naître nos vieux Poëtes n'en avait pas lu un seul en manuscrit . . . Le peu qu'il en dit est copié d'après les notices erronées ou très imparfaites qu'a publiées Fauchet sur quelques-uns d'entre eux; et l'histoire de notre Poësie reste encore à faire en entier.[112]

Certainly the fabliaux at least are little better known and no more appreciated in the first quarter of the eighteenth century than they had been in the last quarter of the sixteenth.

We have said that the first significant advance upon Fauchet comes more than 150 years after the publication of his *Recueil*. It is in July

notes on Durand and "Les trois Bossus" (Fauchet, *Œuvres*, fol. 484 ro; La Croix du Maine, Juvigny re-issue, vol. I, p. 168; du Verdier, *idem*, vol. III, p. 466).

[107] *Dictionnaire étymologique*, nouvelle édition, Paris (Briasson) 1750, vol. I, p. 569: "Fa-bliau. Vieux mot, qui signifie 'Poëme'; Voyez le Président Fauchet. De 'fabula.' Fabula, fabulum, fabulellum, FABLEAU, FABLIAU."

[108] Cf. Nykrog, *Les Fabliaux*, p. ix.

[109] *Histoire de la Poësie françoise*, Paris (Pierre Giffart) 1706, pp. 82–83.

[110] *Histoire de la Poësie françoise*, Paris (Prault fils) 1739, p. 159. Massieu died in 1722.

[111] *Idem*, p. 161. For Fauchet's opinion, see above, p. 202.

[112] See above, pp. 120–121.

1746 that the Comte de Caylus presents his "Mémoire sur les Fabliaux" before the Académie des Inscriptions.[113] For us the originality of this paper lies not in Caylus's opening conjectures upon the probable origins of the fabliaux[114] nor in his realization of the importance of manuscript St.-Germain 1830,[115] rather in his willingness to commit himself not only to a definition of the genre but to some kind of literary appreciation, to something more than what appears to have become the regulation two words, at best two lines, of comment upon odd tales.

Caylus determines the nature of the fabliau by first defining the genre of the "conte" and then examining this particular subsidiary in the light of each item of that definition:

C'est un poëme qui renferme le récit élégant d'une action inventée, petite, plus ou moins intriguée, quoique d'une certaine étendue, mais agréable ou plaisante, dont le but est d'instruire ou d'amuser.[116]

Naturally, he says, not all of the fabliaux match exactly the resulting ideal:

... mais je crois pouvoir assurer qu'il n'y a aucune partie qui, en quelques endroits de ces fabliaux, n'ait été rendue de façon à servir de modèle ....[117]

In defence of this view Caylus, like Le Grand after him, first notes that

---

[113] Published in 1753 in the *Mémoires de l'Académie des Inscriptions*, vol. XX, pp. 352–376.

[114] Caylus considers the genre older than the romances of chivalry, but admits that he had not at first been able to trace it beyond the "ignorance and darkness" preceding the eleventh century. He felt certain, however, that the fabliaux dated from a much earlier period: "... ce que j'en trouvois me paroissoit trop formé quant au fond & aux détails, pour le juger de nouvelle création, s'il m'est permis de me servir de cette expression: d'ailleurs j'étois persuadé que les hommes de tous les temps ont aimé à s'amuser, & que les ouvrages dont je vais parler sont une suite de ce goût."
This notion, he says, led him to look to the ancients, and it is with them, the Hebrews, Homer, Aesop and the rest, he now concludes, that such tales must have originated. But then how did the poets of twelfth and thirteenth-century France come to know the works of the ancients, at that time still lost to the literary world? Caylus cannot say, but he would defend his conjecture by referring the reader to: "... tous les livres grecs traduits en arabe, & portés en Espagne par les Maures: loin d'exclure cette probabilité, je l'admets, ainsi que la communication de pareilles idées revenues par l'Inde. Le 'Dolopathos' en est une trop grande preuve pour s'y refuser, d'autant que ce roman absolument oriental par le style, & ce qu'on appelle le quadre ou la forme, a été infiniment célèbre en Europe." ("Mémoire sur les Fabliaux," pp. 352–356.)

[115] Present *B.N.f.fr. 19152*: "Il nous reste encore un assez grand nombre de manuscrits, dans lesquels on trouve des Fabliaux; il y en a dans différentes Bibliothèques, & sur-tout dans celle du Roi: mais celui qui m'a fourni presque tous les matériaux de ce Mémoire, me paroît le plus considérable en ce genre; on le conserve dans la bibliothèque de St. Germain-des-Prés, no. 1830." (P. 356.)

[116] "Mémoire sur les Fabliaux," pp. 357–360.

[117] P. 360. Cf. Nelly Caullot, *Fabliaux et Contes du Moyen Age* (Les Classiques Hatier) 1967, p. 5: "... il n'est guère de finesses dans l'art difficile du conte que nos auteurs de fabliaux aient ignorées."

these tales have none of the weaknesses of the romances, none of their false erudition, their monstrous verbosity, far fewer anachronisms and utter absurdities, pagans offering mass or glorifying the saints, for example, less repetition and undue prolongation of the narrative, none of those continual geographical errors:

> ... la nature du fabliau a exempté ceux qui les ont composés de ces inconvéniens.[118]

The positive merits of the fabliaux, however, Caylus considers best demonstrated by a few simple analyses and short quotations, although the finest examples of the genre are forbidden to him, "... trop libres pour être cités ...".[119] "Le Chastoiement" is given in a brief extract as the most moral tale imaginable, "La Male Honte" for its criticism of the English sovereign and the play on words. As a superior tale the "Lai d'Aristote" occupies a full page of the "Mémoire":

> ... car il renferme plus de critique & présente plus d'images, en même temps qu'il a plus de philosophie, indépendamment du choix des acteurs qui sont plus intéressans.[120]

"Le Convoiteus et l'Envieus" is dismissed in one short paragraph but "... les caractères en sont assez soutenus."[121] Another page is devoted to "Le Sacristain," "... pour donner une idée du génie des Poëtes de ces temps-là":

> Indépendamment des détails de ce conte, qui certainement ont du mérite, & qui sont remplis d'une grande variété, on voit dans ce fabliau des idées suivies & conséquentes, enfin de la composition.[122]

The extracts close with "Guillaume au Faucon," "... un des plus agréables pour les détails, car le fonds est peu de chose ...",[123] and Caylus completes this part of his "Mémoire," the "illustration," by presenting numerous short quotations as specimens of style, demonstrating the wisdom, clarity and perception of the advice and the reflections on life and love offered by the "fablier," the skill with which, like La Fontaine, he interrupts his narrative to "... mêler son sen-

---

[118] "Memoire sur les Fabliaux", p. 361.
[119] *Ibidem.* The extracts occupy pp. 361–367.
[120] P. 362.
[121] P. 364.
[122] Pp. 365–366.
[123] P. 366.

timent aux choses qu'il a entrepris de conter . . .", finally the aptness of his imagery:[124]

Ce qui me surprend, je l'avoue, c'est qu'avec de tels modèles, notre poësie & nos connoissances soient retombées dans la barbarie où elles ont été fort peu de temps après.[125]

The general impression is a highly favourable one then, and Caylus further enhances it by proceeding to remark that La Fontaine, Molière and Rabelais, amongst others, would not enjoy the reputation they do had they not known the fabliaux in one form or another and made use of them. Then again, the Italians have yet to acknowledge their indebtedness to the authors of these tales:

L'Italie, dis-je, qui se glorifie avec raison d'avoir produit Bocace & quelques autres de ses conteurs, perdroit beaucoup de son avantage, si on rendoit publics ces anciens manuscrits François . . . .[126]

Caylus appears in fact to have only one objection to the fabliaux, their obscenity:

Ma critique ne tombe point tant encore sur des mots qui n'étant que de convention, peuvent être admis ou bannis par l'usage ou par la politesse, mais sur des fonds qu'en saine morale il n'est pas possible d'admettre, encore moins de rendre publics.[127]

Certainly, he concedes, the "fabliers" deal harshly with priests and monks, but then the clergy of their day no doubt deserved no gentler treatment.[128] Moreover, the incredible diversity of the contents of medieval manuscripts is in itself ample testimony to the faith and unaffected piety of a period of endearing simplicity:

. . . celui qui savoit lire avoit pour l'ordinaire un livre chez lui, dans lequel il faisoit écrire ce qui lui convenoit: car souvent il ne le pouvoit lui-même; ainsi tout étoit pêle-mêle, morceaux qu'il croyoit historiques, légendes, prix de marchandises, indication de foires, moralités, romans, contes & fabliaux,

---

[124] Pp. 367–372. Le Grand in his turn will remark upon the beauty of those lines extolling the charms of the "châtelaine" in "Guillaume au Faucon." Cf. *Fabliaux ou Contes*, vol. III, p. 51, note (a).

[125] P. 373.

[126] P. 375.

[127] P. 376. Le Grand will espress an identical view: "Après tout, si l'on n'avait que des mots à reprocher aux Poëtes de ce tems, peut-être pourrait-on entreprendre de les excuser, parce que ces mots étant ,comme tous les autres, de pure convention, ils ont pu être bannis de la bonne société après y avoir été admis. Mais c'est par le fonds des choses que certains Contes sont répréhensibles; & jamais la saine morale n'approuvera, ni la débauche, ni l'adultère." (*Fabliaux ou Contes*, vol. I, preface, p. lxx.)

[128] P. 376. Cf. Le Grand's similar view, cited above, p. 198.

dans les plus libres desquels on voit indifféremment répandues des pieuses & longues tirades, sur-tout de l'Ancien Testament. Une telle simplicité fait peut-être l'éloge de nos pères, & nous doit au moins prouver la foi sincère & la piété naïve des hommes de ce temps-là.[129]

The value of Caylus' paper easily outweighs that of the total achievement of his predecessors in this area. He does more to define and demonstrate the precise nature of the fabliaux and their especial merits than all of his forerunners put together. The "Mémoire" will clearly be an important source for subsequent studies of the genre. Moreover, in as much as Caylus treats these tales solely as works of literature and does not concern himself with their historical utility, his obvious regard for them will surely be an encouragement to those of his successors who might care to take that next logical step, the "vulgarisateurs."[130] For, however highly he esteems this genre, Caylus himself does not take that step. It is not his purpose to popularize the fabliaux, to which end, of course, only a collection would really suffice. For whatever reasons, his own insufficient faith in them perhaps, or the fear of an adverse reaction from an unprepared public, he does not appear ever to have considered such a collection:

Quelques analyses de ces fabliaux, & des citations fidellement extraites mettront le lecteur à portée de juger du mérite de ces ouvrages; j'aurai soin de ne donner que ceux qui fournissent des exemples de morale, de jeu de mots, d'amour, de critique & de sentiment.[131]

A few short extracts of the finer, if not the finest,[132] examples of the genre adequately serve his present object, and not all of these, he suspects, are justified. He must make his excuses to the reader:

J'ai peut-être poussé trop loin des analyses futiles, mais rien n'est indigne de recherches, principalement sur des choses qui regardent notre langue & le progrès que l'esprit a fait dans notre nation.[133]

Caylus' is a scholarly paper written to acquaint a largely scholarly public with one of the least known but by no means least valid branches

---

[129] *Ibidem.* M. le Chevalier de Jaucourt's article on fabliaux in the *Encyclopédie* is a three-paragraph résumé of the Caylus "mémoire," somewhat cynical in tone: "Cependant le meilleur des 'fabliaux' de ce manuscrit [St.-Germain 1830], ainsi que ceux dont le plan est le plus exact, sont trop libres pour être cités; & en même tems, au milieu des obscénités qu'ils renferment, on y trouve des pieuses & longues tirades de l'ancien Testament. Une telle simplicité fait-elle l'éloge de nos pères?" (Vol. VI, p. 349.)

[130] See above, p. 193.

[131] "Mémoire sur les Fabliaux," p. 361.

[132] See above, p. 206.

[133] P. 367.

of medieval literature, and as such it is a work of considerable merit, a valuable contribution to the advancement of knowledge and to the promotion of appreciation of the fathers of the modern "conte." But the "mémoire" is not the medium and Caylus' is clearly not the message of the "vulgarisateur."

In contrast, the one purpose of Etienne Barbazan's *Fabliaux et Contes*[134] is to bring a mass public to an awareness of the delights which medieval French literature still holds in store for the modern reader. Ignorance, insists Barbazan, ignorance ensuing from a general reluctance to penetrate the barrier of their language, has caused the "anciens rimeurs" to be neglected and even despised as the antithesis of all that is desirable in literature. Yet this condemnation is unjustified:

Quoique les Auteurs ne paroissent point s'être formés sur les beaux modèles de l'antiquité, on retrouve néanmoins dans quelques-uns de leurs Ouvrages, des traces des Anciens; & dans ce dont ils ne sont redevables qu'à leur propre fond, il y a des traits qui feroient honneur à notre siècle.[135]

And where is this merit better evidenced than in the "Fabel, Fablel, ou Fabliau,"[136] the genre of the "conte" ideally suited to the character of the French who were first in this field:[137]

Mais c'est dans leurs Fabliaux surtout qu'ils font paroître plus de génie. On y trouve une heureuse simplicité, des narrés intéressans, des images vives, des pensées fines, des réflexions justes, des expressions énergiques, une agréable variété, de la conduite & de l'ordonnance.[138]

In his "Mémoire sur les Fabliaux" Caylus, notes Barbazan, has shown that there is not one aspect of the "conte" of which one does not find

---

[134] *Fabliaux et Contes des Poëtes François des XII, XIII, XIV & XVes siècles*, Paris (Vincent) 1756, 3 vols.; re-issued in a revised and enlarged edition by Méon in 1808 (Paris, Crapelet, 4 vols.). References are to the edition of 1756 unless otherwise indicated.

[135] *Fabliaux et Contes*, vol. I, preface, pp. xxvii-xxviii.

[136] Barbazan sets the origins of the fabliaux somewhere before the twelfth century. Cf. vol. I, preface, p. xii, p. xx: "Quoique nous ne les annoncions que pour des productions des douzième, treizième & quatorzième siècles, parce que les manuscrits dont ils sont extraits sont de ces tems, il s'en trouve quelques-uns parmi eux qui sont d'une date plus ancienne, comme on peut en juger par la différence du langage."

[137] *Idem*, vol. I, preface, p. xvii: "Les François naturellement gais, légers & badins saisirent ce genre de composition avec plus d'avidité que les autres nations, & ils en communiquèrent le goût à leurs voisins."
This is reproduced almost verbatim from Caylus (cf. "Mémoire sur les Fabliaux," p. 356). We might note that Barbazan in fact does little to hide his indebtedness to his predecessor. Compare, for example, Caylus' remarks on the diversity of the contents of manuscript volumes (cited above, p. 207) with those found in the preface to the first volume of the *Fabliaux et Contes*, pp. xlv-xlvi: "Si ce mélange singulier ne peut être approuvé, il fait du moins honneur à nos Pères. Il nous fait connoître leur naïve simplicité & leur attachement à la Religion, à laquelle ils revenoient en toute occassion."

[138] *Fabliaux et Contes*, vol. I, preface, p. xxxiii.

the perfect model somewhere in these tales,[139] and the great writers of the last two centuries, Boccaccio, Rabelais, Molière, La Fontaine, Mlle de Lussan, Renard and the rest, have exploited those models.[140] As for the charge of obscenity which has helped to ensure the neglect of the fabliaux, Barbazan concedes that certain of them are indeed basically obscene and are only to be read for the light they shed upon the history and antiquities of the Nation.[141] But he would point out that it is unjust to dismiss the remainder of these tales as vulgar and licentious simply because their authors employ certain terms offensive to the eighteenth-century ear. At the time of the "fabliers" these terms were in common usage, even in the most polite circles:

On n'étoit point scandalisé des mots, ni des choses qu'ils signifioient ... On étoit alors plus simple, & par conséquent moins mauvais ... En effet l'indécence ne consiste point dans les mots, mais dans les choses & les actions; & les mots dépendans uniquement de l'usage, on ne peut blâmer un Auteur de se servir des termes que cet usage ou que la politesse n'ont point bannis du langage.[142]

Not only has Barbazan no mean opinion of the fabliaux, he intends that the reading public should share his view. His purpose is to popularize the fabliaux:

Prévenus que leurs expressions sont barbares, & que leur langage est obscur, on n'a point cru qu'ils méritassent d'être tirés de la poussière des Bibliothèques dans laquelle ils sont ensevelis; mais on espère que ce recueil de Fabliaux que l'on donne au Public fera tomber ce préjugé ....[143]

This he considers he can best achieve by presenting the tales in their original form with a glossary, completing each of the three volumes of his collection, to facilitate reading. For Barbazan has no faith in even the most literal translations, which not only prevent the reader from ever becoming versed in Old French but not infrequently fail to do justice to the original. It is, he believes

... plus utile d'interpréter les vers les plus obscurs, qui paroissent inintelligibles, et de donner une juste explication des mots hors d'usage ... Nos anciens avoient des mots et des expressions très-énergiques que nous n'avons plus, et qui malheureusement ne sont point remplacés, et que nous ne

---

[139] See above, p. 205.

[140] *Fabliaux et Contes*, vol. I, preface, pp. xxxiv-xxxviii.

[141] *Idem*, pp. xliv-xlv. Similarly, as we have seen, the historical relevance of certain fabliaux is the sole reason for their inclusion in Fauchet's lists and Le Grand's own collection.

[142] *Idem*, pp. xxxviii-xliv. Caylus and Le Grand, of course, express an identical view. See above, p. 207 and note 376 to that page.

[143] *Idem*, p. xlvi.

pouvons plus rendre que par de longues et fades périphrases, en sorte qu'il est très-difficile d'exprimer les beautés qui se rencontrent dans ces originaux par des traductions littérales.[144]

To further assist the reader he had at first intended that his collection should open with a treatise on the origins and progress of the French language. But this, he finally decided, was not the place for so lengthy a discussion which he now promises will appear in his *Nouveau Trésor de Borel, ou Dictionnaire de tous les termes de l'ancienne Langue Françoise usitée dans les XII, XIII, XIV, XV & XVIes siècles*, the completed manuscript of which is already in the hands of his publisher.[145] Basically the treatise will prove that all words in French derive from Latin, "marches" and "markes" not from the German "mark" but from "margo," "bec" from "vectum," participle of the Latin verb "vehere," and so on:

C'est chercher en vain l'origine de notre langue françoise jusqu'à la fin du seizième siècle, que de la chercher dans le Grec, l'Allemand, l'Anglo-Saxon, l'ancien Gaulois, le Theutfranc & le Thiois. Son origine est purement latine; une lettre, ou une syllabe ajoutée, retranchée, ou transposée en fait toute la différence.[146]

This knowledge, the vocabulary given and a little application will render the present collection easily accessible to the modern reader, enabling him to appreciate the very real merits of its contents:

Il reconnoîtra que c'est à tort que l'on a si fort négligé, ou méprisé nos anciens Poëtes; & se familiarisant avec leurs expressions, il découvrira dans leurs Ouvrages de la finesse, de l'élégance, de la justesse & des beautés

---

[144] *L'Ordène de Chevalerie*, Avertissement, pp. ix-x. See above, p. 61.

[145] Cf. the Avis du libraire immediately preceding the preface to the *Fabliaux et Contes*, also reprinted in the Méon edition of 1808, vol. III, pp. i-ii. The "Dissertation sur l'Origine de la Langue françoise" in fact appears in *L'Ordène de Chevalerie* (and is again reprinted in the Méon edition of the *Fabliaux et Contes*, vol. I, pp. 1-58) for Barbazan's *Dictionnaire*, to cover some 25,000 words and their etymologies, remained unpublished.

[146] *Fabliaux et Contes*, vol. I, preface, pp. xlviii-xlix. Thus Pasquier, Fauchet, Borel, Ménage, Du Cange are all rejected in the "Dissertation": "On improuvera peut-être la liberté que j'ai prise, de dire que les grands homes que j'ai cités au commencement, ne possédoient pas notre langue; mais que le lecteur les suive comme je les ai suivis, il sera convaincu qu'ils ne nous ont laissé que d'épais nuages, et des obscurités sur notre langue; et j'assure, avec vérité, qu'ils ne m'ont été d'aucun secours; je n'ai formé mon grand recueil que sur des manuscrits, et non sur des ouvrages imprimés; ils sont, à ce que j'ai vu depuis, trop pleins de fautes. Je n'entends pas pour cela rien diminuer de leur mérite, c'étoient des Sçavans, et non éclairans." ("Dissertation" in *Fabliaux et Contes*, 1808, vol. I, p. 58.)

Cf. in the *Mercure* for November 1759 an amusing article on the "Dissertation," gently ridiculing Barbazan's etymologies: "M. Barbazan, Auteur de cette Dissertation, fait descendre notre Langue en droite ligne de la Langue Latine seule & sans aucun mélange. Je suis tenté de penser comme lui; car le Latin est la seule langue sçavante ou étrangerè dont j'ai quelque teintu re ... [Barbazan admits he has little Greek] ... Ah! que de gens caresseroient M.B. s'il s'étoit attaché à la généalogie des familles comme à celle des mots! "("Lettre sur le livre intitulé 'L'Ordène de Chevalerie,'" pp. 107-118.)

cachées sous ce voile d'expressions dont la signification lui avoit été jusqu'-
alors inconnue.[147]

No other medievalist of the eighteenth century has so commendable a
purpose as that envisaged by Barbazan in his *Fabliaux et Contes*. If, as it
is the enlightened view, the efforts of the "anciens rimeurs" are important, are to be read first and foremost as works of literature, ". . .not
as supporting material for antiquarian studies nor as a fossilised series
of linguistic phenomena . . .",[148] then surely the medievalist is at his
most useful as "vulgarisateur." And what higher goal for the "vulgarisateur" than to popularize this early literature not only in the spirit in
which it was first composed but in its original form. But was the eighteenth century ready for Barbazan and his collection? We know that it
was not. Barbazan has no lesser faith in the "fabliaux ou contes" than
Le Grand will have after him. He is no less anxious to publicize that
faith and to justify it before the masses. But the masses are unwilling to
make the effort required in order to understand the justice of this high
regard for the "anciens rimeurs." Barbazan's mistake is to demand that
the reader meet him half-way:

The public ... was neither anxious to be instructed in Old French, nor
willing to purchase its pleasure at the cost of a little application.[149]

The *Fabliaux et Contes*, particularly in the new edition by Méon, may be
of considerable service to the great scholars of the nineteenth and
twentieth centuries, but in its own time it fails to fulfil the purpose for
which it is intended:

De bonne foi, peut-on se flatter qu'il se trouvera des gens assez courageux
pour entreprendre une lecture, dans laquelle, dix fois à chaque phrase, il
leur faudra consulter un Vocabulaire. Ce n'est pas connaître les Lecteurs
Français, que de leur présenter un pareil travail. Aussi l'Ouvrage est-il resté
inconnu, & il est même ignoré des Gens de Lettres.[150]

This view, we know, is not one peculiar to Le Grand d'Aussy.[151]

Although it has been our concern in this discussion to note precisely
what efforts were made by the French both before and during the
eighteenth century to popularize their early literature, we have as yet
failed to mention that collection generally considered to be the most
significant contribution made in this field. But we know that under the

---

[147] *Fabliaux et Contes*, vol. I, preface, p. lii.
[148] C. E. Pickford, *Changing attitudes towards medieval French literature*, p. 21.
[149] L. Gossman, *Medievalism*, p. 259.
[150] Le Grand, *Fabliaux ou Contes*, vol. I, preface, p. lxxxvii.
[151] See avbove, pp. 61–62 and note 9 to the latter.

direction of the Marquis de Paulmy the *Bibliothèque des Romans* did aim at a certain degree of fidelity and exactitude in what it presented of the literature of the Middle Ages[152] and, although we have stressed the obvious historical bias of the work,[153] it was undoubtedly meant to be entertaining as well as instructive, to be ". . . agréable à l'homme du monde qui veut s'amuser . . ." as well as ". . . utile à l'homme de lettres qui veut s'instruire, féconde pour les Poëtes qui cherchent des fictions heureuses & propres au Théâtre, nécessaire à l'Historien & à l'Observateur des moeurs, des tems & des usages anciens & modernes."[154] There can be little doubt that the first director of the *Bibliothèque des Romans*, this only recently deemed worthy of being reprinted,[155] deserves recognition as ". . . l'un de ceux qui ont contribué le plus à vulgariser le moyen âge."[156] And yet this modern view, we know, is not one to which Le Grand d'Aussy would subscribe. At least, we have seen him dismiss Paulmy's collection as presenting only a much distorted picture of medieval literature.

In the first place, while Le Grand would agree that the skill and ability of some enlightened modern writer can be most effectively demonstrated in the short analysis or extract, he is convinced that to employ this technique with the undisciplined authors of the old romances is to show them to their worst advantage:

. . . c'est à la fois les dépouiller de tous leurs agrémens, & ne les montrer qu'avec leurs seuls défauts.[157]

It is perhaps strange that Le Grand should thus condemn the "miniature"[158] as a method of presenting the romances of chivalry to the general reading public for we know that he had collaborated on the *Bibliothèque des Romans* under Paulmy. Indeed, it was he who composed the extract of "Erec" which immediately precedes the three "fabliaux"

---

152 See above, pp. 64–65.
153 See above, p. 72.
154 *Bibliothèque des Romans*, vol. I (July, 1775) Prospectus, p. 9.
155 Slatkine Reprints, May, 1970.
156 H. Jacoubet, *Le Comte de Tressan*, p. 317. Henry Martin is one of the few to protest about the neglect of Paulmy's *Mélanges tirés d'une grande Bibliothèque*: "Me permettra-t-on, du moins, de protester contre l'abandon dans lequel on laisse aujourd'hui ces 'Mélanges,' qui contiennent, à côté d'études très médiocres, des parties véritablement bonnes, et dont l'érudition moderne pourrait encore faire son profit?" (*Histoire de la Bibliothèque de l'Arsenal*, p. 42.)
157 See above, pp. 165–166.
158 Cf. *Bibliothèque des Romans*, vol. I, Prospectus, p. 5: "Il seroit, sans doute, impossible, & même absurde, de rassembler tous les volumes que le tems a accumulés: il suffit de les faire connoître, en les analysant, d'en donner l'âme, l'esprit, &, pour ainsi dire, la 'miniature'. C'est le plan que nous exécutons."

given in the volume for February 1777. But it seems unlikely that Le Grand was responsible for these latter, "Le Chevalier à l'épée," "La Mule sans frein" and "Le court Mantel,"[159] for he again disagrees with the manner in which the second of these at least is reproduced here and introduces his own version of the tale with the following note:

Ce Conte, ainsi que les deux suivans, a déjà paru, d'après les Manuscrits de M. Sainte-Palaye, dans la 'Bibliothèque des Romans,' mais imité plutôt que traduit. Pour moi, à qui les ornemens étrangers sont interdits, & qui suis sévèrement astreint à la fidélité de la traduction, je le donne ici avec sa phisionomie antique & tous les défauts de l'original.[160]

For Le Grand, then, those extracts of the "anciens rimeurs" featured in the *Bibliothèque des Romans* are too far removed from the reality of the originals for that collection to rank as a serious "oeuvre de vulgarisation":

Ce n'est pas d'après ces extraits infidèles et défigurés qu'on peut prendre une idée de notre poésie ancienne.[161]

Obviously the question of method is all-important here. Le Grand's object is to "faire lire les fabliaux," not to entertain his public with elegant adaptations of medieval "contes." If his collection is to prove that certain of these tales remain viable as literature even by eighteenth-century standards, then he must allow them to stand or fall by their own merits. There must be no misrepresentation. The slightest embellishment or flattering modification and he risks invalidating his efforts. And yet modifications there must be:

Il n'est pas possible de faire lire les Fabliaux autrement, que dans une traduction où l'on se permettra certaines libertés.[162]

Barbazan's experience has demonstrated the necessity of translation.

---

[159] *Bibliothèque des Romans*, February 1777, p. 87: "Le peu d'espace que vient d'occuper l'histoire d'Erec & d'Enide, nous laisse la liberté d'extraire encore trois des Fabliaux, dont les manuscrits nous ont été communiqués par M. de Sainte-Palaye. La scène de ces fictions est placée à la Cour du Roi Artus, & les héros sont des Chevaliers de la Table Ronde. Nous ne pouvons, dans un article consacré aux Romans de Chevalerie, parler des autres Fabliaux, qui, d'ailleurs, doivent faire l'objet d'un Recueil que l'illustre Académicien fait composer sous ses yeux."
These extracts occupy pp. 88–98, pp. 98–112, pp. 112–115 respectively.

[160] *Fabliaux ou Contes*, vol. I, p. 13. The extract of "La Mule sans frein" occupies pp. 13–24 of the first volume of the collection and is followed by Le Grand's own version of 'Le Chevalier à l'épée" and "Le Manteau mal taillé," pp. 34–50 and pp. 60–76 respectively. Three of the four romances he had originally intended to include in the *Fabliaux ou Contes*, it will be remembered, had already appeared in the *Bibliothèque des Romans*.

[161] See above, p. 166, note 208.

[162] *Fabliaux ou Contes*, vol. I, preface, p. lxxxvii.

To appreciate the abilities of an author one must first understand him, and the eighteenth-century reader has shown himself a reluctant student of Old French. Then again, there are certain things which, though acceptable to a medieval audience, are now displeasing to the polite ear. Indeed, there are those modern pieces which one might have wished had undergone some alteration, had been thus emended, before being released upon the general public.[163] So too with the more dubious fabliaux:

> ... il en est que je ne présenterai qu'en extrait, ou dont je retrancherai les détails trop libres. Ce n'est point là dépouiller un Auteur, c'est le mettre en état d'entrer chez les honnêtes gens.[164]

Le Grand must show the utmost consideration both to the "fablier" and to the eventual reader. His problem, of course, is how to reconcile the necessity of modifications with that of fidelity and exactitude, impossible in the opinion of Lévesque de la Ravallière:

> Lorsqu'on entreprend de retoucher le texte d'un auteur, de lui donner une nouvelle forme, de substituer des expressions modernes aux anciennes, il est impossible qu'avec les meilleures intentions et les plus heureux talents ce changement se fasse sans altérer le fond des choses, sans renverser très souvent la pensée de l'auteur original, sans affaiblir son génie et sans gâter son caractère.[165]

If Le Grand could bring about such a reconciliation and render extracts truly representative of the "anciens rimeurs" popular with a wide reading public, then clearly his *Fabliaux ou Contes* would represent no little advance upon the achievement of his predecessors and his contemporaries. It is the proud boast of the twentieth century that, thanks to the efforts of scholars like Joseph Bédier, the validity of medieval literature as literature is now widely recognized. And yet even now it is not difficult to find remnants of the old prejudices. Is it not the case that at certain universities students of French literature are given no encouragement to concern themselves with that which precedes the sixteenth century? Indeed, even amongst the most notable modern specialists in the pre-Renaissance period, even amongst those who have quite recently set themselves to study and publish, with laudably meticulous care, the efforts of France's earliest poets, there are one or two

---

[163] See above, pp. 197–198 &, pp. 199–200.
[164] *Fabliaux ou Contes*, vol. I, preface, pp. lxxii-lxxiii.
[165] *Mémoires de l'Académie des Inscriptions*, vol. XXI, p. 541. Cited from Madeleine Jouglard's "Les Etudes d'Histoire littéraire en France au XVIIIe siècle", p. 437.

who could have insisted rather more heavily upon the literary merits of those texts concerning them. In the interests of relevance, let us take a brief look at one or two modern scholars who have occupied themselves with the fabliaux.

Johnston and Owen, who published a collection of fifteen tales in 1957, may not altogether neglect the literary value of the genre, but this is made subordinate to its historical utility:

> The literary values of the fabliaux, then, are by no means negligible; but there is a greater interest which they hold for us ... It lies in the panorama of medieval life which they present ... It is from the fabliaux that much of our knowledge of life in thirteenth-century France has been gleaned.[166]

Surely a more enlightened view and one more in keeping with a collection aimed particularly at those new to Old French literature, and thus presumably meant to fire their enthusiasm for this new field, is that of T. B. W. Reid, who opens a collection of fabliaux of identical purpose with a prefatory note including the following lines:

> The purpose of this volume is to make available to English-speaking students, in a convenient form and with the necessary aids to their comprehension, some representative examples of a characteristic genre of mediaeval French literature. They have been chosen partly with a view to illustrating what appears to have been the evolution of the genre; but most of them have considerable intrinsic merits as narrative poems, and one or two can justifiably be described as French classics.[167]

Even Per Nykrog, that most erudite authority on the fabliaux, is not entirely guiltless, defending Brunetière's harsh view of the genre:

> ... sans doute, Brunetière a raison. Les fabliaux ont avant tout un intérêt historique. Le lettré médiéviste qui s'y serait fourvoyé une fois dans sa recherche des beautés littéraires, n'y reviendrait probablement pas.[168]

Old texts have a special appeal for the medievalist whereas Brunetière scrutinizes the fabliaux with the same critical eye as he would the works of La Fontaine or Maupassant and, given this, one must agree, says Nykrog, that his opinion is very probably justified. But now Ny-

---

[166] R. C. Johnston and D. D. R. Owen, *Fabliaux* (Blackwell's French Texts) Oxford, 1957, introduction, pp. xii-xiii.

[167] T. B. W. Reid, *Twelve Fabliaux* (French Classics) M.U.P., 1958.

[168] Per Nykrog, *Les Fabliaux*, p. 141. cf. Brunetière's article on Bédier's study of the genre, "Les Fabliaux du moyen âge et l'origine des contes" in *La Revue des deux Mondes*, vol. 119 (1893) p. 191: "En fait de qualités littéraires, nos Fabliaux n'en possèdent que d'uniquement, d'exclusivement, de purement historiques, y compris ce 'naturel' même, et cette 'franchise' ou 'verdeur' de style que M. Bédier veut bien y louer encore."

krog would ask the reader to view these tales from an altogether different standpoint:

Au jugement relatif et comparatiste du critique littéraire du XIXe ou du XXe siècle, nous devons essayer de substituer celui qu'a pu porter un lettré du XIIIe siècle. Nous devons tâcher de former un jugement 'absolu,' qui ne tient pas compte du fait qu'on a fait mieux depuis.[169]

Nykrog is arguing that the fabliaux should be judged by the literary standards of the period of their composition, and his own evaluation concludes thus:

Voilà le fabliau, ses faiblesses, qui sont graves, et ses mérites, qui sont remarquables pour cette époque.[170]

In one respect, then, *Les Fabliaux* not only marks no advance upon Le Grand's collection, it is positively retrogressive. It is an essential part of Le Grand's purpose to gain respect for medieval French literature for what it represented in its own time. But it is no less important to him to prove certain specimens of that literature still valid and enjoyable as works of literature in his own century:

Que serait-ce donc si j'avançais que plusieurs de ces Contes sont tels que j'ose les donner après Bocace & Lafontaine, & que malgré la perfection qu'a dû nécessairement amener un intervalle de cinq siècles, tous les Conteurs qui les ont suivies n'ont peut-être encore, avec beaucoup plus d'art, plus de poésie, plus de grâces dans le style, ni autant de vérité dans la narration, ni autant d'intérêt & de variété dans les sujets.

Certain of the "fabliers" are noteworthy in their own right, not simply because they stand higher than their contemporaries on that ladder which leads to the modern literary ideal.

We cannot insist too heavily upon the difficulties with which Le Grand as "vulgarisateur" was faced. Even in the France of the present day, when the problems of language and public sensibility have perhaps become less acute, one wonders if it is possible to publish a collection of fabliaux in the original Old French and yet expect some success with a non-specialist readership. One such collection in fact appeared in the first decade of the twentieth century, a *Recueil de Fabliaux*[171] strikingly similar in purpose to Le Grand's own *Fabliaux ou Contes*. Somewhat exceptionally, the editors choose to include in their selection

---

[169] *Les Fabliaux*, pp. 141–142.
[170] *Idem*, p. 164.
[171] *Recueil de Fabliaux* (Tous les chefs-d'oeuvre de la littérature française) Paris (La Renaissance du Livre) 1910. The original text is presented with difficult words and phrases translated either in brackets within the text itself or in footnotes.

certain of the poorer examples of the genre, for their intention, like that of their predecessor, is to convey a just impression of the fabliaux to a public as yet unacquainted with them:

> Enfin, nous ne nous sommes pas laissé guider dans notre choix par les mérites exclusivement littéraires des pièces. Nous avouons, pour notre part, que la beauté des fabliaux comme: 'Brunain la Vache au Prêtre,' 'Estula,' ou 'la Vieille qui oint la palme au chevalier,' nous est absolument fermée. Nous ne faisons pas non plus grand cas d'un exercice comme 'la Pâtre Nôtre farcie.' Mais ces poésies nous ont paru caractéristiques, et nous les avons données, de préférence à d'autres qui nous semblaient plus belles. Nous espérons qu'après avoir lu ce petit livre, le lecteur emportera des fabliaux une idée d'ensemble et qu'ainsi nous aurons travaillé dans l'esprit de la collection, qui est de servir les Français curieux de tous nos chefs-d'oeuvre.[172]

It seems unlikely that the *Recueil de Fabliaux* can have enjoyed the same success and therefore have had the same influence as Le Grand's collection in the eighteenth century. Surely critical editions of the fabliaux, Pierre Nardin's edition of nine pieces by Jean Bodel for example,[173] are not popular reading matter with the masses. Certainly there is a place for modern translations. Indeed, there is a place for the *Fabliaux ou Contes* which has only recently been seen to deserve reprinting,[174] this perhaps an indictment of modern scholars who appear to have been reluctant to give themselves to a task still fraught with difficulties well-known to Le Grand, the popularization of the fabliaux.[175] And there can be no doubt that the average English reader of the latter part of the twentieth century, if indeed he is aware of their existence, is by no means as well acquainted with these tales as was his counterpart of the last quarter of the eighteenth when translations of the *Fabliaux ou Contes* were enormously popular on this side of the Channel.[176] Perhaps we must wait until these translations in their turn are reprinted before seeing any improvement in this situation.

---

[172] Avertissement des éditeurs, p. 8.
[173] *Jean Bodel: Fabliaux*, Paris (Nizet) 1965.
[174] Slatkine Reprints, 1971.
[175] Some mention must be made here of an excellent little paperback by Robert Hellman and Richard O'Gorman entitled: *Fabliaux. Ribald Tales from the Old French* (New York, Thomas Y. Crowell Company, 1966, Apollo Editions). The work offers accurate yet most readable translations of twenty-two of the fabliaux and is clearly designed for a non-specialist public. It can without hesitation be described as the best that has been offered to the English public since the translations of Le Grand's collection, presenting these tales purely and simply as literature in an effortless rendering. There are amusing little illustrations and, for those who might wish to further their acquaintance with the fabliaux, a select bibliography, an informative afterword and notes to each tale, the first of which is offered in the original Old French as well as in English. The tragedy is that after six years the work is practically unknown, being almost impossible to obtain in this country.
[176] See bibliography.

As "vulgarisateur" Le Grand would appear to have enjoyed no little success. Certainly he does not leave himself open to the kind of embarrassingly apologetic remark made by the *Mercure* in respect of the *Histoire littéraire des Troubadours*:

On doit s'attendre qu'un ouvrage de ce genre est plus utile à consulter qu'-agréable à lire de suite.[177]

The *Année Littéraire*, for example, finds the collection amongst the most entertaining of the day and is clearly convinced of the literary value, even by contemporary standards, of the fabliaux:

Je vous ai déjà rendu compte, Monsieur, d'une partie de cet ouvrage, & j'y reviens avec plaisir; il en est peu dont la lecture soit aussi agréable, & qui prouve mieux que nos ancêtres n'étoient point aussi grossiers que le prétendent quelques beaux esprits de nos jours, qui pourroient se faire une grande réputation, s'ils avoient autant de naiveté, de sel, de grâce & de finesse, qu'on remarque dans la plupart de ces Contes.[178]

The question is, of course, what relation do these extracts bear to the medieval originals? Is it the essential fabliau that the periodical appreciates or something approaching a Tressan adaptation, as Papon suggests?[179] What remains of the originals, of course, depends solely upon the degree of exactitude Le Grand's own particular method of presentation will allow. But if his extracts do not fall short of his purpose, then for the first time in four centuries the fabliaux, at least some of the fabliaux, are to be widely enjoyed for what they are, not merely sympathetically read for what they once represented nor impartially exploited for their particular utility.

The editor of the third edition of the *Fabliaux ou Contes*, Antoine-Augustin Renouard, is well justified, as we have seen, in emphasizing

---

[177]December 1774, p. 132.

[178] 1780, vol. V, Lettre VII, pp. 145–146. The "fabliers," continues the periodical, remain unsurpassed even by La Fontaine, and in one respect at least are vastly superior to Voltaire: "Nos anciens Conteurs ne vous offriront pas des défauts aussi grossiers; ils ne se tourmentent point pour avoir de l'esprit à contre-temps; & pour tourner en ridicule les objets qui en sont le moins susceptibles." (P. 151.)

Cf. also vol. IV of 1782, Lettre XVII, p. 326: "...c'est donc rendre service à la nation & à la littérature que de tirer de l'oubli nos vieux Poëtes, de les traduire en style moderne en leur conservant les grâces de la naïveté antique; c'est enrichir & peupler notre Parnasse d'une foule d'habitans nouveaux, souvent plus dignes d'y figurer que certains rimeurs de nos jours."

[179] *Voyage de Provence*, 1787, vol. II, p. 170: "Je ne puis me résoudre à lui pardonner la liberté avec laquelle, de plusieurs fabliaux sur le même sujet, composés dans des tems différens, il n'en a fait qu'un seul, retranchant ce qu'il y avoit de mauvais, n'en présentant que l'agréable ou le supportable, transposant, rapprochant & arrangeant à sa manière tous ces morceaux épars, pour en faire un conte, qui ne ressemble à aucune des copies qu'il a eues sous les yeux."

how important a part of Le Grand's purpose it was to prove the French responsible for the medieval literary revival, in emphasizing what value he attached to the notes so abundant in his collection. But Renouard introduces his observations upon the purpose of the *Fabliaux ou Contes* with the remark that its author was "... bien loin de ne prétendre qu'à publier une suite d'historiettes récréatives ...".[180] Yet if these latter accurately represent the fabliaux and if the publication is successful, then this, surely, is the most original and most valuable contribution made by Le Grand, apologist but also popularizer, and the *Fabliaux ou Contes* is not only important today for the light it sheds upon a much neglected area of Enlightenment scholarship, but for what it was in part originally intended, as a serious "oeuvre de vulgarisation."[181]

[180] *Fabliaux ou Contes*, 1829, vol. I, Avis de l'éditeur, p. ii.
[181] It is difficult to understand why the editor of the third edition of Le Grand's collection should have asked Raynouard, a "Provençaliste" with no feeling for the literary value of the fabliaux, to supervise his work. It is perhaps fortunate that the request met with a refusal. Cf. *Fabliaux ou Contes*, 1829, vol. I, Avis de l'éditeur, pp. iii-iv.

CHAPTER IV

THE SOURCES

Just as Imbert would draw upon Le Grand d'Aussy for his *Choix de Fabliaux mis en vers*,[1] so Le Grand before him might have put together a very worthwhile collection of extracts of "fabliaux ou contes" simply from the printed sources available to him, might have drawn upon Etienne Barbazan. In fact, the author of the *Fabliaux ou Contes* relied for only three of his extracts upon the printed word,[2] and upon his most significant predecessor not at all. And yet Le Grand did not work principally form the medieval manuscripts. He had an ideal ready-made fund of source material in a collection of annotated manuscript copies furnished by La Curne de Sainte-Palaye, these superior in many respects, given the nature of the proposed compilation, to the originals and certainly to Barbazan's work which Le Grand was able to disregard.

Je dois à M. de Sainte-Palaye les premiers matérieux avec lesquels j'ai commencé cet Ouvrage, & qui m'en ont même inspiré le projet.[3]

This statement from the preface to the first volume of Le Grand's collection surely gives the lie to those unconvincing protestations of a

---

[1] Geneva and Paris (Prault) 1788, 2 vols.

[2] The three extracts concerned are:

1. "Le Manteau mal taillé" (vol. I, pp. 60–76) which Le Grand takes from a rare printed edition in preference to the manuscripts: "Comme elle est très-rare, qu'elle est d'ailleurs conforme à l'original, & que le style, malgré plusieurs défauts, a une naïveté & une certaine bonhomie charmante, je vais m'en servir ...". (P. 60.)

2. "Le laid Chevalier" (vol. I, pp. 177–178): "J'ai trouvé cette pièce dans le 'Menagiana' ... Quoique postérieure de quelques années à celles qui composent ce recueil, je m'en suis emparé, parce que je crois, avec Molière, que tout ce qui est bon dans mon genre m'appartient ...". (P. 177.)

3. "Des Catins et des Ménétriers" (vol. II, pp. 117–118): "Ce conte manque dans les recueils de M. de Sainte-Palaye, quoiqu'il soit du manuscrit de Berne dont il a une copie; on l'y a sans doute oublié. J'en ai trouvé dans le catalogue des manuscrits de cette Bibliothèque, donné par M. Skinner, un extrait en latin & sans titre. Le voici traduit." (P. 117.)

[3] *Fabliaux ou Contes*, vol. I, preface, p. lxxxix.

genuine aversion to the idea of a literary career reported in a much earlier part of this study, to Le Grand's insistence that he was made to break an almost sacred vow never to write, that he was literally black-mailed into publication.[7] The obvious enthusiasm with which he threw himself into this and subsequent projects makes his alleged initial reluctance difficult to accept. It is much easier to believe that this first endeavour simply suggested itself from materials at hand, that, per-haps, working on Sainte-Palaye's manuscript copies of the fabliaux for the *Glossaire*, Le Grand suddenly realized their potential as a collection of extracts in modern translation. Is it not perhaps even more probable that the suggestion came from Sainte-Palaye himself? This would cer-tainly seem to be implied by the introduction to the section "Fabliaux" in the *Bibliothèque des Romans* for February 1777, where the editors ex-plain precisely why they have thought fit to include only three extracts from Sainte-Palaye's copies of the fabliaux manuscripts:

Nous ne pouvons, dans un article consacré aux Romans de Chevalerie, par-ler des autres Fabliaux, qui, d'ailleurs, doivent faire l'objet d'un Recueil que l'illustre Académicien fait composer sous ses yeux.[5]

We have seen that Sainte-Palaye may not have realized the full histor-ical potential of the fabliaux until sometime after 1759.[6] Had this rea-lization come earlier, it might well have been a "Mémoire sur la lec-ture des anciens Fabliaux" that he read before the Académie des In-scriptions on the 13th December 1743, he might indeed have called here for a "bibliothèque générale & complète de tous nos anciens Fa-bliaux." Is it not possible that the *Fabliaux ou Contes* was conceived by Sainte-Palaye himself as an answer to this very call. Certainly Le Grand's collection meets what would no doubt have been the primary recommendation:

On s'attacheroit par préférence à tout ce qui paroîtroit de quelque usage pour l'Histoire, pour les Généalogies, pour les Antiquités françoises & pour la Géographie: sans rien omettre de ce qui donneroit quelques lumières sur les progrès des Arts & des Sciences.[7]

Whether or not Le Grand was in fact more or less commissioned by Sainte-Palaye to compile the *Fabliaux ou Contes*, the materials with which his teacher and benefactor furnished him, drawn from a vast

---

[4] See above, pp. 7–8.
[5] P. 87.
[6] See above, p. 104, note 180.
[7] "Mémoire sur la Lecture des anciens Romans de Chevalerie," p. 798.

fund of copies, extracts, notices and glossaries of manuscripts, the fruit of a lifetime of private researches altogether out of proportion with with Sainte-Palaye's published work, provided an excellent foundation for the task in hand.[8] Others, of course, had looked to the manuscripts of the fabliaux before Sainte-Palaye and have left notices, extracts and partial copies amongst their papers. It is well-known that Claude Fauchet owned and annotated the manuscript *B.N.f.fr. 1593*.[9] Caylus, it appears, had for his own purposes, very probably for his "Mémoire sur les Fabliaux," taken extracts with quotations from every item in *B.N.f.fr. 19152*,[10] while manuscript papers left by La Vallière include what purports to be a *Recueil de Fabliaux, copiés d'après le manuscrit N.2 de l'Eglise de Paris*.[11] But even Barbazan's considerable five manuscript volumes of notices, extracts and copies of fabliaux collections, from which he prepared his own ill-fated *Fabliaux et Contes*, cease to impress when set beside the great bulk of Sainte-Palaye's collated transcripts.[12]

It was probably in the summer of 1770 that Sainte-Palaye wrote to

[8] Some notion of the volume of Sainte-Palaye's manuscript work, copies, extracts, notices and glossaries, can be had from a "Liste des Ouvrages préparés ou composés par La Curne de Sainte-Palaye" concluding volume X of Lucien Favre's edition of the *Dictionnaire historique de l'ancien langage françois* (pp. 25–28). Cf. also L. Gossman, *Medievalism*, appendices 2–4, pp. 362–366. For a more detailed list of Sainte-Palaye's manuscripts and copies of manuscripts, cf. *Ms. Paris, B.N. fonds Moreau 1436*, ff. 41–44: "Manuscrits de La Curne de Sainte-Palaye. Catalogue des manuscrits soit originaux soit copiés"; *Moreau 1439* pp. 508–510: "Catalogues des livres imprimés et manuscrits appartenant au Dépot des Chartes et confiés au Sieur Mouchet, rédacteur et continuateur du 'Glossaire françois.' Accroissement à la partie in-4° de la bibliothèque de M. de Sainte-Palaye." These lists are reproduced by H. Omont, *Inventaire des manuscrits de la Collection Moreau*, Paris (Picard) 1891, pp. 207–213 and pp. 222–223 respectively.

[9] *B.N.f.fr. 25545* also bears notes in Fauchet's hand. Cf. Espiner-Scott, *Claude Fauchet*, p 199.

[10] Le Grand makes use of one of these for his own extract of "Blancandin" which appears in the third edition of the *Fabliaux ou Contes*. Cf. a note to the tale, vol. V, p. 201.

[11] Present *B.N.f.fr. 25545*. This *Recueil* is at present preserved in the Bibliothèque Sainte-Geneviève in Paris, *Ms. 2474* (Suppl. Y.F. in -4°.774), and contains the following: "La Chastelaine de Vergi" (fol. 2), "Le Chevalier au barizel" (fol. 18), "La Confession du Renard et son pèlerinage" (fol. 34), "Marguet convertie. Dialogue entre un vieillard et une femme débauchée" (fol. 47).
The first folio bears a note in Mercier de Saint-Léger's hand: "Toutes ces pièces en vers ont été copiées sur un ms. de l'Eglise de Paris, qui est aujourd'huy à la Bibliothèque du Roy, par une personne très intelligente et fort habile dans l'art de déchiffrer et dans l'ancienne langue françoise. M. le duc de la Vallière m'a donné ces copies, qui méritent d'être conservées soigneusement, an 1762."

[12] On Barbazan's collection of notices and extracts of manuscripts, by no means all of which are devoted to the manuscripts of the fabliaux, cf. Henry Martin, *Histoire de la Bibliothèque de l'Arsenal*, pp. 198–201: "Pour la préparation de ses trois volumes des 'Fabliaux,' il fit d'un grand nombre de manuscrits des notices et des extraits, qui forment aujourd'hui les nos. 3123, 3124, 3125, 3138 et 3519 de l'Arsenal. A cette liste, on peut encore ajouter le manuscrit 7079, dans lequel se trouvent des notices sur la vie et les oeuvres de beaucoup d'anciens poètes français." (P. 200.)

his friend de Brosses requesting him to do all in his power to obtain from La Clayette the loan for a period of three months of a certain manuscript which had come to his attention and with which he thought to complete his collections of copies of fabliaux and of French songs before 1300. His letter began thus:

Il y a 50 ans de bien comptés que je me donne tous les soins imaginables pour rassembler les anciens contes ou fabliaux anciens que j'ai pu découvrir ....[13]

The carefully annotated manuscript copies which Sainte-Palaye was only too willing to place at the disposal of Le Grand d'Aussy for the preparation of the *Fabliaux ou Contes* may have been the hard-won fruits of long years of painstaking research, but they were never meant to give rise to scholarly editions of texts and Paul Meyer is mistaken in believing that only the indifference of the reading public thwarted Sainte-Palaye's plans for publication.[14] We have already observed that eighteenth-century medievalists did not themselves consider the careful editing of medieval literary texts a worthwhile occupation, that the scholars themselves were no less indifferent than the reading public.[15] We know that Sainte-Palaye's copies of manuscripts were originally meant only to provide material for his historical undertakings, for the *Glossaire* and for the *Dictionnaire des Antiquités*. And we do not need Le Grand to vouch for this.[16] We have seen that the very manner in which these copies are annotated can leave no doubt as to the purpose they were originally to serve.[17] There can similarly be little doubt but that the bias of these annotations determined the particular bias of the *Fabliaux ou Contes*.

Once a scribe had surrendered to him the completed copy of a manuscript Sainte-Palaye appears to have set about the task of annotating it in three separate phases. We cannot know the exact sequence in which he worked but he very probably began by ensuring that he fully

---

[13] *Ms. Paris, B.N. fonds Bréquigny 65*, fol. 168.

[14] Cf. "Notice sur deux anciens manuscrits français ayant appartenu au Marquis de La Clayette" in *Notices et Extraits*, vol. XXXIII (1890) p. 2: "D'ailleurs, il faut bien le reconnaître, si Sainte-Palaye n'a rien publié de l'immense recueil de textes qu'il avait formé, la faute en est moins à lui qu'à son temps: il n'y avait point alors de public pour nos anciens auteurs ...".
Meyer also publishes here the letter from Sainte-Palaye to de Brosses cited above ("Notice," pp. 4-5).

[15] See above, pp. 59-61.

[16] *Fabliaux ou Contes*, vol. I, preface, p. lxxxix: "Dans la collection d'anciennes poésies, que depuis soixante ans ce Savant si estimable a pris soin de faire copier dans toutes les Bibliothèques pour composer le Glossaire qu'il va donner au Public, j'ai trouvé ...".

[17] See above, pp. 88-89.

understood every text contained in the copy. Lionel Gossman speaks of Sainte-Palaye's "meticulous linguistic control of the text" in referring to these copies,[18] and there can be little doubt that Le Grand's task was much facilitated by the notes to points of linguistic interest which fill the right-hand margins of these transcripts. Wherever there could be doubt as to the sense of a particular word or phrase that word or phrase is underlined in the text of the copy and its meaning given in the margin. If himself in doubt, Sainte-Palaye is careful only to suggest a possible translation which is then introduced by "pe," no doubt "peut-être." Only on the rarest occasions is Sainte-Palaye lost for a translation, but where this does occur he states categorically:

Je n'entends pas le sens de ce mot.[19]

The left-hand margins of his transcripts Sainte-Palaye reserved almost exclusively for notes to points of historical and geographical interest. Signalizing such points probably represented the second phase in the work of annotating a copy, but it was undoubtedly the most important. Sainte-Palaye was merely practising what he had preached in the "Mémoire sur la Lecture des anciens Romans de Chevalerie" where he had advocated the systematic study of the literary sources of medieval history and recommended that the first concern be "... tout ce qui paroîtroit de quelque usage pour l'Histoire, pour les Généalogies, pour les Antiquités françoises et pour la Géographie ...". Such was the material required for the *Dictionnaire des Antiquités* and clearly the greatest care was taken to ensure that nothing of relevance was overlooked in these copies. One may take any annotated folio from Sainte-Palaye's transcripts and be sure that the notes to points of historical interest will be the first to strike the eye, bracketed, underlined and, more often than not, marked "A," no doubt for "Antiquités." These notes, of course, cover all those subjects to be treated in the *Dictionnaire* and this, as we know, was to be an encyclopaedic survey of French society from the thirteenth to the seventeenth century.[20] We might recall here that the *Année Littéraire* was to remark of the *Fabliaux ou Contes*:

... on croit ne lire que des Contes, & l'on fait un cours d'antiquité ....[21]

[18] *Medievalism*, p. 264.
[19] Cf. for example, *Ms. Paris, Arsenal 2765*, fol. 200 vo.
[20] See above, p. 88.
[21] See above, p. 110. We have said that the "bulletins" collected by Le Grand for the preparation of his *Histoire de la Vie Privée des Français* probably owed much to the *Dictionnaire des Antiquités* (see above, p. 95). It is quite possible that the notes to "antiquités" in the

As we have said, the very rare literary judgements found in the margins of Sainte-Palaye's copies, the non-committal and almost disinterested "Jolie pièce," go unnoticed.[22]

The final phase in Sainte-Palaye's work of annotating the transcript was to collate the individual texts it contained with other versions of which he had copies and to note variant readings where these facilitated comprehension. Although it does not appear to have been Sainte-Palaye's practice always to have copied every available version of any item, a large number are headed by notes giving references to several copies after other manuscripts. Such is the heading to the copy of "Du Chevalier qui fist parler . . ." from *B.N.f.fr. 19152*:

Voy une autre copie de ce fabliau sur le ms. du Roy 7625 f.209 R. c.2 et une autre sur le ms. N. D. de Paris no 2 f.77 Vo c. 1-82 Vo. c.2 dont les variantes sont rapportées ci-après marquées par N.D.[23]

And when Sainte-Palaye does not trouble to have a second, or perhaps third or even fourth, version copied, we find more often than not that the variant readings of this latter are noted in the margin of the copy of the first, as in the case of "La Bataille de Charnage et de Karesme" from *B.N.f.fr. 25545*:

Ce fabliau n'a point été copié d'après ce ms. mais les variantes en ont été portées sur ma copie du ms. de St. Germain des Près – fol. 90 vo. c.3. J'en ai encore deux autres copies, une sur le ms. du Roi, no 7989[2] f.84 vo et l'autre sur le ms. du Roi 7615 fol. 120–122 vo.[24]

Not infrequently, then, Le Grand d'Aussy might work from two, three or even four versions of a particular piece without once referring to the medieval manuscripts. Finally it is to be remembered that where Sainte-Palaye does have copies of several versions of a piece, only one copy will usually have been scrutinized for materials useful to the *Glossaire* and the *Dictionnaire des Antiquités*:

margins of Sainte-Palaye's copies of manuscripts had led Le Grand to seek information for his own notes to the *Fabliaux ou Contes* in the *Dictionnaire*.

[22] See above, p. 89.

[23] *Ms. Paris, Arsenal 2771*, fol. 82 vo.

[24] *Ms. Paris, B.N. fonds Moreau 1691*, fol. 86 ro. There are occasions when Sainte-Palaye simply notes the title of a piece and gives a reference to another copy without bothering to mark variant readings on this latter. Cf. *Ms. Paris, B.N. fonds Moreau 1727*, fol. 260 vo:
"'Li regnes Nostre Dame Sainte Marie.'
Cette pièce n'a point été copiée sur ce ms. [Turin, L.V. 32] J'en ai une copie parmi les Fabliaux ms. du Roy 7218 f. 93 R. c. 2.''

'De Karesme et de Charnage.'

Conférez cette copie avec une autre que j'ai faite sur le ms. de S. Germ. C'est celle sur laquelle j'ai fait mes extraits de mots et autres.[25]

We have seen Sainte-Palaye suddenly stop "extracting" a tale upon realizing that he already possesses a copy after some other manuscript "... dont j'ai fait les Extraits de Mots, Antiq., Geogr. &c.".[26]

The care with which Sainte-Palaye's transcripts were executed has been called into question on a number of occasions. Etienne Barbazan has no qualms about publishing his own edition of *L'Ordène de Chevalerie* within a year of the appearance of Marin's edition after a Sainte-Palaye copy:[27]

... cette copie n'a point été faite par M. de Sainte-Palaye lui-même, mais par un Copiste qui ne sçait point lire les anciens manuscrits, & qui les entend encore moins: elle fourmille de fautes de lecture & d'intelligence; la ponctu-ation n'est rien moins qu'exacte.[28]

B. de Roquefort-Flaméricourt, however much he may have gleaned from the *Fabliaux ou Contes* for his *De l'Etat de la Poésie françoise dans les XIIe et XIIIe siècles*,[29] rebukes Le Grand d'Aussy for failing to go to the medieval manuscripts for his extracts:[30]

Le Grand d'Aussy a traduit quelques-uns de nos Fabliaux en prose; il les a enrichis de notes curieuses. Mais cet auteur, au lieu de consulter les manu-scrits originaux, a fait sa traduction d'après des copies, souvent fautives, de la Curne de Sainte-Palaye; elles l'ont fait tomber dans d'énormes contre-sens, et il s'est égaré dans une prolixité de notes sur des objets qui n'existoient point.[31]

Méon, who makes use of certain of these copies in his *Nouveau Recueil de Fabliaux et Contes*,[32] feels obliged to forewarn his readers of their in-accuracies:

---

[25] *Ms. Paris, Arsenal 2768*, fol. 190 ro.

[26] See above, p. 89.

[27] In volume II of Marin's *Histoire du Grand Saladin*, Paris (Tilliard) 1758.

[28] Barbazan, *L'Ordène de Chevalerie*, Lausanne and Paris (Chaubert & Hérissant) 1759, Avertissement, p. vi.

[29] Paris (Fournier) 1815.

[30] Le Grand, of course had criticized a number of his own predecessors for a similar failing. See above, p. 121, note 39.

[31] *De l'Etat de la Poésie françoise*, pp. 5–6.

[32] *Nouveau Recueil de Fabliaux et Contes inédits, des Poétes français des XIIe, XIIIe, XIVe et XVe siècles*, Paris (Chasseriau) 1823, 2 vols.

... une partie de ces Contes ayant été prise sur des copies faites pour M. de Sainte-Palaye, on y trouvera quelques mots évidemment mal copiés, et qu'il a été impossibles de rectifier faute du manuscrit original.[33]

An inaccurate copy is far better than nothing, of course, and Méon's name must be added to the lengthy inventory of nineteenth and twentieth-century medievalists who have come to appreciate and be thankful for the enterprise of their most illustrious predecessor. A number have turned to Sainte-Palaye's transcripts principally for the annotations they bear, Achille Jubinal, for example, in his *Jongleurs et Trouvères*, dismissing as "fort infidèle" the copy of *B.N.f.fr. 837* and *f.fr. 1553*, but acknowledging the help gained from the marginal notes:

Nous n'avons point fait difficulté de nous aider quelquefois de cette copie pour le sens de certaines phrases, et nous avons profité d'une partie des annotations qu'elle renferme, annotations qui sont, je crois, de la main de M. de Sainte-Palaye.[34]

Not a few modern scholars, as Lionel Gossman notes, have found it possible to place the same reliance in Sainte-Palaye's copies of certain texts as in the medieval originals.[35] To the names mentioned by Gossman we might add those of Montaiglon and Raynaud who for their *Recueil général et complet des Fabliaux* take a number of texts and variant readings from Sainte-Palaye's transcript of *Ms. Berne, Stadt- und Universitätsbibl. 354* and partial transcript of *Ms. Bibl. Univ. de Turin, L.V. 32*.[36] The destruction of the original *Ms. Bibl. Univ. de Turin, L.V. 32* in a fire at the Turin University library in January 1904 and the disappearance of two manuscripts formerly in Noblet's library at La Clayette make Sainte-Palaye's copies of these especially precious.[37]

Although Le Grand might have compiled a weighty collection of extracts of "fabliaux ou contes" solely from the transcripts made available to him by Sainte-Palaye, he did not begin work without first making some effort to ensure that the Bibliothèque du Roi held no other relevant manuscript collections overlooked by his teacher:

---

[33] Vol. I, Avertissement, p. v.

[34] A. Jubinal, *Jongleurs et Trouvères, ou Choix de Saluts, Epîtres, Rêveries et autres pièces légères des XIIIe et XIVe siècles*, Paris (Merklein) 1835, avis de l'Editeur, p. 14.

[35] Cf. L. Gossman, *Medievalism*, pp. 264–267.

[36] For texts from Sainte-Palaye's copy of *Ms. Berne, Stadt-und Universitätsbibl. 354*, see Montaiglon & Raynaud, nos. LXXV, LXXVI and LXXVII; for variants from this copy see nos. LXX, LXXIV, LXXX and LXXXVI. The text taken from Sainte-Palaye's copy of *Ms. Bibl. Univ. de Turin, L.V. 32* is no LXIX.

[37] On the Turin manuscript, cf. C. Brunel, "David d'Ashby, auteur méconnu des 'Faits des Tartares'" in *Romania*, vol. LXXIX (1958) p. 39. On Noblet's manuscripts, cf. Paul Meyer, "Notice de deux anciens manuscrits français ayant appartenus au Marquis de La Clayette."

Comment deviner au milieu d'une telle multitude, quels volumes contenai-
ent des Fabliaux? Il m'a donc fallu fouiller en aveugle dans cette mine, de
laquelle enfin, l'impatience & le dégoût m'ont chassé, malgré la complaisance sans bornes que m'ont fait éprouver les Gens de Lettres, attachés à la
garde ou au service de la Bibliothèque.[38]

Of those manuscripts discovered by Le Grand during the course of
this search and listed by him in his preface,[39] only one contains fabliaux
proper and Sainte-Palaye had a partial copy of this. From the remainder Le Grand drew the "miracles," "fables," "contes dévots" and
romances. Finally, there is evidence to suggest that Le Grand very
probably knew and used for the first edition of his collection two other
medieval manuscripts, not listed by him in his preface, containing recognized fabliaux.[40]

[38] *Fabliaux ou Contes*, vol. I, preface, p. xci.
[39] *Ibidem.*
[40] See Appendix.

CHAPTER V

THE METHOD. AN EXAMINATION OF LE GRAND'S EXTRACT FORM: THE "COPIE REDUITE".

If, as there is evidence to suggest, we should rightly give La Curne de Sainte-Palaye credit for the original notion of a collection of *Fabliaux ou Contes*,[1] then clearly, having once accepted the idea, Le Grand d'Aussy firmly imposed his own will upon the enterprise. There was really no question of a "bibliothèque générale & complète de tous nos anciens Fabliaux" of exactly the kind that Sainte-Palaye would no doubt have recommended: a uniform series of extracts all carefully executed after one archetype, giving a definitive répertoire of all the historical data to be found in the fabliaux, this to save contemporaries the "painful" task of actually reading them.[2] Le Grand, of course, is most anxious not only to prove medieval literature a reliable and invaluable source for the antiquarian, but to provide those with a less scholarly interest in the national past with as many insights as possible into it. However, he is no less anxious to demonstrate those literary merits by which, as he finds, the "trouvères" reigned supreme in their own day and even remained valid in the eighteenth century. Le Grand is committed to the rehabilitation of the fabliaux as worthwhile literature. The *Fabliaux ou Contes* as Sainte-Palaye would no doubt have envisaged it might have proven a long and painstaking labour, but it could have had nothing to match the problems inherent in Le Grand's conception of the undertaking. How could one ensure a just appreciation of the fabliaux by a public set at a linguistic and cultural distance of five centuries?

---

[1] See above, p. 222.

[2] Cf. "Mémoire concernant la lecture des anciens Romans de Chevalerie," p. 798: "... qu'il me soit permis de souhaiter que quelques gens de Lettres se partagent entre eux le pénible travail de lire ces sortes d'ouvrages, dont le temps détruit tous les jours quelques morceaux ,d'en faire des extraits qu'ils rapporteront à un système général & uniforme; afin que cessant de prendre des routes différentes, on ne soit point obligé de recommencer souvent les mêmes lectures."

While the *Fabliaux ou Contes* must surely have taken a quite different direction at Sainte-Palaye's hand, there can be little doubt that what Le Grand had learnt in the employ of his friend and benefactor and, indeed, the experience gained collaborating on the *Bibliothèque des Romans*, served him well in his first independent enterprise. Firstly there is the question of source material. Le Grand, it will be remembered, attributed his contemporaries' disdain for medieval literature in great part to the reluctance of historians like Massieu to consult the manuscripts before decrying the efforts of the "anciens rimeurs."[3] How much more important then for those who would revive these latter to go to the manuscripts and not take the easy course of some late corrupt, printed edition, which could give no true impression of the original:

Tressan, la Bibliothèque des Romans, Meyer &c. ont donné des extraits de nos R. de Chevalerie; mais ils n'ont travaillé que sur les versions imprimées, c'est à dire sur des imitations ....[4]

Only three times will Le Grand himself take the printed word as his source in his own collection, and on each occasion he is careful to state his particular reasons for doing so.[5] But it is easy for the author of the *Fabliaux ou Contes* to criticize his contemporaries. He himself could not have been in a stronger position, with a collection of very carefully annotated manuscript copies made readily available to him by the foremost medievalist of the day.

The medieval originals would no doubt have proven far less of a problem for Le Grand, a former researcher for the *Glossaire*, than for many of his contemporaries. But the diligence and care which Sainte-Palaye had employed in the annotation of his transcripts meant that his disciple rarely if ever needed to struggle for linguistic control of any text. If the right-hand margin of Sainte-Palaye's copy did not offer a translation for some particularly obscure word or phrase, then Le Grand could usually rest assured that there was little point to further search.[6] Equally important, he need only glance down the left-hand margin of the copy to know at once whether a text merited attention for its historical insights.[7] We know what importance Le Grand gave these latter, that he was quite prepared to include in his collection

---

[3] See above, p. 121, note 39.
[4] *Ms. Paris, B.N.n.a.f. 6227*, fol. 164.
[5] See above, p. 221.
[6] See above, p. 225.
[7] See above, *ibidem*.

pieces which had nothing else to recommend them but the light they shed upon the manners and customs of the period of their composition, even tales which he himself found actually to detract from the literary reputation of the "anciens rimeurs."[8] It may well have been the first phase in Le Grand's work of selecting texts for his collection simply to list those transcripts with the least amount of blank space in the left-hand margin. One disappointing feature of Sainte-Palaye's copies, for us at least, is the absence of any real literary criticism. But did Le Grand see this as a deficiency? Would he not in any case have preferred to follow his own judgement? The author of the *Fabliaux ou Contes* needed no guidance in matters of taste. There can be little doubt that Sainte-Palaye's linguistic and historical annotations were of much greater use to Le Grand than any literary appreciations might have been. The real work of the *Fabliaux ou Contes* did not therefore begin with the amassing of source materials, but only with the adaptation of these to the author's particular purposes.

These latter, as we have seen, were the yardstick against which Le Grand measured the "fabliaux ou contes," selecting or rejecting individual items according to their utility. A particular tale need not necessarily be the ideal medium for all three aims envisaged by the author in order to be considered for inclusion in the collection, as we know, but it will invariably serve at least one of his purposes, indirectly if not directly. The note on the use of French in medieval England which concludes "Des deux Anglais"[9] might easily have been inserted elsewhere in the collection and does not explain the inclusion of this tale. There is no evidence that it was a source of inspiration to others, no list of Italian or even French writers who have at some time adopted and adapted the anecdote. Moreover, there is no suggestion that the piece was in any way outstanding even by medieval literary standards. Then why should Le Grand go to the trouble of preparing an extract? Paradoxically, the tale is included for its lack of merit. Le Grand, we know, is above all anxious to convey an accurate impression of the "fabliaux ou contes," a considerable number of which are less than mediocre. He cannot therefore concern himself exclusively with the finest examples of the genre. One might say that "Des deux Anglais" and similar items are the setting to show the stone.[10]

Having once found a particular item in some way useful to the pur-

[8] See above, pp. 108–109.
[9] *Fabliaux ou Contes*, vol. II, pp. 107–109.
[10] See above, p. 200.

poses of the proposed collection, Le Grand's first concern is to bring together and collate as many versions of this as he can find. No doubt he
had learnt the importance of this procedure from Sainte-Palaye, the
first to recommend that scholars who would acquaint themselves with
and publish medieval French texts not only mistrust early printed
editions but go beyond the first manuscript versions they came upon:

Je crois devoir recommander également aux Savans qui voudront connoître
les écrits de nos anciens auteurs, et à ceux qui voudront les publier, non
seulement de ne point se fier aux anciens imprimés, mais de ne point se
contenter de la lecture d'un seul manuscrit et d'en conférer le plus qu'ils
pourront les uns avec les autres.[11]

The object of the *Fabliaux ou Contes* is not the scholarly edition in Old
French, of course, but Le Grand is concerned with accuracy and it is
hardly less important for him that "... all the elements of a text could
be reconstituted in their entirety ...".[12] Yet the search for variants did
not entail too great an effort on his part. The bulk of the work, as we
know, had been done for him. It may not have been Sainte-Palaye's
practice always to have copied every available version of any particular
item, but he would never fail to give references for any one purposely
omitted from his transcripts and very often took the trouble to note
variant readings from it in the margin of the copy of some other version.[13] We know that Le Grand did spend some time in the manuscript
room of the then Bibliothèque du Roi searching for collections of fabliaux that Sainte-Palaye might have overlooked, occasionally finding
odd items useful to him,[14] and clearly, having once selected a tale for
his collection, he took great pains to ensure that this great repository
had not held other versions secret from his illustrious predecessor. Not
infrequently, however, his effort was in vain[15] and the extract composed from two, three or even four separate versions of the piece without Le Grand having once been obliged to refer to the medieval originals.

It was largely as a result of La Curne de Sainte-Palaye's industry,
then, that Le Grand was acquainted with a far greater number of
manuscript collections of fabliaux than any of his predecessors who

---

[11] Cited by L. Gossman, *Medievalism*, p. 226.
[12] *Ibidem.*
[13] See above, p. 226.
[14] See above, pp. 228–229.
[15] For example, cf. a note to "L'Ordre de Chevalerie," vol. I, p. 140, (a). Le Grand had
thought to find a version unknown to Sainte-Palaye only to discover the piece totally unrelated.

publicly gave their attention to this genre, that his choice of materials was much improved even upon that of Barbazan.[16] A large number of tales, their existence ignored by this latter, appear for the first time in the *Fabliaux ou Contes*.[17] Moreover, when Le Grand was dealing with some item already published by Barbazan, he not infrequently had two versions to Barbazan's one, four to his two. "Le Prestre qui menga les Meures" was known to the author of the *Fabliaux et Contes* in only one form, that appearing in *B.N.f.fr.19152*.[18] Le Grand, however, was acquainted with and made use of a second version contained in *Berne 354*.[19] Barbazan had the choice of two manuscripts for his edition of "Constant du Hamel," *B.N.f.fr.837* and *B.N.f.fr. 19152*.[20] Le Grand had a choice of four in the transcripts furnished by Sainte-Palaye, this tale also featuring in *B.N.f.fr. 1553* and the Berne manuscript again.[21]

In the present day, of course, we should expect an editor reproducing some medieval French text in its original form to be more concerned with variants than one interested only in presenting an extract of this in a modern translation. But it is the eighteenth century that concerns us here. Even La Curne de Sainte-Palaye, although he carefully entered variants in the margins of his transcripts, had no notion of reconstructing correct readings on the basis of the manuscript tradition. At this time an editor would usually establish his text after one "authoritative" manuscript:

A good manuscript was one which had been copied faithfully and which had suffered few alterations, interpolations, and stylistic or linguistic corrections. A bad manuscript was almost invariably a late one, which had been altered to suit the requirements of a later generation of readers.[22]

It was not therefore unusual that Barbazan should in fact take only one manuscript for each tale, merely noting the existence of other versions.[23] Where two or more equally authoritative manuscripts existed

[16] See table in Appendix.

[17] For example, "Brifaut," "Le povre Clerc," "Le Pré tondu" and those other tales which appear only in the Berne manuscript.

[18] Barbazan published the tale in his *L'Ordène de Chevalerie*, pp. 161–167.

[19] Cf. a prefatory note to Le Grand's extract of this piece, *Fabliaux ou Contes*, vol. I, p. 222: "Dans la version du manuscrit de Saint-Germain, qui est celle qu'a imprimée Barbasan, l'Auteur se nomme; dans celle du manuscrit de Berne il ne le fait pas; & celle-ci a encore bien d'autres différences. Je les ai fondues toutes deux ensemble pour faire cet extrait."

[20] Cf. *Fabliaux et Contes*, vol. II, pp. 204–252.

[21] Le Grand's extract appears in the third volume of his collection, pp. 356–368.

[22] L. Gossman, *Medievalism*, p. 229. In part 3 of his book Gossman devotes a most interesting chapter (ch. IV) to the problems faced by eighteenth-century editors of medieval texts and the solutions they contrived to find.

[23] Cf. the table of contents to each volume of the *Fabliaux et Contes*, e.g. vol. I, p. liv: "De la Bourse pleine de sens, par Jehan li Galois d'Aubepierre. Extrait du Ms. 7218. Il est aussi dans le Ms. 7615."

it was the practice to select one of these and simply note variants in the text, a procedure which Barbazan would no doubt have adopted had he intended his collection for a purely scholarly public. But if Barbazan did not need to look very far to find a "good" manuscript, then certainly Le Grand did not carefully scrutinize three or even four versions of a particular tale simply in order to find the most authoritative text, not for an extract in modern translation. Certainly, as we have said, the author of the *Fabliaux ou Contes*, much concerned with exactitude, was anxious to be aware of all the elements of any item selected for his collection. But very often he might gather these from only one or two "good" manuscripts, needing only to scan quickly through the rest to ensure that nothing had been missed. What was the purpose of his industry? Why extend the very detailed examination of variants even beyond Sainte-Palaye's transcripts? Clearly Le Grand would not add to the weight of his task without some specific object:

... j'en multipliais aussi les difficultés à un point dont on n'a pas d'idée. Il n'y a presque pas de Fabliaux dont je n'aie trouvé plusieurs copies; & presque toujours ces copies différaient entre elles, soit par un certain nombre des vers, soit par des morceaux entiers, plus ou moins considérables. Quelquefois elles n'avaient que le titre de commun, & quelquefois le fonds du Conte était entièrement le même, sans qu'il y eût un seul vers de semblable.[24]

The complexity of Le Grand's task may, as he insists, have increased proportionately to the number of variants consulted, but the advantage to be gained was seen as adequate compensation:

J'en ai tiré parti en les refondant ensemble; & me suis permis, toutes les fois que je l'ai pu, d'insérer dans la version principale que je suivais, les traits les plus agréables qui se rencontraient dans les autres. C'était pour moi une nouvelle peine; mais les Contes y ont gagné, & ce motif m'a suffi.[25]

A number of extracts are drawn from only one version of a particular tale, when this, for whatever reason, especially recommends itself to Le Grand. Here he notes the existence of variants and analogous pieces, not infrequently summarizing these in the notes.[26] But for the majority of his extracts Le Grand selects one version of the chosen piece as a basis and proceeds to add to this the best features from others. These

---

[24] *Fabliaux ou Contes*, vol. I, preface, pp. xci–xcii.

[25] *Idem*, p. xciv.

[26] A large number of "contés dévots" end with notes summarizing similar tales, and the fables often with short extracts, in translation of course, from the Latin and Greek originals. Cf. also the notes to "Du Prud'homme qui donna des Instructions à son Fils, alias Du Prud'homme qui n'avait qu'un Ami," vol. II, p. 384, and to "De la Demoiselle qui ne pouvait, sans se pâmer, entendre un certain jurement, alias De la Demoiselle ...", vol. III, pp. 435–436.

may differ to the extent of being unrecognizable as variants of the same item, no matter:

Ces trois versions sont absolument différentes … J'ai suivi la première comme la meilleure, quoique le manuscrit en soit imparfait; & me suis permis, à mon ordinaire, d'y insérer les traits les plus agréables des deux autres, quand le sens l'a permis.

This note introducing the extract of "Huéline et Eglantine, alias Le Jugement d'Amour, alias Florance et Blanchefleur"[27] demonstrates also that a tattered and torn manuscript, rejected by compilers of scholarly editions, could be valued and put to some use by Le Grand, that the version selected as the basis for an extract need not be the best preserved. The "version principale" would no doubt be that best suited to the purposes of his collection, not necessarily the most complete.[28] Finally, where there is nothing to choose between the two equally useful versions of a particular item, they are simply fused into one piece, as in the case of "Du Curé qui mangea des mûres":

Dans la version du manuscrit de Saint-Germain, qui est celle qu'a imprimée Barbazan, l'Auteur se nomme; dans celle du manuscrit de Berne il ne le fait pas; & celle-ci a encore bien d'autres différences. Je les ai fondues toutes deux ensemble pour faire cet extrait.[29]

The method was clearly open to criticism and it will be no surprise to learn from what quarter that criticism came. If the Provençalistes were somewhat embarrassed by the absence of "pièces justificatives" to substantiate their own claims for the troubadours, then they must do all in their power to discredit the case for the "trouvères." Papon seizes upon Le Grand's explanations to denounce the *Fabliaux ou Contes* as inadmissible evidence:

Je ne puis me résoudre à lui pardonner la liberté avec laquelle, de plusieurs fabliaux sur le même sujet, composés dans des tems différents, il n'en a fait qu'un seul, retranchant ce qu'il y avoit de mauvais, n'en présentant que l'agréable ou le supportable, transposant, rapprochant & arrangeant à sa manière tous ces morceaux épars, pour en faire un conte, qui ne ressemble à

---

[27] Vol. I, p. 230. In a note introducing "Le Mariage, alias Le Jeu d'Adam le Bossu d'Arras" (vol. I, p. 367) Le Grand promises always to give the differing titles of variants used.

[28] The following note interrupts the extrait of "Huéline et Eglantine": "Ici le manuscrit se trouve déchiré, & le dénouement manque. Je vais y suppléer par un extrait de celui de la troisième version." (Vol. I, pp. 235–236.)

[29] Vol. I, p. 222. Le Grand is prepared to take this one step further. Cf. "De l'Herberie, alias Le Dit de l'Herberie," vol. III, p. 349: "Tels sont les deux titres de deux pièces, totalement différentes, & fort ordurières, que j'ai réunies & fondues ensemble, parce que le sujet en est le même; ne contenant toutes deux que des propos de charlatan dans une place publique."

aucune des copies qu'il a eues sous les yeux. Je conviens qu'il n'a pas toujours usé d'une liberté si grande; mais soyez persuadé qu'il y a peu de pièces dans son recueil qui soient une copie fidelle de l'original. Il les a toutes embellies par quelques changements.[30]

Time and time again in the collection, as we know, Le Grand insists that his first concern has been exactitude, even at one point claiming to have rejected certain illustrations because of the engraver's wish to improve upon the originals.[31] The most serious and most damaging charge that can be brought against him, as he well knows, is that of conveying a false impression of the fabliaux, Papon's charge. Le Grand protests his innocence in advance:

Je me flatte qu'on ne blâmera point de pareilles restitutions. J'ai cru néanmoins devoir en prévenir, & je répéterai ailleurs cet avertissement plus d'une fois, afin de rassurer sur mon exactitude, ceux qui rencontrant par hazard l'original de quelque Fabliau, croiraient voir dans ma traduction l'apparence d'une infidélité.[32]

His defence, of course, is quite simply that his collection is not intended as a definitive scholarly edition of the fabliaux. His method appears quite acceptable when seen in the light of this much less pedantic object, "faire lire les fabliaux." After all, he is introducing no foreign matter when he borrows from variants. Le Grand later redefines his purpose in a "Notice sur les Enseignemens du Chevalier Geoffroi de la Tour-Landri à ses filles":

... je me suis fait une méthode de travail pour laquelle je demande grâce, parce qu'il m'en coûteroit un peu trop d'y renoncer. Ce n'est point tel ou tel manuscrit que je veux faire connoître; c'est tel ou tel ouvrage, tel ou tel auteur d'après plusieurs manuscrits; et cet auteur, cet ouvrage, mon plan est principalement de le considérer en masse, tant sous le point de vue littéraire, que sous ce qu'il peut présenter d'intéressant concernant les usages et les mœurs de la nation.[33]

Clearly it was only once he had put aside scissors and paste and begun to set down his translations that Le Grand felt himself seriously threatened by possible charges of misrepresentation. We have noted Lévesque de la Ravallière's most discouraging comments upon the inherent

[30] *Voyage de Provence* (1787) vol. II, pp. 170–171.
[31] Cf. *Fabliaux ou Contes*, vol. I, concluding note to "Le Médecin de Brai," p. 414: "Le Graveur s'est imaginé sans doute que de pareils dessins déshonoreraient son talent. Il a voulu les corriger, les embellir; il y a mis de l'esprit; enfin ce n'était plus une copie, & il a fallu y renoncer."
[32] *Idem*, vol. I, preface, pp. xciv-xcv.
[33] *Notices et Extraits des Manuscrits de la Bibliothèque nationale*, vol. V, p. 160.

dangers of translation.[34] The author of the *Fabliaux ou Contes* was well aware of these. But he must translate. Barbazan had failed because he refused to do so and Le Grand was too well acquainted with contemporary tastes to imagine that the public was now any more willing to take up the study of Old French than it had been twenty years previously. How easy it would have been for the author of the *Fabliaux ou Contes* simply to emulate the editors of the *Bibliothèque des Romans*, and no doubt be assured the kind of success that Tressan enjoyed. But Le Grand has set himself to rehabilitate the fabliaux as literature worthy in its own right and must invalidate his efforts if he follows the example of his less serious contemporaries:

Ce n'est pas d'après ces extraits infidèles et défigurés qu'on peut prendre une idée de notre poésie ancienne.

The problem is how to reconcile the considerable modifications dictated by the limitations of an uninstructed public with the necessity of fidelity and exactitude essential to the purpose of the *Fabliaux ou Contes*. The answer can only be some kind of compromise:

Il n'est pas possible de faire lire les Fabliaux autrement, que dans une traduction où l'on se permettra certaines libertés. Il faut en réformer le style, en retrancher beaucoup de longueurs & des choses de mauvais goût, en resserrer quelquefois la narration; en un mot, ce sont des métaux tirés de la mine, qui doivent être purgés de leurs scories, fondus & travaillés: mais qu'il faut bien se garder aussi de dénaturer.[35]

The *Fabliaux ou Contes* may have been quite a sizeable collection but Le Grand could without any difficulty have filled twenty and more volumes had he chosen to translate in full all those tales of which he gives only an abridged version. It is the brevity of many of Le Grand's extracts that perhaps strikes one most when first glancing through his work. A note introducing the first tale, "Merlin," summarizes in a few short lines the original prologue, "... trivial & fort long que je supprime, comme je ferai toujours en pareil cas sans en prévenir ...".[36] Lest the reader become bored, lengthy preambles and digressions and repetitive conclusions are reduced to an absolute minimum and not infrequently excluded, when the extract will be abruptly interrupted with a brief synopsis of what has been omitted. The "Lai du buisson d'épine" concludes this way:

[34] See above, p. 215.
[35] *Fabliaux ou Contes*, vol. I, preface, pp. lxxxvii-lxxxviii.
[36] *Idem*, vol. I, p. 1.

Le reste du Conte, dans lequel, selon le costume d'alors, le Poëte fait marcher ensemble le courage & l'amour, ne contient plus qu'un long récit de plusieurs combats successifs.[37]

Similar reductions are made to a piece when Le Grand has already presented, or is later to present, a tale with what he sees as possibly tiresome similarities:

Je n'ai donné qu'une analise de ce Conte, parce qu'on lira plus bas un Roman qui offre des situations à-peu-près semblabes, avec plus d'intérêt encore.[38]

This note concludes one of many extracts of the poorer or better known anecdotes where the author wishes only to give the briefest possible outline of the original. These Le Grand specifically terms "extraits" or "analyses" in a note, either introducing or interrupting the piece, announcing the lack of merit of the tale[39] or reminding the reader that he has come upon this or a very similar story a dozen times before:

Je n'ai pas besoin d'en dire davantage. Tout le monde connaît ce Conte ....[40]

The above concludes an extract of a mere half page, a by no means unusual length for a Le Grand "analyse."[41] In the third volume Haisiau's "De l'Anel qui faisoit les ... grans et roides" is reduced to only the first three words of the title and is only mentioned because it has proven a source of inspiration to others[42]—nothing that might in any way help the case for the "trouvères" can be omitted!

Haisiau's tale, of course, is drastically "abridged" not because it has no literary merit nor because it is already too well known to the public, rather for its obscenity. Le Grand's fear of boring his readers appears to have been matched only by his dread of offending their sensibilities. Or so he would have us believe:

---

[37] Vol. III, pp. 244–250.

[38] "De la bonne Impératrice qui garda loyalement la foi du mariage," vol. IV, p. 120. Cf. also the note introducing "Le Sacristain," vol. III, p. 401: "Tout le commencement du Fabliau différent très-peu des trois ou quatre précédens, il suffira d'en donner l'analyse."

[39] Cf. the note introducing "De l'Ombre et de l'Anneau," vol. I, p. 179: "Ce Conte, d'une longueur mortelle, peut se réduire à cette analyse."

[40] "Du Curé qui posa une pierre," vol. II, p. 374.

[41] Cf. for example, in vol. II: "Les deux Parasites," p. 238, "Du Villain et de sa femme," p. 330; vol. III: "Ammelot," p. 168, "Lai d'Idoine," p. 170, "Lai d'Isabeau," p. 171, etc. Quite a number of the fables in vol. IV occupy no more than half a page.

[42] Vol. III, p. 425: "Quoique le grave Président Fauchet ait donné l'extrait de ce Fabliau, je n'en parlerais point si je n'avais à remarquer ... qu'il a été imité."

Il est des Contes licentieux que je supprimerai en entier; il en est que je ne présenterai qu'en extrait, ou dont je retrancherai les détails trop libres. Ce n'est point là dépouiller un Auteur, c'est le mettre en état d'entrer chez les honnêtes gens.[43]

It is not to the directness of the "fabliers" in calling a spade a spade that Le Grand objects. Like Caylus and Barbazan he can excuse them those unselfconscious terms now banished from polite society. But with his predecessors he condemns those tales which centre upon some gross obscenity[44] and chooses, as in the case of Haisiau's "De l'Anel ...", to suppress them.[45] Elsewhere he simply modifies or omits an offending passage. The extract of "De la Dame qui fut corrigée"[46] Le Grand interrupts without a qualm just before the dénouement:

La décence ne me permet pas d'en traduire davantage. Je préviens aussi que par le même motif j'ai changé le dernier mot du titre, qui, dans l'original, annonce crument l'endroit que je supprime.

For quite a number of these less delicate tales the author resorts once more to the "analyse," offering only the skeleton of the narrative.[47] But rarely is the reader at a loss to see beyond the omission or through the modification to the original, especially since Le Grand considers it essential in the interests of exactitude always to account for what has been suppressed or recast:

La décence me défend de traduire le reste de l'aventure, contée dans l'original d'une manière aussi plaisante que naïve. Mais je me permettrai, à l'ordinaire, d'en donner l'extrait; & je suis cette méthode d'autant plus volontiers, qu'en ôtant à un tableau trop licentieux le danger qu'il pourrait avoir, elle m'acquitte de l'exactitude qu'attendent de moi les gens de lettres.[48]

Le Grand, of course, was well aware of contemporary tastes and knew that such inclusions could do the collection little harm. Whether or not we accept his protestations of an overriding concern with exactitude,

---

[43] Vol. I, preface, pp. lxxii-lxxiii.

[44] Caylus, Barbazan and Le Grand had identical views on this question. See above, pp. 207, 210.

[45] The notes prepared by Le Grand for a third edition of the *Fabliaux ou Contes* include a series of extracts headed "Fabliaux Licencieux" (*Ms. Paris, B.N.n.a.f. 6227*, ff. 1–16). Several of these, amongst them "Gauteron et Marion," "Le Fout ..." and "Des trois Dames qui trouvèrent un ...", are included by Renouard in his edition of Le Grand's collection, now couched in language rather more acceptable than that to be found in the original extracts. "Le Fout ...", for example, becomes "Le Consolateur." Cf. *Fabliaux ou Contes* (1829) vol. I, p. 287, vol. III, pp. 284–287 and vol. IV, pp. 196–198.

[46] "De la Dame escoillée," vol. II, pp. 336–349.

[47] For example, cf. "De la Demoiselle qui rêvait," vol. III, p. 426.

[48] The note interrupts the extract of "Le Meunier d'Aleus," vol. II, pp. 413–419.

he certainly spared no effort to ensure that the "honnêtes gens" of the
eighteenth century had little difficulty in reading between the lines.
Moreover, there are occasions when he himself regrets the interruption[49] and one at least where the periphrastic note must be more than a
match for the original![50] On the other hand, it would be unfair for us
to insist that Le Grand's refusal to suppress those more dubious passages which in some way shed light upon the manners and customs of
the past is really but an excuse to offer his readers further titillation. Le
Grand, as we know, was a true disciple of Sainte-Palaye. He had no
qualms about boring or shocking his public when the alternative was
to lose some valuable insight into the national past:[51]

Quelqu'étranges que soient les moeurs des Fabliaux, il est de mon devoir
de les représenter telles qu'elles sont, puisqu'elles peignent leur siècle.[52]

We have noted already that Le Grand would take this historical scru-
ple so far as to include in his collection tales which he himself considered devoid of all literary merit. But these he presents in a concise and
unembellished form, offering them simply as documentary evidence
with no thought that they should provide anything but instruction:

Cette Pièce, composée alternativement d'un vers de huit syllabes & d'un
vers de quatre, est ce que nous appelons un amphigouri. Je ne la rapporte
que pour faire connaître les principaux genres de plaisanterie usités alors, &
il suffira d'en extraire quelques lignes.[53]

[49] Cf. the note concluding "Du Chevalier qui faisait parler . . .", vol. III, p. 424.
[50] Cf. "Béranger," vol. II, p. 365: "Ici je me vois forcé d'interrompre mon récit pour
réclamer l'indulgence de mes Lecteurs. Me pardonneront-ils de dire que la belle guerrière
propose au Chevalier de venir embrasser ce qu'on ne baise guères ordinairement, & que
le poltron s'y soumet; que l'une descend & présente sans voile l'objet du baiser, tandis que
l'autre ôtant son heaume, s'avance, un genou en terre, pour sa respectueuse cérémonie, qui
lui fait faire une remarque & une réflexion bien singulières."
[51] Or, of course, the opportunity to list half a dozen tales inspired by some medieval piece.
For example, cf. "Les deux Parasites" (vol. II, pp. 238–239) where the list of imitators is
longer than the extract itself.
[52] See above, p. 108. Cf. also a note on "Audigier" in Le Grand's manuscript papers: "J'ai longtemps hésité si je devais annoncer ce poëme . . . Cependant je me suis
dit que dans un ouvrage tel que le mien, le premier devoir est de ne rien omettre de ce qui
caractérise le génie de nos pères, et que pour apprécier ce génie, il faut connaître le genre de
plaisanteries dont ils s'amusaient, comme on a connu leurs lois, leurs usages et leurs moeurs."
(*Ms. Paris, B.N.n.a.f. 6226,* fol. 13.)
[53] Introductory note to "Rêverie," vol. III, p. 100. Cf. also, for example, "L'Indigestion
du Villain," vol. II, pp. 112–113, or those items given as examples of early French theatre,
e.g. "Le Miracle de Théophile," vol. I, pp. 333–336. "Le Jeu de S. Nicolas" which follows
(pp. 339–345), although a little more substantial, concludes: "D'après le prologue on devine
le reste de la pièce, & ce qu'on vient d'en lire suffit pour en donner l'idée."
    An unusual note introducing "Les deux Ménétriers" (vol. I, p. 299) forewarns the reader
that what follows might best be omitted by those with a lesser interest in the history of early
French poetry.

We have perhaps already dwelt at undue length upon those items which Le Grand himself announces to be of only secondary interest. It was hardly with such tales as "Rêverie" or "L'Indigestion du Villain" that he hoped to resuscitate and rehabilitate the "trouvères" and their fabliaux, and it is time, therefore, that we looked to those extracts which were indeed intended as a means to this end. It was here that Le Grand's ability as popularizer was put to the test, and it is by these more studied pieces that his success must be measured. His task, again, to convey to a non-specialist and even lazy public an accurate impression of the fabliaux, was no easy one. He must translate and abridge. But how could he do this without a breach of that first and all-important law of exactitude, by which he must invalidate his efforts:

... ce sont des métaux tirés de la mine, qui doivent être purgés de leurs scories, fondus & travaillés: mais qu'il faut bien se garder aussi de dénaturer. C'est à quoi je me suis spécialement attaché. J'ai conservé, autant que je l'ai pu, le caractère original de ces vieux Poëtes, leur manière naïve de narrer, leur simplicité touchante. Quoique par fois leurs sujets soient plaisans, leur expression l'est peu; je ne me suis pas permis de l'être davantage. J'ai poussé le scrupule jusqu'à donner à quelques-uns de leurs Contes, un style, ou plus rapide, ou plus élégant, quelquefois même plus poëtique, selon que pouvaient l'autoriser les faibles nuances qui distinguaient les Auteurs.[54]

There can be no question of a literal translation then, as this would strip the piece of its original appeal. Too liberal a rendering must distort it out of all recognition. The answer, of course, is a compromise, the "miniature" or "copie réduite" as Le Grand terms it:

Enfin, leur langage étant devenu inintelligible, je me suis fait leur interprète; & sans jamais dire autrement qu'eux, j'ai cru dans certains endroits pouvoir dire mieux. Ce n'est donc point une traduction littérale que je donne, on ne la supporterait pas; ce n'est point une traduction libre, elle les altérerait; c'est une copie réduite, pour laquelle il a fallu employer des couleurs nouvelles, & qui, sans rendre trait pour trait l'original, est cependant fidèle, parce qu'elle n'y ajoute rien.[55]

Our task now must be to evaluate the "copie réduite," and to this end we have chosen to select and examine in some detail one particular example of this form, Henri d'Andeli's "Lai d'Aristote," an extract to which the author of the *Fabliaux ou Contes* clearly gave much thought

[54] Vol. I, preface, pp. lxxxviii-lxxxix.
[55] *Ibidem.*

and care and one, amongst several, which can be said to represent what we might term the Le Grand method.[56]

ELEMENTS OF THE "COPIE REDUITE"

A summary history of the anecdote

To begin at the very beginning, we should perhaps first note briefly that Le Grand considers the anecdote to be Arabic in origin, remarking upon its appearance under the title "Le Visir sellé et bridé" in D. D. Cardonne's *Mélanges de littérature orientale*.[57] Maurice Delbouille, in his own edition of the "Lai d'Aristote," cites this same piece, although from a different collection, in support of the same case.[58] But whatever its origins the story concerning Aristotle appears to have enjoyed no little success both during and after the Middle Ages,[59] although Le Grand himself makes reference to only one work composed before his own century in which the episode appears, the *Amours d'Euriale et de Lucrèce* of AEneas Sylvius Piccolomini which dates from the fifteenth century.[60] Other more recent works offering some version of the tale, *La Bibliothèque amusante et instructive*,[61] Imbert's *Historiettes ou Nouvelles en vers*,[62] the comedy *Le Tribunal domestique*,[63] are listed and a short account given of this latter. Finally, this summary history of the anecdote includes reference to and brief descriptions of several artistic representations of the final "chevauchée triomphale," by Spranger, Sadeler, Van Bossuit and some master then unknown to Le Grand:

Un Amateur m'a assuré avoir vu à Paris, il y a plusieurs années, un groupe en marbre représentant le même sujet. Il appartenait alors à M. le Marquis de Vence.

---

[56] The extract appears in vol. I, pp. 197–211.

[57] Paris, 1770, vol. I, p. 16. As is always the case in the *Fabliaux ou Contes*, these notes on the history of the anecdote, filling two pages, follow immediately upon the extract.

[58] Cf. Maurice Delbouille, *Le Lai d'Aristote de Henri d'Andeli, publié d'après tous les manuscrits*, Paris, (Les Belles Lettres) 1951 (Bibliothèque de la Faculté de Philosophie et Lettres de l'Université de Liège-Fascicule CXXIII) pp. 53–56.

[59] Cf. Delbouille, pp. 5–6 and Bédier, *Les Fabliaux*, pp. 446–447.

[60] Cologne (Ulrich Zell) 1468.

[61] Paris, 1755, vol. II, p. 15.

[62] Paris (Delalain) 1774.

[63] Apparently first staged in 1777.

The Manuscripts

Caylus' extract and Barbazan's edition of the "Lai d'Aristote"[64] are both mentioned in the first of the notes proper which, indeed, exposes some confusion on Le Grand's part concerning the manuscripts used by his predecessors:

Le Comte de Caylus, dans l'extrait qu'il a donné de ce Fabliau, dit que la Maîtresse d'Alexandre lui fait prendre le déguisement d'Abbé. Cette mascarade inutile ne se trouve ni dans l'édition qu'a donnée du Fabliau Barbassan, d'après le manuscrit cité par M. de Caylus; ni dans deux autres versions un peu différentes de celle-ci, que j'ai entre les mains, & d'après lesquelles cet extrait est fait.

It should be made clear here that the "Lai d'Aristote" is preserved in five manuscripts: A, *B.N.f.fr. 837*; B, *B.N.f.fr. 1593*; C, *B.N.n.a.f. 1104*; D, *B.N.f.fr. 19152*; E, *Arsenal 3516*. C and E were unknown to Le Grand and his predecessors. The line included but misinterpreted by Caylus as a request that Alexander disguise himself

Or soiez demain en abé

in fact appears in only one of the three manuscript versions of the tale known to Le Grand and his contemporaries, D,[65] that obviously employed by Caylus, whereas Barbazan, for his edition, made use of A, as he states in the table of contents to the first volume of his collection.[66] Le Grand, who clearly worked from A and B, obviously needed no help with readings since he cannot have examined Barbazan's edition closely.[67] It is similarly curious that the author of the *Fabliaux ou Contes* should have failed to realize the very simple explanation for Caylus' error. Le Grand, of course, knew the manuscript used by Caylus, then *St.-Germain 1830*, very well, and the copy with which Sainte-Palaye furnished him does not omit the "Lai d'Aristote."[68]

In attempting to account for Le Grand's confusion we can perhaps suggest an answer to a much more important question. Why should Le Grand choose to compose his extract of this particular tale from A and B, especially when it is deliberately omitted from Sainte-Palaye's copy

---

[64] Cf. Caylus, "Mémoire sur les Fabliaux," pp. 362–363; Barbazan, *Fabliaux et Contes*, vol. I, pp. 155–178.
[65] Cf. Delbouille, *Le Lai d'Aristote*, p. 75, note to lines 255–264.
[66] P. lv.
[67] But how can he have overlooked the manuscript number given in the table of contents?
[68] Cf. *Ms. Paris, Arsenal 2773*, fol. 21 ro.

of the former?[69] The answer would seem to be that Sainte-Palaye's transcript of D bears almost no annotations, whereas if we turn to that from B[70] we find what must have been a much more attractive proposition for a would-be editor. Moreover, the right-hand margin of this latter bears the following note:

Cette pièce se trouve dans le ms. du Roy 7218 qui est plus conforme au ms. du Roy 7615 qu'à celui de St. Germain des Prés.[71]

It would seem that Le Grand, taking account of this, did not examine the St.-Germain transcript too carefully, preferring in any case to work from two manuscripts in the same group. Maurice Delbouille informs us that the version offered by DE is superior to that of ABC.[72] But again it must be remembered that C and E were unknown to Le Grand to whom AB promised more than what he must have regarded as an independent D. Moreover, the two manuscripts Le Grand used, A and B, do in fact form a separate "sous-groupe."[73] Perhaps, given the nature and purpose of the *Fabliaux ou Contes*, we can excuse the author's uncharacteristic step in almost totally disregarding D in this instance.

The preservation of the narrative

The narrative line of the "Lai d'Aristote" is preserved almost intact in Le Grand's extract. The conquests of the powerful Alexander have been brought to an abrupt halt, not by the superior strength of some enemy army, but by the irresistible force of love. With the king totally engrossed in his lady his followers become restless and secretly censure their lord for his neglect of them. Aristotle, Alexander's tutor, becomes their spokesman and reproaches his master for the unseemly way in which he treats his men. Here Le Grand's extract differs from the manuscript versions for Alexander heeds the words of the old sage and remains apart from his love until she, unable to restrain herself any longer slips to his side under cover of darkness. Hearing the king's story, she swears to be avenged:

La belle irritée contre le pédagogue jura qu'elle s'en vengerait. Elle pria son

---

[69] Cf. *Ms. Paris, Arsenal 2763*, fol. 178 ro: "On voit ici depuis le f. 80 v. c2 jusqu'au f. 83 r.cl 'Li Lais d'Aristote' dont je n'ai pas pris de copie parce que j'en avais deux autres, l'une sur le ms. de S-G.d.Pr., et la 2e sur le ms. du Roy 7615."

[70] Cf. *Ms. Paris, Arsenal 2769*, fol. 90 vo.

[71] *Ibidem*.

[72] *Le Lai d'Aristote*, p. 11.

[73] *Ibidem*.

amant de se trouver le lendemain matin à l'une des fenêtres de la tour, &
promit de le lui faire voir dans un tel appareil que le précepteur à son tour
aurait besoin d'une leçon.

Disporting herself in the open air the following morning, she attracts
Aristotle's attention with her sweet voice. The sight and sound of the
"belle Indienne" prove too much for the old man who finally lays hold
of her, vowing that he would risk anything for her favours. Here the
extract again deviates from the manuscript versions, for in the former
the maid's complaint is not that malicious tongues have set her at
variance with the king, but that Alexander, "... devenu, comme tous
les amans, ingrat par trop de bontés ...", has grown cold towards her.
The effect, nevertheless, is the same, Aristotle promising, in the hope of
an obvious reward, to use his influence to set things to rights. But if he
loves her he will surely grant her one desire, to ride upon his back
across the grass. To this Aristotle willingly agrees and, as arranged, the
scene is observed by Alexander who proceeds to upbraid his tutor in his
turn. This latter takes the point, but in the extract fails to note that the
trick has also proven him justified in fearing for his king. Nevertheless,
there is the same happy outcome and Le Grand concludes:

> Amour vainc tot & tot vaincra
> Tant com li monde durera.

Abréger

The basic narrative line is preserved with few modifications then, but
the manuscript versions are drastically condensed in the extract.To
begin with, Le Grand docks a number of passages which he clearly dismissed as "longueurs" despite their obvious relevance. Such is the case
at the opening of the tale where we have nothing of d'Andeli's invec-
tives against slanderous tongues, which would seem to set the tone of
the whole piece.[74] In view of the attention which Le Grand will later
give to the scene of Aristotle's humiliation, it is particularly surprising
that he should omit from his extract that prophetic remark made by
the old sage when censuring the king:

> Or croi que vos ne veez goute,
> Rois, fait Aristotes ses maistre,
> Si vos porra on mener paistre
> Ausi com une beste en pré![75]

---

[74] Cf. *Le Lai d'Aristote*, ed. Delbouille, lines 20–37. All references concerning the original
text are to Delbouille's edition.
[75] Lines 164–167.

Repetitions and digressions are similarly omitted, with no mention made, for example, of Alexander's generosity.[76] Lengthy descriptive passages are reduced to an absolute minimum and the exposition of a mood or state of mind will occupy Le Grand for no more than a line or two. Alexander's reply to Aristotle's stricture[77] becomes a simple exclamation:

> Ah! je vois bien qu'ils n'ont pas aimé!

A lengthy passage, evoking the king's torment at the enforced separation from his love, which we find in D, the manuscript used by Caylus, is absent from A and B and we cannot therefore look for it in the extract.[78] Little, in any case, would have remained of this for Le Grand does not even care to slow the pace of his "copie réduite" while Alexander, now reunited with his love, makes his excuses:[79]

> Alexandre l'embrassa mille fois en l'assurant d'une constance éternelle; mais il convint que les remontrances sévères d'Aristote l'avaient à regret séparé d'elle pendant quelque tems.

Thus he continues, avoiding repetitions and anything that smacks of a digression, condensing those passages which he feels are not essential to the preservation of the original character of the piece, reducing the whole to the barest essentials necessary for the reader to obtain an accurate impression of Henri d'Andeli's tale. The conclusion he dispatches with the same haste as the prologue. Aristotle is quick to admit his error and the whole of the rather lengthy, somewhat involved concluding discourse on the power of love is summarized thus:

> Cet exemple doit nous apprendre à ne blâmer ni les amies ni leurs amans: car amour est le maître de tous les hommes.

An impression of the original style

It is of course impossible for Le Grand to mirror exactly and completely the style found in the manuscript versions and his conclusion might justifiably be taken as typical of the extract as a whole, simple, concise, unembellished. Thus the account of Alexander's total preoccupation with his newly found love,

---

[76] In fairness to Le Grand it should be made clear that the manuscript versions he used do omit here some fourteen lines (71–84) of the reading from D.

[77] Lines 146–154.

[78] Lines 191–214.

[79] Lines 225–237. Lines 235–236 are in fact omitted in A and B.

Li rois avuec s'amie maint.
S'en parolent maintes et maint,
De ce qu'il en tel point s'afole
Et qu'il maine vie si fole
Que d'avuec li ne se remuet
Com cil qui amender nel puet.[80]

is reduced by Le Grand to the simple statement of fact:

Alexandre ne pouvait plus se séparer de sa mie.

He retains little of the direct speech found in the manuscript versions
and thereby further increases the pace of the narrative, merely reporting:

Elle parut surprise de cet amour que jusques-là on lui avait laissé ignorer;
elle s'y montra sensible cependant, & se plaignit avec une rigueur apparente
de la froideur d'Alexandre, devenu, comme tous les amans, ingrat par trop
de bontés. Aristote enchanté de cet aveu, & persuadé sans doute que le
dépit allait lui livrer cette beauté charmante promit d'employer, pour
ramener à ses pieds l'infidelle, tout le pouvoir qu'il avait sur son esprit; mais
il demandait une récompense, & sans façon il pria la dame d'entrer chez lui.

In deference to his readers Le Grand must translate and abridge and
thus he cannot hope to retain fully the style used in the originals. But
what then becomes of his desire to preserve the original character of
these early poets?
   The answer to this question is given in the second note to the extract:

Cependant son style en plusieurs endroits a quelque sorte d'emphase; on
peut en juger par la traduction, où j'ai tâché de lui conserver ce caractère.

In certain passages, then, Le Grand will make an effort to reproduce
the style of the manuscript versions used, sufficient at least to convey
what he sees as a proper impression of this particular aspect of d'Andeli's tale. Elsewhere, as for example in the prologue, he will feel
obliged to adapt his source materials so as not to discourage the reader,
or perhaps feel compelled to sacrifice the preservation of style to the
greater concern, the preservation of what he sees as the original character as a whole. In other words, it may be essential that he make
modifications to the style if the impression made by a particular fabliau
is to be retained as it goes through the process of translation:

[80] Lines 115–120.

... c'est une copie réduite, pour laquelle il a fallu employer des couleurs nouvelles.

Le Grand is fully justified in reducing the account of Alexander's infatuation to that summary statement of fact:

Alexandre ne pouvait plus se séparer de sa mie.

This in fact follows immediately upon a passage in which the absolute power of love is reasserted and where Le Grand has clearly attempted to retain something of the original "emphase":

Qu'amour est redoutable & puissant, puis-qu'il humilie à ce point les maîtres du monde, & qu'il leur fait oublier ainsi le soin de leur gloire! Ne les blâmons pas cependant. Ils sont hommes comme nous, & l'amour a autant de pouvoir sur eux que sur le dernier de leurs sujets.

The modern prose rendering one might offer for those lines on Alexander's infatuation could do nothing to enhance d'Andeli's literary reputation and might easily detract from this unjustifiably.

Having once established what is the essential style of the original, Le Grand then selects those passages which appear to him most representative of this and for which he can hope to find some approximation in a modern prose rendering. An example is the delightful picture of the "belle Indienne" as she sets out to ensnare Aristotle:

Le lendemain, dès que le soleil parut, & avant que personne fût levé, elle descendit au verger; car le désir de la vengeance l'avait éveillée de bonne heure. Une longue chevelure blonde flottait à l'abandon sur ses épaules. Nulle guimpe, nul voile qui cachât sa tête ou son visage, & pour tout vêtement elle portait sur sa chemise un simple bliaut qu'elle avait laissé entr'-ouvert comme pour respirer plus à l'aise. Dans cet ajustement voluptueux, elle vint se promener près de la fenêtre du philosophe en chantant doucement cet air . . . .

It may well seem improper of Le Grand to thus impose his own interpretation of the "Lai d'Aristote" upon his public. But it is precisely because of the nature of this public that he must intervene to guide it. Paradoxically, the author of the *Fabliaux ou Contes* must as it were "cheat" his readers in order to have the least hope of being fair to d'Andeli.

To convey a notion of the language and versification of the original

The simplest solution to a yet more obvious problem posed by the necessity of translation, how to convey some notion of the manner in which the fabliaux were first written down, was clearly to present a number of texts in the original Old French. This was Antoine-Augustin Renouard's answer, each of the five volumes of his third edition concluding with "Choix et extraits d'anciens fabliaux." Le Grand himself had added copies of the originals to those first translations he offered his sceptic friends:

> ... et j'apportois en même temps une copie des originaux; afin que si l'on me faisoit un crime d'avoir élagué chez eux quelques défauts, on ne m'accusât pas au moins d'avoir ajouté à leurs beautés.[81]

But this, as we see, was only that a very small and clearly very learned readership might verify the fidelity of his renderings. The public for which the *Fabliaux ou Contes* was intended, on the other hand, would no doubt have found page upon page of Old French a very daunting prospect, and a series of "Choix et extraits" as used by Renouard half a century later was evidently no way to acquaint the uninitiated eighteenth-century reader with the language of his medieval ancestors. Similarly, there was little sense in a preface offering a lengthy and detailed analysis of the language and versification of the fabliaux. This might well interest other "savants" but could only discourage the greater number who could not be expected to acquire in a few days weeks or even months what for Le Grand was the fruit of a lifetime of careful study. The author of the *Fabliaux ou Contes* knew that he must be much more gentle with his public and chose therefore a gradual accumulative process whereby the reader is permitted to assimilate information at a leisurely pace, slowly adding to and improving his knowledge from brief quotations and notes as he progresses through the collection.

The foundation is laid in the preface where Le Grand, although he gives most of his time to a summary history of French literature, does have a few, very few words to say on the versification of the fabliaux:

> Je me contenterai de dire que ces vers sont ordinairement de huit syllabes, rimant deux à deux, sans faire alterner régulièrement, comme aujourd'hui la règle l'ordonne, des rimes masculines & des rimes féminines. Ce n'est pas qu'on méconnût cette sorte d'agrément, il était au contraire fort en usage; mais on n'en avait pas encore fait une loi.[82]

It is similarly in the preface that the reader is first introduced to the language of these early poets. Many of the points which Le Grand feels

---

[81] *Observations sur les Troubadours*, p. 5.
[82] *Fabliaux ou Contes*, vol. I, preface, pp. ci-cii.

he must make here are effectively illustrated or substantiated with a few lines in Old French. On the question of whether or not the poets of Provence could formerly have enjoyed any success in northern France, for example, he finds it useful to introduce a footnote emphasizing the distance that separated "romane provençale" from "romane française." He cites short passages in both, supplying a complete rendering into modern French in the first case, translating individual words or phrases which might cause difficulty in the second:

> Quant florist la violette
>   fleur
> La rose & la flor de glai, (glayeul, iris)
>
> Que chante li papegai, (sorte d'oiseau)
>   me   amourettes
> Lors mi poignent amorettes
>
> Qui me tiennent gai.
> Jamais jusqu'ici
> Mès pieca ne chantai;
>
> Or chanterai,
>
> Et ferai
>
> Chanson joliette
>
>   ma mie
> Pour l'amour de m'amiette
> (A laquelle depuis long-tems je me suis donné.)
> Où grand pieca me donnai.[83]

The extracts to follow will give Le Grand ample opportunity to build upon this foundation with notes on the language and composition of the fabliaux prompted by a large number of quotations from the manuscripts:

Les citations seront faites avec la fidélité la plus scrupuleuse, afin qu'on puisse connaître le langage du tems.[84]

Every effort will be made to ensure that the reader need never struggle for a translation. Accents and punctuation marks will be added, words running together separated, abbreviations expanded fully, the letter u

[83] *Idem*, pp. lvii-lix.
[84] *Idem*, p. xcviii.

replaced by the v as demanded by modern usage, and the meaning of any difficult word or phrase supplied as above.[85] On the very rare occasions when Le Grand will offer a relatively lengthy passage in Old French he will divide his page into two columns in order that his readers might follow the original and the translation simultaneously.[86] The bitter pill which Barbazan's readers refused to swallow has now been made quite palatable.

Some mention must be made in passing of the words and short phrases we find italicized in this as in other extracts. These are usually "key" terms or antique turns of phrase recurrent in the literature of the "anciens rimeurs" and with which Le Grand would have his readers well acquainted. "Chevalerie," "chevalier," "baron," these will quickly lose their curious ring as one progresses through the collection. Similarly, then, we find "sans villenie" for "sanz vilanie" and "qui fut si roi" for "qui tot fu sire." By modernizing and incorporating these in the narrative proper and yet signalizing them with the use of italics, Le Grand not only makes certain that they are noted by the reader, he also demonstrates precisely how they were used.

Purposeful quotations

Le Grand, of course, does not interrupt his narrative with quotations arbitrarily but appears rather to select these first and foremost for their contribution to the preservation of the original character of his tales into which they are effectively integrated. As in the manuscript versions, the songs as retained by Le Grand in the "Lai d'Aristote" greatly enhance the scene in which the old sage is seduced and literally brought to his knees by the "belle Indienne." Similarly, the quotation used to bring the extract to a close is not only interesting from a linguistic point of view. These two lines effectively summarize for Le Grand all that has gone before, enabling him to avoid a lengthy and repetitive conclusion. Moreover, they provide him with an excellent opportunity to enlighten his readers further, in a note following the extract, on the "préjugés de ces siècles sur l'amour."

---

[85] Cf., for example, the first extract, "Merlin," vol. I, p. 5.
[86] Cf., for example, the prologue to "Les trois Chevaliers et la Chemise," vol. I, pp. 151–153 where the Old French is given to prove the fidelity of the translation. Cf. also "Description d'un Siège," vol. II, pp. 226–228.

Certaines libertés

Le Grand's treatment of the songs found in the manuscript versions of the "Lai d'Aristote" is of particular interest. For whereas the author of the *Fabliaux ou Contes* protested the most scrupulous fidelity in his quotations, he in fact preserves only two of the four songs in more or less their original form, replaces one completely and retains only the first line of the last. But before we attempt to evaluate these modifications it would be useful to pause for one moment and examine the composition and purpose of the "chansons," to which end we shall cite what is generally the best reading, from D.

"C'est la jus desoz l'olive," like "Ci me tienent amoretes" and "Ainsi va qui amors mainent," is an example of the "chanson de carole" or dance-song. T. B. W. Reid informs us[87] that this consisted of two parts, a rhymed or assonanced narrative couplet,

> C'est la jus desoz l'olive^{a1}
> La fontaine i sort serie^{a2}

and a lyrical refrain, normally two unrhymed lines of different length,

> La la voi, la voi, la voi^{b} ⎱ accidental
> La belle blonde, a li m'otroi^{c} ⎰ rhyme

To combine these two parts a line based on b but of the metrical form, length and rhyme or assonance of a was inserted between a^1 and a^2, and a new line of the metrical form of c between a^2 and b:

> C'est la jus desoz l'olive^{a1}
> La la voi venir, m'amie!^{a3}
> La fontaine i sort serie,^{a2}
> El jaglolai (de) soz l'aunoi.^{c2}
> La la voi, la voi, la voi!^{b}
> La bele blonde, a li m'otroi.^{c1}

It was very often so arranged, however, that the first line of the lyrical refrain rhymed with the narrative couplet and was used as the second line of the song:

> Aaliz main se leva.^{a1}
> Bon jor ait qui mon cuer a.^{A3}
> Biau se vesti et para^{a2}
>   Desoz l'aunoi.^{b2}
> Bon jor ait qui mon cuer a,^{A3}

---

[87] *Twelve Fabliaux* (M.U.P.) French Classics, 1958, p. 117.

N'est pas o moi.[b1] [88]

This is the form of "Ci me tienent amoretes" and "Ainsi va qui amors mainent." Maurice Delbouille points out that only in such cases did the "roondet" comprise six lines:

> ... sinon, il comptait quatre vers dont le troisième ... se rattachait au second par une rime (ou assonance) intérieure et au quatrième par la rime (ou assonance) finale.[89]

In view of this Delbouille would have had the first song printed in four lines were it not for the accidental rhyme in the first part of the lyrical refrain.[90]

In the five manuscripts offering the "Lai d'Aristote" we find in fact only two complete examples of the "roondet" as defined above. This is the first song, "C'est la jus desoz l'olive," as preserved in D and E. Working, as we know he does, from A and B, Le Grand cannot then be expected to reproduce even one song in full. But this first lyric he replaces entirely with what he claims to be a slightly modified version of a "chanson" taken from the manuscript poems of Eustache Deschamps:

> Enfant j'estais & jeunette
> Quand à l'escole on me mit:
> Mais je n'y ai rien appris
> Fors qu'un seul mot d'amourette;
> Et nuit & jour le répete
> Depuis qu'ai un bel ami.

The original he condemns as unworthy of reproduction[91] and certainly A at least offers a particularly poor version:

> Or la voi la voi la voi
> La fontaine i sort serie
> Or la voi la voi m'amie
> El glaiolai desouz l'annoi
> Or la voi la voi la bele
> Blonde or la voi.[92]

The second "roondet," "Ci me tienent amoretes," is retained, with only slight modifications to spellings, as it appears in the manuscript versions used, where not only a first line but also the third, "Dras i

---

[88] A rondeau from *Guillaume de Dole* as reproduced by Delbouille, *Le Lai d'Aristote*, p. 23.
[89] Delbouille, *Le Lai d'Aristote*, p. 23.
[90] Cf. p. 98.
[91] See note (c) to Le Grand's extract.
[92] Delbouille, *Le Lai d'Aristote*, p. 77.

gaoit meschinete," is missing. Of the final song, as we know, only the second line,[93] "Ainsi va qui amors mainent," is retained by Le Grand.

Although the first and third "roondets" do vary considerably in the two manuscripts used, although neither of these latter offers a complete example of this form, the author of the *Fabliaux ou Contes* must yet have realized from his close examination of A and B that these three songs are composed on similar lines. The first as preserved in B lacks only the initial line:

> . . . .
> Or la voi la voi m'amie
> La fonteune i cort serie
> A glaiolat desoz l'anoi
> Or la voi la voi la voi
> La bale blonde et li m'ostroi.[94]

Both A and B omit two lines from the second but it remains recognizable as of the same type:

> . . . .
> Ci me tienent amoretes
> . . . .
> Douce trop vos aim
> Ci me tienent amoretes
> Ou je tieng ma main.

Again the third as found in A lacks only the initial line:

> . . . .
> Ainsi va qui amors maine
> Pucele blanche que laine
> Maistre musart me soutient
> Ainsi va qui amors maine
> Et ainsi qui les maintient.

Le Grand clearly understood how much songs enhance the narrative. Why otherwise should he go to the trouble of replacing the first "roondet"? What he does not seem to have realized, however, is that this one particular type, the "chanson de carole," is particularly apt here:

Jeu de rimes et de rythmes où la gaieté et la plaisanterie s'alliaient à l'élégance, ces 'chansonnettes' menues et allègres animaient d'abord le mouvement des ronds, mais en dehors de la danse on les reprenait aussi lors des promenades et des marches, pour aller d'un pas plus léger ... Vives et

---

[93] All manuscripts omit a first line.
[94] Delbouille, *Le Lai d'Aristote*, p. 77.

gaies, ces chansons de danse convenaient à merveille pour donner à la scène
l'allure de farce q'elle devait avoir.[95]

The author of the *Fabliaux ou Contes*, as we have said, can hardly have
failed to realize that the three songs were of the same type. We have
seen that quite acceptable versions of two of them were available in the
manuscripts used. As for the remaining one, "Ci me tienent amoretes,"
Le Grand would surely not have found it too difficult a task to compose
for himself that line so obviously lacking in view of the composition of
the others. He has no qualms about the "légers changements" brought
to those lines taken from Deschamps and clearly did not refrain
through an excess of scruples. From the manuscripts used he could not,
of course, have known that the initial line is missing from each of the
songs, but these omissions do not in any case greatly diminish their effectiveness. No doubt Le Grand had his reasons for not approaching the
"chansons" in the manner outlined above, but these are not particularly obvious.[96] All we can do is note in his favour that the effect of the
songs is not entirely lost in the extract. The second, of course, remains
more or less intact, but the gaiety and lightheartedness at least of
"C'est la jus desoz l'olive" is well preserved in the substituted "Enfant
j'estais & jeunette," and although only one line of the third and final
"roondet" is retained, it is the centre-point, the triumphant refrain
"Ainsi va qui amors mainent."

It is interesting that Le Grand should adopt a totally different procedure for the first strophe of the "chanson de toile" contained in the
"Lai d'Aristote." Delbouille offers the following reading:

> En un vergier, lez une fontenele
> Dont clere est l'onde et blanche la gravele,
> Siet fille a roi, sa main a sa maissele.
> En soupirant son doz ami apele:
> Hai, cuens Guis amis!
> La vostre amor me tolt solaz et ris.[97]

The extract, however, presents an abridged and slightly altered modern version:

> Dans un verger, sur l'herbette nouvelle,
> Fille à un Roi triste & mate s'assit:
> En soupirant elle appelle

---

[95] *Idem*, pp. 25 and 28.
[96] It is especially baffling when we remember that he might so easily have turned for
help to a third manuscript, D.
[97] *Le Lai d'Aristote*, p. 81.

Son doux ami.
Ah! Comte Gui,
Pour votre amour ai perdu joie & ris.

Known from the *Chansonnier de Saint-Germain*, the song concerns a prin-
cess who, married to an old man, sighs longingly for the handsome
Count Gui, her love. Surprised by her husband, who beats her, she
begs of God that he preserve Gui's love for her and bring him to her
that night. The request is granted and Gui arrives to comfort the lady.
The original audience, of course, might have known the tale well
enough to realize the resemblance of the husband to the old sage Aristotle as he appears in the "Lai d'Aristote," similarly demanding "un
amour impossible."[98] Although Le Grand's readers could hardly have
been aware of this, they could not fail to realize the effect of such a
melancholy air upon the ears of the old philosopher. He had been
hesitant. Now the plaintive song of the young seductress finally draws
him completely into the snare. The song, then, loses nothing of its effect in the extract. But why this modernized version when the original,
with one or two annotations, could have presented no real difficulty?
Le Grand would appear to have asked himself a similar question for
the third edition of his *Fabliaux ou Contes* reproduces, with a few modifications to spellings, that version found in A.[99]

The notes

Before concluding our analysis of this particular "copie réduite" and
turning, as we must, to an examination of Le Grand's interpretation of
the "Lai d'Aristote" as brought to light by the manner in which he
presents this tale, some mention must be made of the copious notes
with which it concludes. These offer a veritable mine of information,
ranging from remarks upon the numerous anachronisms to be found in
medieval poetry, through a discussion of the former use of the "capiel,"
"capel" or "chapel" as mentioned in this piece, to a short dissertation
on the "préjugés de ces siècles sur l'amour," prompted by the final quotation. Nor are these notes in the least burdensome for the reader,
spiced as they are with interesting little anecdotes, and often quotations, by way of illustration:

Dans un Conte que je supprimerai parce qu'il ne contient qu'une belle ré-
partie, on reproche à une femme d'avoir pour amant un Chevalier fort laid;

[98] *Idem*, pp. 28–29.
[99] *Fabliaux ou Contes* (1829) vol. I, p. 277.

il est si brave, répond-elle, que je n'ai pas regardé son visage: (réponse absolument la même que celle de Louis XIV à la Duchesse de Bourgogne, qui
se moquait d'un Officier hideux par sa laideur: Madame, il est à mes yeux
un des plus beaux de mon Royaume, car c'est un des plus braves).[100]

Le Grand was well aware of contemporary tastes and, as we know,
would himself later acknowledge that such notes do much to explain
the success of the *Fabliaux ou Contes*:

Dans ce grand nombre de notes, il y en aura beaucoup probablement que
les gens instruits trouveront superflues, comme expliquant des mots trop
aisés à entendre, ou des usages connus. Mais qu'ils songent quelle est la
classe de Lecteurs qui s'occupe des Contes; & quels sont ceux par conséquent pour qui j'ai dû travailler.[101]

Justice for all

The basic conditions of accessibility and exactitude which Le Grand
was to impose upon his *Fabliaux ou Contes* in view of the aims envisaged
in this collection and the public he intended it should reach, these conditions resulted in a particular kind of extract, then, the "copie réduite" such as we have seen in the "Lai d'Aristote." Given the complexity of the task in hand it is not too difficult to see the justice of Le
Grand's approach. Reproducing as he does the original texts of the
fabliaux, Barbazan can, it is true, lay claim to a certain impartiality.
But Le Grand finds no advantage in this when his fabliaux remain inaccessible to the majority of readers. Moreover, even were these prepared to struggle for linguistic control of medieval texts, the author of
the *Fabliaux ou Contes*, we feel, would yet insist upon his own particular
method, realizing that an attempt to be impartial on his part might so
easily result in a false or unwarranted interpretation on the part of his
public. Acutely aware of the limitations of this latter when it came to
the language and literature of the Middle Ages, Le Grand thus selects
that method by which he can best hope to be fair both to the original
poet and to his readers. However, justifiable and proper as this method
may be in view of the conditions imposed upon the collection, it is not
without an element of risk. Clearly, any misinterpretation on Le
Grand's part could only be amplified by such an approach. Convinced
of the reader's need of "guidance," he must be careful that his extracts
do not in fact prove misleading. Central to Le Grand's task in the

[100] Note (e).
[101] *Fabliaux ou Contes*, vol. I, preface, pp. xcvii-xcviii.

Fabliaux ou Contes, then, is the question of interpretation. If he is properly to preserve a poet and his work he must first himself be sure of his
own impression of these:

> ... ce sont des métaux tirés de la mine, qui doivent être purgés de leurs
> scories, fondus & travaillés: mais qu'il faut bien se garder aussi de déna-
> turer.

THE QUESTION OF INTERPRETATION

Principally, of course, the originators of the fabliaux impressed Le
Grand as narrators, as storytellers:

> Je pris la liberté de dire que, pour le style, le goût, la critique, pour tout ce
> qui tient à l'art, il ne falloit point le chercher dans les ouvrages de ce temps;
> mais que si l'on vouloit se contenter d'esprit et d'imagination, on pourroit,
> à une certaine époque, en trouver chez nos vieux poètes ....[102]

This for Le Grand constitutes the originality of the contribution made
by these authors, their "caractère original" which must be preserved in
the extracts, "... leur manière naïve de narrer, leur simplicité touchante ...". Certainly there can be no doubt that the impression Le
Grand intends us to obtain of the author of the "Lai d'Aristote" is that
of d'Andeli the "conteur." Reducing both prologue and epilogue to an
absolute minimum, only once does Le Grand interrupt the narrative
proper, to proclaim the absolute power of love.[103] In fact, it would
appear that he came to much the same conclusion as Delbouille, who
remarks of d'Andeli:

> ... dès qu'il cesse de disserter pour conter, on le sent plus alerte et plus sûr
> de lui-même. Il est à l'aise.[104]

With the exception of this brief interruption, those sections of the
manuscript versions which Le Grand obviously destined for particular
attention in his extract are invariably ones in which he thought to see
the real talent of this poet, the essential d'Andeli, d'Andeli the "conteur."

Such a passage is the exposition, the introduction to the narrative
proper, where we learn of the reason for the sudden change in this
great conqueror Alexander:

---

[102] *Observations sur les Troubadours*, p. 4.
[103] See above, p. 249.
[104] *Le Lai d'Aristote*, p. 17.

Amour qui maîtrise l'univers, Amour qui tout lie & tout soumet venait de le faire entrer dans ses chaînes. Il lui avait trouvé une amie jeune & charmante; & dès ce moment le damoiseau avait renoncé aux conquêtes, pour ne plus s'occuper que de sa belle.

The note of pained disbelief which marks the king's reaction to the shock of Aristotle's chastising words is similarly well retained in that single exclamation:

Ah! je vois bien qu'ils n'ont pas aimé.

Indeed, the picture of the lover rendered almost frantic by the anxiety and grief which separation from the loved one brings, this picture is more dramatically evoked in the extract than in the manuscript versions used, A and B omitting twenty-four lines, where Alexander gives vent to his anguish, included in D and E.[105] In the extract, of course, it is not Alexander but the "belle Indienne" who is responsible for the reunion. Ignorant of the reason for her lover's absence, she has all the more cause to be distressed:

Celle-ci qui l'aimait tendrement, & qui croyait avoir perdu son coeur fut bien affligée de cette absence. Elle pleura, elle gémit; enfin, hors d'état de résister davantage aux inquiétudes de son amour, elle se glissa chez le prince un soir à la faveur des ténebres; &, toute en larmes, lui demanda par quel malheur elle avait donc pu lui déplaire.

Like d'Andeli, Le Grand similarly takes pleasure in the delightful picture of this beautiful young woman as she sets out, aware now of the situation, to take her revenge, employing all her feminine wiles.[106] Indeed, the whole of the seduction "scene" has obviously been the object of Le Grand's particular attention, for it is here he sees at work the "esprit et imagination" of this poet, the real talent of d'Andeli. The old philosopher, "lais et noirs et pales et maigres," is fascinated by the sight and sound of the guileful young beauty:

Peu-à-peu elle s'avança ainsi de la fenêtre, sans paraître s'en apercevoir. Elle se baissait, se relevait alternativement pour déployer avec plus d'avantage ses graces piquantes; & elle chantait en même-tems cette autre chanson . . . .

Torn between the demands of reason and the call to love, he is more than a little perplexed:

Aristote était hors de lui-même. Ses yeux enflammés suivaient la belle dans tous ses mouvemens. Ils s'enfonçaient avidement par-dessous son bliaut,

---

[105] Cf. *idem*, p. 73.
[106] See above, p. 249.

quand le hasard le faisait entr'ouvrir; & comme s'il eût craint de se déceler
& de la faire fuire, il osait à peine respirer. Cent fois la raison lui conseilla
de retourner à ses livres; cent fois elle lui représenta ses rides, sa tête chauve,
sa peau noire & son corps décharné, faits pour éloigner l'espérance & effa-
roucher l'amour. La raison parla en vain, il l'obligea de se taire.

In order better to preserve the effect of the final confrontation of the
decrepit old sage and the young temptress, Le Grand retains the direct
speech he found in the manuscript versions. How "surprised" is the
"belle Indienne" by Aristotle's sudden appearance and forthright declaration of love:

Le philosophe qui la guettait la saisit alors par son bliaut, & l'arrêta au
passage. 'Qui me retient, s'écrie-t-elle en se retournant? – Ma douce dame,
c'est celui qui ne peut plus vivre sans vous, & qui pour vous plaire exposerait
avec plaisir âme & vie, corps & honneur.' Elle parut surprise de cet amour
que jusques-là on lui avait laissé ignorer . . . .

Although the complaint she has to make is altered by Le Grand, the
result remains the same, the bargain is struck:

Aristote enchanté de cet aveu, & persuadé sans doute que le dépit allait lui
livrer cette beauté charmante promit d'employer, pour ramener à ses pieds
l'infidelle, tout le pouvoir qu'il avait sur son esprit; mais il demandait une
récompense, & sans façon il pria la dame d'entrer chez lui.

But the old philosopher is duped and the climax is reached as, blinded
by his passion, by the delights he has been promised, he goes down on
all fours for the maid to ride upon his back:

Il sort dans le verger, se courbe vers la terre, & appuyé sur les mains, présente le dos. Une selle était-là toute prête, on la lui met; on lui passe la bride
autour du cou; & la belle, triomphante, s'asseoit avec fierté, & se promène
ainsi sur l'herbe, chantant à haute voix

> Ainsi va celui qu'amour maine.

The only criticism here might be that Le Grand could have preserved
the effectiveness of the seduction scene even more successfully had he
seen fit to retain the final song as he must have known it from A. Similarly, as we have said, he might have given added weight to the moral
by including in his extract that prophetic remark made earlier by
Aristotle when chastising the king.[107] Nevertheless, the lesson is effectively driven home and Le Grand, unlike d'Andeli, declines to insist
further. The tale is quickly brought to a close with Aristotle, humbled

[107] See above, p. 246.

into an admission of his earlier injustice, making no attempt to regain
his former authority. Only now does Le Grand care to intervene once
more, reducing the rather long and involved concluding section of the
tale to a few simple lines.

Signalized in this way, the particular care and attention which Le
Grand devotes to the preservation of the narrative proper and the
manner in which this is presented, his reluctance to retain the various
observations and conclusions the poet offers in anything but a highly
condensed form, all this can leave us in little doubt as to the impression
we are meant to obtain of Henri d'Andeli author of the "Lai d'Aristote." Clearly for Le Grand the "caractère original" of this particular
poet is to be seen in his ability as a teller of tales. Thus the minimum of
interruption to the flow of the narrative, seen as sufficient in itself to
convey whatever intentions might underlie it. Certainly the extract,
like the manuscript versions used, remains "riche de sens divers et multiple dans son unité foncière."[108]

Above all, of course, the "Lai d'Aristote" would appear to be a
hymn to the absolute power of love, and certainly Le Grand's extract is
successful as such. For it we reduce the original fabliau to its barest
essentials, to the tale it tells, then we are left with the example to fit the
maxim:

> Amour vainc tot & tot vaincra
> Tant com li monde durera.

Precisely these two lines Le Grand sees as adequate to summarize not
only the lengthy concluding discourse he found in the manuscript versions but, it might be suggested, the whole of his extract. To the extent
that the piece can be seen as asserting the sovereignty of love, to this
extent we might suggest that the extract remains "une oeuvre courtoise." As the notes to the quotation closing the extract show, Le Grand
was by no means ignorant of the "préjugés de ces siècles sur l'amour":

> ... une passion qui enfantait les héros, quoique souvent par la faiblesse
> humaine elle dégénérât en libertinage, dans ses principes cependant était
> infiniment estimable.[109]

However, if Le Grand's treatment of the originals ensures that this
hymn to the greater glory of love remains central to the piece, this is
not to the exclusion of those other facets of d'Andeli's work which ap-

---

[108] Delbouille, *Le Lai d'Aristote*, p. 21.
[109] P. 211.

pear as the tale progresses, giving it new and different emphases and thereby making alternative interpretations equally possible. Indeed, the moral example illustrating the dangers of the feminine ruse, which seems to emerge from the originals, is if anything given added weight in the extract.

Delbouille discerns in three of the manuscript versions of the "Lai d'Aristote," including the two used by Le Grand, what appears to be a definite attempt to eliminate the word "nature" from that section of the tale where the "belle Indienne" vows to be avenged and later from the description of her beauty as she sets out to ensnare Aristotle.[110] Whether or not this is in fact a conscious effort, these omissions make it easier for us to lose sight of the real motivating force behind the act of vengeance, the seduction. Add to this the effectiveness of the song, however greatly modified, and Le Grand's reluctance to interrupt the narrative by including the observations d'Andeli has to make, and it is not difficult to understand how easily we might see in the seduction scene the classic picture of the spider and the fly, the helplessness of man in the hands of woman:

Elle savait trop bien, la rusée, ce qu'il fallait pour l'attirer dans ses pièges.

But if the impression made by the moral example is thus enhanced, then the farcical tone in which this is conveyed is similarly amplified. D'Andeli's avowed intention was to relate "chose qui puist valoir et plaire,"[111] and, instructive as it may be, the "Lai d'Aristote" is very amusing. Indeed, we might well be excused for regarding it principally as a "conte à rire." Certainly it is successful as such as it appears in the extract.

Thus the piece remains "riche de sens divers et multiple dans son unité foncière" as Le Grand succeeds in preserving what for him is the original character of this poet. For this richness, this multiplicity of meanings, as we have seen, results not from any great literary technique d'Andeli may have but rather from his imagination and "esprit naturel" as a story-teller. For Le Grand the authors of the fabliaux are first and foremost tellers of tales:

Joignez à cela une manière de narrer simple, claire & naïve, du sentiment, des peintures du coeur humain vraies jusqu'à étonner ... nulle affectation, pas une seule antithèse: quelquefois un proverbe sensé; jamais de ces maximes tranchantes & à prétention, si communes dans nos écrits modernes;

[110] Cf. *Le Lai d'Aristote*, p. 96, note to lines 255–264.
[111] *Idem*, p. 67, line 58.

enfin, souvent du mauvais goût & bien des défauts, mais au moins aucun des défauts du bel esprit.[112]

It is in fact surprising to note how closely Le Grand's conception of the essential merit of these poets resembles that of Joseph Bédier:

Ainsi – et tel est bien le caractère essentiel des fabliaux – le poète ne songe qu'à dire vitement et gaiement son conte, sans prétention, ni recherche, ni vanité littéraire. De là ces défauts: négligence de la versification et du style, platitude, grossièreté. De la aussi des mérites, parfois charmants: élégante brièveté, vérité, naturel.[113]

There remains one aspect of d'Andeli's piece, however, which we have until now avoided but which, by its very absence from the extract, demands our attention. This concerns the note of satire to be found in the "Lai d'Aristote." Le Grand himself certainly saw in d'Andeli something of a satirist, for when examining the reasons why this latter chose to replace the "visir" of the original oriental tale with Aristotle,[114] he remarks:

Peut-être aussi n'a-t-il choisi Aristote que parce que c'était de son tems le dieu des universités & des écoles d'Europe.[115]

But if he is aware of the satire and himself takes pleasure in it, he does not see it as conflicting with the assurances d'Andeli gives in his prologue, the repeated observations with which he interrupts the narrative and the conclusions he draws at the end of his tale. In any event, there is no incongruity in the extract, and one of the many qualities attracting Le Grand to the fabliaux was indeed the apparent complete sincerity of their authors:

... cette sorte de bon-hommie d'un narrateur convaincu de ce qu'il vous raconte, & dont l'effet est de séduire, même au milieu des invraisemblances, parce qu'à son ton de franchise il vous paraît incapable de tromper ...[116].

But does this really apply in the case of the "Lai d'Aristote"?

In fact, by reducing both prologue and epilogue to an absolute minimum, by declining to preserve d'Andeli's interruptions, Le Grand removes a basic incongruity from the tale. For is the poet sincere in his criticism of the "mesdisant":

---

[112] *Fabliaux ou Contes*, vol. I, preface, pp. lxiv-lxv.
[113] *Les Fabliaux*, p. 347.
[114] On this question, cf. Delbouille, *Le Lai d'Aristote*, pp. 57-61.
[115] *Fabliaux ou Contes*, vol. I, p. 205.
[116] Preface, p. lxv.

Ne ja jor que ge vive, en m'uevre
N'orroiz vilanie remuevre,
Qu'ainz ne l'enpris ne n'enprandrai,
Ne vilain mot n'i reprandrai,
En oeuvre n'en dit que ge face.[117]

Can this tale really be regarded as "une oeuvre courtoise"? The very weight of d'Andeli's assurances casts doubt upon his candour:

Pourtant, alors même qu'il affiche ainsi le souci d'écrire avec ferveur ad majorem amoris gloriam, on se demande encore si ses intentions courtoises n'étaient pas simple prétexte, pur alibi ou malicieuse excuse, si tant de bonne volonté trop fortement affirmée, tant de précautions oratoires et tant de formules conventionnelles n'étaient pas appelées, en vérité, à donner le change sur les vrais desseins du conteur, à pallier l'irrévérence d'une anec-dote où, pour la plus grande joie de certains, mais au grand scandale de tels autres, se trouvait outrageusement compromise, avec Aristote, la dignité de la philosophie elle-même.[118]

What we have in the "Lai d'Aristote," then, would seem to be a fabliau in the guise of a lay.

The tone and style adopted by d'Andeli were decreed by the "gens de qualité" figuring in the tale:

On ne pouvait parler de héros aussi illustres que sur le mode courtois con-venant à leur dignité.[119]

Thus such "digressions" as that made upon Alexander's generosity are quite to be expected. Since little space is given to this particular "trait courtois" of the king's character in the manuscript versions used by Le Grand, we should not perhaps be surprised to find no reference to it in the extract. But such an omission is characteristic of Le Grand's ap-proach. For him the essential d'Andeli is d'Andeli the "conteur" and this is the impression he intends we should obtain of this poet. Yet the obvious ease and pleasure with which d'Andeli tells his story, the de-light he takes, for example, in the picture of the aged Aristotle brought to his knees by the wiles of the "belle Indienne," precisely this appears so out of keeping with his avowed "intentions courtoises." Le Grand, for his part, has no qualms in making modifications to the narrative which the "arts poétiques" of d'Andeli's day would not have permitted. Similarly he appears to have no doubts as to the sincerity of the as-

[117] *Le Lai d'Aristote*, p. 67, lines 46–51.
[118] *Idem*, p. 17.
[119] *Ibidem*.

surances given in the prologue. What we have in the extract, then, is not a fabliau written in the guise of a lay, but purely and simply a fabliau.

In dealing with the method of presentation which Le Grand adopted for his *Fabliaux ou Contes* we were able to justify the use of the extract form and acknowledge its suitability given the aims envisaged by the author and the needs of his public. But if Le Grand's presentation of the "Lai d'Aristote" is defensible, to what extent can we justify his interpretation of the piece, imposed upon the reader as it is precisely because of the method of presentation employed?

Perhaps the best defence of Le Grand's interpretation is to be found in the evidence we have as to how the "Lai d'Aristote" was received by its medieval audience. This appears, like Le Grand himself, to have been unconcerned about the doubtful sincerity of d'Andeli's assurances, to have been unaware of or indifferent to the basic incongruity in the tale. Like the author of the *Fabliaux ou Contes*, d'Andeli's contemporaries appear simply to have enjoyed the humour of the piece, to have noted the lesson and the satirical element it contained – they received it simply as a fabliau, albeit of the highest quality.

In discussing this question Maurice Delbouille remarks:

On voit d'abord les scribes attentifs à délester le lai des réflexions et des conclusions dont Henri avoit chargé son récit, ou même à marquer davantage le caractère bouffon de l'aventure.[120]

For in that version of the "Lai d'Aristote" represented by A, B and C, as opposed to that of D and E, he discerns "... l'oeuvre d'un scribe appliqué à réduire la longueur du poème par l'élimination de développements apparemment oiseux ...."[121] A number of passages which would appear to give added weight to the assurances d'Andeli makes in the prologue, to his "intentions courtoises," are in fact missing from the manuscript versions used by Le Grand, as for example the section which includes the following observation:

> Et s'il fait iluec demoree,
> Ce n'est mie molt grant merveille,
> Puis que volentez li conseille:
> Il li covient, ce n'est pas doute,
> Parfornir sa volenté tote,

---

[120] *Idem*, p. 18.
[121] *Idem*, p. 11.

> Ou il desferoit le commant
> Qu'Amors commande a fin amant.[122]

The author of the *Fabliaux ou Contes* thus sees no reason why he should not modify the originals and have the "belle Indienne" come to Alexander. For in A and B it is not made particularly clear that by listening to Aristotle and remaining at a distance from his lady the king would in fact be disobeying the commands of love:

> Et ge sai bien que g'ai mespris
> Qu'onques por lui defis amis
> La volenté de fin ami.[123]

Moreover, Alexander's sudden change of mind, the decision to disobey his tutor, lacks justification in the manuscript versions used by Le Grand, which omit a relatively lengthy passage where the king bemoans the injustice done to him:

> Mes maistres et mi home ensanble
> Ne sentent pas ce que ge sent,
> Et se ge plus a ax m'asent,
> Tot ai perdu, ce m'est avis.
> Vielt Amors vivre par devis?
> Nenil, mais a sa volenté.[124]

In the light of this it is similarly not difficult to understand why Le Grand should feel justified in altering the complaint which the "belle Indienne" makes to Aristotle. With the diminished emphasis upon the "aspect courtois" of the "Lai d'Aristote" which we find in the manuscripts used for the extract, it is perhaps more in keeping that the lady should complain of coldness on Alexander's part rather than of having been set at variance with him by malicious tongues. Although we have had cause to question Le Grand's knowledge of the "Lai d'Aristote" as it appears in D, he may have known it well enough to discern in A and B that tendency noted by Delbouille, "... l'oeuvre d'un scribe appliqué à réduire la longueur du poème par l'élimination de développements apparement oiseux." But whether or not the extract presents a conscious extension of this, the result is the same. Totally preoccupied with the narrative proper, Le Grand reacted to the "Lai d'Aristote" in much the same way as the scribes of the manuscript versions he used.

When reference was made to the "Lai d'Aristote" later in the thir-

---

[122] *Idem*, p. 70, lines 130–136.
[123] *Idem*, p. 74, lines 234–236. Text of D.
[124] *Idem*, p. 73, lines 208–213.

teenth century this invariably concerned the seduction of Aristotle and his ensuing humiliation, whether used to illustrate the dangers of the feminine ruse or cited in the great "débats" of the period.[125] Similarly, the attention of those artists who found inspiration in the tale was usually arrested by the picture of the old sage down on all fours.[126] If we turn to those works Le Grand mentions in his short history of the anecdote, the same emphasis becomes obvious. The title "Le Visir sellé et bridé" makes clear the interpretation proper to this piece. AEneas Sylvius Piccolomini cites the tale "comme un exemple du pouvoir de l'amour," and the following résumé is given of the eighteenth-century comedy, *Le Tribunal domestique*:

Un Vénitien las des intrigues & de la coquetterie de sa femme, veut faire revivre une ancienne loi de Rome, qui permettait aux maris de juger les leurs; & dans ce dessein il convoque la famille de l'accusée. Mais une suivante, de concert avec sa Maîtresse qu'elle a prévenue, dérange ce projet. Le Vénitien s'était épris pour elle; il lui demande d'être son Favori. Ce mot rapelle à la soubrette un chien qui se nommait ainsi, & qu'elle dit avoir perdu. Elle exige de l'époux qu'il le remplace; lui attache au cou un ruban couleur de rose, le fait sauter, japper, &c. Le dénouement se devine sans peine.

As we know, Le Grand himself did not fail to note the lasting popularity of the scene of the "chevauchée triomphale" amongst artists of successive generations.

There is, then, something traditional in the way this anecdote has been treated by artists and writers over the centuries. There is a clear parallel to be drawn between the manner in which the scribes of A, B and C approached the "Lai d'Aristote," the uses to which it was put by d'Andeli's contemporaries and the impression it made, for example, upon the author of *Le Tribunal domestique*. Far from breaking with this tradition Le Grand's interpretation of the piece as a fabliau, although "riche de sens divers et multiple dans son unité foncière," is totally in keeping with it and helps to ensure its survival.

---

[125] Cf. *idem*, pp. 19–21.
[126] *Idem*, pp. 18–19: "De leur côté, les artistes qui cherchent un motif décoratif dans l'évocation de cet épisode de la vie d'Aristote s'arrêtent invariablement à la scène bientôt fameuse de la chevauchée ridicule."
Cf. also J. Bédier, *Les Fabliaux*, pp. 446–447.

A MODEL EXTRACT

It must be said once again that the "Lai d'Aristote" is one of the more outstanding extracts in the collection of *Fabliaux ou Contes*. This is not to suggest that Le Grand was a writer of uneven talent. It is simply that he found this one of the more outstanding fabliaux. He had, as we well know, no wish to present only the finest specimens and thereby totally misrepresent the genre. As literature a number of fabliaux are less than mediocre and so must appear no better in his extracts. Moreover, setting aside those tales included for their very mediocrity, it would be improper to seek great artistry in those extracts presented as no more than historical documents or for reasons of provincial or national prestige. Given the aims of the *Fabliaux ou Contes*, these are no less valid than the "Lai d'Aristote." Nevertheless, it is in such extracts as this latter that we see Le Grand at his most effective, for with Henri d'Andeli's tale, rich in historical insights, a source of inspiration to later generations of writers and a challenge to the "beaux esprits" of the 18th century, he can serve all three of his primary objectives. To this extent we have in the "Lai d'Aristote" an example of the Le Grand extract par excellence.

CHAPTER VI

CONCLUSION: THE POPULARITY
AND ENDURING VALIDITY OF THE
FABLIAUX OU CONTES

Whatever his appreciation of contemporary tastes, even Le Grand must have been a little surprised by the success of his *Fabliaux ou Contes*.[1] The *Bibliothèque des Romans* was well subscribed to at the time, of course, but it relied for much of its appeal, as we have seen, upon pseudo-medieval texts and was thus no yardstick by which to measure the eventual popularity of a "serious" collection such as Le Grand proposed. Only once before had a work of similar intent and on a similar scale been offered to the public and this had been shunned. Was the *Fabliaux ou Contes* to repeat the failure of the *Fabliaux et Contes*? Perhaps the very title, recalling an earlier disappointment, would be enough to discourage those who had known Barnazan's work. Le Grand need have had no qualms:

Voici encore une preuve que ce ne sont pas les Livres les moins importans ni les moins accueillis du Public que nous allons renfermer dans cet unique Extrait. Cet Ouvrage, de M. le Grand, a eu beaucoup de succès & en méritoit beaucoup. Les Fabliaux qui en forment le fond, sont bien choisis, racontés & abrégés avec goût; les Préfaces & les Notes de l'Auteur sont sçavantes & ne le sont pas trop. Ce livre est un fort beau pendant à l'histoire des Troubadours de M. l'Abbé Millot.[2]

The reviews praise every aspect of Le Grand's work, not the least its subtle contribution to the historical and linguistic education of the general reading public:

Il ne faut pas que ce titre de 'Contes' & de 'Fabliaux' vous fasse regarder ce Recueil comme frivole; il y en a peu d'aussi instructifs: c'est vraiment ici que l'utile se trouve uni avec l'agréable, on croit ne lire que des Contes, & l'on

---

[1] Cf. *Le Journal des Sçavans*, August 1780, p. 571: "Nous rendrons compte le plutôt qu'il nous sera possible de cet Ouvrage, dont le succès est à présent très-décidé."
[2] *Idem*, July 1781, pp. 481–482. This remark was clearly meant to be complimentary, but the two works, we know, had little in common.

fait un cours d'antiquité; on apprend les moeurs, & les usages des siècles passés; par le moyen des notes savantes qui accompagnent les Fabliaux, on trouve dans ces jeux d'une imagination Romanesque un fonds prodigieux de Doctrine, & l'on peut retirer autant de fruit de ces petits Romans, que de la lecture du 'Glossaire' de Ducange, avec cette différence que l'érudition qu'ils nous procurent, n'est point achetée par l'ennui.[3]

These lines bring immediately to mind Edmond Estève's definition of Sainte-Palaye's genius:

... il donne la littérature en apparence la plus légère pour base à l'érudition la plus solide, et il fait de la poésie l'auxiliaire de la science.[4]

Equally gratifying no doubt was that vote of confidence in the Le Grand method which came from the *Journal Encyclopédique*. The editors of the *Annales Poétiques* had rightly judged it futile to recall anything earlier than Villon. But the author of the *Fabliaux ou Contes* has found the means to go far beyond him:

L'homme de lettres qui donne aujourd'hui au public trois volumes des anciens fabliaux, fait mieux encore: il les traduit, prend la liberté de les abréger, liberté nécessaire pour les faire lire, supprime quelques détails licencieux ou impies ... enfin, il n'a rien négligé pour que des richesses si long-tems enfouies ne fussent pas perdues pour nous.[5]

Moreover, here at last is public recognition of the contribution made by the "anciens rimeurs" to the progress of letters in France, these "richesses si long-tems enfouies" monuments of French literary history. But are they all museum pieces? Are not certain items from the répertoire of the "trouvères" still viable as literature even by eighteenth-century standards? As if to reply to Le Grand's ultimate request, the *Année Littéraire* calls upon modern literary sophisticates to emulate their ancestors and learn from them the art of the narrative:

... ils pourroient se faire une grande réputation, s'ils avoient autant de naiveté, de sel, de grâce & de finesse, qu'on remarque dans la plupart de ces Contes. Ils y apprendront sur-tout une chose qu'ils ne savent plus, c'est la manière de narrer avec naturel & vérité, en oubliant de faire parade de leur esprit, pour s'occuper seulement de leur sujet. On peut assurer que nos vieux Ecrivains sont nos maîtres dans cette partie; & si la Fontaine les a surpassés

---

[3] *Année Littéraire*, 1782, vol. IV, pp. 326–327.
[4] See above, p. 88.
[5] *Journal Encyclopédique*, 1780, vol. II, pt. 1, p. 73.

dans tout le reste, il n'est que leur égal & leur imitateur dans l'art de conter.[6]

In thus censuring the "beaux esprits" of his day the author of the above review does much to explain Le Grand's success. As we might expect, the object of his disapproval is Voltaire who, it is said, has been concerned only to parade his own wit, and this at the expense of his narrative and of the characters there portrayed. The result is a cynical, mocking tone which destroys all naturalness and interest:

... il n'a songé qu'à y mettre de l'esprit. C'est toujours lui qui se montre, & qui cherche à briller, aux dépens de son récit & de ses personnages ... vous ne voyez jamais que Voltaire qui se moque des choses qu'il vous conte, & qui fait passer ce ton moqueur dans la bouche de ceux qu'il fait parler ....[7]

It was largely as a reaction to what were seen as the intellectual excesses of Voltaire and his bretheren that the eighteenth century sought a return to the "unaffected simplicity" of a bygone age. The position is made clear in an article concerning Sauvigny's *Histoire amoureuse de Pierre le Long et de sa très honorée dame Blanche Bazu*[8] appearing in the *Esprit des Journaux François et Etrangers* in September 1778:

... ce qui est factice étourdit et étonne, mais ce qui est naturel et vrai s'empare toujours de l'âme et la charme même sans qu'on s'en aperçoive. Or rien ne paraît moins participer à l'art que les moeurs et les sentiments de nos bons aïeux. Lorsqu'on sait les peindre, on est donc sûr du succès ... En lisant cette histoire, on ne peut s'empêcher de regretter vivement qu'on ne fasse plus usage aujourd'hui et presque point de cas d'un style si propre à chanter l'amour et ses délices.[9]

Poetry and prose in the "vieux style," more particularly the "style marotique," did in fact enjoy some considerable success at this time.[10] The *Année Littéraire's* one criticism of Le Grand is that he has preserved far too few of those delightful antique turns of phrase characteristic of these early poets:

Il faut convenir que ce vieux style s'accorde mieux avec l'ingénuité piquante qui règne dans ces fabliaux, que notre françois moderne ... J'aurois donc désiré que l'éditeur nous eût présenté plusieurs de ces fabliaux sous une partie de leur forme primitive, & de leur vieux langage; quoique son style

---

[6] *Année Littéraire*, 1780, vol. V, p. 146.
[7] *Idem*, pp. 146–147. The reviewer is clearly no friend of Voltaire and continues: "... je pourrois vous citer une foule d'exemples de ce défaut le plus contraire de tous à la vérité du récit; mais il n'est pas toujours facile de citer Voltaire à des Lecteurs honnêtes."
The "fabliers," it seems, have nothing to match Voltaire's indelicacy!
[8] London, 1765.
[9] Cited by H. Jacoubet, *Le Comte de Tressan*, pp. 99–100.
[10] Cf. *idem*, part II, ch. IV: "Le culte du bon vieux temps de la naïveté et de l'héroîsme."

soit fort agréable, je ne doute pas qu'on eût vu avec plaisir un plus grand nombre de ces traits naïfs & originaux qui caractérisent nos fabliers.[17]

"Le Manteau mal taillé," which Le Grand, as we know, reproduces in a slightly modernized and abridged version of an edition printed some short time after La Fontaine's tales, is highly praised by the reviewer as a fine example of what is required. It is interesting to note that Caylus had included this same version of the piece in his collection *Les Manteaux*[12] but without those modifications deemed necessary by Le Grand. The editor of the third edition of the *Fabliaux ou Contes* prefers Caylus' version:

> Le conte tel que le reproduit en entier le comte de Caylus étant d'une naïveté qui n'est pas sans agrément, j'ai cru que bien qu'un peu prolixe il pourroit être substitué avec avantage à l'extrait qu'en avoit fait Legrand ....[13]

The "amour du naïf" was clearly revived in the early nineteenth century!

Le Grand's collection would appear then to have been ideally suited to contemporary tastes. Well before the publication of the *Fabliaux ou Contes* Caylus had appreciated this quality of simplicity, of naturalness in the work of the "fabliers" and had similarly regretted its passing:

> ... enfin on y connoissoit pleinement la simplicité & la naïveté, qui seront toujours la base du goût vrai, & dont il semble qu'on s'écarte un peu trop aujourd'hui.[14]

But whereas Caylus had been content merely to enable the learned readership of the *Mémoires de l'Académie des Inscriptions* to sample this, Le Grand set out to restore it to full vigour for the public at large, his primary concern to preserve what he saw as the essential merit of the "fabliers," "... leur manière naïve de narrer, leur simplicité touchante ...". He would appear to have succeeded. The *Année Littéraire* now finds these early poets more than competition for some of the greatest men of literature that the eighteenth century would produce:

> ... ils ne se tourmentent point pour avoir de l'esprit à contre-temps; & pour tourner en ridicule les objets qui en sont le moins susceptibles. Cependant ils ne manquent pas de sel & de plaisanterie; mais ce sel est piquant sans âcreté; leur plaisanterie naïve, & jamais forcée. Ils avaient même le talent

---

[11] *Année Littéraire*, 1780, vol. V, p. 174.
[12] La Haye, 1746.
[13] *Fabliaux ou Contes*, 1829, vol. I, footnote, p. 126.
[14] "Mémoire sur les Fabliaux," p. 373.

d'envelopper la critique ou la satyre, sous le voile de l'allégorie qui la rend plus ingénieuse & plus forte.[15]

The mood, of course, would change dramatically as France neared that period of her greatest unrest.[16] But while the Middle Ages continued to be viewed with a sympathetic, nostalgic eye, so the *Fabliaux ou Contes* continued in popularity.

In France it was Barthélemy Imbert who profited most from Le Grand's success. Already in July 1780 the *Mercure* had begun to publish a series of his verse adaptations of the *Fabliaux ou Contes*. In 1785 "Aucassin et Nicolette," "Auberée," "Le Chevalier à l'Epée," "La Châtelaine de Vergy" and "Le Chevalier à la Trappe" are offered in a little volume entitled *Fabliaux choisis mis en vers*,[17] to be followed three years later by a more comprehensive *Choix de Fabliaux mis en vers* in two volumes.[18] It is interesting to note that Le Grand himself took a hand in this latter, receiving due acknowledgement from Imbert:

L'ouvrage de M. Legrand étant public, tout le monde avoit, comme moi, le droit d'y puiser. Mais je lui dois un remercîment personnel pour une obligation absolument particulière. Ayant appris que je m'occupois de mettre en vers un choix de nos Fabliaux, il a eu l'honnêteté de m'offrir & de me communiquer quelques autres sujets, qu'il vient de découvrir en faisant des recherches pour une nouvelle édition de son ouvrage; ainsi je lui dois l'avantage d'avoir ajouté à mon recueil quelques Fabliaux absolument nouveaux pour mes lecteurs.[19]

La Curne de Sainte-Palaye, of course, had not thought twice before furnishing authors like Tressan and Mlle de Lubert with the materials for new adaptations. But Sainte-Palaye was not concerned with the survival, let alone the popularization, of medieval French literature as literature. Le Grand most decidedly was and had even reproached the editors of the *Bibliothèque des Romans* for their pseudo-medieval offerings. Then what is the explanation for this apparent change of heart? The date of Imbert's *Choix de Fabliaux*, 1788, is perhaps the key. It may well have been that at a time of increasing hostility towards all that the Middle Ages represented, Le Grand was grateful to anyone who cared to recall the literature of that period, caring only that the fabliaux, in one form or another, should survive.

The Revolution may well have caused Le Grand to postpone in-

---

[15] *Année Littéraire*, 1780, vol. V, p. 151.
[16] See above, pp. 42–43.
[17] Amsterdam and Paris (Belin) 1785.
[18] Geneva and Paris (Prault) 1788.
[19] *Choix de Fabliaux mis en vers*, vol. I, Avertissement, p. xi.

definitely the publication of a third edition of the *Fabliaux ou Contes*, but the collection had by this time become popular with readers across the channel in England. W. Carew Hazlitt's *The Feudal Period: illustrated by a series of tales romantic and humorous*[20] had first appeared in 1786 as *Tales of the XIIth and XIIIth centuries. From the French of Mr. Le Grand*,[21] re-issued in 1789 to appear as *Norman Tales from the French of Mr. Le Grand*[22] and again in 1800 under the title *Tales of the Minstrels*.[23] Le Grand's notes are not reproduced in these volumes but the very title of the fourth edition indicates clearly the value placed upon the historical insights afforded by the fabliaux.[24] What is disappointing is that, while this collection of stories had obviously enjoyed no little success since its first appearance nearly a century earlier, Hazlitt does not think for one moment to connect this with the literary ability of the "fabliers":

Such tales ... kept a limited circle of readers amused, till a better fare was provided for them by men of a higher stamp and of loftier literary pretensions.[25]

In Hazlitt's favour, however, is his concern that Le Grand's fabliaux be rendered exactly into English. It was this, it would seem, which decided him against a re-edition of G. L. Way's verse translation of 1796:

... the fidelity of the translation was almost unavoidably sacrificed to the exigencies of verse, and in a lame, though harmonious paraphrase we too often miss the truth of the original picture which, with all its faults on its head – its rough colouring, its homely design, and, to boot, its not over-nice detail, we get with greater force and veracity in a prose book.[26]

His judgement here, however, is much too harsh. Way's *Fabliaux or Tales abridged from French manuscripts of the XIIth and XIIIth centuries*,[27] which had reappeared in 1800 in two volumes[28] and in 1815 in three,[29]

---

[20] London (Reeves and Turner) 1873.
[21] London (Egerton) 2 vols. The translations were by John Williamson.
[22] London, 1789.
[23] London, 1800.
[24] Cf. *The Feudal Period*, preface, p. ix: "To those who are without inclination to inquire more deeply, this series of medieval stories and anecdotes may serve a useful purpose, as depicting roughly, but faithfully the state of Western society a century before Chaucer, when the most humanising influence was the spirit of gallantry with all its faults, the homage offered by men to women."
[25] *The Feudal Period*, preface, p. xi.
[26] *Idem*, p. viii.
[27] London (R. Faulder) 1796.
[28] *Ibidem*.
[29] London (J. Rodwell).

was in many ways a much more exact rendering of Le Grand's collection, as even the title would suggest.

In the first place, the notes are retained, here thrown to the end of the volume. These, together with the preface and a glossary, were the responsibility of G. Ellis who took the trouble to abridge them, to omit those he found trivial or of interest only to the French, to add others of relevance and finally to refer whenever possible to English instead of French examples. It is not to be expected that Ellis concern himself in his preface with the question of the "trouvères" and the troubadours, which could be of only scant interest to English readers, but he does replace this with a dissertation on the rise and progress of chivalry, ". . . that leading institution of the dark ages, and which had an influence so considerable on manners and literature . . .",[30] in his view an important omission on Le Grand's part. Finally, his glossary will help clarify the numerous antique terms which the translator, in the true Le Grand manner, has borrowed from these early writers. For Way, too, was concerned to convey an accurate impression of the "fabliers":

In short, he has endeavoured to adapt the colouring and costume of language to the manners he describes: to give an exact copy in miniature of the works of antiquated masters; not to rival or eclipse them by the superior brilliancy of his tints, or by the nicer artifice of his composition.[31]

Way's method, then, is the "copie réduite" in verse and, whatever Hazlitt's findings, it is surprisingly effective.

In view of the success of Way's translations it is most disappointing that Ellis should conclude his preface by remarking that the fabliaux, and he makes no exceptions, cannot in honesty be set against modern works of literature:

With these more finished productions of a polished age it is not the intention of the translator to compare his Fabliaux: he offers them as the first rude essays in a species of composition which the pedantry of criticism has vainly attempted to discredit, which has employed the pens of a Richardson and a Fielding, and in which many female writers of the present day have successfully blended the allurements of fiction with much useful instruction and pure morality.[32]

No doubt Le Grand would have been most gratified to see his translators so keenly aware of, and so concerned to further publicize, the

---

[30] *Fabliaux or Tales*, 1796, preface, p. viii.
[31] *Idem*, p. vi.
[32] *Idem*, p. xxxvii.

invaluable contribution of the "anciens rimeurs" to the progress of literature. But did any, like him, value at least some of the productions of these early poets as more than just monuments of literary history? Only one it seems, William Stewart Rose, who gave his attention not to the fabliaux but to *Parténopex*, his translation appearing in London in 1807:[33]

> If the author of this history has not produced so rich a tissue of adventure as characterises some of the ancient romances, the web which he spins is, at least, less involved; and perhaps what is wanting in imagination is more than compensated in the interest excited by the story, in the unity of action, and the simplicity of its design.[34]

It is unfortunate that Rose, who in his title announces a "free translation," did not similarly share Le Grand's concern for exactitude that *Partenopex* might have been allowed to stand or fall by its own merits.[35]

No doubt we are expecting far too much of the nineteenth century when we have seen that our own has thus far done comparatively little to follow Le Grand's example and rehabilitate the "anciens rimeurs," has even produced a number of specialist students of medieval French literature whose appreciation of this as literature not only marks no advance upon Le Grand but is positively retrogressive.[36] It could be argued that it is unjust to judge a work of literature outside its historical context, to compare its author with those who have been enlightened by the passing of centuries. But it is foolish not to do so when only greater honour can ensue from that comparison. It was for this reason that Le Grand set certain of the fabliaux beside the efforts of the great eighteenth-century "conteurs." It is for this reason that we now set Le Grand beside his successors of the nineteenth and twentieth centuries. Le Grand d'Aussy ranks with such great scholars turned "vulgarisateurs" as Paulain Paris with his *Romans de la Table Ronde* in modern French,[37] Albert Pauphilet with his slightly modernized texts in the

---

[33] *Partenopex de Blois, a romance in four cantos. Freely translated from the French of M. le Grand; with notes: by William Stewart Rose*, London (Longman, Hurst, Rees, and Orme) 1807.

[34] Preface, p. vi.

[35] It would be interesting to know in what spirit Lückenmüller published his German translation of Le Grands' collection, *Erzählungen aus dem 12ten und 13ten Jahrhundert von Le Grand, mit historischen und kritischen Anmerkungen*, Halle (Ruff) 1795–8, 5 parts. This work is mentioned both in Gustav Gröber's *Grundriss der romanischen Philologie* (vol. I, p. 41) and in Sommervogel's *Bibliothèque de la Compagnie de Jésus* (vol. IV, cols. 1660–1663), but it has proven impossible to trace a copy.

[36] See above, pp. 215–217.

[37] *Les Romans de la Table Ronde mis en nouveau langage et accompagnés de recherches sur l'origine et le caractère de ces grandes compositions*, Paris (L. Techner) 1868–1877, 5 vols.

"Bibliothèque de la Pléiade" series[38] and, of course, Joseph Bédier whose popular versions of medieval classics, all based upon his editions for the "Société des anciens Textes français" and running into hundreds of editions,[39] are published in the same spirit as the *Fabliaux ou Contes*:

> Le livre que voici ne s'adresse pas aux seuls érudits; il convient que tous les lettrés puissent lire le poème vénérable et s'y plaire.[40]

This is not to suggest that Le Grand's translations are invariably a match for those of the modern popularizer. Louis Brandin's prose rendering of "Les Trois Aveugles de Compiègne,"[41] for example, is, as we should expect it to be, a considerable improvement upon that version found in the *Fabliaux ou Contes*.[42] It is a question of scale. Is it not a little shameful that the slim volume of modern French translations in the Classiques Hatier series, *Fabliaux et Contes du Moyen Age*,[43] remains amongst the best that one can recommend to the non-specialist reader, to those who might enjoy the fabliaux simply as literature?[44] It does offer a most excellent introduction to the genre but it cannot compare with Le Grand's *Fabliaux ou Contes* which, in the original French and in the English translations, remains the most comprehensive collection of medieval "contes" available to non-specialists on both sides of the Channel.[45] As we have already hazarded to suggest, Le Grand's col-

---

[38] *Jeux et Sapience du Moyen Age, Poètes et Romanciers du Moyen Age, Historiens et Chroniqueurs du Moyen Age.*

[39] For example *Le Roman de Tristan et Iseut* and *La Chanson de Roland* in the series "L'Edition d'Art."

[40] *La Chanson de Roland publiée d'après le manuscrit d'Oxford et traduite par Joseph Bédier*, Paris (L'Edition d'Art) 1944, avant-propos, p. xi. Like Le Grand before him, Bédier stresses the complexities and frustrations of the popularizer's art: "Des traductions telles que la mienne ne prétendent qu'à l'exactitude littérale, et cette prétention même vise trop haut. On est inexact, et de la pire des inexactitudes, du seul fait que l'on transcrit en prose un ouvrage la poésie." (*Ibidem.*)

[41] Cf. *Lais et fabliaux du 13e siècle*, Paris (E. de Boccard) "Poèmes et récits la vieille France," 1932, pp. 87–88.

[42] Vol. II, pp. 149–159.

[43] First published in 1946 with translations by Mlle A. Perrier, and more recently, in 1967, with texts by Nelly Caullot.

[44] Children would appear to have fared rather better than adults here. Especially worthy of note is J. Sablière's *Fabliaux adaptés pour la Jeunesse*, Paris (Les Nouvelles Presses Françaises) 1948. Sablière's tales, complete with illustrations, are in fact adaptations from Le Grand's collection which, of course, was meant to serve an identical purpose: to acquaint an uninstructed public with the delights afforded by the fabliaux.

Also worth mentioning is Marcelle and Georges Huisman's *Contes et Légendes du Moyen Age*, Paris (Fernand Nathan) "Collection des Contes et Légendes de tous les Pays," 1962. Featured here, again with illustrations, are "La housse partie," "Le pauvre clerc," "La folle largesse" and "Les trois aveugles de Compiègne."

[45] Once again, it is most regrettable that Richard O'Gorman's *Fabliaux* should be so difficult to obtain in this country. See above, p. 218, note 175.

lection is important today not only for the light it sheds upon a much neglected area of Enlightenment scholarship, but, according to its original purpose, as a serious "oeuvre de vulgarisation."

* * *

For well over a century and a half the efforts of the great Enlightenment medievalists have been exploited by an unending stream of successors who have extracted what they required, curtly noted their gratitude, more often than not apologizing to their readers at the same time for the inaccuracies to be found in this source, and gone on their way. Achille Jubinal, who made use of Sainte-Palaye's copies of *B.N. f.fr. 837* and *f.fr. 1553* for his *Jongleurs et Trouvères ou Choix de Saluts, Epîtres, Rêveries et autres pièces légères des XIIIe et XIVe siècles*,[46] is one example amongst the many:

Une copie fort infidèle, quant à l'orthographe et même quant au nombre de pièces, en existe à la Bibliothèque de l'Arsenal, parmi les manuscrits du marquis de Paulmy. Nous n'avons point fait difficulté de nous aider quelquefois de cette copie pour le sens de certaines phrases, et nous avons profité d'une partie des annotations qu'elle renferme, annotations qui sont, je crois, de la main de M. de Sainte-Palaye.[47]

Others may have been less grudging in applauding their precursors, even to the extent of proclaiming them worthy of attention in their own right.[48] But it was not until 1968 that the greatest of all the eighteenth-century medievalists, La Curne de Sainte-Palaye, to whom nineteenth and twentieth-century scholars owe an inestimable debt, became the object of an independent study.[49] His fellows, Caylus, Barbazan, Le Grand d'Aussy, continue almost unknown.

---

[46] Paris (J. A. Merklein) 1835.

[47] *Idem*, Avis de l'Editeur, p. 14. B. de Roquefort-Flaméricourt, who leans heavily upon Le Grand d'Aussy for his *De l'Etat de la Poésie françoise dans les XIIe et XIIIe siècles* (Paris, Fournier, 1815), is even less gracious:

"Le Grand d'Aussy a traduit quelques-uns de nos Fabliaux en prose; il les a enrichis de notes curieuses. Mais cet auteur, au lieu de consulter les manuscrits originaux, a fait sa traduction d'après des copies, souvent fautives, de la Curne de Sainte-Palaye; elles l'ont fait tomber dans d'énormes contre-sens, et il s'est égaré dans une prolixité de notes sur des objets qui n'existoient point. C'est par suite de cette négligence à recourir aux originaux que le Grand d'Aussy a souvent pris pour des Fabliaux détachés des pièces extraites de Romans ou d'autres ouvrages, sans indiquer d'où elles étoient tirées.

Ainsi l'homme de lettres qui traitera la question proposée aura à travailler sur un terrain neuf; car jusqu'à présent aucun auteur ne lui a tracé la route qu'il devra suivre." (P. 6.)

Roquefort's work took the prize offered in 1810 by the Classe d'Histoire et de Littérature ancienne of the Institut de France for the best study under this title.

[48] Cf. L. Gossman, *Medievalism*, p. 355.

[49] L. Gossman's study is sub-titled "The World and Work of La Curne de Sainte-Palaye."

For those engaged upon editions of medieval texts there was, of course, much more to be gleaned from Sainte-Palaye than from the author of the *Fabliaux ou Contes*. Montaiglon and Raynaud did, it is true, have recourse to his collection for their *Recueil général et complet des Fabliaux*,[50] but generally speaking it could have offered little to those concerned with presenting scholarly editions to a scholarly public. If Le Grand has been largely overlooked, then this is because his ambitions as popularizer were altogether foreign to the greater number of his immediate successors. The *Fabliaux ou Contes* very soon came to be seen as no more than a collection of mediocre adaptations of the fabliaux. And this view prevails for Le Grand's achievement remains unsung today. It is paradoxical that one who was so ahead of his time should be scorned and neglected precisely because of his originality. Le Grand d'Aussy, like La Curne de Sainte-Palaye, must finally be given credit for his contribution to the advancement of medieval studies, for his pioneering efforts to promote medieval literature for what it is.

---

[50] Cf. vol. I, Avant-propos, p. vi and "Notes et Variantes," passim. In the notes to "Le Dit dou Soucretain" (vol. VI, pp. 239–254) a "new" fabliau, "Dou Sacretaig," is introduced by a few lines borrowed from Le Grand's extract of this (*Fabliaux ou Contes*, vol. III, pp. 401–409).

APPENDIX: THE SOURCES OF THE
FABLIAUX OU CONTES

A. MANUSCRIPT COPIES USED BY LE GRAND D'AUSSY

1. *Fabliaux Manuscript Copies:*

Medieval manuscripts		Eighteenth-century copies made for Sainte-Palaye
B.N. f.fr. 837	(anc. Bib. du Roi 7218)	Arsenal 2763–2767.
Berne Stadt- und Universitätsbibliothek 354		B.N. f. Moreau 1720–1721.
B.N. f.fr. 19152	(anc. St.-Germain 1830)	Arsenal 2771–2775.
B.N. f.fr. 1593	(anc. Bib. du Roi 7615)	Arsenal 2768–2769.
B.N. f.fr. 2168	(anc. Bib. du Roi 7989[2])	Arsenal 2770.
B.N. f.fr. 25545	(anc. Notre-Dame no. 2)	B.N. f. Moreau 1691.
Turin Bib. Univ. L.V. 32	(anc. Bib. Reg. G.I. 19[1])	B.N. f. Moreau 1727.

2. *Other Manuscript Copies* – Fables, Contes dévots etc.:

Arsenal 3142	(anc. Ms. de Gaignat)	B.N. f. Moreau 1680–1683, 1728.
Original Ms. lost	(anc. Mss. de la Clayette)	B.N. f. Moreau 1715–1719, Arsenal 6361.
Berne Litt. 113		B.N. f. Moreau 1727.

Notes

1. *Ms. Turin L.V. 32* was destroyed in a fire at the Turin University library in 1904, making Sainte-Palaye's copy particularly precious.

2. La Curne de Sainte-Palaye also had copies made of the following manuscripts which contain fabliaux but which Le Grand d'Aussy did not use:

a. *B.N.f.fr. 1553 (anc. Bib. du Roi 7595).* Cf. *B.N.f.fr. 9218:* "Copies de poésies françaises faites pour Le Curne de Sainte-Palaye, et avec notes de sa main, tirées des mss. français 1553, 1569 et 2201 (anc. nos. 7595, 7604 et 7999)." A partial copy then.

b. *B.N.f.fr. 375 (anc. Bib. du Roi 6987).* Cf. *Arsenal 3313–3318:* "Copie du ms. du roy no. 6987 *(Bibl. nat. f.fr. 375)* – 6 volumes. Copies faites pour Lacurne de Sainte-Palaye, avec annotations de sa main."

3. La Curne de Sainte-Palaye had made glossaries of the following manuscripts of which he possessed copies:

Medieval Mss.	Glossary
B.N. f.fr. 25545	B.N. f. Moreau 1559, fol. 148 and 1560, fol. 133 and fol. 217
Berne 354	B.N. f. Moreau 1560, fol. 1.
Turin L.V. 32	B.N. f. Moreau 1559, fol. 12.
Arsenal 3142	B.N. f. Moreau 1559, fol. 209 and 1561, ff. 1, 27, 73, 123.
Berne Litt. 113	B.N. f. Moreau 1559, fol. 1.

Cf. also *B.N. f. Moreau 1558*, fol. 132: "Glossaire de mots contenus dans le fabliau de 'La Vieille escoillée'."

4. La Curne's transcripts, of course, contain a number of items other than fabliaux, that is "contes dévots," fables, romances, which may have been useful to Le Grand for the preparation of the *Fabliaux ou Contes*. Only the principal items are given.

   a. *Vie des Pères*

B.N. f. Moreau 1717, ff. 1ro–368vo and *1718*, ff. 1ro–192ro: a copy of the *Vies des Pères* after a manuscript formerly in the possession of Noblet de La Clayette and now lost.

   b. *Miracles de Notre Dame*

B.N. f. Moreau 1719, ff. 251ro–334ro: a copy of the *Miracles* after the same manuscript of La Clayette.

   c. *Fables de Marie de France*

Arsenal 2772, ff. 46ro–103vo: a copy of the *Fables* after *B.N. f.fr. 19152*.

B.N. f. Moreau 1683, ff. 1ro–51ro: a copy of the *Fables* after *Arsenal 3142* with variants from *B.N. f.fr. 19152* marked by Caylus and from *B.N. f.fr. 25545* by La Curne. La Curne did not possess a full copy after this latter.

Arsenal 2768, ff. 48vo–125vo: a copy of the *Fables* after *B.N. f.fr. 1593*.

A note to the above shows that Sainte-Palaye possessed a fourth copy of the *Fables* after *B.N. f.fr. 2168*, but this appears to be missing from his collections. Cf. *Arsenal 2768*, fol. 48vo: "On trouvera les extraits de ces fables dans ma copie qui a esté faite sur le ms. Fabliaux de l'Abbaye de St. Germ. des Pr. J'en ai une autre copie avec des variantes parmi les pièces jointes au 'Cléomades' et autres mss. de M. de Sardière et une autre sous le titre de 'Bestiaire' ms. Baluze 572 et du Roy 7989[2]."

   d. *Romans*

In the fourth volume of the *Fabliaux ou Contes* (p. 255) Le Grand promises his readers four romances. Two of these are *Parténopeus* and *Florès et Blanche-Fleur* and a third very probably *Blancandin*, since this appears in an extract by Le Grand in the third edition of his collection. The identity of the fourth romance is uncertain.

   1) *Parténopeus*

Arsenal 5871, ff. 13ro–17ro: "Extrait du roman de Parténopex de Blois" with annotations by Sainte-Palaye.

Arsenal 2774, ff. 22ro–308vo: a copy of *Parténopeus* after *B.N. f.fr. 19152*.

Sainte-Palaye's partial copy of *Berne Litt. 113* does not include this romance.

   2) *Florès et Blanche-Fleur*

Arsenal 2775, ff. 111ro–188vo: a copy of *Floire et Blancheflor* after *B.N. f.fr. 19152*.

Cf. a note to the above: "Voi une autre copie de ce roman sur le ms. du Roy no. 6987 f.247vo c.1. jusqu'au f.254ro c.4." We have already noted Sainte-Palaye's copy of *B.N. f.fr. 375* (anc. 6987).

   3) *Blancandin*

Arsenal 2775, fol. 1ro: a copy of *Blancandin* after *B.N. f.fr. 19152*.

Again a note to the above shows that Sainte-Palaye had a second copy after *B.N. f.fr. 375*: "Voi une autre copie de ce Roman sur le ms. du Roy no. 6987 depuis le f.254vo c.1. jusqu'au f.267ro c.4."

Le Grand admits to having reproduced more or less verbatim Caylus' version of *Blancandin* from the latter's unpublished collection of extracts from *B.N. f.fr. 19152*: "C'eût été un travail inutile que de recommencer celui du comte de Caylus, je l'ai donc à-peu-près employé, sauf plus de retranchements encore sans lesquels cette pièce auroit probablement paru trop longue à beaucoup de mes lecteurs." (*Fabliaux ou Contes*, 1829, vol. V, pp. 201–202.)

5. A "Catalogue alphabétique des fabliaux et autres pièces en vers ou en prose tirées de divers manuscrits copiés pour Sainte-Palaye" can be consulted in *B.N. f. Moreau 1564*, fol. 1.

6. It will have been noticed that a number of the manuscript copies used by Le Grand are now held in the Bibliothèque de l'Arsenal. In fact, nearly 200 manuscript volumes from Sainte-Palaye's collection are preserved here today. Paulmy himself, founder of the Arsenal, was responsible for their acquisition.

In 1763 La Curne de Sainte-Palaye bequeathed his library to the Cabinet des Chartes on condition that he might retain it until his death. In recognition he was granted a pension of 4,000 livres for himself and for his twin brother. The bequest was officially approved on the 5th May 1765. In 1762 Bréquigny and others had persuaded Sainte-Palaye to postpone publication of his *Glossaire* and to modify the plan of the work. It was very probably this setback which caused Sainte-Palaye to think of leaving his manuscripts to the King in the hope that somebody might complete the work which he himself could not hope to finish.

In 1780, about a year before Sainte-Palaye's death on the 1st March 1781, Paulmy offered Jacob-Nicolas Moreau, director of the Cabinet des Chartes, a number of manuscripts highly relevant to the work of the Cabinet in exchange for certain of those of Sainte-Palaye. Paulmy was a member of the Comité des Chartes and no doubt had the interests of the Cabinet at heart when proposing the exchange. The volumes he requested bore no relation to the work of the Cabinet. A full 230 volumes were to be surrendered by either side, but Paulmy promised to add to his part "plusieurs autres recueils manuscrits et livres précieux" if the exchange was agreed.

The transaction was approved and Paulmy surrendered his manuscripts in the last days of June or early days of July 1780, asking to be met with the same deference. The situation must have been embarrassing since Sainte-Palaye had been assured that his library would remain intact while he lived. Yet Paulmy, it appears, did not have to await the death of his fellow medievalist before taking possession of a considerable part of the latter's most treasured belongings. At least, it is clear from Paulmy's register of bindings that, amongst numerous other items, the copies of fabliaux manuscripts used earlier by Le Grand were already in the Arsenal by the 20th November 1780. In his last months, then, Sainte-Palaye met with the same treatment he himself had once dealt "minor" scholars like Barbazan.

According to Henry Martin, Paulmy's library now holds precisely 194 manuscript volumes from Sainte-Palaye's collection. It is perhaps time that Delisle's suggestion was acted upon: "Les recueils de Sainte-Palaye sont donc aujourd'hui divisés entre deux établissements littéraires de Paris. Cette circonstance est d'autant plus regrettable que les différentes parties de la collection sont remplies de renvois dont les savants ne pourront guère tirer parti tant que ces différentes parties ne seront pas rapprochées les unes des autres." (*Le Cabinet des Manuscrits*, vol. I, p. 572.)

On the history of Sainte-Palaye's library cf.:

L. Delisle, *Le Cabinet des Manuscrits*, vol. I, pp. 557–575.

H. Omont, *Inventaire des Manuscrits de la Collection Moreau*, pp. 201–221.

H. Martin, *Histoire de la Bibliothèque de l'Arsenal*, pp. 216–227.

For lists of the manuscripts to be exchanged cf.:

a. *B.N. f. Moreau 1436*, fol. 20bis: "Etat des manuscrits de M. de Sainte-Palaye vendus au Roy et que M. le marquis de Paulmy désireroit échanger pour pareil nombre de manuscrits anciens relatifs à l'histoire de France." (This list reproduced by Omont, *Inventaire*, p. 214 and Martin, *Hist. Bib. Ars.*, pp. 220–221.)

b. *B.N. f. Moreau 1436*, fol. 20ter: "Etat des recueils et volumes manuscrits, tous concernant l'histoire de France, et utiles au nouveau Dépot des Chartes, que M. le marquis de Paulmy offre en échange de pareil nombre de volumes manuscrits tirés de la bibliothèque cédée au Roy par M. de Sainte-Palaye." (This list reproduced by Omont, *Inventaire*, p. 215 and Martin, *Hist. Bib. Ars.*, pp. 221–222.)

B. MEDIEVAL MANUSCRIPTS USED BY LE GRAND D'AUSSY

1. *Manuscripts listed by Le Grand in his preface:*

Of the manuscripts listed by Le Grand in the preface to the first volume of the *Fabliaux ou Contes* (p. xci) only one contains recognized fabliaux. It is the first entry below. Sainte-Palaye, we know, had a partial copy of this but Le Grand makes no mention of it. From the remainder he extracted "miracles," "contes dévots," etc.:

B.N. f.fr. 1553	(anc. Bib. du Roi 7595).
B.N. f.fr. 818	(anc. Bib. du Roi 7208).
B.N. f.fr. 1444	(anc. Bib. du Roi 7534).
B.N. f.fr. 1569	(anc. Bib. du Roi 7604).
B.N. f.fr. 1586	(anc. Bib. du Roi 7612).
B.N. f.fr. 2161	(anc. Bib. du Roi 7985).
B.N. f.fr. 2162	(anc. Bib. du Roi 7986).
B.N. f.fr. 2163	(anc. Bib. du Roi 7987).
B.N. f.fr. 2188	(anc. Bib. du Roi 7996).

2. *Manuscripts probably known and used by Le Grand but not listed in his preface:*

1. *B.N. f.fr. 1635 (anc. Bib. du Roi 7633).*

"Le Testament de l'Asne" is preserved only in *B.N. f.fr. 1635* and since the tale appears in the first edition of the *Fabliaux ou Contes* (vol. II, pp. 249–251) then Le Grand either knew the original manuscript or took his extract from Barbazan (1756, vol. I, pp. 113–122). Since Barbazan lists all the manuscripts used, in tables introducing each of the three volumes, we can probably take it that Le Grand looked to the original of this tale. Nevertheless, it is strange that "Charlot le Juif," again preserved only in *B.N. ffr. 1635*, should not have appeared in the earlier editions of Le Grand's collection although again included by Barbazan (vol. I, pp. 140–147), and indeed that the manuscript, containing as it does five fabliaux, should not have been listed by Le Grand. It should be noted that Caylus, too, mentions "Charlot le Juif" and gives the manuscript reference ("Mémoire sur les Fabliaux," p. 374).

2. *B.N. f.fr. 1446 (anc. Bib. du Roi 7834³⁻³).*

"Le Clerc qui fu repus derriere L'Escrin" is preserved only in *Arsenal 3524* and *B.N. f.fr. 1446*. It is included by Le Grand in his first edition (vol. II, pp. 423–424). The tale does not appear in Barbazan, so that Le Grand must have taken his extract from the original. It seems unlikely that he knew Arsenal 3524 as "Le Sentier battu," which is only preserved here, does not appear in the earlier editions of the *Fabliaux ou Contes*.

There is some evidence to suggest that Le Grand knew the manuscript *Berlin, Hamilton 257* in which are preserved 30 fabliaux:

a. The editors of the *Recueil Général* consider Le Grand's reference to "le vin de Saint-Pourçain" in his *Histoire de la Vie Privée des Français* (1815, vol. III, p. 5, note), cited by A. Héron in a note to his edition of "La Bataille des Vins" (*Les Œuvres de Henri d'Andeli*, Rouen, Imprimerie de Espérance Cagniard, 1880, p. 105), proof of Le Grand's acquaintance with this manuscript. Cf. Montaiglon-Raynaud, *Recueil général et complet des Fabliaux*, vol. VI, p. 159.

b. The third edition of the *Fabliaux ou Contes* includes a tale entitled "L'Oie" (vol. IV, p. 37), that is "L'Oue ou Chapelain," which only appears in *Berlin, Hamilton 257*.

c. The above proves at best that Le Grand came to know this manuscript after the publication of the second edition of his collection. However, "Le Vallet aus douze Fames" appears in four manuscripts according to Per Nykrog (*Les Fabliaux*, p. 322), *B.N. f.fr. 837*,

Berlin, Hamilton 257, B.N. f.fr. 1593 and *B.N. f.fr. 25545,* and Le Grand, introducing this tale in the third volume of his first edition (p. 67), claims knowledge of four versions, excluding that in the manuscript poetry of Eustache Deschamps.

The evidence remains puzzling. Had Le Grand known *Berlin, Hamilton 257* in 1779 he would surely have listed so important a manuscript.

C. TABLE OF FABLIAUX MANUSCRIPTS
KNOWN TO LE GRAND D'AUSSY AND HIS PREDECESSORS

Ms. reference and number of fabliaux contained there	Fauchet	Caylus	Barbazan	La Curne	Le Grand
B.N. f.fr. 837 (59)	—	—	—	—	—
B.N. f.fr. 1593 (23)	—		—	—	—
B.N. f.fr. 25545 (6)	—		—	—	—
B.N. f.fr. 19152 (27)		—	—	—	—
B.N. f.fr. 1635 (5)		—	—	—	—
B.N. f.fr. 2168 (6)			—	—	—
Arsenal 3524 (2)			—		
B.N. f.fr. 12603 (12)			—		
Turin L.V. 32 (2)				—	—
Berne 354 (42)				—	—
B.N. f.fr. 1553 (6)				—	
B.N. f.fr. 375 (1)				—	
B.N. f.fr. 1446 (1)					—

1. Per Nykrog assumes that Caylus did not know *B.N. f.fr. 837* since he describes *B.N. f.fr. 19152* as the largest collection of manuscript fabliaux (Nykrog, *Les Fabliaux,* p. xi). Yet Caylus specifically mentions *B.N. f.fr. 837* under its old number, *anc. Bib. du Roi 7218,* in his "Mémoire sur les Fabliaux" (p. 374). *B.N. f.fr. 837, f.fr. 19152* and *f.fr. 1635* are the only fabliaux manuscripts actually named by Caylus, although he clearly knew of others: "Il nous reste encore un assez grand nombre de manuscrits, dans lesquels on trouve des Fabliaux; il y en a dans différentes Bibliothèques, & sur-tout dans celle du Roi ..." ("Mémoire sur les Fabliaux," p. 356).

2. In a "Table d'autres Fabliaux qui se trouvent dans les mêmes Manuscrits" concluding the third volume of his *Fabliaux et Contes* Barbazan names four tales contained in *B.N. f.fr. 12603,* but he lists them incorrectly under *anc. Bib. du Roi 7534.* This latter is present *B.N. f.fr. 1444. B.N. f.fr. 12603* was formerly *anc. suppl. fr. 180.*

3. L. Gossman lists *B.N. f.fr. 1446* in his third appendix, "Sainte-Palaye's Collations of Manuscripts of Fabliaux" (*Medievalism,* p. 364). I have been unable to trace any reference to this manuscript in Sainte-Palaye's copies.

4. A far from comprehensive "Table de Manuscrits contenant des Fabliaux," which clearly formed part of preparations for a third edition of the *Fabliaux ou Contes,* shows that by the time Le Grand came to undertake this new edition he knew one other manuscript containing a recognized fabliau. This was *B.N. f.fr. 1588 (anc. Bib. du Roi 7609)* in which is preserved "Fole Larguesce." The "Table" can be consulted in *B.N. n.a.f. 10859,* ff. 271–336.

BIBLIOGRAPHY

SECTION I. MANUSCRIPT WORKS

LE GRAND D'AUSSY

Unless otherwise stated the manuscript is in Le Grand's hand.

Paris, Bibliothèque de l'Arsenal:

Ms. 3415   *Le Grand d'Aussy: 'Histoire de la Vie Privée des Français.' Manuscrit en partie autographe.*
Paper, 227 leaves (numbered) 230 × 190 mm. Half-bound in mottled calf. Draft of the *Histoire de la Vie Privée des Français* with corrections and additions in Paulmy's as well as Le Grand's hand.

Ms. 6498   *Pièces relatives aux restitutions des bibliothèques des condamnés, émigrés, etc.*
Paper, 325 leaves (numbered) 250 × 180 mm. Half-bound in brown morocco.

Fol. 217:   Letter from the Minister of the Interior to Le Grand regarding the return of his father's library. Le Grand acknowledges receipt at the foot of the letter. Dated "le 16 frimaire, an 6."

Ms. 6588   *Papiers de Le Grand d'Aussy.*
Paper, 91 leaves (numbered) 240 × 190 mm. Half-bound in green parchment.

Ff. 1–30:   Draft of the *Histoire de la Langue française depuis son origine jusqu'à nos jours.*

Ff. 32–51:   "Fragments sur les Sépultures." Rough draft.

Ff. 53–61:   "Fouilles à faire dans la ci-devant église de St.-Germain." Rough draft.

Ff. 62–74:   "Fouilles à faire dans les départements." Rough draft.

Ff. 76–91:   "Correspondance et pièces relatives au différend survenu entre Le Grand d'Aussy et le marquis de Paulmy, au sujet de 'L'Histoire de la Vie Privée des Français,' 1779–1781."

Ms. 6608   *Recueil.*
Paper, 120 leaves (numbered) 340 × 230 mm. Half-bound in green parchment.

Ff. 1–22:   "Extraits de romans faits sous la direction du marquis de Paulmy pour la 'Bibliothèque des Romans.' "
A series of brief extracts prepared for Paulmy's collection by Le Grand.

Paris, Bibliothèque nationale, fonds français:

Ms. 20842   *Notes et papiers personnels de Dom Poirier.*

Paper, 180 leaves (numbered) in-folio. Half-bound.

Fol. 54:   Letter from Le Grand to Dom Poirier thanking him for information as to the location of the Saint-Germain manuscripts, which were to be scoured for materials useful to the *Histoire de la Littérature française*. Dated "le 22 ventôse, an 4."

Paris, Bibliothèque nationale, nouvelles acquisitions françaises:

Ms. 3328   *Traité historique de la nourriture des Français.*

Paper, 176 leaves (numbered) 350 × 220 mm. Half-bound.

Draft of the *Histoire de la Vie Privée des Français.*

Ms. 6226   *Papiers divers de Le Grand d'Aussy.*

Paper, 222 leaves (numbered) 205 × 158 mm. Half-bound in hard-back. "Notes, analyses, extraits de contes, dits, fabliaux, romans et pièces diverses de toute sorte." Materials collected by Le Grand for his numerous publications, principally the *Fabliaux ou Contes.*

Ms. 6227   *Suite du précédent.*

213 leaves (numbered). Format and binding as in ms. 6226.

Ff. 1–17:   "Notes pour la nouvelle édition des 'Fabliaux.'" A series of extracts of "fabliaux licentieux."

Ff. 164–167:   Notes on the romances for the proposed *Histoire de la Littérature française.*

Ms. 6228   *Suite du précédent.*

370 leaves (numbered). Format and binding as in ms. 6226.

Ff. 49–80:   "Notice sommaire sur les trois ouvrages auxquels je travaille." An analysis of the three major histories upon which Le Grand engaged in his last years.

Ms. 6229   *Essai sur la langue, les Sciences & la littérature françaises.*

117 leaves (numbered). Format and binding as in ms. 6226. "Seconde époque: depuis la conquete des Francs jusqu'à Charlemagne." Part of Le Grand's preparations for his histories of language, literature and the arts and sciences.

Ms. 6230   *Suite du précédent.*

354 pages. Format and binding as in ms. 6226. "Troisième époque: depuis le règne de Charlemagne jusque vers le milieu du XIe siècle."

Ms. 6231   *Suite du précédent.*

82 leaves (numbered). Format and binding as in ms. 6226. "Quatrième époque."

Ms. 10124   *Recueil de lettres ou pièces signées par divers fonctionnaires de la Bibliothèque royale ou divers érudits (XIVe-XIXe siècle).*

Parchment and paper, 105 leaves (numbered) in folio. Half-bound.

Ff. 70–71:   Letter from Le Grand to Citizen Poupard de la Croiserie thanking him for his help in matters arising from the death of his brother, Pierre-Théodore. Dated "le 14 floréal, an 8."

Ms. 10855   *Arts et usages en France.*

Paper, 387 leaves (numbered) in-folio. Half-bound. "Matérieux recueillis par Le Grand d'Aussy pour ses Ouvrages sur la Langue, la Littérature, et les Usages, Arts et Sciences en France." These notices or "bulletins" are in alphabetical order, this first volume covering A-D.

Ms. 10856   *Suite du précédent.*
             423 leaves (numbered). Format and binding as in ms. 10855.
             "Arts et usages en France: E-N."
             Ff. 69–70:   A concise history of the progress of language and literature
                           in France to the time of the "fabliers" including remarks on
                           the possible origins of the fabliaux.
Ms. 10857   *Suite du précédent.*
             375 leaves (numbered). Format and binding as in ms. 10855.
             "Arts et usages en France: O-V."
Ms. 10858   *Essai sur la langue et la littérature française.*
             323 leaves (numbered). Format and binding as in ms. 10855.
             Some scholar has taken the trouble to preface the text with a detailed
             analysis of the work.
Ms. 10859   *Papiers divers de le Grand d'Aussy.*
             418 leaves (numbered). Format and binding as in ms. 10855.
             "Notice sur ses ouvrages, objets figurés dans les miniatures, 'Vie d'Apollo-
             nius de Tyane,' fabliaux, etc."
             Ff. 2–54:   A lengthy article on Le Grand's published and unpublished
                           works by an unknown scholar.
             Ff. 69–128:   Lists of "objets de gravures" and of manuscripts containing
                           miniatures preserving these.
             Ff. 130–270: Draft of the *Vie d'Apollonius de Tyane.*
             Ff. 271–326: "Table de manuscrits contenant des fabliaux."
Ms. 11123   *Essai sur la langue, les sciences et la littérature françaises.*
             Paper, 174 leaves (numbered) 205 × 150 mm. Full-bound in hard-back.
             A carefully executed copy of the first part (vol. I) of the *Essai*, clearly pre-
             pared for publication.
Ms. 21536   *Recueil de lettres autographes de divers personnages du XIXe siècle.*
             Paper, 431 leaves (numbered) in-folio. Half-bound.
             Fol. 124:   Letter from Le Grand to Citizen De Villiers regarding cer-
                           tain works held in the Bibliothèque nationale. Dated "le
                           11 ventôse, an 8."

Paris, Bibliothèque nationale, fonds Bréquigny:
Ms. 165   *Correspondance de Bréquigny.*
             Paper, 233 leaves (numbered).
             Ff. 208–209: Letter from Le Grand to Bréquigny remarking upon the
                           kindness shown him by La Curne de Sainte-Palaye.

Paris, Bibliothèque de l'Institut de France:
Ms. 4740   *Autographes de personnalités diverses.*
             Paper, 63 items of varying format (unnumbered). Portfolio.
             A letter from Le Grand to Citizen Poupard de la Croiserie concerning
             matters arising from the death of Le Grand's brother, Pierre-Théodore.
             Dated "le 14 frimaire, an 8."

For the sake of completeness the following should be added to the list of
Le Grand's manuscripts

Paris, Bibliothèque de l'Arsenal:
Ms. 6505   *Pièces relatives aux livres choisis dans les Dépôts littéraires pour différentes biblio-
             thèques.*

Paper, 378 leaves (numbered) 380 × 240 mm. Half-bound in brown morocco.

Fol. 54: A letter from Le Grand at the Bibliothèque nationale acknowledging receipt of a number of books to be forwarded to the school of artillery at La Fère. Dated "le 11 vendémiare, an 4."

Ms. 6508 *Pièces relatives aux livres choisis dans les Dépôts littéraires pour les bibliothèques des Ecoles centrales des départements et pour les colonies.*

Paper, 500 leaves (numbered) 400 × 250 mm. Binding as in ms. 6505.

Fol. 398: A letter from Le Grand at the Bibliothèque nationale acknowledging receipt of several books to be forwarded to the Ecole Centrale de Tours. Dated "le 3 vendémiaire, an 4."

Ms. 6510 *Pièces relatives aux livres choisis dans les Dépôts littéraires pour les bibliothèques militaires.*

Paper, 384 leaves (numbered) 390 × 250 mm. Binding as in ms. 6505.

Fol. 6: A letter from Le Grand at the Bibliothèque nationale acknowledging receipt of two volumes to be forwarded to the school of artillery at Châlons. Dated "le 21 messidor, an 3."

Contemporary Medievalists

Barbazan, Etienne

Paris, Bibliothèque de l'Arsenal:

Mss. 3081–3084 *Dictionnaire ou glossaire de l'ancienne langue françoise, avec l'explication des mots justifiée par des citations extraites de différens manuscrits et leurs étymologies.*

Paper, 1,365, 1,014, 944 and 1,085 pages, 350 × 225 mm. Full-bound in gold-tooled marbled calf.

Barbazan's *Nouveau Trésor de Borel* which remains unpublished to this day.

Ms. 3123 *Anciennes poésies extraites de différens manuscrits de la Bibliothèque royale et autres.*

Paper, 726 pages, 290 × 220 mm. Full-bound in mottled parchment.

The first volume of Barbazan's collection of "notices et extraits" from which he prepared the *Fabliaux et Contes.*

Ms. 3124 *Suite du précédent.*

399 pages. Format and binding as in ms. 3123.

Volume two.

Ms. 3125 *Suite des précédents.*

Paper, 375 pages, 265 × 190 mm. Full-bound in marbled calf.

Volume three.

Ms. 3138 *Anciens romans et fabliaux – copies de Barbazan avec notes.*

Paper, 232 pages, 293 × 220 mm. Full-bound in gold-tooled marbled calf.

Further materials for the *Fabliaux et Contes.*

Ms. 3519 *Notices et extraits de manuscrits par Barbazan.*

Paper, 635 pages, 287 × 217 mm. Full-bound in marbled calf.

Further materials for the *Fabliaux et Contes.*

Ms. 7079 *Notices sur la vie et les oeuvres des anciens poètes françois.*

Paper, 186 pages, 290 × 220 mm. Full-bound in gold-tooled marbled calf.

This volume must be added to those collections from which Barbazan prepared his *Fabliaux et Contes.*

Paris, Bibliothèque nationale, nouvelles acquisitions françaises:

Ms. 1790   *Notices de différents manuscrits anciens des bibliothèques de l'église de Notre-Dame de Paris, de la Sorbonne et de M. de Bombarde.*
Paper, 74 leaves (numbered) 255 × 190 mm. Half-bound.
A collection of notices and extracts, very probably part of materials amassed for the *Fabliaux et Contes.*

LA CURNE DE SAINTE-PALAYE

Paris, Bibliothèque de l'Arsenal:
Mss. 2763–2767 *Copie des fabliaux ms. du roy no. 7218.*
Paper, 428, 314, 298, 327 and 294 leaves (numbered) 255 × 190 mm. Half-bound in sheep-skin.
A copy after present *B.N.f.fr. 837* with annotations in Sainte-Palaye's hand.
Mss. 2768–2769 *Copie des fabliaux tirés du manuscrit du roy no. 7615.*
Paper, 204 and 251 leaves (numbered) 250 × 185 mm.
Binding as in mss. 2763–2767.
A copy after present *B.N.f.fr. 1593* with annotations in Sainte-Palaye's hand.
Ms. 2770   *Copie des fabliaux qui sont dans le manuscrit du roy 7989,*[2] *Baluze 572, in-4.*
Paper, 144 leaves (numbered) 255 × 190 mm. Binding as in mss. 2763–2767.
A copy after present *B.N.f.fr. 2168* with annotations in Sainte-Palaye's hand.
Mss. 2771–2775 *Fabliaux manuscrits de la bibliothèque de St-Germain des Prés.*
Paper, 162, 235, 192, 308 and 188 leaves (numbered) 250 × 190 mm.
Binding as in mss. 2763–2767.
A copy after present *B.N.f.fr. 19152* with annotations in Sainte-Palaye's hand.
Mss. 3313–3318 *Copie du 'ms. du roy no. 6987' (Bibl. nat. f.fr. 375) – 6 volumes. Copies faites pour La Curne de Sainte-Palaye, avec annotations de sa main.*
Paper, 288, 413, 343, 489, 441 and 381 leaves (numbered) 385 × 255 mm.
Binding as in mss. 2763–2767.
Mss. 4277–4353 *Antiquités françoises.*
Paper, 77 vols., 255 × 190 mm. Binding as in mss. 2763–2767.
A second version of the *Dictionnaire des antiquités françoises.*
Mss. 4354–4370 *Antiquités françoises.*
Paper, 17 vols., 255 × 195 mm. Binding as in mss. 2763–2767.
Supplement to the *Dictionnaire des antiquités.*
Ms. 5871   *Recueil de notices et d'extraits d'anciens romans.*
Paper, 89 leaves (numbered) 370 × 250 mm. Half-bound in green parchment.
Ff. 13–17:   "Extrait du roman de 'Parténopex de Blois.' "
Annotations by Sainte-Palaye.
Ms. 6361   *Copie des chansons françoises tirées du manuscrit de la Clayette, suivies de la table des anciens mots françois tirés de ces mêmes chansons.*
Paper, 92 leaves (numbered) 385 × 250 mm. Half-bound in sheep-skin.
Copy annotated by Sainte-Palaye.

Paris, Bibliothèque nationale, fonds français:
Ms. 9218   *Copies de poésies françaises, faites pour La Curne de Sainte-Palaye, et avec notes de sa main, tirées des mss. français 1553, 1569 et 2201 (anc. nos. 7595, 7604 et 7999).*
Paper, 536 leaves (numbered) 380 × 180 mm. Half-bound.
A partial copy of the fabliaux manuscript *B.N.f.fr. 1553* with annotations by **Sainte-Palaye.**

Paris, Bibliothèque nationale, fonds Moreau:

Ms. 1436 *Recueil de pièces relatives à la cession au Roi de la bibliothèque et des papiers de Sainte-Palaye, et à l'échange fait avec le marquis de Paulmy.*
Paper, 44 leaves (numbered).

Ff. 1–15: "Mémoires de la Curne de Sainte-Palaye sur ses travaux et sa bibliothèque."

Fol. 20bis: "Etat des manuscrits de Sainte-Palaye vendus au Roy et que M. le Marquis de Paulmy désireroit échanger pour pareil nombre de manuscrits anciens relatifs à l'histoire de France."

Fol. 20ter: "Etat de recueils et volumes manuscrits, tous concernant l'histoire de France, et utiles au nouveau Dépôt des Chartes que M. le marquis de Paulmy offre en échange de pareil nombre de volumes manuscrits tirés de la bibliothèque cédée au Roy par M. de Sainte-Palaye."

Ff. 41–44: "Catalogue des manuscrits soit originaux soit copies de La Curne de Sainte-Palaye."

Mss. 1437–1440 *Catalogue de la bibliothèque et des papiers de La Curne de Sainte-Palaye.*
Paper, 187 and 122 leaves (numbered), 520 and 749 pages.

Mss. 1511–1523 *Dictionnaire des antiquités françoises, par La Curne de Sainte-Palaye. Recueil de notes sur l'histoire, les usages et les institutions de la France au moyen âge et dans les temps modernes.*
Paper, 13 vols. in-folio.
First version of the *Dictionnaire des antiquités.*

Ms. 1558 *Glossaires.*
Paper, 137 leaves (numbered).

Fol. 132: "Glossaire de mots contenus dans le fabliau de 'la Vieille excoillée.' "

Ms. 1559 *Glossaires.*
Paper, 214 leaves (numbered).

Fol. 1: "Glossaire du ms. de Berne, Litt. 113."

Fol. 12: "Glossaire du ms. de Turin, G.I.19." *(Turin L.V. 32).*

Fol. 148: "Glossaire du ms. de Notre-Dame, N.2." *(B.N.f.fr. 25545).*

Fol. 209: "Glossaire de plusieurs fabliaux du ms. de M. de Paulmy." *(Arsenal 3142).*

Ms. 1560 *Glossaires.*
Paper, 218 leaves (numbered).

Fol. 1: "Glossaire du ms. de Berne 354."

Ff. 133, 217: "Glossaire du ms. de Notre-Dame, N.2."

Ms. 1561 *Glossaires.*
Paper, 147 leaves (numbered).

Ff.1,27,73,123:"Glossaire du ms. de Gaignat." *(Arsenal 3142).*

Ms. 1564 *Catalogue alphabétique des fabliaux et autres pièces en vers ou en prose tirées de divers manuscrits copiés pour Sainte-Palaye.*
Paper, 200 leaves (numbered).

Ms. 1653 *Supplément aux Mémoires sur l'ancienne Chevalerie.*
Paper, 192 leaves (numbered).

Ff. 39–51: "Note pour un mémoire sur le fabliau de la Canise.

Mss. 1654–1661 *Notices de manuscrits relatifs à l'histoire de France, conservés dans les bibliothèques de France et d'Italie, rédigées par Sainte-Palaye, Secousse, etc.*
Paper, 8 vols. in-folio.
Mss. 1662–1676: a second version, 15 vols. in-quarto.

Mss. 1680–1683 *Copie figurée du ms. de Guyon de Sardière, puis de Gaignat, aujourd'hui à la Bibliothèque de l'Arsenal, no. 3142.*
Paper, 216, 258, 206 and 194 leaves (numbered) in-folio.
Copy annotated by Sainte-Palaye.

Ms. 1691   *Copie d'une partie des pièces contenues dans le ms. N.2 de Notre-Dame.*
Paper, 292 leaves (numbered) in-quarto.
A partial copy after present *B.N. f.fr. 25545* with annotations by Sainte-Palaye.

Mss. 1715–1719 *Copie de deux mss. appartenant au marquis Noblet de La Clayette.*
Paper, 304, 277, 368, 311 and 336 leaves (numbered) plus 92 pages, in-quarto.
A copy of the La Clayette manuscripts now lost, annotated by Sainte-Palaye.

Mss. 1720–1721 *Copie du ms. 354 de Berne.*
Paper, 420 and 153 leaves (numbered) in-quarto.
Copy annotated by Sainte-Palaye.

Ms. 1727   *Extraits de mss. de Paris, Berne et Turin.*
Paper, 459 leaves (numbered) in-quarto.
Ff. 91–134vo: Copy of a number of items from *ms. Berne Litt.*
113 with annotations by Sainte-Palaye.
Ff. 195–375vo: Copy of a number of items from *ms. Turin L.V.*
32 with annotations by Sainte-Palaye.

Ms. 1728   *Copie de plusieurs pièces du ms. de Baluze 572, du Roi 7989² du Lucidaire en vers, ms. de M. Gibert: des fabliaux qui se trouvent à la suite des Congés de Jehan Bodel, dans le ms. de M. le Mis. de Paulmy (Arsenal 3142).*
Paper, 281 leaves (numbered) in-quarto.
Copy annotated by Sainte-Palaye.

Paris, Bibliothèque nationale, fonds Bréquigny:
Ms. 62   *Rapports de Bréquigny avec l'Académie des Inscriptions et principalement avec La Curne de Sainte-Palaye.*
Paper, 258 leaves (numbered).
Fol. 212: "Projet d'étude sur l'histoire de France."

Ms. 154   *Mélanges d'histoire littéraire.*
Paper, 224 leaves (numbered).
Ff. 2–43:   "Observations générales sur le caractère de notre ancienne langue et sur le style de nos anciens auteurs."

La Valliere, Duc de

Paris, Bibliothèque Sainte-Geneviève:
Ms. 2474   *Recueil de FABLIAUX, copiés d'après le manuscrit coté N.2 de l'Eglise de Paris (aujourd'hui, Biblioth. nationale, ms. franç. 25545).*
Paper, 57 leaves (numbered) 275 to 278 × 200 mm.

Paulmy, Marquis de

Paris, Bibliothèque de l'Arsenal:
Ms. 6408   *Portefeuille de M. d'Argenson et de Paulmy.*
Paper, 137 leaves (numbered) 320 × 230 mm. Half-bound in green parchment.
Ff. 78–80:   "Pièces relatives au différend survenu entre M. de Paulmy,

le comte de Tressan et M. de Bastide, à propos de la 'Bibliothèque des romans.' "

SECTION II. PRINTED WORKS

PRINCIPAL EIGHTEENTH-CENTURY JOURNALS TO WHICH REFERENCE IS MADE

L'Année Littéraire, ou Suite des Lettres sur quelques écrits de ce temps. Par M. Fréron, Amsterdam and Paris, 1754–1789, 292, vols., Slatkine Reprint, Geneva 1966.

Correspondance littéraire et critique, adressée à un souverain d'Allemagne, depuis 1770 jusqu'en 1782, par le baron de Grimm et par Diderot, ed. Tourneux, Paris (Garnier frères) 1877–1882, 16 vols.

L'Esprit des Journaux Français et Etrangers, ouvrage périodique et littéraire par une Société de Gens de Lettres, Liége, Paris, Brussels, 1772–1814, 480 vols.

Le Journal de Littérature, des Sciences et des Arts, par M. l'Abbé Grosier, Paris, 1779–1783, 30 vols.

Le Journal de Monsieur, frère du Roi, par M. l'Abbé Royou, Paris, 1776–1783, 30 vols.

Le Journal de Paris, ou Poste du Soir, Paris, 1777–1811, the first French daily.

Le Journal des Sçavans, Paris, 1665–1792, 111 vols.

Le Journal Encyclopédique ou Universel, par une Société de Gens de Lettres, Liége, Bouillon, 1856–1793, 306 vols., Slatkine Reprint, Geneva 1968.

Le Magasin Encyclopédique, ou Journal des Sciences, des Lettres et des Arts, Paris, 1795–1816, 122 vols.

Le Mercure de France, Paris, 1672–1791, 977 vols., Slatkine Reprint, Geneva 1972.

AUTHORS BEFORE 1700

Borel, Pierre: *Trésor de recherches et antiquitez gauloises et françoises,* Paris (A. Courbé) 1655.

Brice, Germain: *Description nouvelle de ce qu'il y a de plus remarquable dans la ville de Paris,* Paris (N. Legras) 1684.

Cassan, Jacques de: *La Recherche des droits du roy et de la couronne de France,* Paris (F. Paneray) 1632.

Chantereau-Lefebvre, Louis: *Traité des Fiefs et de leur Origine. Avec les preuves tirées de divers autheurs anciens et modernes,* Paris (L. Billaine) 1662.

Chapelain, Jean: "De la Lecture des vieux Romans," ed. A. C. Hunter, *Opuscules Critiques,* Paris (Droz) 1936, pp. 205–241.

Chasteuil, Pierre de: *Apologie des anciens Historiens et des Troubadours ou Poëtes Provencaux,* Avignon (J. du Périer) 1704.

Du Cange, Charles du Fresne: *Glossarium ad Scriptores Mediae et Infimae Graecitatis,* Lyon (Anisson, J. Posuel and C. Rigaud) 1688, 2 vols.

Glossarium ad Scriptores Mediae et Infimae Latinitatis, Paris (L. Billaine) 1678, 3 vols.

Duchesne, André: *Antiquitez et recherches des villes, chasteaux et places plus remarquables de toute la France,* Paris (J. Petit-Pas) 1609.

Histoire généalogique de la Maison de Montmorency, Paris (R. Cramoisy) 1624.

Du Verdier, Antoine: *Les Bibliothèques Françoises,* Paris (Honorat) 1585.

Fauchet, Claude: *Les Œuvres de Feu M. Claude Fauchet,* Paris (David Leclerc et Jean de Hugueville) 1610.

Origines des dignitez et magistrats de France, recueillies par Claude Fauchet, Paris (J. Périer) 1600.

Recueil de l'origine de la langue et poësie françoise, ryme et romans. Plus les noms et sommaire des oeuvres de CXXVII poetes françois, vivans avant l'an M.CCC, Paris (M. Patisson) 1581.

Recueil des antiquitez gauloises et françoises, Paris (J. du Puys) 1579.

Favyn, André: *Le Théâtre d'Honneur et de Chevalerie,* Paris (R. Fouet) 1620, 2 vols.

Godefroy, Théodore: *Traitez touchant les droits du roy très chrestien sur plusieurs estats et seigneuries possédées par divers princes voisins*, Paris (A. Courbé) 1655.

Huet, Pierre Daniel: *Traité de l'Origine des Romans* (Faksimiledrucke nach der Erstausgabe von 1670 und der Happelschen Ubersetzung von 1682) Stuttgart (J. B. Metzlersche) 1966.

La Croix du Maine, François Grudé: *Les Bibliothèques Françoises*, Paris (L'Angel) 1584.

La Noue, François de: *Discours Politiques et Militaires*, Geneva (Droz) 1967 (Textes Littéraires Français).

Le Laboureur, Jean: *Histoire de la Pairie de France et du Parlement de Paris*, London (S. Harding) 1740.

Ménage, Gilles: *Dictionnaire étymologique de la Langue françoise*, Paris (Briasson) 1750, 2 vols. *Les Origines de la Langue françoise*, Paris (A. Courbé) 1650.

Mézeray, François: *Histoire de France depuis Pharamond jusqu'au règne de Louis le Juste*, Paris (D. Thierry) 1685, 3 vols.

Montaigne, Michel de: *Essais*, Texte établi et présenté par Jean Plattard, Paris (Les Belles Lettres) 1946 (Les Textes Français).

Nostredame, Jean de: *Les Vies des plus célèbres et anciens poètes provençaux*, Lyon (A. Marsilii) 1575.
— ed. Chabaneau-Anglade, Paris (Champion) 1913.

Pasquier, Etienne: *Les Œuvres choisies d'Etienne Pasquier*, ed. Léon Feugère, Paris (Firmin Didot) 1849, 2 vols. *Recherches de la France, revues et augmentées de quatre livres*, Paris (J. Mettayer & P. L'huillier) 1596.

Piccolomini, Aeneas Sylvius: *Les Amours d'Euriale et de Lucrèce*, Cologne (Ulrich Zell) 1468.

Vincent, Jacques: *L'Histoire amoureuse de Flores et Blanchefleur samye avec la complainte que fait un amant contre Amour et sa dame, le tout mis d'espagnol en français*, Paris, 1554.

Vulson de la Colombière, Marc: *Le Vray Théâtre d'Honneur et de Chevalerie, ou le Miroir Héroique de la Noblesse*, Paris (A. Courbé) 1648, 2 vols. in-folio.

CONTEMPORARIES OF LE GRAND D'AUSSY

Barbazan, Etienne: *Fabliaux et Contes des Poëtes françois des XII, XIII, XIV et XVes siècles, tirés des meilleurs auteurs*, Paris (Vincent) and Amsterdam (Arkstée and Merkus) 1756, 3 vols.
— a new edition, by M. Méon, Paris (Crapelet) 1808, 4 vols.
L'Ordène de Chevalerie, Paris (Chaubert & Hérissant) 1759.

Bénédictins de la Congrégation de Saint-Maur:
1. Bouquet, Dom Martin: *Recueil des Historiens des Gaules et de la France*, Paris, 1738–1752, vols I–VIII. Continued first by others of the Congrégation de Saint-Maur and later by the members de l'Académie des Inscriptions, vols IX–XXIV, Paris, 1757–1904.
2. Rivet, Dom Antoine: *Histoire littéraire de la France*, Paris, 1733–1763, 12 vols. Continued by the members de l'Académie des Inscription.
3. Sainte-Marthe, le P. Denis de: *Gallia christiana*, Paris, 1715–1789, 13 vols in-folio.

Bonafous: *Le Parterre du Parnasse françois, ou Nouveau recueil des pièces les plus rares et les plus curieuses des plus célèbres poëtes françois, depuis Marot jusqu'à présent*, Amsterdam (E. Roger) 1710.

Cambry, Jacques: *Contes et Proverbes, suivis d'une Notice sur les Troubadours*, Amsterdam, 1784.

Caylus, Comte de: *Les Manteaux*, La Haye, 1746.
"Deux Mémoires sur Guillaume de Machault, poète et musicien dans le XIVe siècle, avec une notice de ses principaux ouvrages," *Mém. Acad. Inscr.*, vol. XX, pp. 399–439.
"Mémoire sur les Fabliaux," *Mém. Acad. Inscr.*, vol. XX, pp. 352–376.

Chaudon, Abbé Louis-Mayeul: *Bibliothèque d'un homme de gout*, Avignon (J. Bléry) 1772, 2 vols.
— a new edition, Avignon and Paris, 1779, 2 vols.

Contant d'Orville, André Guillaume: *Ancienne chronique de Gérard d'Euphrate, duc de Bourgogne*, Paris, 1783, 2 vols.

Du Fresnoy, Abbé Nicolas Lenglet: *Le Roman de la Rose, par Guillaume de Lorris et Jean de Meun dit Clopinel, revu sur plusiers éditions et sur quelques anciens manuscrits*, Amsterdam, 1735, 3 vols.
— revised edition, Paris (J. F. Bernard and J. B. Lantin de Damerey) 1798.

Falconet, Camille: "Sur nos premiers traducteurs françois, avec un Essay de Bibliothèque françoise," *Mém. Acad. Inscr.*, (partie historique) vol. VII, pp. 292–300.

Goujet, Abbé Claude Pierre: *Bibliothèque française, ou Histoire de la Littérature française*, Paris (P. J. Mariette) 1740–1756, 18 vols.

Imbert, Barthélemy: *Historiettes ou Nouvelles en vers*, Paris (Delalain) 1774.

Imbert, B. and Sautreau de Marsy, C. S.: *Annales poétiques, ou Almanach des Muses depuis l'origine de la poésie françoise*, Paris, 1778–1788, 40 vols.

Jaucourt, M. le Chevalier de: "Fabliaux," *Encyclopédie* (Paris, Briasson, 1751–1777, 11 vols.) vol. VI, p. 349.

Juvenal de Carlencas: *Essai sur l'Histoire des Belles-Lettres*, Lyon (Duplain) 1740–1744, 2 vols.

La Curne de Sainte-Palaye: *Dictionnaire historique de l'ancien langage françois ou Glossaire de la langue françoise depuis son origine jusqu'au siècle de Louis XIV*, Niort (L. Favre) 1875–1882, 10 vols.

Histoire littéraire des Troubadours, contenant leurs vies, les extraits de leurs pièces, & plusieurs particularités sur les moeurs, les usages, & l'histoire du douzième & du treizième siècles, Paris (Durand neveu) 1774, 3 vols.
— a reprint by *Slatkine Reprints*, Geneva, 1967.

Les Amours du bon vieux temps, Vaucluse and Paris (Duchesne) 1756.

Mémoires historiques sur la Chasse, Paris (Duchesne) 1781.

Mémoires sur l'ancienne Chevalerie considérée comme un établissement politique et militaire, *Mém. Acad. Inscr.*, vol. XX, pp. 597–847; also Paris (Duchesne) 1759, 2 vols.
— a new edition, Paris, 1781, 3 vols.
— a new edition, by A. P. Barginet with notes and an introduction by Charles Nodier, Paris (Girard) 1826, 2 vols.

Projet d'un glossaire françois, Paris (H. L. Guérin and L. F. Delatour) 1756.

Table chronologique des diplômes, chartes, titres et actes imprimés concernant l'histoire de France, Paris, 1769–1876, 8 vols.

"La Romance d'Aucassin et Nicolette," *Mercure*, February 1752, pp. 10–64.

"Mémoire concernant la Lecture des anciens Romans de Chevalerie," *Mém. Acad. Inscr.*, vol. XVII, pp. 787–799.

"Remarques sur la Langue Françoise des XIIe et XIIIe siècles comparée avec les Langues Provençale, Italienne et Espagnole, dans les mêmes siècles," *Méd. Acad. Inscr.*, vol. XXIV, pp. 671–686; also published in Favre's edition of the *Glossaire*, vol. X, pp. 377–382, and by J. M. C. Leber in *Collection des meilleures dissertations*, Paris, 1826–1838, vol. XIV, pp. 278–300.

La Dixmerie, Bricaire de: *Cléomir et Dalia*, Paris, 1763.

Le Beuf, Abbé Jean: *L'Etat des sciences en France, depuis la mort du roy Robert ... jusqu'à celle de Philippe le Bel*, Paris (Lambert et Durand) 1741.
"Notice sommaire de deux volumes de poésies françoises et latines conservés dans la Bibliothèque des Carmes-Déchaux de Paris," *Mém. Acad. Inscr.*, vol. XX, pp. 377–398.

Le Fort de la Morinière, A.-C.: *Bibliothèque poétique, ou Nouveau choix des plus belles pièces de vers en tout genre, depuis Marot jusqu'aux poëtes de nos jours*, Paris, 1745, 4 vols.

Lévesque de La Ravalière: *Les Poésies du Roi de Navarre*, Paris (H. L. & J. Guérin) 1762, 2 vols.

Lhéritier, Marie Jeanne: *La Tour ténébreuse*, Paris (Vve de C. Barbin) 1705.

Marin, François Louis Claude: *Histoire du Saladin, sulthan d'Egypte et de Syrie*, Paris (Tilliard) 1758.

Massieu, Abbé Guillaume: *Histoire de la Poésie françoise*, Paris (Prault) 1739.

Mervesin, Dom Joseph: *Histoire de la Poésie françoise*, Paris (Pierre Giffart) 1706.

Monnet, Jean: *Anthologie françoise, ou Chansons choisies depuis le XIIIe siècle jusqu'à présent*, Paris, 1705, 3 vols.

Montfaucon, Bernard de: *Monuments de la Monarchie françoise*, Paris (J. M. Gandouin et P. F. Giffart) 1729–1733, 5 vols.

Noblot de la Clayette, Charles: *L'Origine et les Progrès des Arts et des Sciences*, Paris (H. L. Guérin) 1740.

Papon, le P. de Jean Pierre: *Histoire générale de Provence*, Paris (Moutard) 1776–1786, 4 vols.

Paulmy, Marquis de: *La Bibliothèque universelle des Romans*, Paris, 1775–1789, 112 vols.

   Mélanges tirés d'une grande Bibliothèque, Paris (Moutard) 1779–1788, 69 vols.

   Paulmy's claims to the disputed *Histoire de la Vie Privée des Français*:

   1. "Précis d'une histoire générale de la vie privée des Français dans tous les temps et dans toutes les provinces de la monarchie, formant le volume C des *Mélanges tirés d'une grande Bibliothèque*," Paris (Moutard) 1779.

   2. *Lettre à l'auteur des Fabliaux*, n.p. n.d., 6 pages, B.N. ref. 8°Li¹6.

   3. *Le Journal de Paris*, no. 33, Friday 2nd February, 1781 (volume for January–June 1781, p. 143); no. 46, Thursday 15th February, 1781 (*idem*, p. 183).

Rigoley de Juvigny: *Les Bibliothèques françoises de La Croix du Maine et de du Verdier*, Paris (Saillant et Nyon) 1772–1773, 6 vols.

Saint-Foix, Germain de: *Essais historiques sur Paris*, London, 1754.

— nouvelle édition augmentée, London and Paris (Duchesne) 1759, 3 vols.

Sallier, Abbé Claude: "Observations sur un recueil manuscrit des poésies de Charles d'Orléans," *Mém. Acad. Inscr.*, vol. XII, pp. 580–592.

Sauvigny, Billardon de: *Histoire amoureuse de Pierre le Long et de sa très honorée dame Blanche Bazu*, London, 1765.

Sinner, Jean Rodolphe: *Extraits de quelques poésies du XIIe, XIIIe et XIVe siècle*, Lausanne, 1759.

Tencin, Mme de: *Le Siège de Calais*, La Haye (J. Neaulme) 1739, 2 vols.

Tressan, Comte de: *Les Œuvres choisies du Comte de Tressan*, Paris, 1787–1791, 12 vols.

"La Chanson de Roland," *Bibliothèque des Romans*, December 1777, pp. 210–216.

"L'Histoire amoureuse de Florès & de Blanche-Fleur," *idem*, February 1777, pp. 151–225.

"Ursino le Navarin," *idem*, January 1779, vol. II, pp. 47–142, February 1779, pp. 3–106.

Velly P. F. and Villaret C.: *Histoire de France, depuis l'établissement de la monarchie jusqu'au règne de Louis XIV*, Paris (Desaint et Saillant) 1769–1799, 33 vols.

Voltaire: *Œuvres Complètes*, Paris (Garnier Frères) 1877–1885, 52 vols.

Le Grand d'Aussy

Works other than the *Fabliaux ou Contes*, listed in chronological order of first appearance, with subsequent editions, translations and other works extracted from or inspired by Le Grand, and with details of contemporary criticism

Histoire de la Vie Privée des Français, depuis l'origine de la nation jusqu'à nos jours, Paris (PH. D. Pierres) 1782, 3 vols.

   Nouvelle édition avec des notes – par J. B. B. de Roquefort, Paris (Laurent-Beaupré) 1815, 3 vols. (The Brynmor Jones Library of the University of Hull possesses a copy of this second edition: ref. DC33L5).

Extracted: *Versuch einer Geschichte des Obstbaues in Frankreich, aus dem franzosischen des Herrn Le Grand d'Aussy*, Frankfurt am Mayn (P. H. Guilhauman) 1800.

Inspired: *Tableau historique des Monumens, Costumes et Usages des Français, depuis les Gaullois jusqu'à nos jours: ouvrage rédigé d'après Ducange, Montfaucon, Legendre, Saint-Foix et Legrand d'Aussy. Par M. de Roquefort*, Paris (Thiériot et Belin) 1824.

Vie publique et privée des François, à la ville, à la cour et dans les provinces, depuis la mort de

Louis XV jusqu'au commencement du règne de Charles X, pour faire suite à la 'Vie privée des François' de Legrand d'Aussy, par une société de gens de lettres, Paris (Mlle Sigault) 1826, 2 vols.

Cf. *Année Littéraire*, 1781, vol. V, pp. 252–253.

Idem, 1783, vol. II, pp. 217–251.

L'Esprit des Journaux Français et Etrangers, May 1783, pp. 3–45.

Journal de Monsieur, 1783, vol. I, pp. 250–281.

Mercure, May 1783, pp. 59–70.

Voyage d'Auvergne, par M. Le Grand d'Aussy, Paris (E. Onfroy) 1788.

Nouvelle édition, revue et augmentée, Paris (chez le directeur de l'Imprimerie des Sciences et Arts) an III (1795) 3 vols.

Translated: *Reisen durch Auvergne von Legrand. Umgearbeitet mit Anmerkungen und Zusätzen von Heinr. Fr. Link, Professor zu Rostock*, Göttingen (Vandenhöck und Ruprecht) 1797.

Documents retrospectifs sur l'Auvergne. Lettre sur la communauté des Guittard-Pinon, Clermont (Imprimerie de Thibaut-Landriot frères). The work is signed and dated 1788.

Second Voyage dans l'Intérieur de l'Afrique, par le Cap de Bonne-Espérance; dans les années 1783, 84 and 85; par F. Levaillant, Paris (H. J. Jansen) an III (1795) 3 vols.

Nouvelle édition, Paris (H. J. Jansen) an IV, 2 vols.

Nouvelle édition, Paris (Crapelet) 1803, 3 vols.

Translated: *New Travels into the interior parts of Africa – translated from the French*, London, 1796, 3 vols.

Vie d'Apollonius de Tyane, par Pierre-Jean-Bapt. Legrand d'Aussy, précédée d'une notice historique sur Legrand d'Aussy, par M. Lévesque, Paris (L. Collin) 1807, 2 vols.

Extracts, articles, "mémoires," "notices"

Bibliothèque universelle des Romans:
Extracts composed by Le Grand d'Aussy and prepared for publication by the Marquis de Paulmy:

1. "Les Prophéties de Merlin," July 1775, vol. I, pp. 134–140.
2. "Le Triomphe des Neuf Preux," *idem*, pp. 140–165.
3. "Le Saint-Gréaal, Roman de la Table Ronde," August 1775, pp. 88–110.
4. "Lancelot du Lac, Chevalier de la Table Ronde," October 1775, vol. I, pp. 62–117.
5. "Perceval le Gallois," November 1775, pp. 37–85.
6. "Perceforest, Roi de la Grande-Bretagne," January 1776, vol. I, pp. 23–74.
7. "Le Roman du Roi Artus & des Compagnons de la Table Ronde," July 1776, vol. I, pp. 90–118.
8. "Gyron le Courtois, Chevalier de la Table Ronde," October 1776, vol. I, pp. 48–96.
9. "Erec et Enide," February 1777, pp. 49–86.
10. "Histoire des quatre frères Chevaliers de la Table Ronde," July 1777, vol. I, pp. 87–122.
11. "Hugues Capet, roman manuscrit," January 1778, vol. I, pp. 5–70.

Le Journal de Paris, no. 36, Monday 5th February, 1781 (volume for January-June 1781, p. 143). A letter from Le Grand to the editors of the *Journal de Paris* regarding the disputed *Histoire de la Vie Privée des Français* and replying to a letter from the Marquis de Paulmy published three days previously in the same journal.

Mémoires de l'Institut national des Sciences et Arts. Sciences morales et politiques (Paris, Baudouin):
1. "Notice sur l'état de la marine en France au commencement du XIVe siècle, et sur la tactique navale usitée alors dans les combats de mer, par le citoyen Legrand

d'Aussy – Lu à l'Institut national le 17 thermidor an VI (1798)." *Mém. Inst.*, vol. II
(Paris, fructidor, an VII – 1799) pt. II, pp. 302–375.
Published separately: Paris (Baudouin) n.d.

2. "Mémoire sur les anciennes sépultures nationales et les ornemens extérieurs qui en
divers temps y furent employés, sur les embaumemens, sur les tombeaux des rois
francs dans la ci-devant église de Saint-Germain-des-Près, et sur un projet de
fouilles à faire dans nos départemens, par le citoyen Legrand d'Aussy – Lu à l'Institut national le 7 ventôse an VII (1799)."
Idem, pt. II, pp. 411–680.
Published separately: Paris (Baudouin) an VII.
A new edition: *Des Sépultures nationales, et particulièrement de celles des Rois de France,
par Legrand d'Aussy – suivi des Funérailles des rois, reines, princes et princesses de la
monarchie française, depuis son origine jusques et y compris celles de Louis XVIII, par M.
de Roquefort*, Paris (J. Esneaux) 1824.

3. "Mémoire sur l'ancienne législation de la France, comprenant la loi salique, la loi
des Visgoths, la loi des Bourguignons – Lu à l'Institut national le 22 frimaire an
VII." *Mém. Inst.*, vol. III (Paris, prairial, an IX – 1801) pt. II, pp. 382–366.

4. "Voyage d'outremer et retour de Jérusalem en France par la voie de terre, pendant
le cours des années 1432 et 1433, par Bertrandon de la Brocquière, conseiller et
premier écuyer tranchant de Philippe-le-Bon, duc de Bourgogne; ouvrage extrait
d'un manuscrit de la Bibliothèque nationale, remis en français moderne, et publié
par le citoyen Legrand d'Aussy ... Lu à l'Institut national le 22 messidor an
VIII." *Mém. Inst.*, vol. V (Paris, fructidor, an XII – 1804) pt. II, pp. 421–637.
Translated: *The Travels of Bertrandon de la Brocquière – published by Le Grand d'Aussy
in the Vth volume of the 'Mém. de l'Institut,' translated by Thomas Johnes*, at the
Haford press, by J. Henderson, 1807.
* Lack of time at a particular session of the Institut prevented Le Grand from
reading a "notice" introducing this "mémoire." This "notice" appeared in the
Magasin Encyclopédique, 6e an (1800) vol. III, pp. 482–489.

Unpublished "mémoires":
1. "Histoire de l'Etablissement du Droit coutumier en France." Cf. *Magasin Encyclopédique*, 5e an (1799) vol. I, p. 118.
2. "Mémoire sur les Voyageurs français antérieurs au quinzième siècle." Cf. *idem*,
6e an (1800) vol. IV, p. 91.
3. "Mémoire sur l'Etablissement des Dixmes en faveur du Clergé." Cf. *idem*, 6e an
(1801) vol. V, p. 376.
4. "Mémoire sur les Pèlerinages en France." Cf. *idem*, 6e an (1801) vol. V, p. 376;
vol. VI, p. 368.

Notices et Extraits des Manuscrits de la Bibliothèque nationale et autres Bibliothèques, vol. V, Paris
(Imprimerie de la République) an VII:

1. "Notice de neuf manuscrits de la Bibliothèque nationale, contenant 'Alexandre,'
roman historique et de chevalerie." Pp. 101–131.
2. "Notice d'un manuscrit contenant 'Le Lucidaire.' " P. 155.
3. "Le Jeu spirituel de la paume ou de l'éteuf." Pp. 156–157.
4. "Enseignements du chevalier Geoffroi de la Tour-Landri à ses filles." Pp. 158–166.
5. "Notice d'un manuscrit contenant 'La Branche au royaux lignages.' " Pp. 238–242.
6. "Notice sur l'ouvrage intitulé 'Image du Monde.' " Pp. 243–266.
7. "Notice sur le 'Volucraire.' " P. 267.
8. "Notice sur le 'Trésor de Brunetto-Latini.' " Pp. 268–274.
9. "Notice sur deux ouvrages manuscrits du XIIIe siècle intitulés 'Bestiaire.' " Pp.
275–278.

10. "Notice sur deux pièces en vers intitulées 'Bibles.'" Pp. 279–293.
11. "Notice des manuscrits contenant le poëme intitulé 'Le Renard.'" Pp. 294–320.
12. "Notice des manuscrits contenant 'Le nouveau Renard.'" Pp. 321–328.
13. "Notice du 'Renard le bestourné' de Rutebeuf." Pp. 328–329.
14. "Notice du 'Renard Contrefait.'" Pp. 330–357.
15. "Notice des manuscrits de La Salle." Pp. 392–397.
16. "Notice du 'Dit d'Aventures.'" Pp. 398–403.
17. "Notice d'un manuscrit contenant 'La Bataille des Vices contre les Vertus.'" Pp. 404–411.
18. "Notice du 'Brichemer' de Rutebeuf." Pp. 412–414.
19. "Notice du 'Mariage des Sept Arts.'" Pp. 490–495.
20. "Notice de 'La Bataille des Sept Arts.'" Pp. 496–511.
21. "Notice de quelques ouvrages intitulés 'Doctrinal.'" Pp. 512–541.
22. "Notice d'un manuscrit contenant 'Le Débat de Félicité.'" Pp. 542–545.
23. "Notice de 'L'Anti-Claudien.'" Pp. 546–559.
24. "Notice du manuscrit intitulé 'La Folle et la Sage.'" Pp. 560–563.
25. "Notice du manuscrit intitulé 'Le Chevalier errant.'" Pp. 564–580.

Cf. also:
1. *Notices et Extraits*, vol. IX, p. 6: "Erreur plaisante de Le Grand d'Aussy dans sa traduction du 'Lay de Graelant.'"
2. *Ibidem:* "N'ayant travaillé que d'après les extraits faits par Paulmy ou Sainte-Palaye est tombé dans de graves erreurs; opinion singulière qu'il fonde sur la fausse leçon 'Gesdefer.'"
3. Vol. XIII, p. 194: "Son opinion erronée sur le poëme d'Alexandre par Lambert li Cors."
4. *Idem*, pp. 196–197: "Porte un faux jugement sur Thomas de Kent."
5. Vol. XX, p. 110: "Son mémoire sur une expédition en Hollande en 1304."

The *Fabliaux ou Contes*

1. The editions:
First edition:
Fabliaux ou Contes du XIIe et du XIIIe siècle, traduits ou extraits d'après divers manuscrits du tems; avec des notes historiques et critiques, et les imitations qui ont été faites de ces Contes depuis leur origine jusqu'à nos jours, Paris (Eugène Onfroy) 1779, 3 vols. in-8.
Contes dévots, Fables et Romans anciens; pour servir de suite aux Fabliaux. Par M. Le Grand. Tome quatrième, Paris (chez l'Auteur, quai de l'Ecole, maison de M. Juliot; et aux Adresses ordinaires. Et pour les Pays Etrangers chez Dufour, Libraire, à Mastricht) 1781, 1 vol.in-8.
Observations sur les Troubadours, par l'Editeur des Fabliaux, Paris (E. Onfroy) 1781, 1 vol. in-8.
*Second edition:
Fabliaux ou Contes du XIIe et du XIIIe siècle, Fables et Roman du XIIIe, traduits ou extraits d'après plusieurs manuscrits du tems; avec des notes historiques et critiques, et les imitations qui ont été faites de ces Contes depuis leur origine jusqu'à nos jours. Nouvelle Edition augmentée d'une Dissertation sur les Troubadours. Par M. Le Grand, Paris (E. Onfroy) 1781, 5 vols. in-12.
Third edition:
Fabliaux ou Contes, Fables et Romans du XIIe et du XIIIe siècle, traduits ou extraits par Legrand d'Aussy. Troisième édition, considérablement augmentée, Paris (Jules Renouard) 1829, 5 vols. in-8. Edited by Antoine-Augustin Renouard.
*Reprinted by *Slatkine Reprints*, Geneva, 1971.

2. Translations and adaptations of the *Fabliaux ou Contes* in chronological order of first appearance:

Imbert, B.: A series of Imbert's verse adaptations from Le Grand appeared in the *Mercure de France* between July and September 1780:

"La Bourse trouvée," July 1780, pp. 5–8.
"On ne s'y reconnaîtra pas," *idem*, pp. 51–57.
"L'Envieux et le Convoiteux," *idem*, pp. 100–103.
"Le Chien et le Serpent," *idem*, pp. 146–153.
"Le laid Chevalier," *idem*, pp. 195–196.
"Le Siège prêté et rendu," August 1780, pp. 4–7.
"Le Dépositaire," *idem*, pp. 99–102.
"Le Noyé," *idem*, pp. 147–149.
"Les Jambes de Bois," September 1780, pp. 5–7.
"Etula," *idem*, pp. 55–58.
"Le Dialogue," *idem*, pp. 101–102.
"Le Fablier," *idem*, pp. 147–149.

Imbert, B.: *Fabliaux choisis mis en vers*, Amsterdam and Paris (Belin) 1785.

Williamson, J.: *Tales of the XIIth and XIIIthe centuries. From the French of Mr. Le Grand*, London (Egerton) 1786, 2 vols.
A new edition: *Norman Tales. From the French of Mr. Le Grand*, London, 1789.
A new edition: *Tales of the Minstrels*, London, 1800.
A new edition: *The Feudal Period; illustrated by a series of tales romantic and humourous*, London (Reeves and Turner) 1873. Edited by W. C. Hazlitt.

Imbert, B.: *Choix de Fabliaux mis en vers*, Geneva and Paris (Prault) 1788, 2 vols.

Lückenmüller: *Erzählungen aus dem 12ten und 13ten Jahrhundert, von Le Grand, mit historischen und kritischen Anmerkungen*, Halle (Ruff) 1795–1798, 5 parts.

Way, G. L.: *Fabliaux or Tales abridged from French manuscripts of the XIIth and XIIIth centuries by M. Le Grand, selected and translated into English verse, by G. L. Way, with a preface, notes and appendix by G. Ellis*, London (R. Faulder) 1796.
A new edition, London (R. Faulder) 1800, 2 vols.
A new edition, corrected – by G. L. Way, London (J. Rodwell) 1815, 3 vols.

Rose, W. S.: *Partenopex de Blois, a romance in four cantos. Freely translated from the French of M. Le Grand; with notes: by William Stewart Rose*, London (Longman) 1807.

Sablière, J.: *Fabliaux adaptés pour la Jeunesse*, Paris (Les Nouvelles Presses Françaises) 1948.

3. Works inspired by the *Fabliaux ou Contes:*

Jubinal, Achille: *Nouveau recueil de contes, dits, fabliaux et autres pièces inédites des XIIIe, XIVe et XVe siècles, pour faire suite aux collections de Legrand d'Aussy, Barbazan et Méon, mis au jour pour la première fois par Achille Jubinal d'après les mss. de la Bibliothèque du Roi*, Paris (E. Pannier) 1839–1842, 2 vols.

Roquefort-Flaméricourt, B. de: *De l'Etat de la Poésie françoise dans les XIIe et XIIIe siècles*, Paris (Fournier) 1815.

4. Contemporary criticism:

Année Littéraire: 1780, vol. V, pp. 145–179.
1781, vol. V, pp. 217–253.
1782, vol. IV, pp. 325–331.

Bérenger, L. P.: *Porte-Feuille d'un Troubadour, ou Essais Poétiques, suivis d'une Lettre à M. Grosley, de l'Académie des Inscriptions & Belles-Lettres, sur les Trouvères & les Troubadours*, Marseille and Paris (Nyon) 1782, pp. 81–110.

L'Esprit des Journaux Français et Etrangers: February 1780, pp. 59–90.
September 1781, pp. 134–150.
January 1783, pp. 271–274.

Grimm: *Correspondance Littéraire*, vol. V (January 1780) 1812, pp. 99–102.
Le Journal de Littérature, des Sciences et des Arts: 1779, vol. VI, pp. 73–103.
1782, vol. IV, pp. 49–62.
Le Journal de Monsieur: 1782, vol. III, pp. 289–327.
Le Journal des Savants: August 1780, p. 571.
July 1781, pp. 481–482.
November 1782, pp. 742–743.
Le Journal Encyclopédique: 1780, vol. II, pt. I, pp. 72–82.
1781, vol. IV, pt. III, pp. 464–476.
Le Journal Etranger: February 1780, p. 72.
Le Mercure de France: April 1780, pp. 103–110.
Idem, pp. 147–160: Mayer's "Observations critiques."
February 1781, pp. 107–126.
June 1781, p. 30.
May 1782, pp. 127–133.
Papon, le P. Jean-Pierre: *Voyage littéraire de Provence, contenant tout ce qui peut donner une idée de l'état ancien & moderne des Villes, les Curiosités qu'elles renferment, la position des anciens Peuples, quelques Anecdotes littéraires, l'Histoire Naturelle, &c. & cinq Lettres sur les Trouvères & les Troubadours*, Paris (Barrois l'aîné) 1780.
A new edition, Paris (Moutard) 1787, 2 vols.

Biographies and bibliographies of Le Grand d'Aussy

Biographie Universelle Ancienne et Moderne, nouvelle édition, revue, corrigée et considérablement augmentée d'articles omis ou nouveaux, Paris (Mme C. Desplaces) and Leipzig (Libraire de F. A. Brockhaus) n.d. vol. XXIII, pp. 640–641.
Daire, Abbé: *Histoire littéraire de la ville d'Amiens*, Paris (P. Fr. Didot) 1782, pp. 401–402.
Dictionnaire des Lettres Françaises – Le dix-huitième Siècle, Paris (Librairie Arthème) 1960, vol. II, pp.79–80.
Dictionnaire historique, critique et bibliographique contenant les vies des hommes illustres, célèbres ou fameux de tous les pays et de tous les siècles, Paris (Ménard et Desenne) vol. XVI (1822) pp. 88–89.
Lévesque, Pierre Charles: "Notice historique sur Legrand d'Aussy," *Mém. Inst.*, vol. IV (Paris, Baudouin, 1802) pp. 84–95. The "Notice" also prefaces Le Grand's *Vie d'Apollonius de Tyane.*
Nouvelle Biographie Générale, depuis les temps les plus reculés jusqu'à nos jours, Paris (Firmin Didot frères) vol. XXX (1862) cols. 429–430.
Sommervogel, Carlos: *Bibliothèque de la Compagnie de Jésus*, vol. IV, (Paris, Picard, 1893), cols. 1660–1663.

On Le Grand's education and the Jesuit colleges he attended:

Daniel, Le P. Charles: *Les Jésuites instituteurs de la jeunesse française au XVIIe et au XVIIIe siècle*, Paris (Victor Palmé) and Brussels (J. Albanel) 1800.
Delattre, P.: *Les Etablissements des Jésuites en France depuis quatre siècles*, Enghien (Institut supérieur de Théologie) and Wetteren (Imprimerie de Meester frères) vol. I (1949) cols. 180–202, 991–1009.

Modern students of the fabliaux who mention or use Le Grand d'Aussy

Montaiglon A. de and Raynaud G.: *Recueil général et complet des Fabliaux des XIIIe et XIVe siècles*, Paris (Librairie des Bibliophiles) 1872–1890, 6 vols, "Notes et Variantes," *passim.*
Nardin, Pierre: *Jean Bodel. Fabliaux*, Paris (Librairie A. G. Nizet) 1965, pp. 33, 38.

Nykrog, Per: *Les Fabliaux: étude d'histoire littéraire et de stylistique médiévale*, Copenhagen (Munksgaard) 1957, p. xiii.

Reid, T. B. W.: *Twelve Fabliaux*, Manchester (M.U.P.) 1958 (French Classics) pp. 99, 101, 105, 107.

Cf. also:

Bossuat, Robert: *La Poésie Lyrique au Moyen Age*, Paris (Librairie Larousse) n.d. (Les Classiques Larousse) p. 98.

Lafitte-Houssat, J.: *Troubadours et Cours d'Amour*, Paris (Presses Universitaires de France) 1966 ("Que sais-je," no. 422) pp. 30–31.

Woledge, B.: "Une Branche d'Armes: poème anonyme du XIIIe siècle" in *Mélanges de Langue et de Littérature médiévales offerts à Pierre Le Gentil*, Paris (Société d'Edition d'Enseignement Supérieur) 1973, pp. 899–900.

Modern works concerned with eighteenth-century medievalism

*denotes some mention of Le Grand d'Aussy

Baldensperger, F.: *Etudes d'Histoire Littéraire*, Paris (Hachette) 1907, pp. 110–146: "Le Genre Troubadour."

Estève, Edmond: "Le moyen âge dans la littérature du XVIIIe siècle," *Revue de l'Université de Bruxelles*, 1923, pp. 352–382.

*Gossman, Lionel: *Medievalism and the Ideologies of the Enlightenment. The World and Work of La Curne de Sainte-Palaye*, Baltimore (Johns Hopkins) 1968.
"Old French scholarship in the eighteenth century: the 'Glossary' of La Curne de Sainte-Palaye," *French Studies*, vol. XII (1958) pp. 346–358.

*Jacoubet, Henri: *Le Comte de Tressan et les origines du genre troubadour*, Paris (Presses Universitaires de France) 1923.

*Jouglard, Madeleine: "La connaissance de l'ancienne littérature française au XVIIIe siècle," *Mélanges offerts par ses amis et ses élèves à M. Gustave Lanson*, Paris (Hachette) 1922, pp. 268–276.
"Les études d'histoire littéraire en France au XVIIIe siècle," *La Revue du Mois*, 10th April, 1915, pp. 424–443.

*Lanson, René: *Le Gout du Moyen Age en France au XVIIIe siècle*, Paris and Brussels (G. van OEst, editor) 1926.

*Martin, Henry: *Catalogue des Manuscrits de la Bibliothèque de l'Arsenal*, vol. VIII, *Histoire de la Bibliothèque de l'Arsenal*, Paris (Plon) 1899.

Mornet, Daniel: *Le Romantisme en France au XVIIIe siècle*, Paris (Hachette) 1912.

*Nykrog, Per: *Les Fabliaux*, pp. ix–xiv.

Pauphilet, Albert: *Le Legs du Moyen Age*, Melun (Librairie d'Argences) 1950, pp. 23–49.

*Pickford, C. E.: *Changing attitudes towards medieval French literature*, Hull (University of Hull Publications) 1966, pp. 12–15.

On seventeenth-century medievalism, cf. Edelman, Nathan: *Attitudes of Seventeenth-Century France toward the Middle Ages*, New York (King's Crown Press) 1946.

Miscellaneous modern works to which reference is made

Bédier, J.: *La Chanson de Roland publiée d'après le manuscrit d'Oxford et traduite par Joseph Bédier*, Paris (L'Edition d'Art) 1944.
Le Roman de Tristan et Iseut renouvelé par Joseph Bédier, Paris (L'Edition d'Art) 1926.
Les Fabliaux, 6th edition, Paris (Champion) 1964.

Brandin, L.: *Lais et Fabliaux du treizième siècle*, Paris (E. de Boccard) 1932 (Poèmes et récits de la vieille France, no. 15).

Brunel, C.: "David d'Ashby, auteur méconnu des 'Faits des Tartares,'" *Romania*, vol. LXXIX (1958) pp. 39–46.

Brunetière, M. F.: "Les Fabliaux du moyen âge et l'origine des contes," *La Revue des deux Mondes*, vol. CXIX (1893) pp. 189–213.

Caullot, N.: *Fabliaux ou Contes du Moyen Age*, Paris (Les Classiques Hatier) 1967.

Cioranescu, A.: *Bibliographie de la Littérature française du dix-huitième Siècle*, Paris (Editions du Centre National de la Recherche Scientifique) 1969, 3 vols.

Delbouille, M.: *Le Lai d'Aristote de Henri d'Andeli, publié d'après tous les manuscrits*, Paris (Les Belles Lettres) 1951 (Bibliothèque de la Faculté de Philosophie et Lettres de l'Université de Liége-Fascicule CXXIII).

Delisle, L.: *Le Cabinet des Manuscrits*, Paris (Imprimerie Impériale) 1868–1881, 4 vols.

Espiner-Scott, J. G.: *Claude Fauchet: sa vie, son oeuvre*, Paris (Droz) 1938.

Gröber, G.: *Grundriss der romanischen Philologie*, Strassburg (K. J. Trübner) 1888–1902, 3 vols.

Guerlin de Guer: "Le comique et l'humour à travers les âges. Les fabliaux," *Revue des Cours et Conférences*, (1926–1927) Paris (Boivin) 1927, pp. 325–350.

Hauvette, H.: *La France et la Provence dans l'oeuvre de Dante*, Paris (Boivin) 1930 (Bibliothèque de la Revue des Cours et Conférences).

Hellman, R. and O'Gorman, R.: *Fabliaux. Ribald Tales from the Old French*, New York (Thomas Y. Crowell Company) 1966 (Apollo Editions).

Héron, A.: *Les Œuvres de Henri d'Andeli*, Rouen (Imprimerie de Espérance Cagniard) 1880.

Hoepffner, E.: *Les Troubadours dans leur Vie et dans leurs Œuvres*, Paris (A. Colin) 1955.

Huisman M. and G.: *Contes et Légendes du Moyen Age*, Paris (Fernand Nathan) 1962 (Collection des Contes et Légendes de tous les Pays.)

Jeanroy, A.: *La Poésie lyrique des Troubadours*, Toulouse (E. Privat) and Paris (H. Didier) 1934, 2 vols.

Johnston R. C. and Owen, D. D. R.: *Fabliaux*, Oxford (Basil Blackwell) 1957 (Blackwell's French Texts).

Joly, A.: "De la condition des vilains au moyen âge d'après les fabliaux," *Mémoires de l'Académie nationale des Sciences, Arts et Belles-Lettres de Caen*, 1882, pp. 445–492.

Jubinal, A.: *Jongleurs et Trouvères, ou Choix de Saluts, Epîtres, Réveries et autres pièces légères des XIIIe et XIV siècles*, Paris (Merklein) 1835.

Ledieu, A.: *Les Vilains dans les oeuvres des Trouvères*, Paris (J. Moisonneuve) 1890.

Lee, A. C.: *The Decameron. Its Sources and Analogues*, London (David Natt) 1909.

Méon, D. M.: *Nouveau Recueil de Fabliaux et Contes*, Paris (Chasseriau) 1823, 2 vols.

Méray, A.: *La vie au temps des cours d'amour; croyances, usages et moeurs intimes des XIe, XIIe et XIIIe siècles, d'après les chroniques, gestes, jeux partis et fabliaux*, Paris (A. Claudin) 1876.

Meyer, P.: "Notice de deux anciens manuscrits français ayant appartenu au Marquis de La Clayette," *Notices et Extraits*, vol. XXXIII (1890) pp. 1–90.

Omont, H.: *Inventaire des Manuscrits de la Collection Moreau*, Paris (Picard) 1891.

Paris, P.: *Les Romans de la Table Ronde mis en nouveau langage et accompagnés de recherches sur l'origine et le caractère de ces grandes compositions*. Paris (L. Techner) 1868–1877, 5 vols.

Pauphilet, A.: *Jeux et Sapience du Moyen Age*, Paris (Bibliothèque de la Pléiade) 1951.
Poètes et Romanciers du Moyen Age, Paris (Bibliothèque de la Pléiade) 1952.
Historiens et Chroniqueurs du Moyen Age, Paris (Bibliothèque de la Pléiade) 1952.

Pickford, C. E.: *La Farce de Maistre Pathelin*, Paris (Les Petits Classiques Bordas) 1967.

Scott, Sir Walter: *Catalogue of the Library at Abbotsford*, Edinburgh (T. Constable) 1838.

Williams, G. S.: *The Amadis Question*, New York and Paris, 1909.

Zumthor, P.: *Histoire littéraire de la France médiévale*, Paris (Presses Universitaires de France) 1954.

Anon.: *Recueil de Fabliaux*, Paris (La Renaissance du Livre) 1910 (Tous les chefs-d'oeuvre de la littérature française).